THIS PLEASANT LAND

NEW PHOTOGRAPHY OF THE BRITISH LANDSCAPE

Written by Rosalind Jana

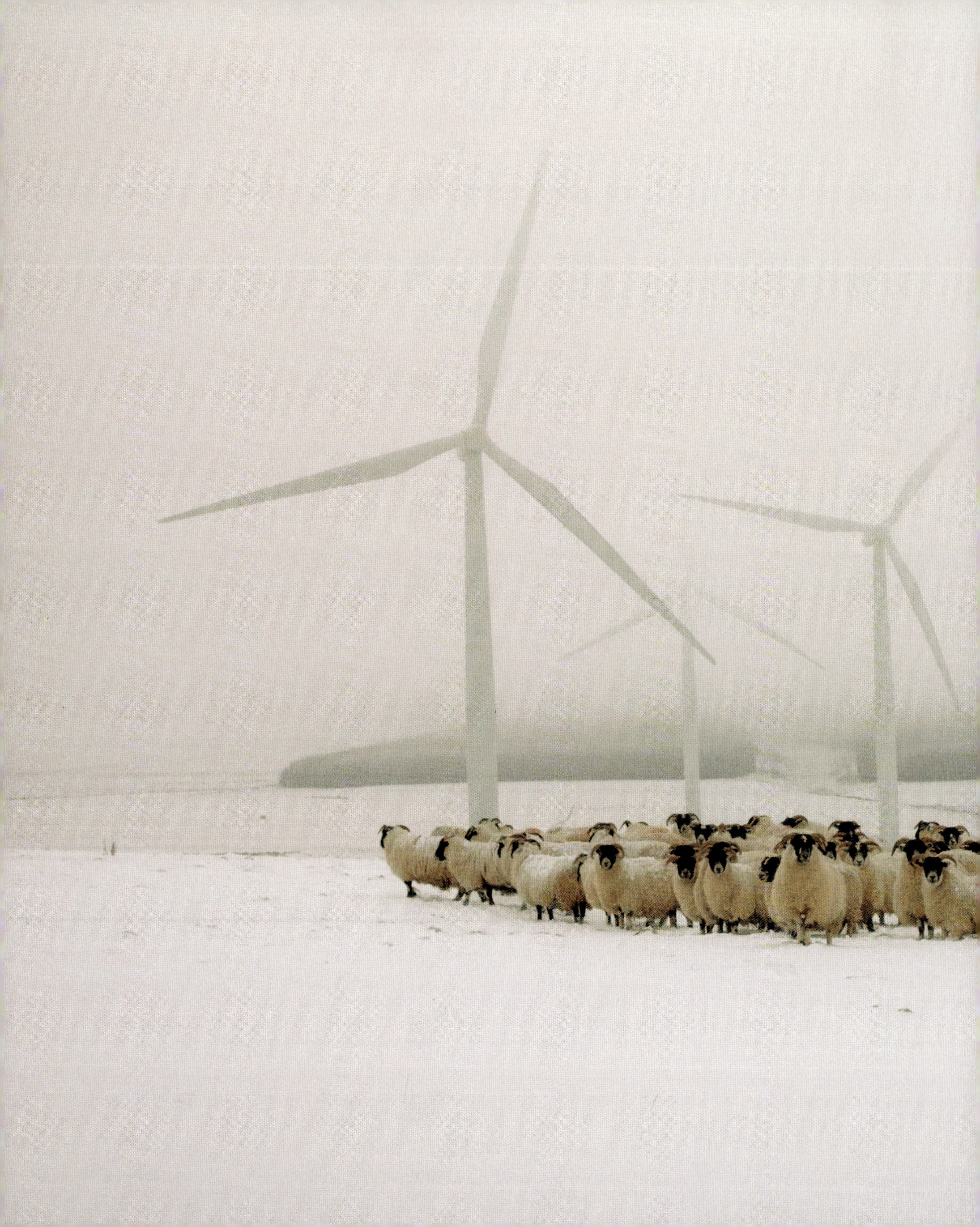

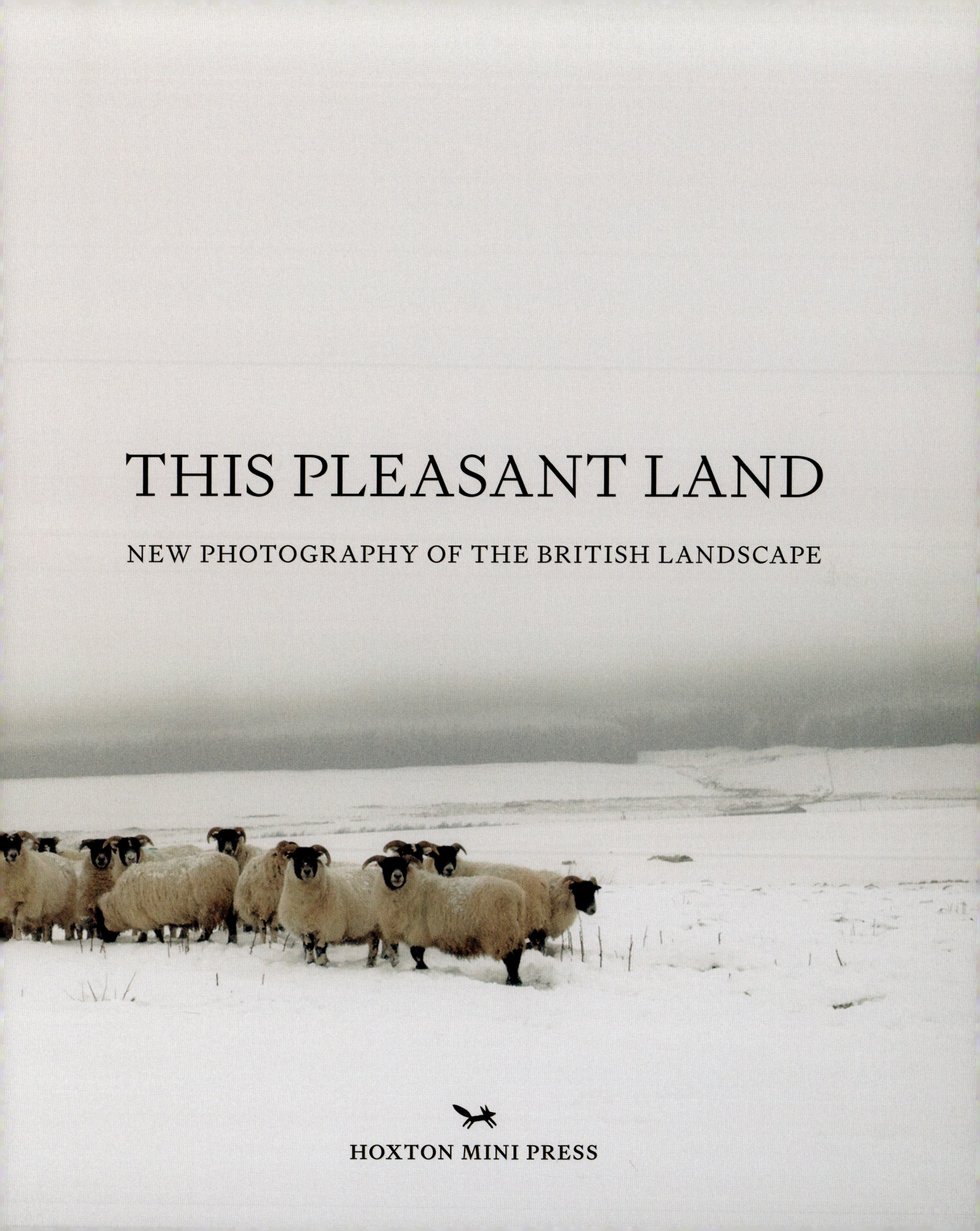

THIS PLEASANT LAND

NEW PHOTOGRAPHY OF THE BRITISH LANDSCAPE

HOXTON MINI PRESS

Rosalind Jana

Rosalind Jana is an arts and culture writer based in London. She writes for publications and platforms including *British Vogue*, *The Guardian*, *Apollo*, *Elephant*, *Prospect*, *Wired*, *British Journal of Photography*, *Magnum Photos* and *BBC Culture*. Rosalind has previously introduced two photobooks for Hoxton Mini Press: *An English Summer* by Chanel Irvine and *The Hackney Marshes* by Freya Najade.

Hoxton Mini Press

Hoxton Mini Press is a small indie publisher based in east London. It began when Ann and Martin met walking their dogs in Hoxton Square and then went on to get married and start a publishing company. Their goal is to make books that are beautiful but also accessible – not aloof – filled with great photography and personal stories. They want both collectors and everyday folk to keep their books in neat piles on wooden shelves, and pass them down to future generations. For books are no longer about information, but objects in their own right: things to collect and own and inspire.

Front cover photograph: Toby Coulson
Back cover photograph: Robin Friend
Previous spread: Sophie Gerrard

Contents

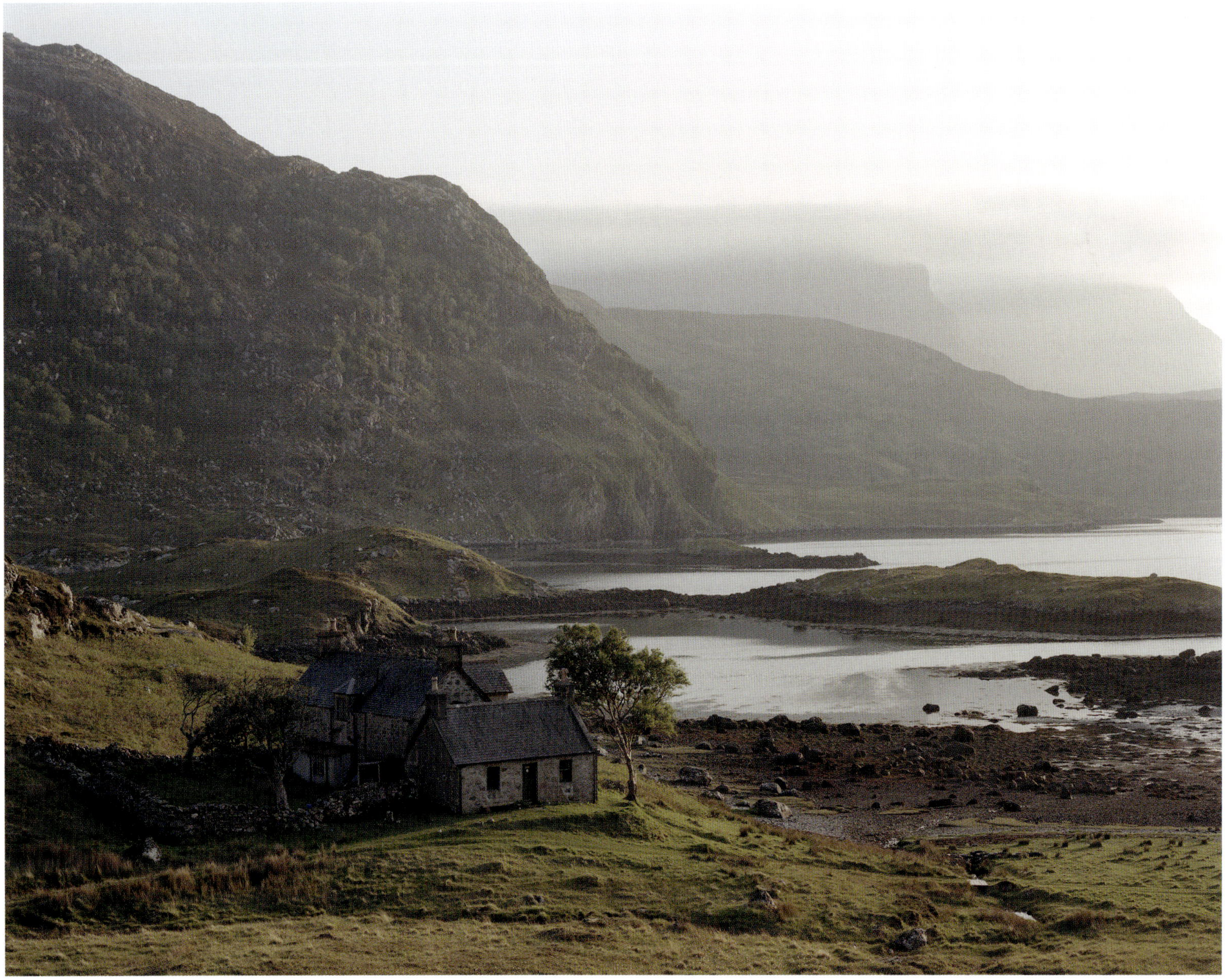

Nicholas J R White, Black Dots, Glencoul, Northern Highlands, Scotland, May 2016

The Sensation of Place

by Rosalind Jana

The photographs gathered in this book might be varied in location and focus, but they all share an initial moment of open-air absorption. Close to home or following day-long hikes, shot early in the morning or during gathering dusk, caught in passing or building on repeat visits, this is the kind of work that requires a state – however brief – of absolute immersion.

When writing about landscape photography, much of the discussion tends to focus on the content and technicalities of the final image, rather than the sensation of taking it. But, when talking to the photographers featured here, several paused when faced with the initial question: 'Why landscape?'

They felt that their answers were too simplistic, that it was somehow cliché to speak of a desire to find something that felt more rooted, more present-tense, than other areas of their photographic practice. There was a quality of *being* to many of these projects and ongoing bodies of work, reflecting not only their creators' political concerns or artistic sympathies, but also a powerful desire to be outside.

Many also spoke about personal connections: the places they grew up, the circuitous paths that brought them towards particular projects or preoccupations. Simon Schama writes in *Landscape and Memory*, 'If our entire landscape tradition is a product of a shared culture, it is by the same token a tradition built from a rich deposit of myths, memories, and obsessions.' Elsewhere the historian describes landscape as a 'work of the mind', its strata 'built up... as much of memory as from layers of rock.' We all bring ourselves into the landscape, overlaying it with our own half-formed map of associations, recollections, interests and urges. It is at once beyond us and beneath us. In its wilder hinterlands we might like to think that it remains untouched, but our fingerprints – real and imagined – are all over it.

'Why landscape?' is a question that could also be asked about this book. The photographs in its pages have been taken in the last two decades or so, forming a post-millennium portrait of Britain. They build on earlier photographic traditions to present their own, time-bound view of the nation's terrain. From its meadows and mountains to scrapheaps and amusement arcades, its winding, mineral-rich rivers and woods to far-reaching fens, this selection of fine art landscape photography captures the beautiful, the bleak, the uncontainable and the marginal. It also offers a series of windows into recent history. Only a handful of these projects feature people – Sophie Gerrard's female farmers, Simon Roberts' Stonehenge tourists, Alex Ingram's island wardens – but every project has something to say about the era in which we live. Gerrard embarked on her project while thinking about the Scottish independence referendum. Ingram explores idealised spaces on the edge of civilisation, now facing the brunt of our changing climate. Roberts' work pokes around notions of Britishness, dwelling on nationhood in the context of austerity politics and, more recently, Brexit.

A landscape is a thing that is constantly changing. Places are occupied and abandoned. Boundary lines are redrawn. A landscape is not merely a reflection, but an embodiment, of contemporary concerns, cutting to the heart of how we live together and understand ourselves as a country. Who is welcome here? Who is excluded? Who is maintaining the borders and gates, and to what ends? How is the land itself – rural, urban, suburban – cared for or neglected? The last twenty years have been turbulent in Britain, though maybe we say that of every era. This book features work made during a time of uncertain, often polarised, national identity, capturing the public realm in a state of both flux and stagnation.

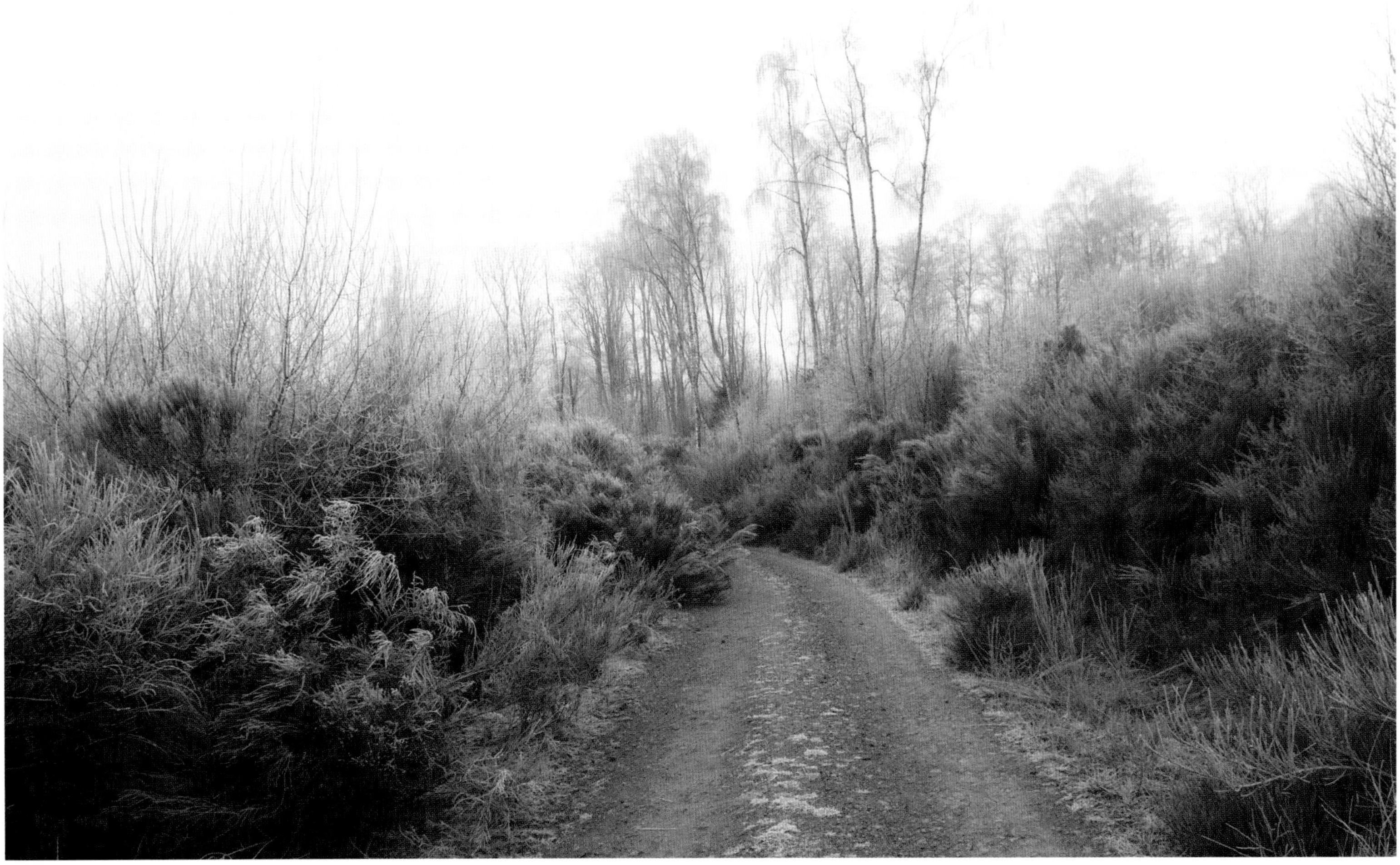

Iain Sarjeant, Close to Home, near Strathpeffer, Ross-shire, Scotland, 2017

Even where there isn't an explicit political context, most of these photos aren't interested in merely depicting the land as a point of visual fact or interest. Instead, they raise questions about how we inhabit it, own it, work it, protect and destroy it. Paul Hart's stark, atmospheric photos of the Fens capture large-scale agribusiness in action; vast expanses of land given over to tilled fields and monocultural crops. Jethro Marshall's images of quarries trace the dusty scars left behind by industrial extraction. While taking these photos, he was frequently asked to leave by private security personnel. Much of this land is not as free to explore as we might hope or assume. It's a well-rehearsed argument to say that the classical bucolic vista is not only a purely human invention, but one buttressed by wealth, power and 'no trespassing' signs (even now, half of England is owned by just 1 percent of its population).

Older incursions into the landscape leave their marks too. Nature might begin her slow process of reclamation, veiling quarries with grass or sucking buildings beneath the waves, but history's leftovers remain. Kaveh Rostamkhani's year-long documentation of former mining towns in South Wales focuses not only on the communities still enduring a decades-old aftershock, but the reminders of that once thriving industry – hulking machinery, capped mineshafts – embedded in the surrounding area. Richard Brine's images of pillboxes recall the brief period in 1940 when the threat of German invasion felt serious enough to construct nearly 30,000 defensive structures to slow their progress. Now these concrete blocks stand empty, alluding to dystopic events that never came to pass.

Military use of land also forms a substantial strata of projects here. Conflict both near and far has been a decisive factor in shaping our understanding of place and nation. From Donovan Wylie's ominous photos of decommissioned British watchtowers in Northern Ireland, taken from the vantage point of a helicopter,

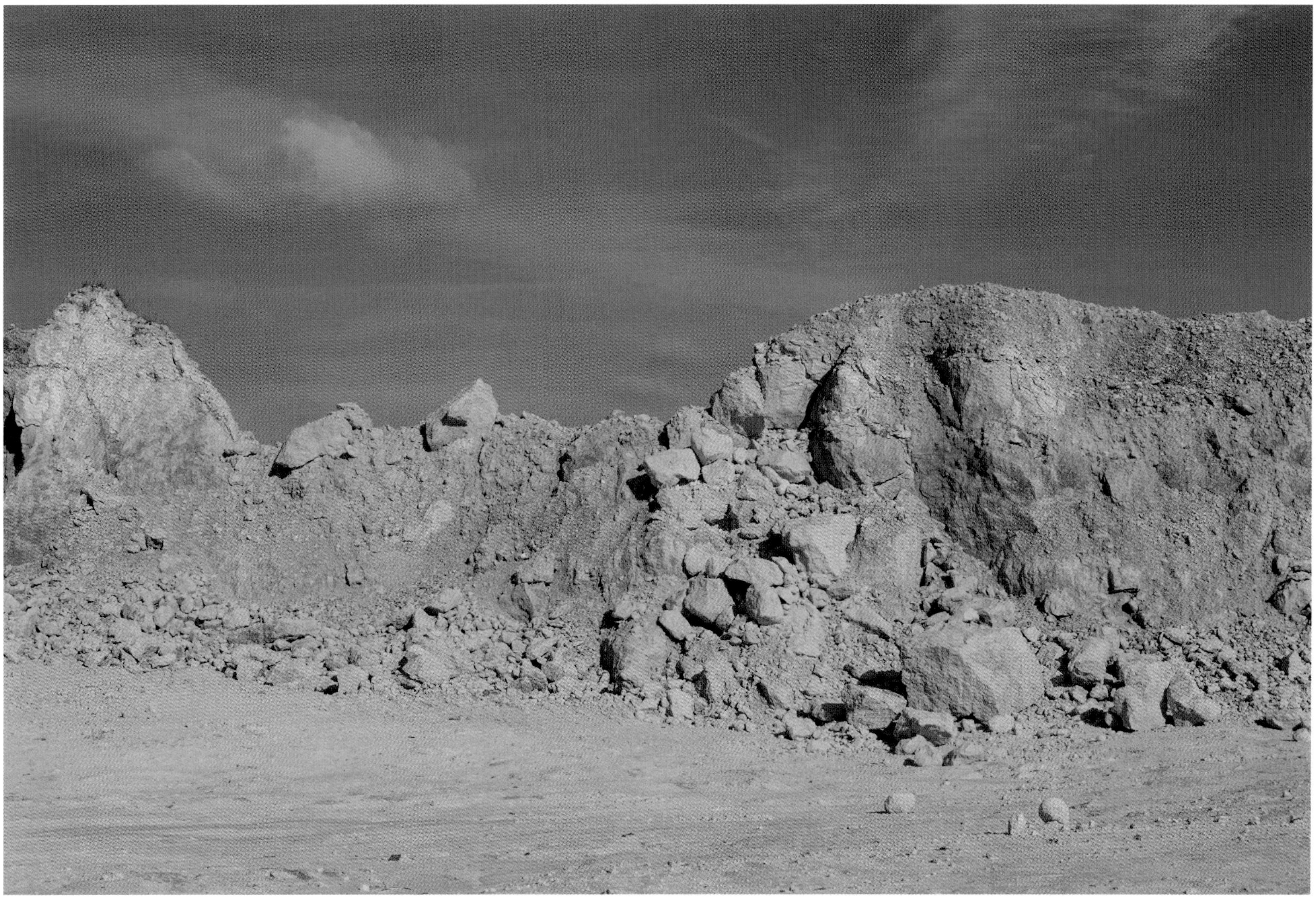

Jethro Marshall, Rocky, Chalk Quarry, Shapwick, England, 2019

to Melanie Friend's on-the-ground observations of the air show displays of RAF pilots and Sarah Pickering's surreal images of simulation pyrotechnics mid-explosion, one is never far away from a reminder of war (even if the intense privacy of army bases also obscures them from public view). Here we see war as spectacle, as threat, as backdrop. In England, the military can facilitate a pleasant day out for families keen to see the sky-high aerobatics of the Red Arrows; in Northern Ireland, their presence forms a deep and painful part of living memory.

The spectre of climate change lurks behind many of these works. Spencer Murphy's wildfires and Joseph Wright's floods are two sides of the same coin, capturing the consequences of extreme weather events. Max Miechowski's elegiac portraits of the places and people affected by coastal erosion observe a process that has been happening for thousands of years but is being sped up by rising sea levels and increased rainfall. And a project like Robin Friend's *Bastard Countryside*, with its beached whales and rubbish, contains a grim commentary about our destructive relationship with the planet.

In this context, photography is often offered as both a salve and call to action. If we not only see the harder realities of the land, but also its extraordinary splendour (Harry Cory Wright's hazy sunrises, for example) will we be encouraged to change our ways to preserve what we still have? One can always be hopeful that people will see, as they wonder at the pale light and green hedgerows, something worth protecting, but it would also be limiting to view the photography presented here as possessing any one purpose or message. Rather, it is an open-ended anthology of the land and those who move through it. 'Sometimes a landscape seems to be less a setting for the life of its inhabitants than a curtain behind which their struggles, achievements and accidents take place,' John Berger writes in *A Fortunate Man*. 'For those who, with the inhabitants,

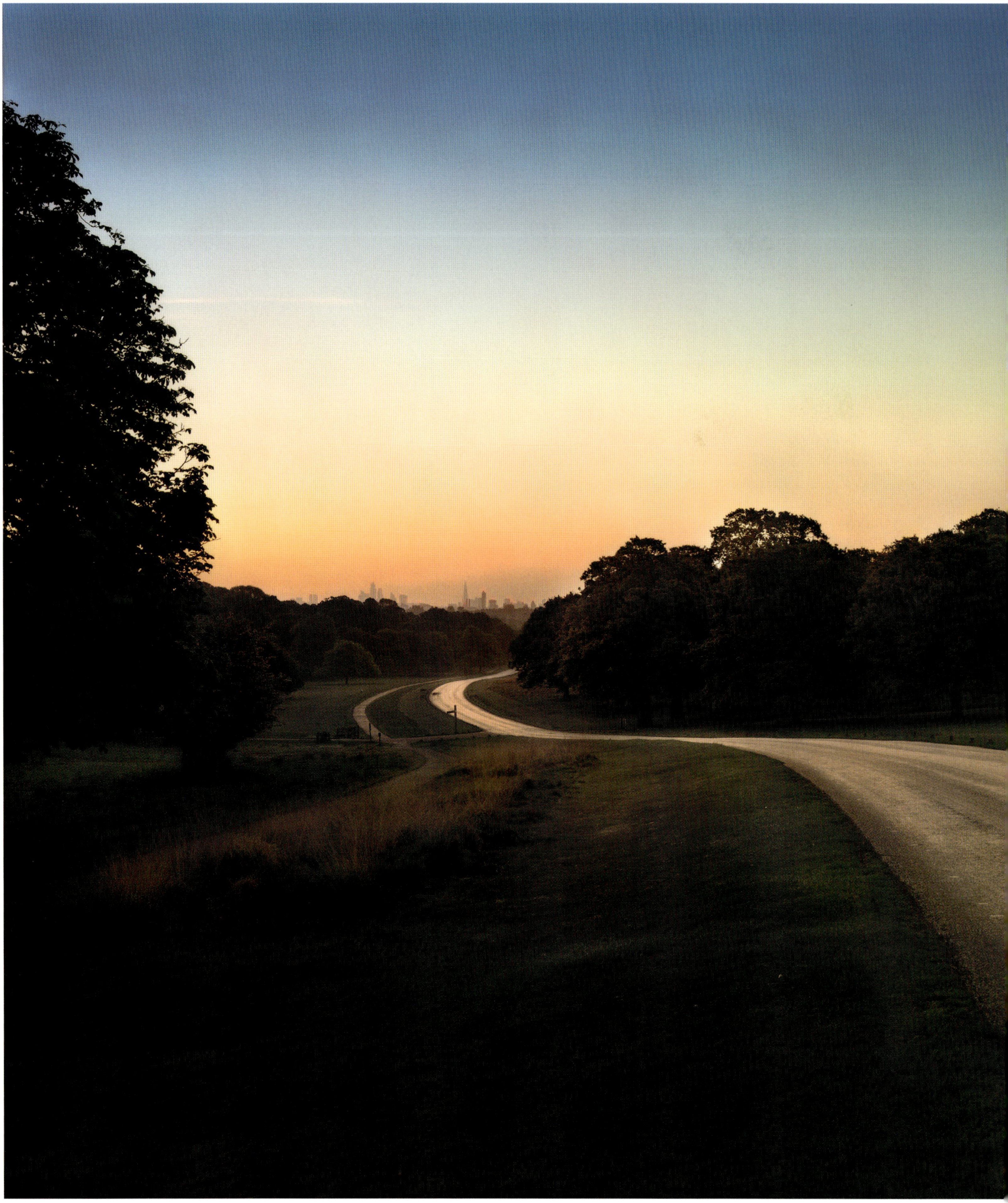

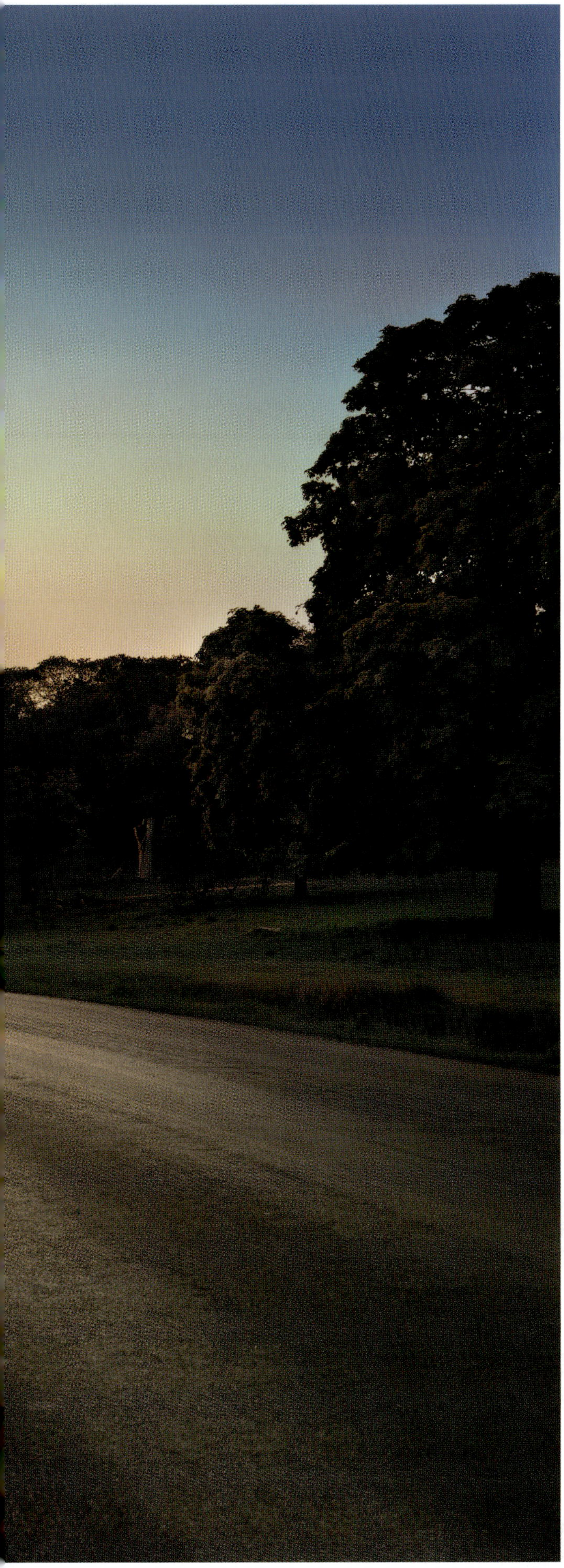

are behind the curtain, landmarks are no longer only geographical but also biological and personal.' Here, hopefully, we are ushered behind the curtain, each photographer twitching it back to reveal their own, carefully chosen set of landmarks and preoccupations. Their bodies of work tell story after story, whether these are autobiographical or documentary, abstract or immediately legible. For photographers such as Jem Southam or Robert Darch, those stories stray towards the spacious possibilities of fiction, with landscape not so much a backdrop as a stage setting.

I said previously that the physical aspect of landscape photography is often forgotten, its present-tense moment of image-taking replete with practical concerns (light, weather, attire, timing) as well as the sheer sensation of being there. But any kind of photography – especially landscape – engages with all the tenses at once. To photograph a landscape is to think about the history that stands before you: geological, cultural, political. It is to make a choice about how you compress time. The weight of the past and the reality of the present are held together in the frame, preserved for future viewing. 'Why landscape?' is a question that can be posed continuously, gathering different reasons and responses with each new asking. It is a question that each of these twenty-four projects holds a different answer to. Come back tomorrow and they may tell you something new again.

Harry Cory Wright, Sensation of Landscape, Richmond Park with Metropolis Behind, London, England, 2018

Bastard Countryside

Robin Friend

'[Bastard countryside] has always got this element of danger, wrapped up in a beautiful image. Almost like a poison chalice. It should be otherworldly to look at, but at the same time, uneasy.'

In *Les Misérables*, Victor Hugo describes the land surrounding Paris as 'bastard countryside'. It is 'amphibian' and 'bizarre': a place where city and countryside clash and overlap – 'the end of the beaten track, the beginning of the passions, the end of the murmur of things divine, the beginning of the noise of humankind.' When Robin Friend first heard this phrase used by nature writer Robert Macfarlane, during his MA at the Royal College of Art, it suddenly seemed to make sense of the work he had been creating. Having grown up in Australia before returning to the UK as a teenager, Friend often found himself looking for harsh landscapes reminiscent of the Australian bush. He was also drawn to places where nature was encroaching – or reclaiming – manmade ground.

'Bastard countryside' became a unifying principle, a way of seeing, a narrative impulse. Friend began travelling around the country in search of this elusive quality. He found it in rusted skips, and in mines holding scrapped cars, light spilling down from the shafts overhead like stage spotlights. He found it in the image of a beached sperm whale on Hunstanton beach in Norfolk, the sea dyed red near the grey bulk of its body.

Hard to define but immediately recognised when he found it, 'bastard countryside' offered a route into thinking about industrialisation and waste, as well as the uncertain future of our planet as we push it towards a dystopic end. These are not straightforwardly ugly images though. Rather, they arrest the viewer with their curious, almost celestial splendour. Friend describes this quality as remorse, but it is not especially quiet or sombre. There is an epic cast to these photos, an embrace of scale and chaos that offers a dismal majesty.

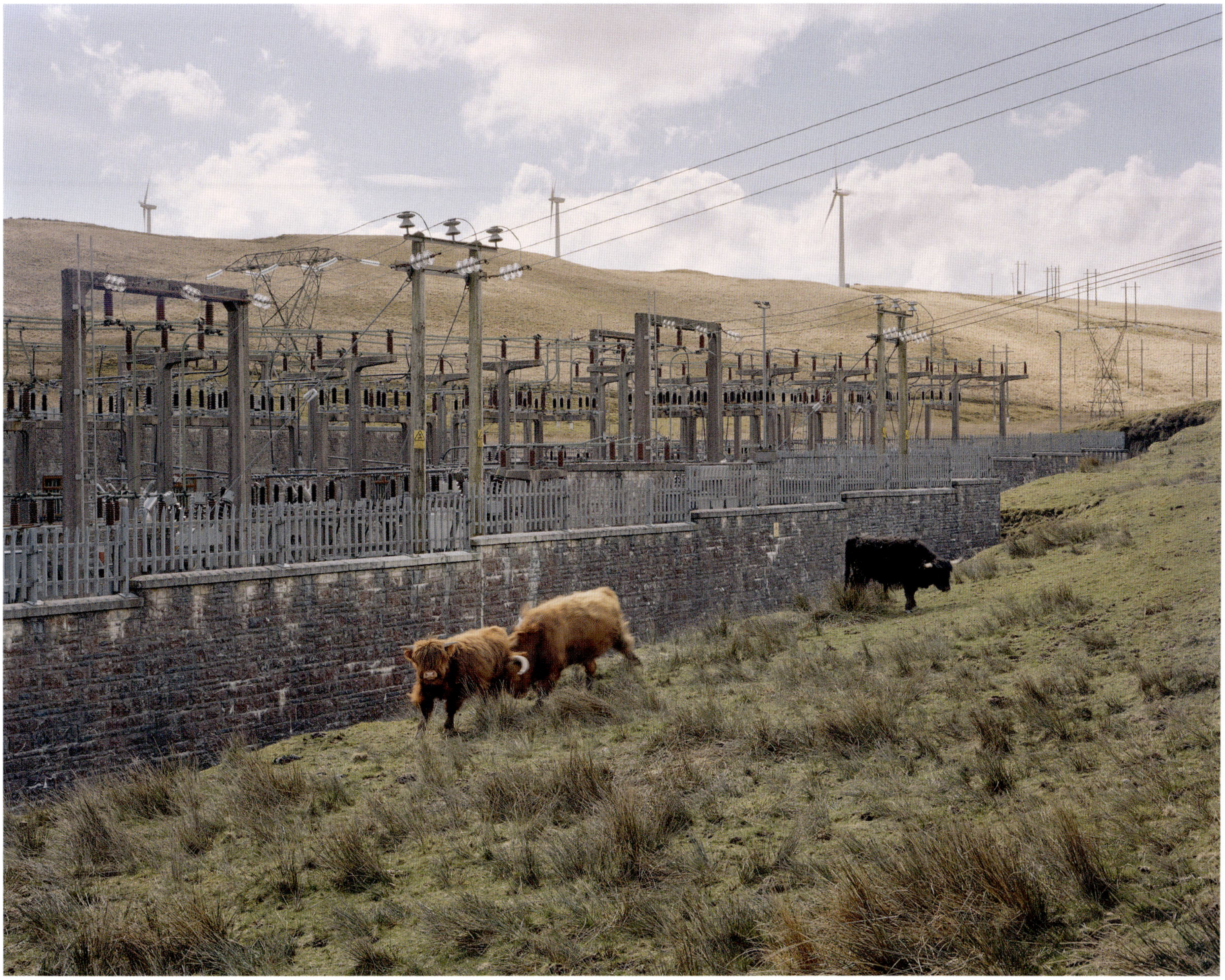

Substation near Ystumtuen, Wales, 2016

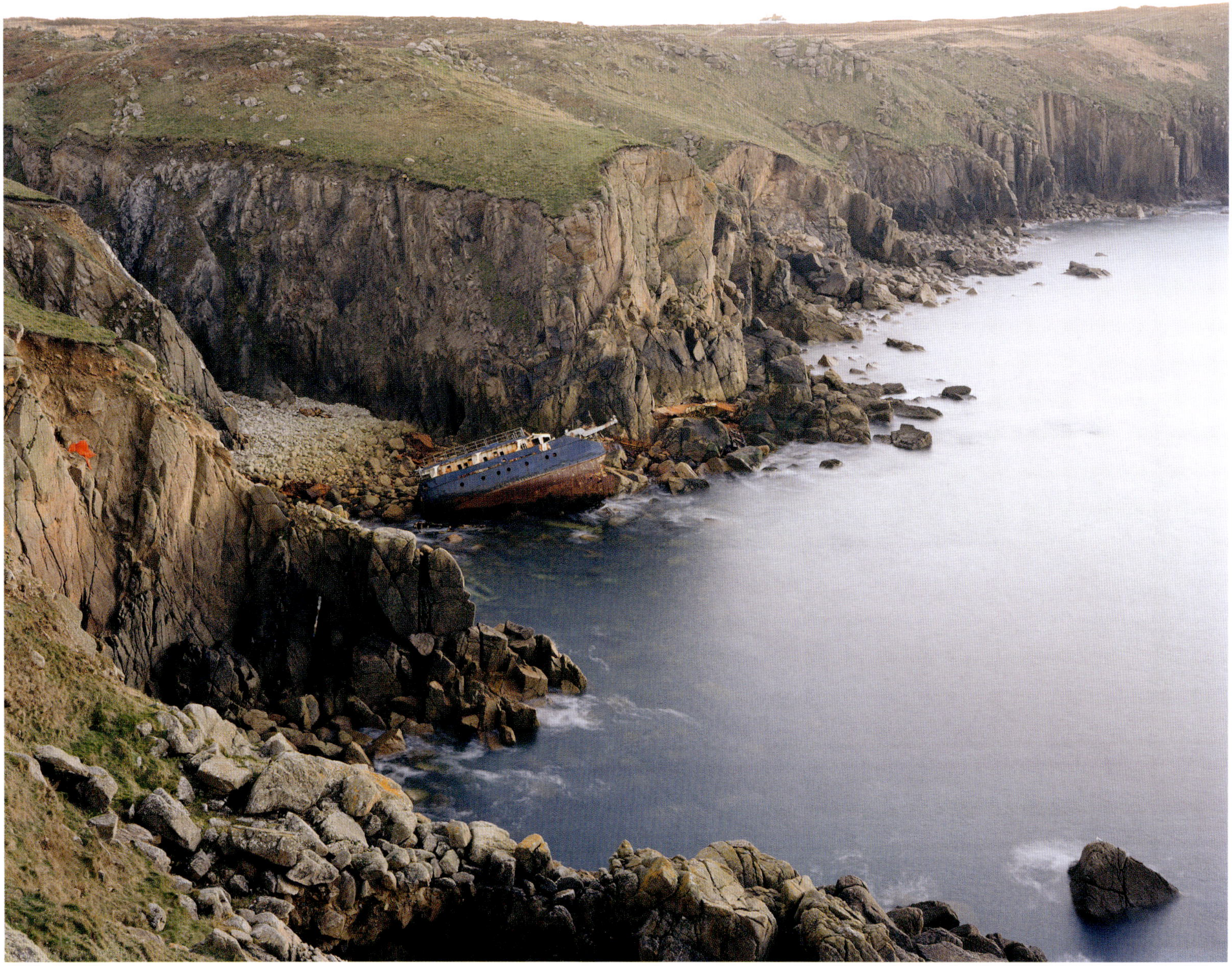

Land's End, England, 2003

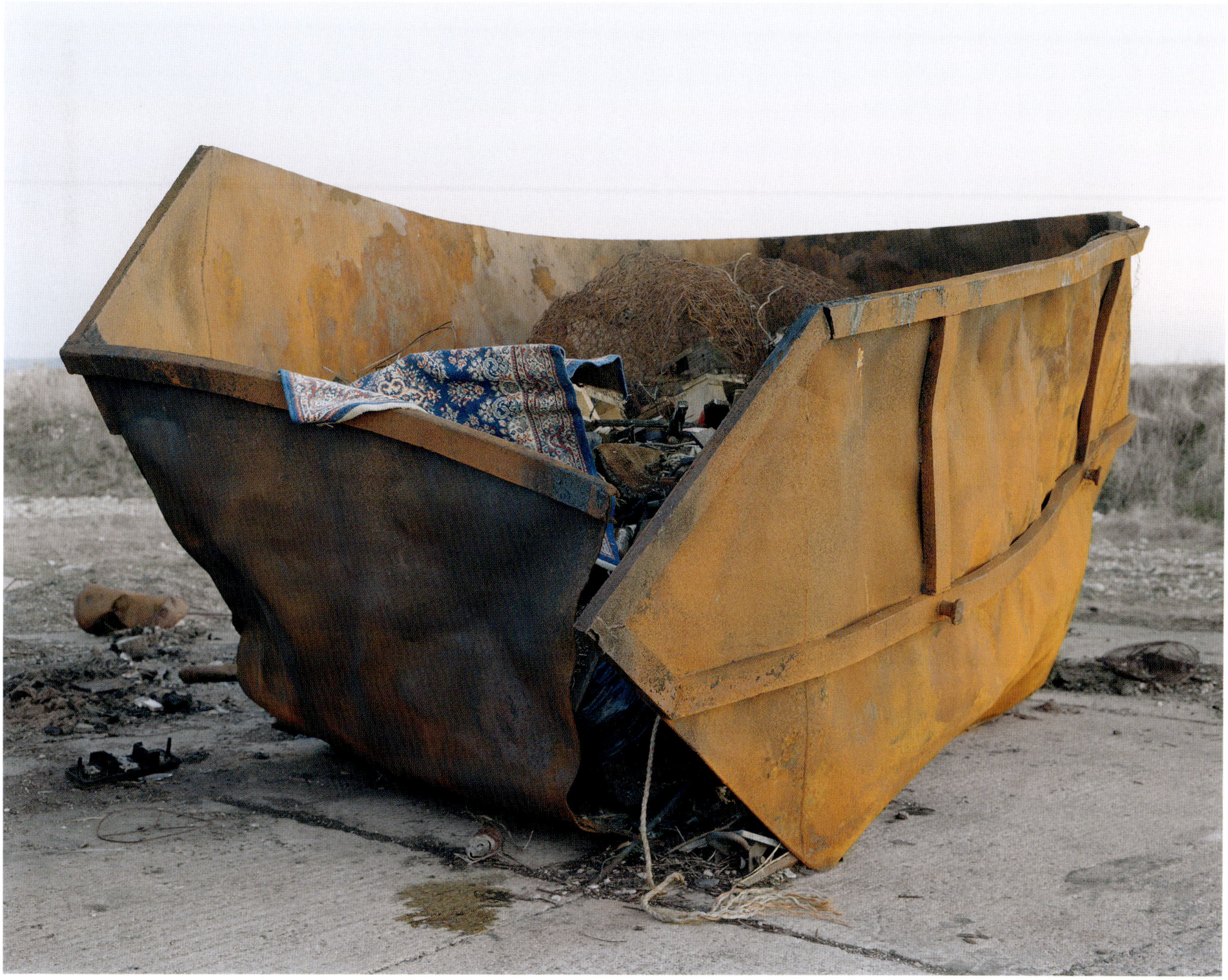

Skip, Newhaven, England, 2008

Birch & Steel, Brokenhurst, Hampshire, England, 2008

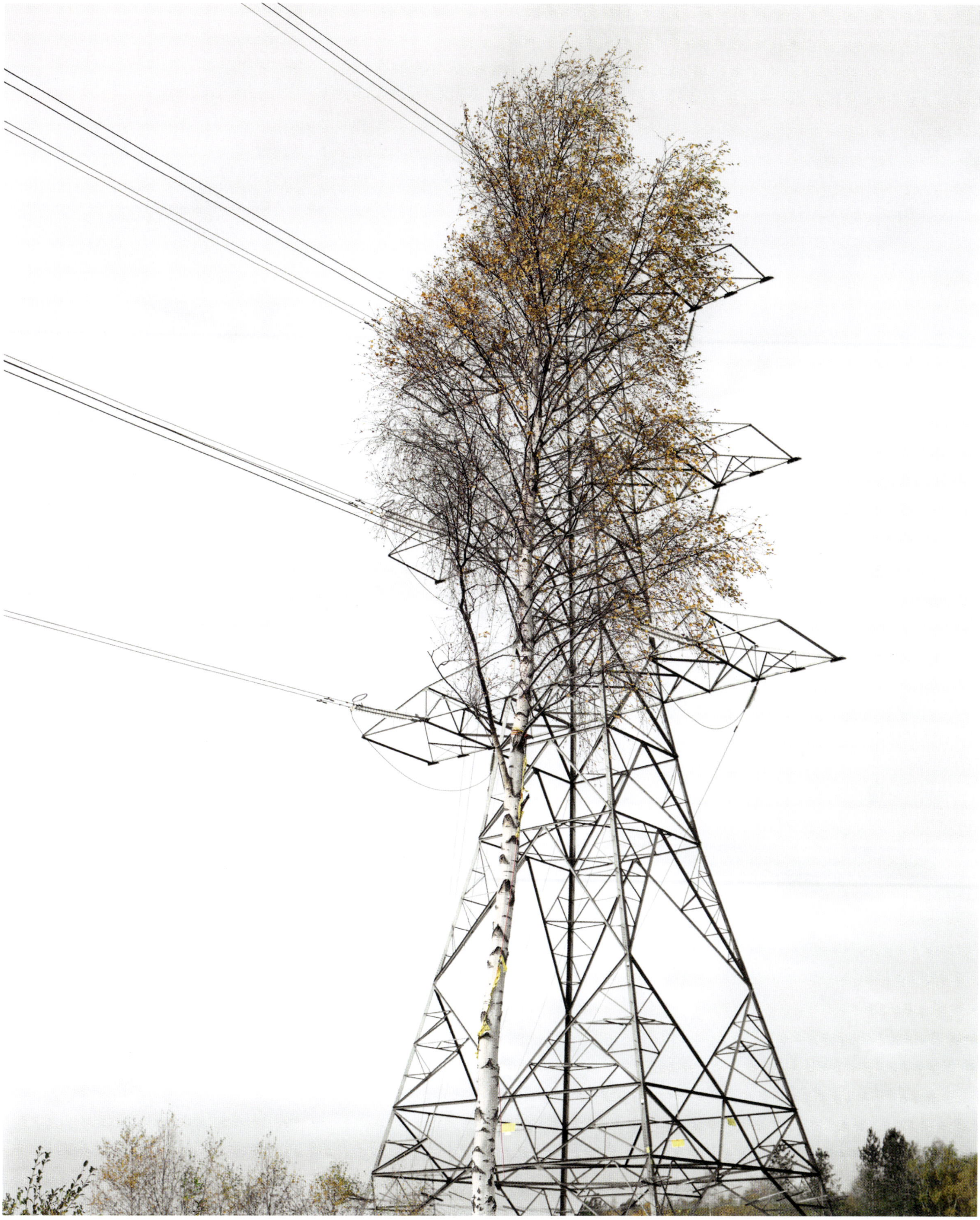

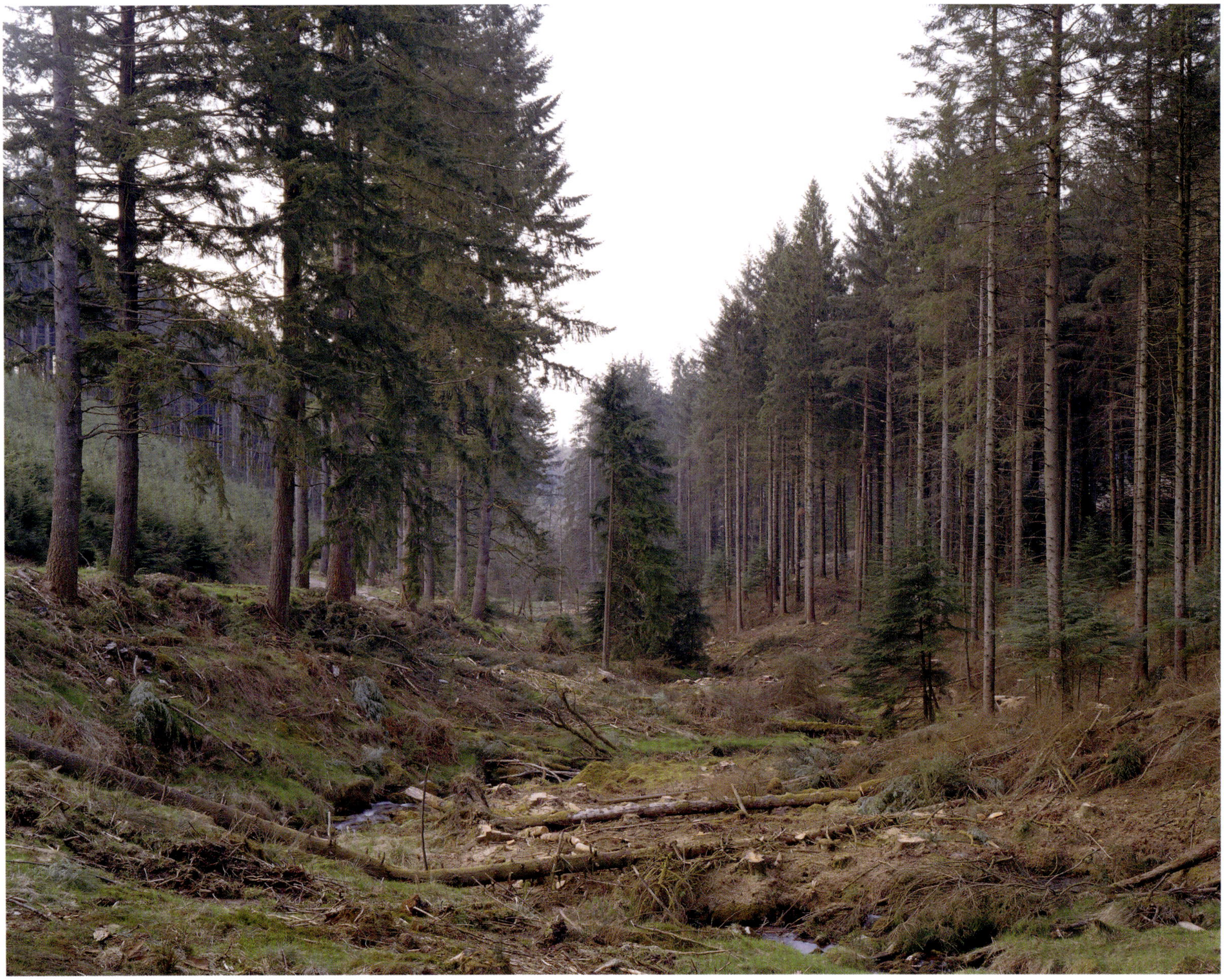

Forestry Plantation, Dartmoor, England, 2005

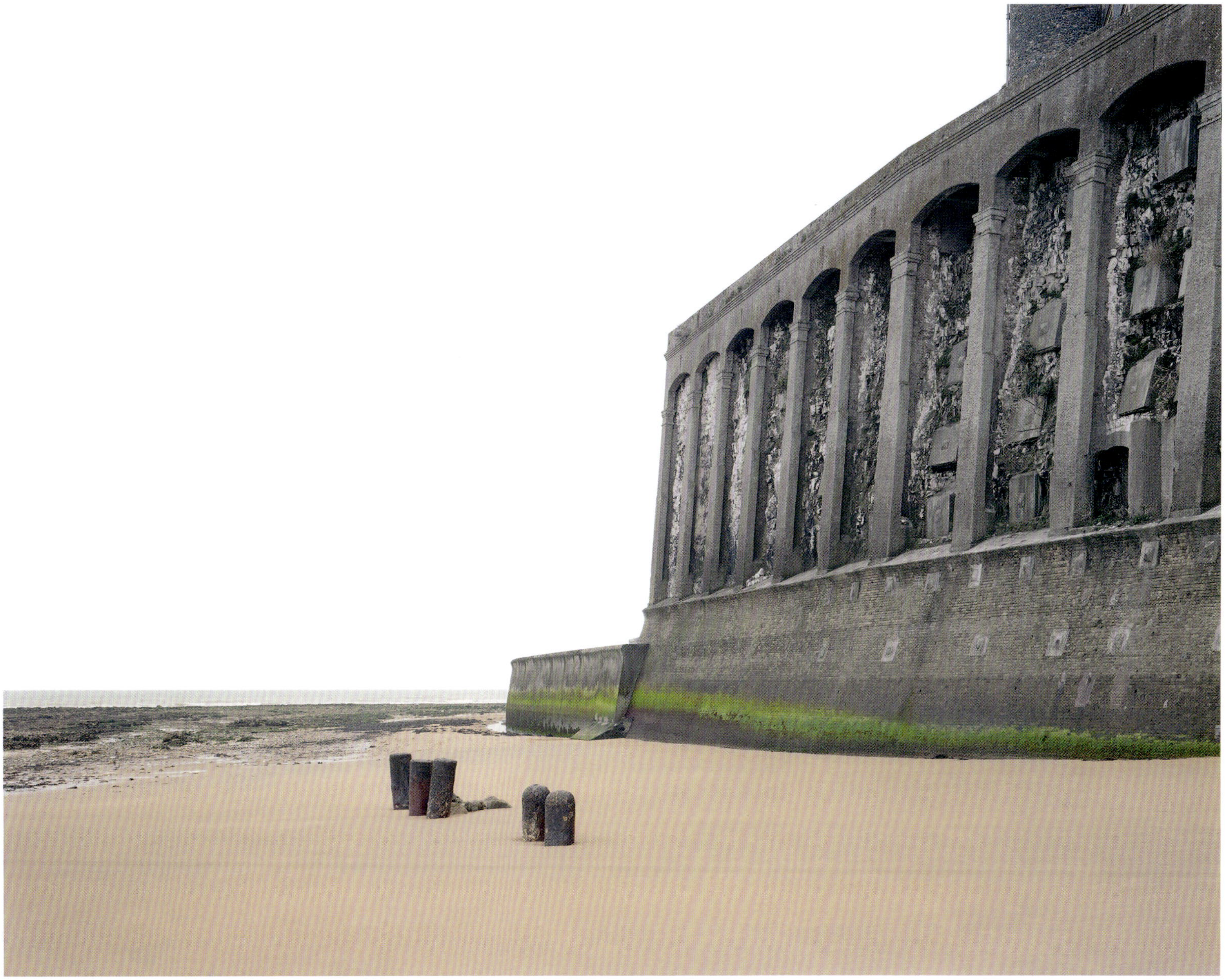

Kingsgate Bay, England, 2016

Gaewern Slate Mine, Corris, Wales, 2014

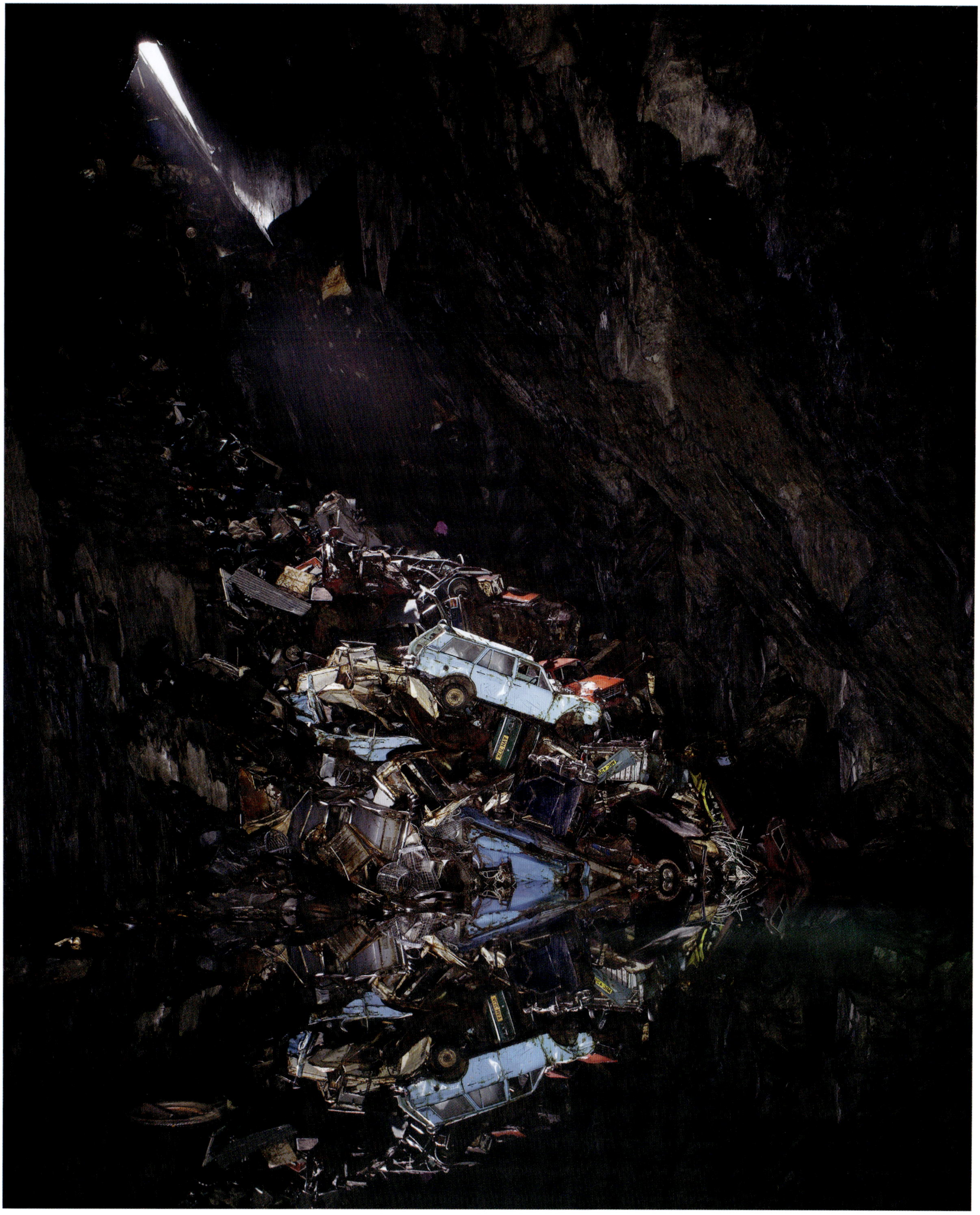

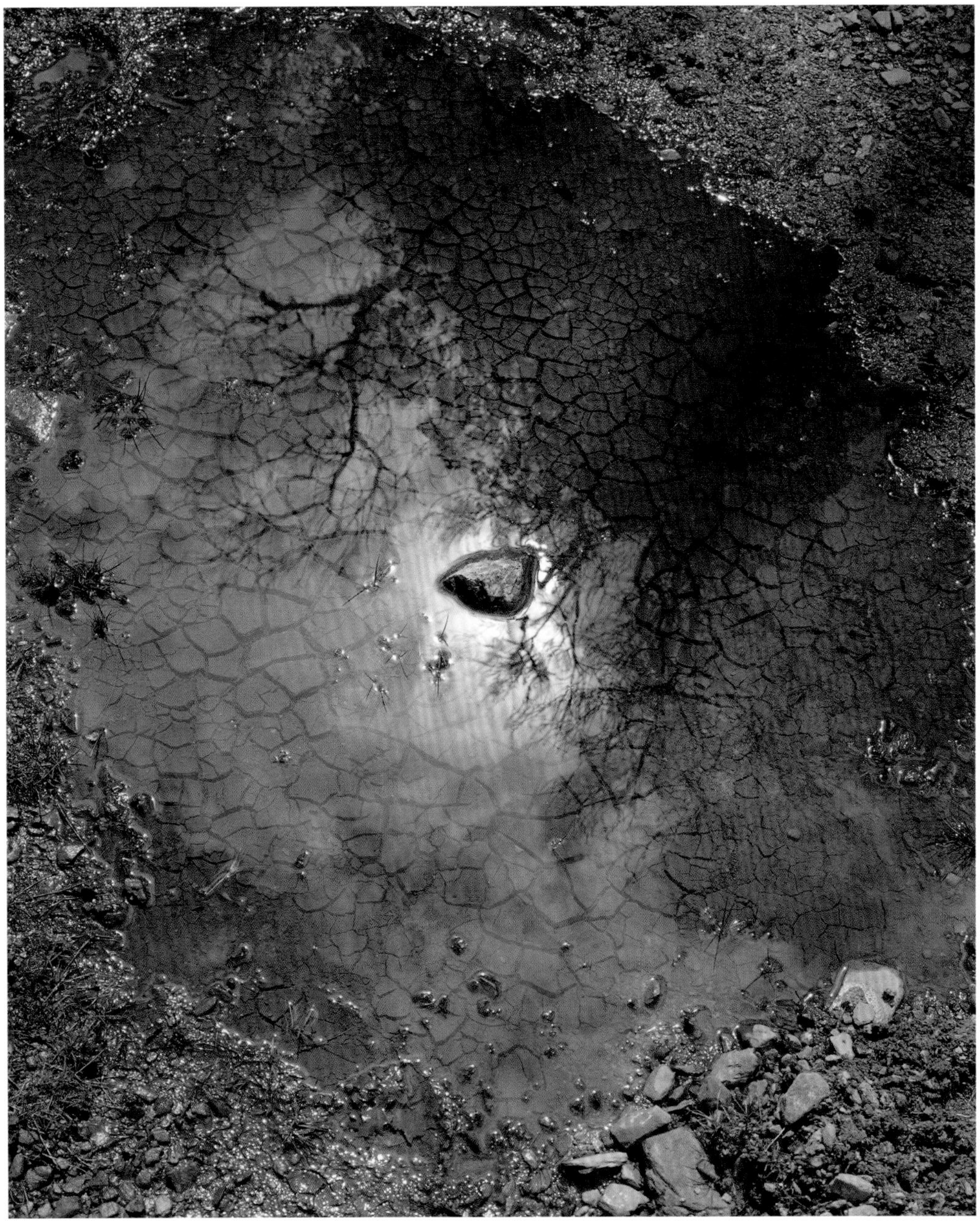

Hodge Close Quarry, Coniston, England, 2018

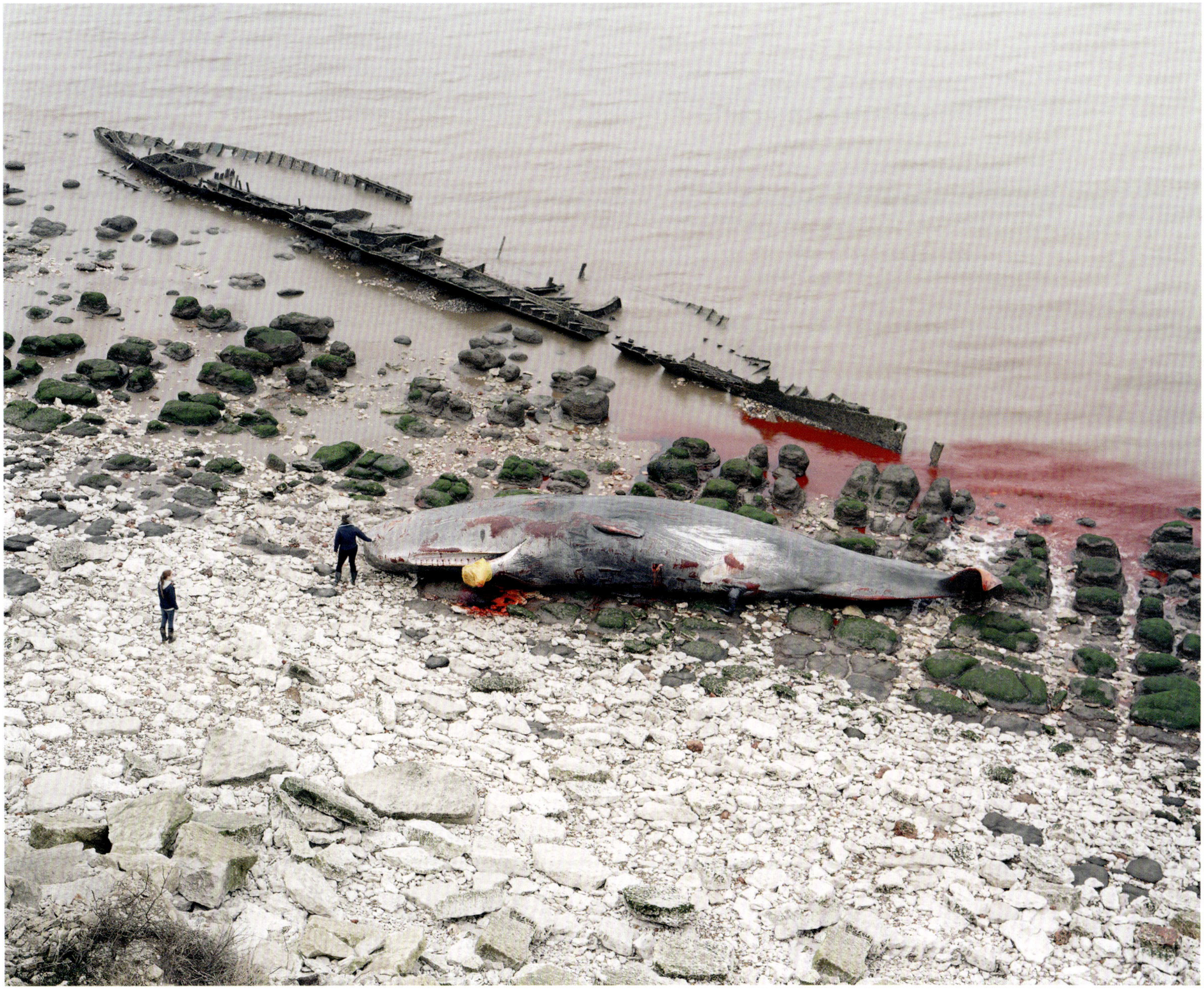

Sperm Whale, Hunstanton, England, 2016

Black Dots

Nicholas J R White

'[The process] is stripped back to the bare bones. I have a chat with a stranger, build a fire, and then we walk off the next morning and never see each other again.'

A bothy is a small, basic hut or cottage in a remote place. The door is left unlocked, ready to welcome weary travellers in need of somewhere to stay. Many of them are located in the Scottish Highlands, though others exist in Wales and the Lake District. The terrain where they are built is equally varied, ranging from mountains and meadows to sweeping coastline. For Nicholas J R White, bothies weren't just a point of interest in the landscape, but the very thing that allowed him to explore it. Being able to move between these entirely free forms of accommodation allowed him to cover much more ground as he travelled through some of Britain's wilder reaches on foot – capturing the images that would eventually become part of *Black Dots*.

White's childhood holidays were spent hillwalking on Dartmoor, where he now lives. Taking a camera out with him felt like a natural progression. What began as a method of documenting friends and family in the outdoors later became a profession. Today his work is still attentive to secluded spaces where walkers can find shelter. The bothies provide a sense of scale: something to focus on against the vastness of mist-capped mountains and distant lakes. In a few images, the buildings themselves are (aptly) little more than black dots. On one trip, after a six-hour hike through the Cairngorms, White camped out for three days to photograph a bothy against a white expanse of snow, its silhouette tiny beneath The Devil's Point. With all the photos taken on a large format camera, White only took two sheets of film for the entire trip – packing light so as to carry everything with him. This explains the sparing quality of each image, the considered sense of stillness in this project devoted to places that can only be reached by walking.

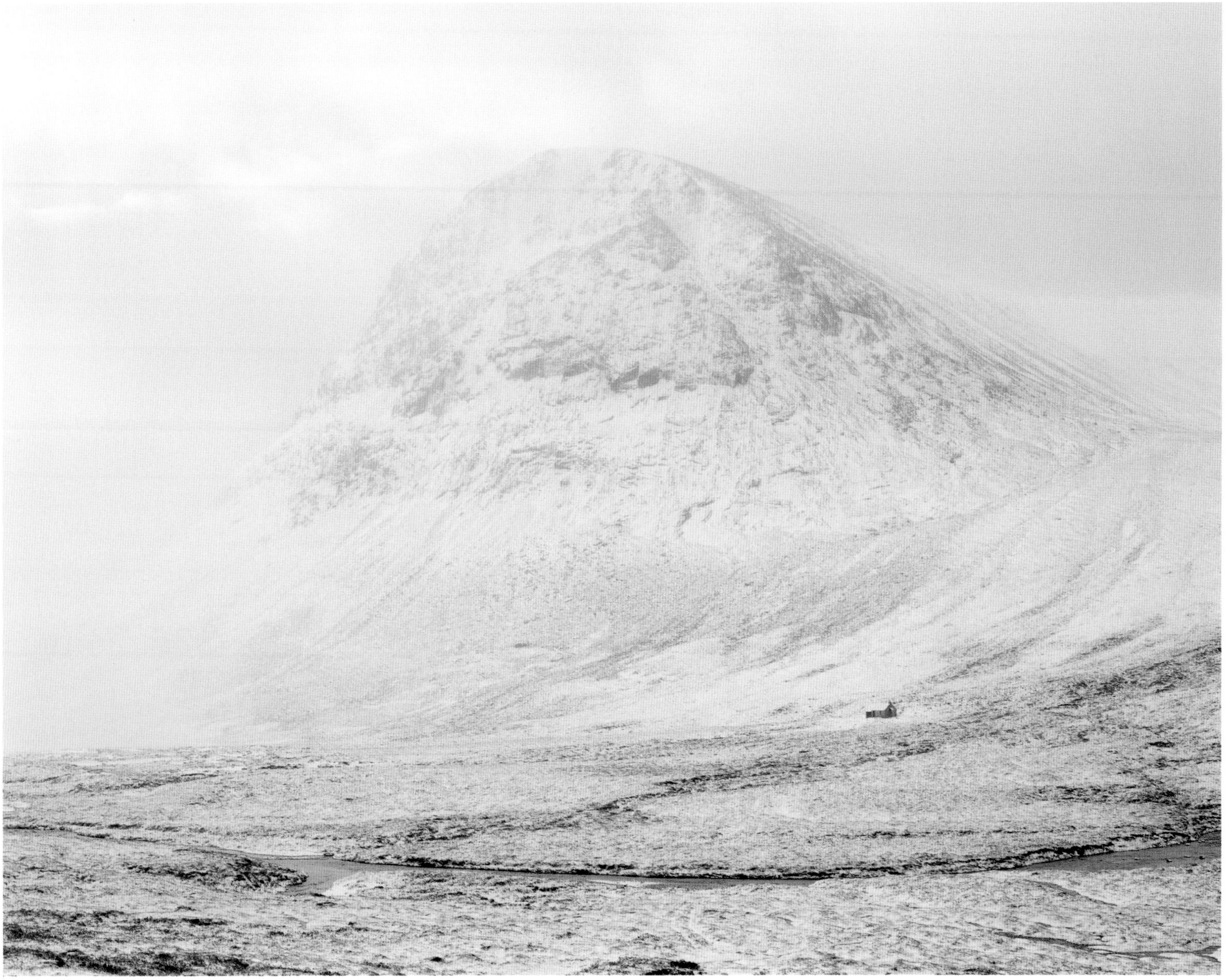

Corrour Bothy and The Devil's Point, Cairngorms, Scotland, January 2017

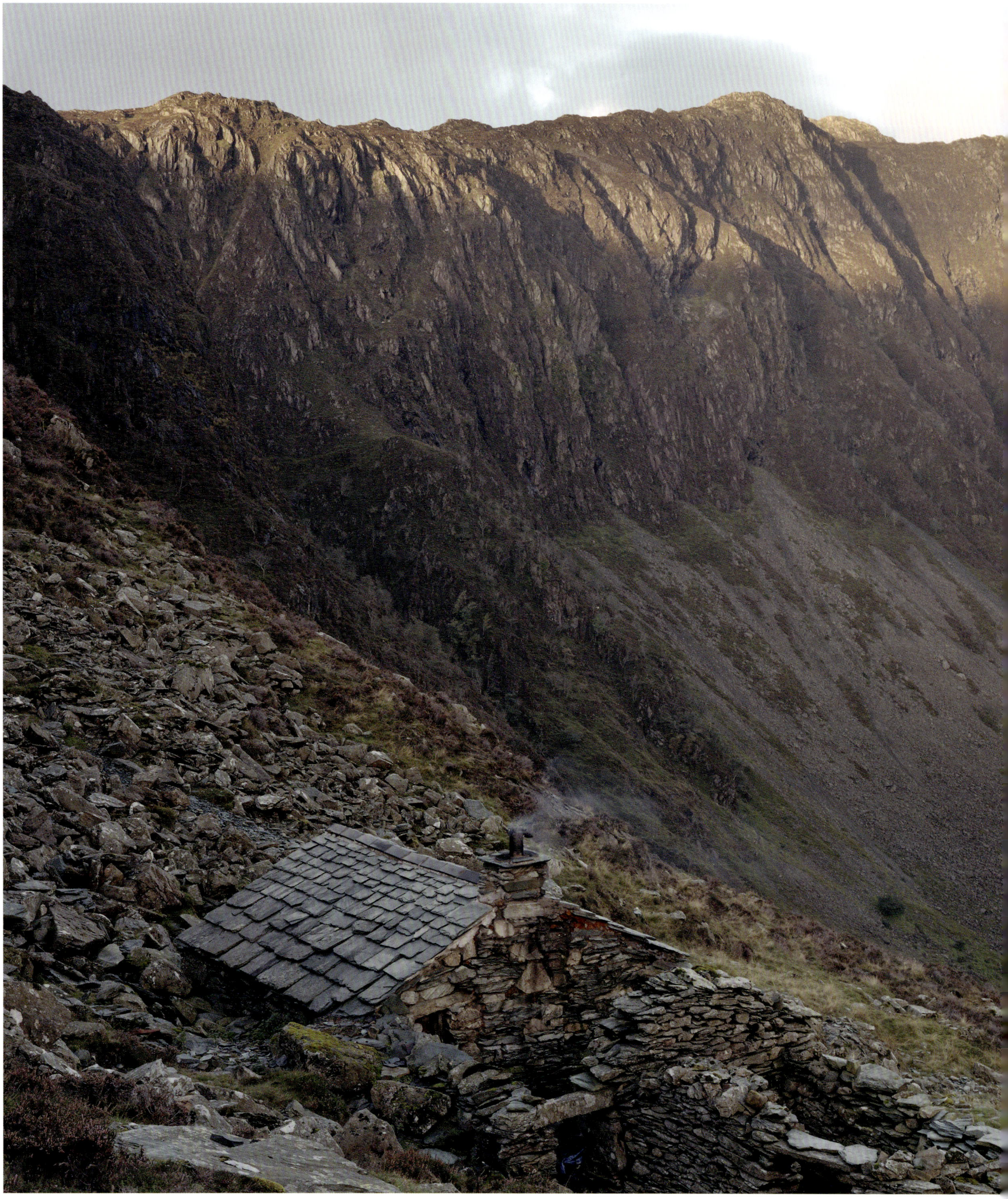

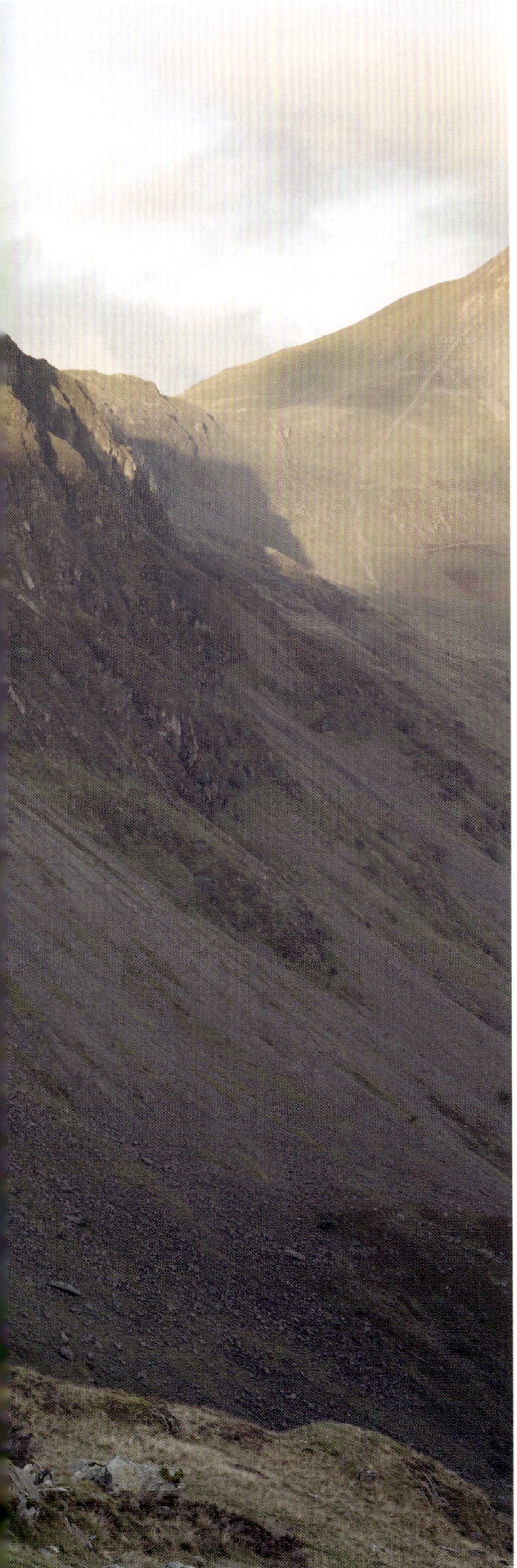

Warnscale Head and Haystacks, Lake District, England, October 2015

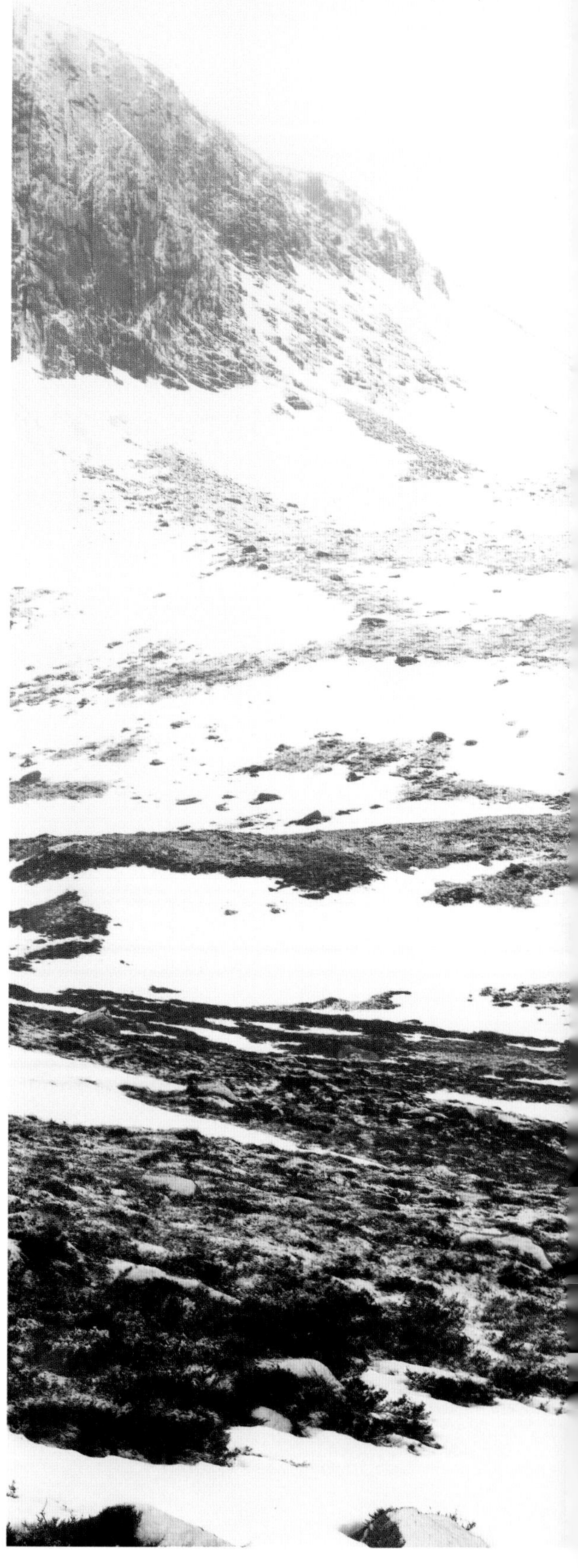

Hutchinson Memorial Hut, Cairngorms, Scotland, March 2016

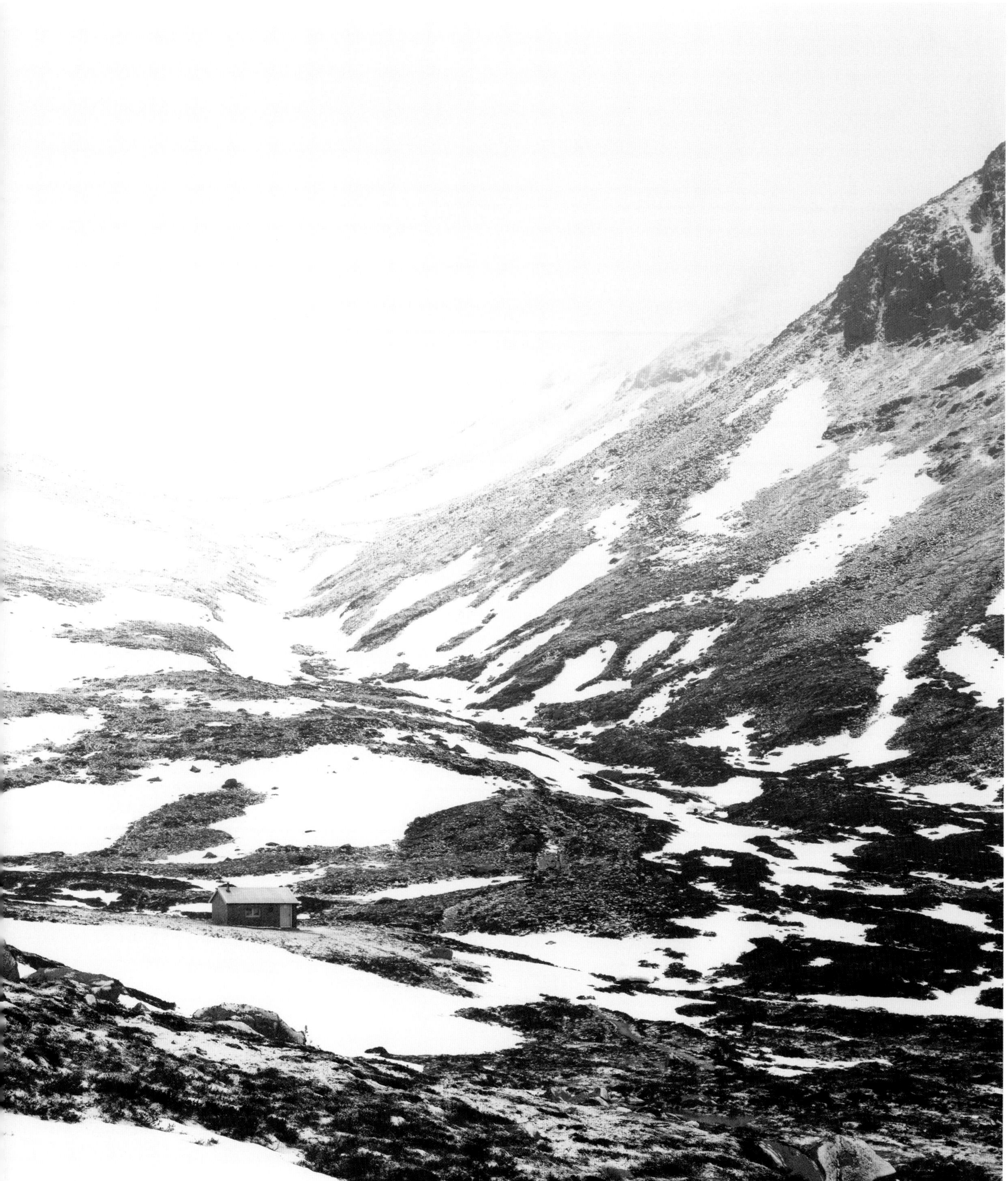

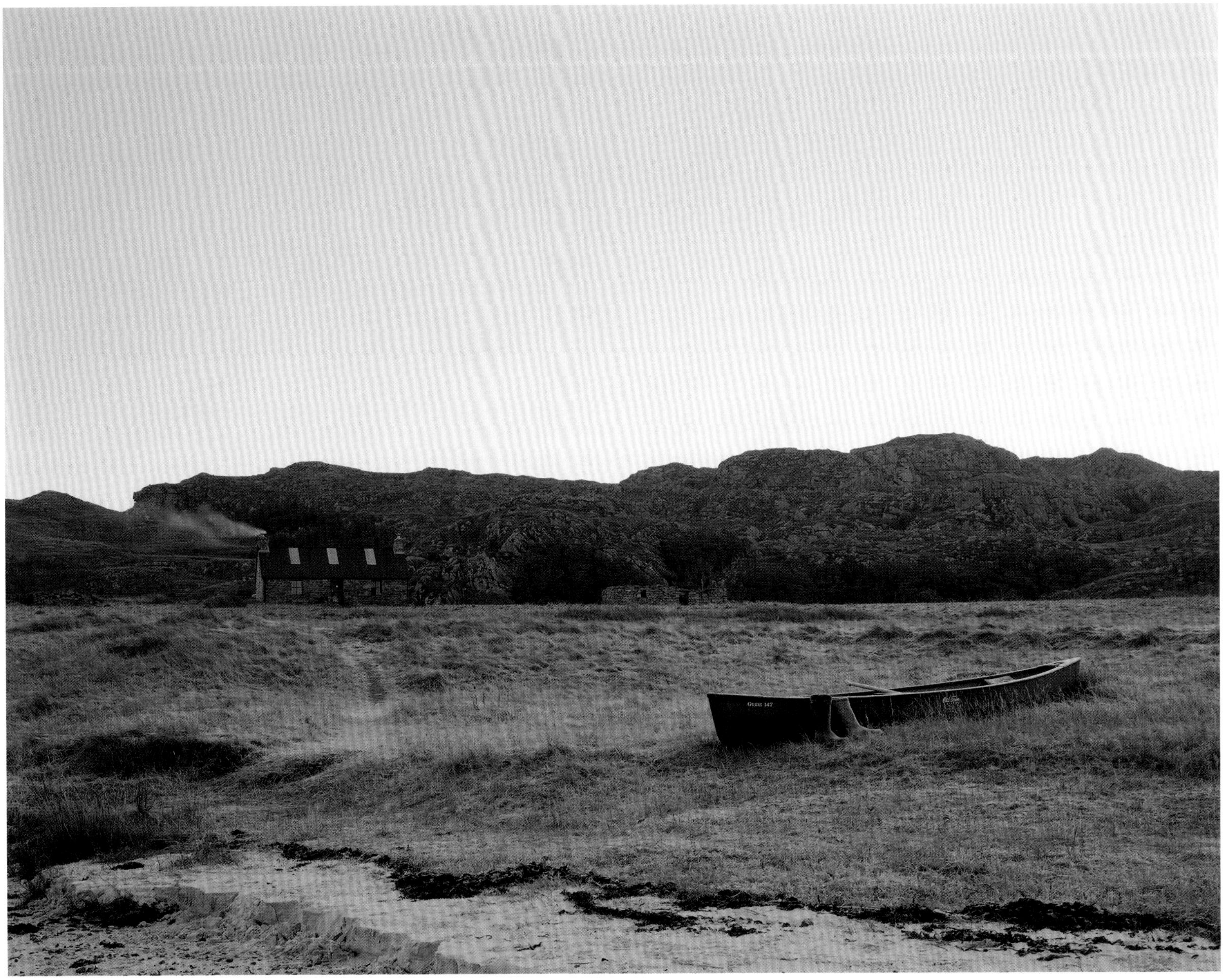

Sandy's canoe at Peanmeanach, Ardinsh peninsula, Scotland, October 2016

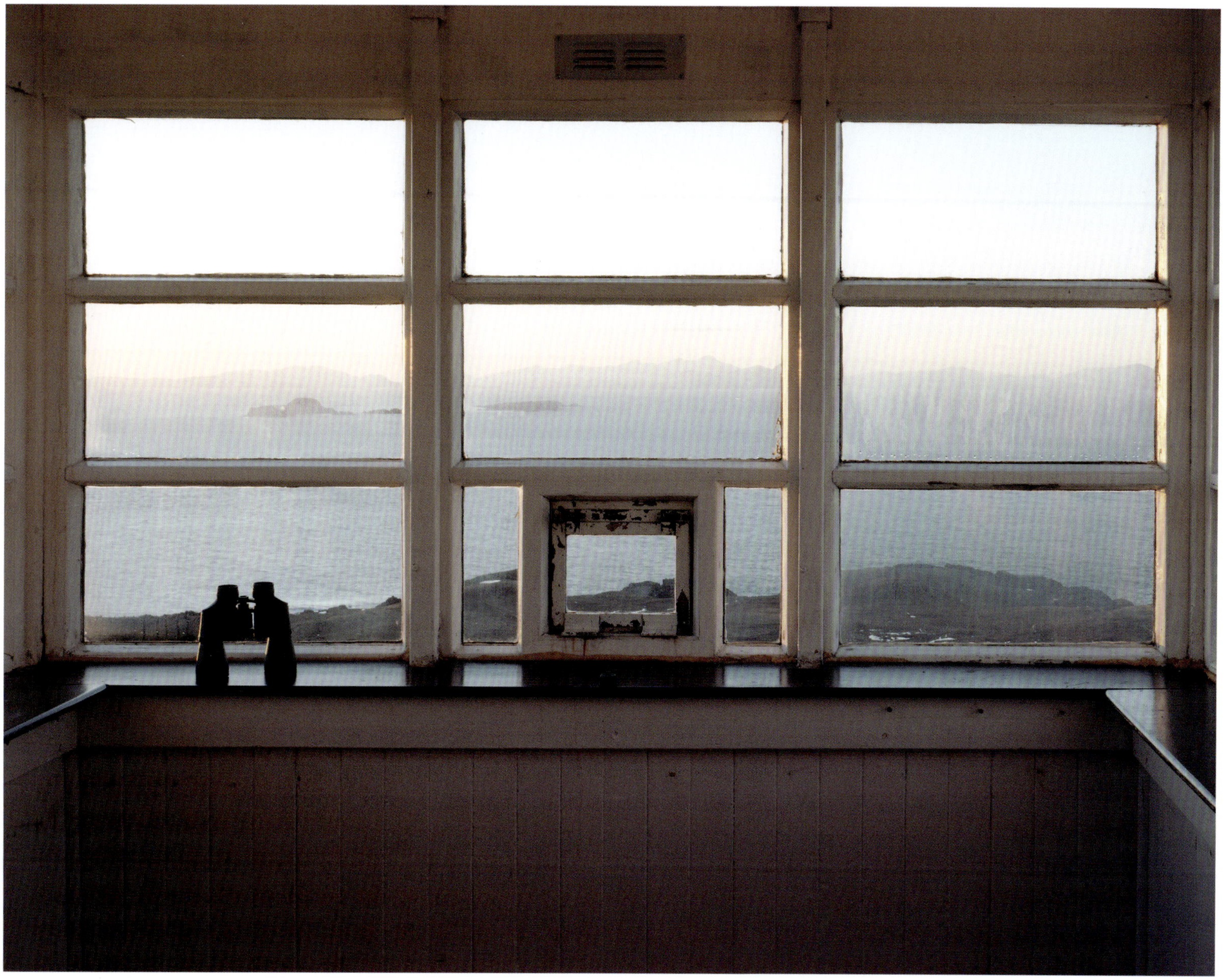

The Lookout bothy, Isle of Skye, Scotland, March 2016

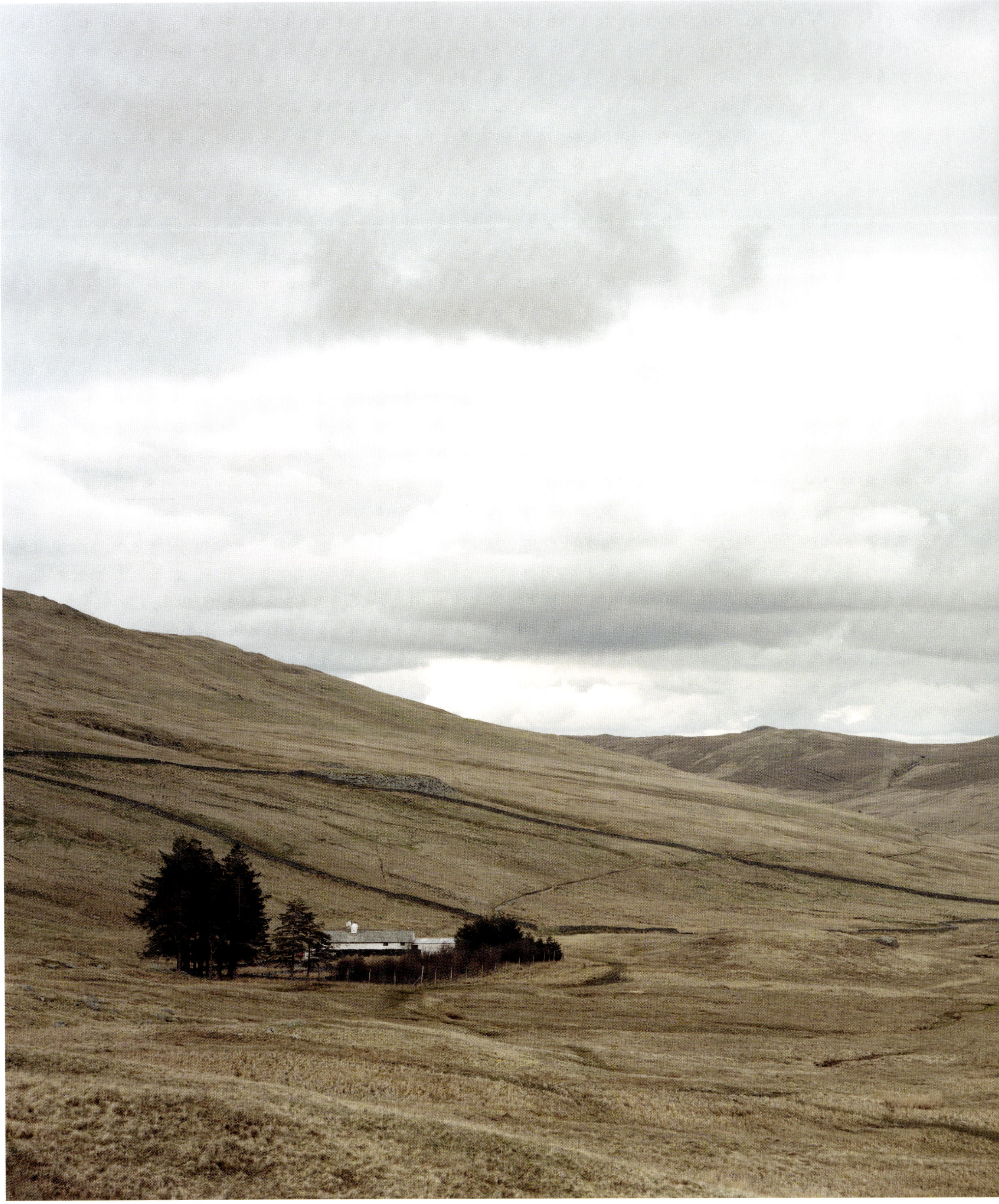

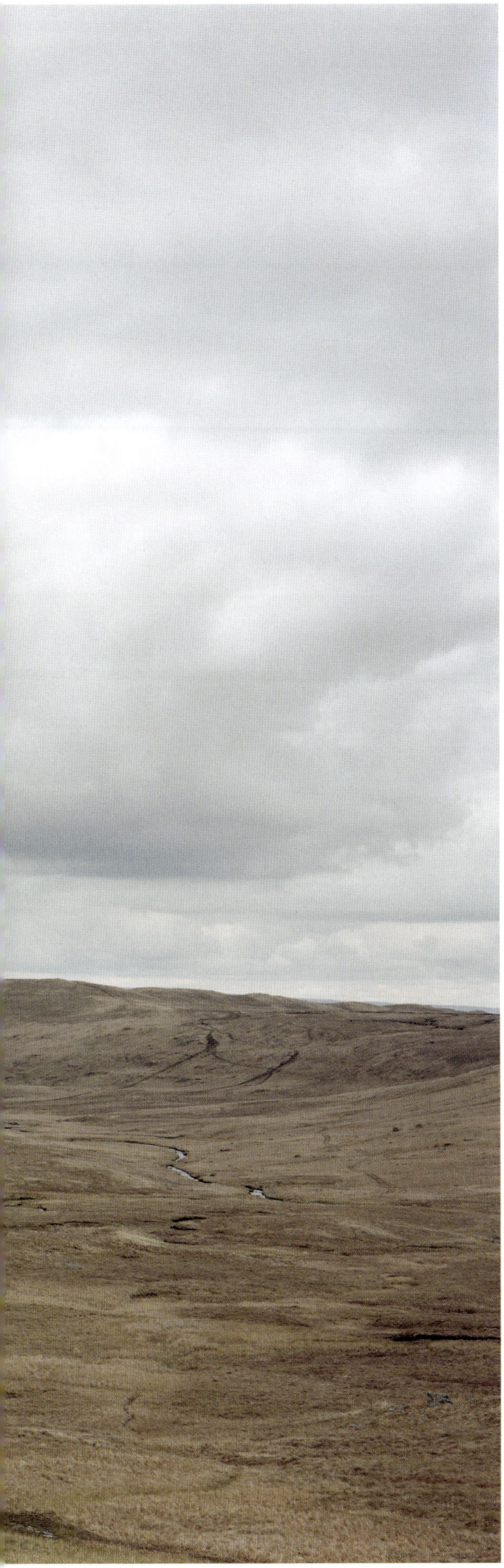

Mosedale Cottage, Lake District, England, May 2015

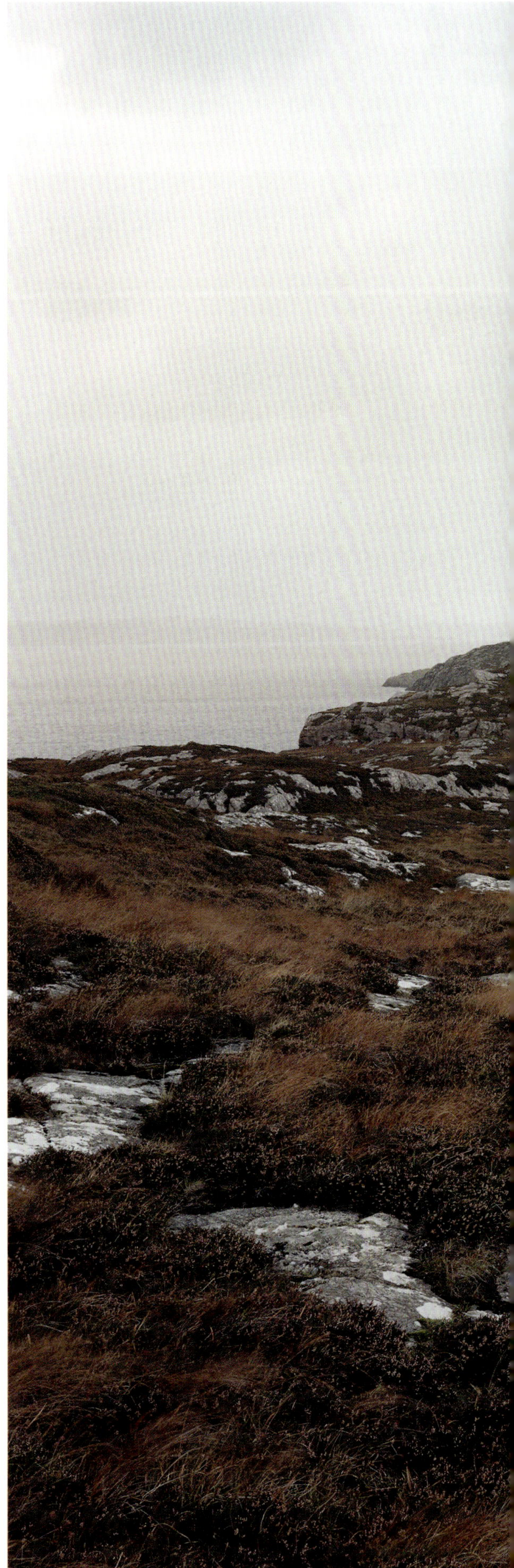

Taigh Thormoid Dhuibh, Raasay, Scotland, October 2016

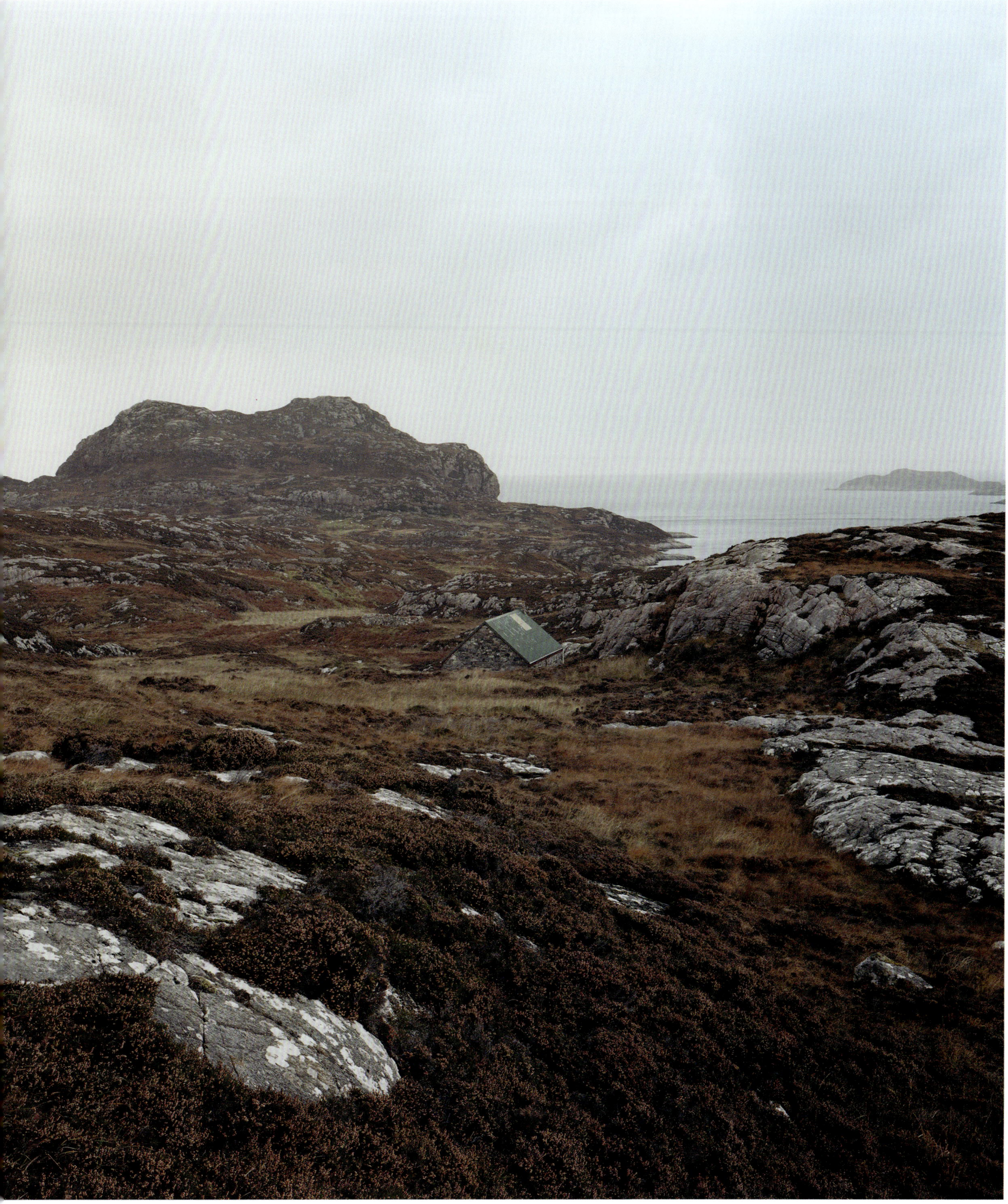

The Gatekeepers

Alex Ingram

'Each island has its self-contained story... If you do a portrait of someone, you spend time with them, get to know them. It's the same with a portrait of an island.'

Much as we might dream of living beyond easy reach, island life is not for everyone. It requires a stoic willingness to accept that if the weather cuts you off from supplies and civilisation, you'll just have to manage. Alex Ingram's *The Gatekeepers* is an ongoing project documenting the wardens of Britain's small islands. Skomer, Bardsey, Flat Holm, Lundy, the Isle of May – they all host remarkable populations of wildlife, as well as a few humans tasked with their stewardship.

Ingram grew up in St Davids in Wales, relatively near a handful of islands, including Skomer. Curious about what it might take to live and work somewhere so remote, Ingram reached out to a couple living there and asked if he could stay with them. In 2017 he spent several days on Skomer, just a mile off the Welsh coast, finding himself among acres of volcanic rock, craggy bays, grasslands and puffin colonies. When he was due to return home, a storm delayed his journey by another week. It was an apt immersion. In a place where there are no cars, supermarkets or even, sometimes, fresh water, one must be resourceful – and relatively at peace with moving to the rhythms of the natural world.

Ingram has since documented many islands, hosted each time by their wardens. Often employed by wildlife organisations, they complete important tasks including scientific research. Sometimes it is gruelling work. Recently they have faced harrowing outbreaks of avian flu, which threaten rare bird colonies. Ingram has also had to adapt to the demands of these isolated locations; *The Gatekeepers* is shot on film not only for aesthetic reasons, but also practical ones. A mechanical camera is easier to fix if it breaks and easier to dry if it's caught in a rainstorm. The resulting photos are sensitively observed, recording the gentleness of the changing light as the winds shift and waves break over a rocky inlet.

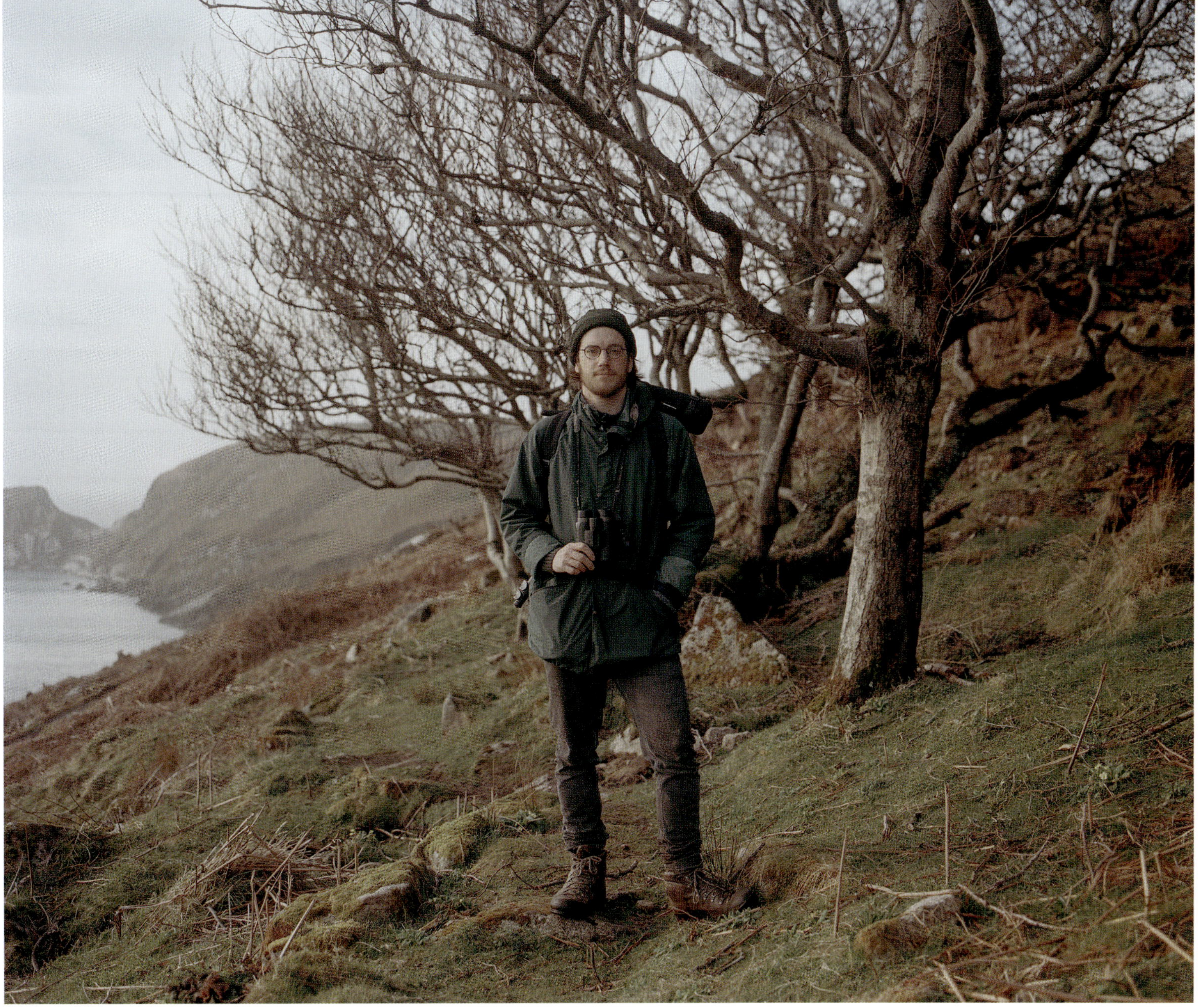

Dean Woodfin Jones, Lundy Island, England, 2018

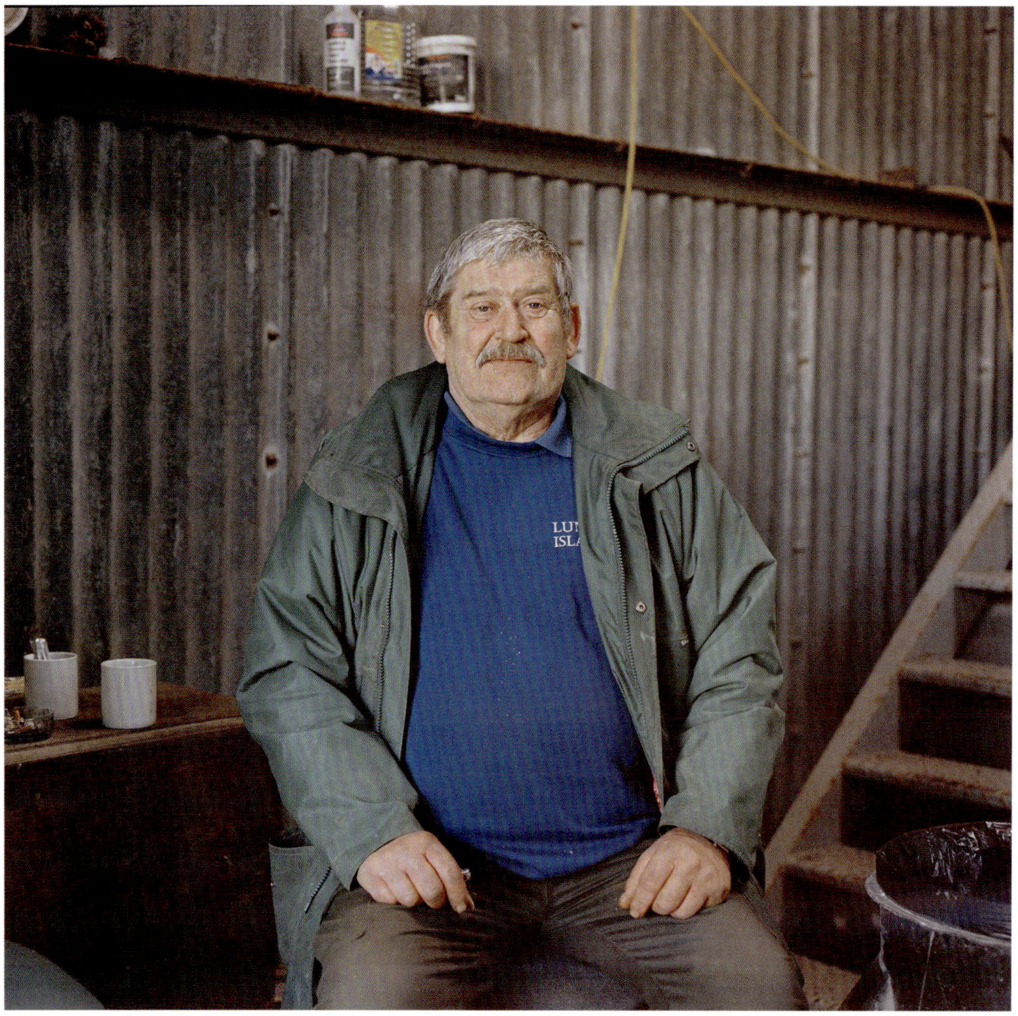

Kevin Walsh, Lundy Island, England, 2018

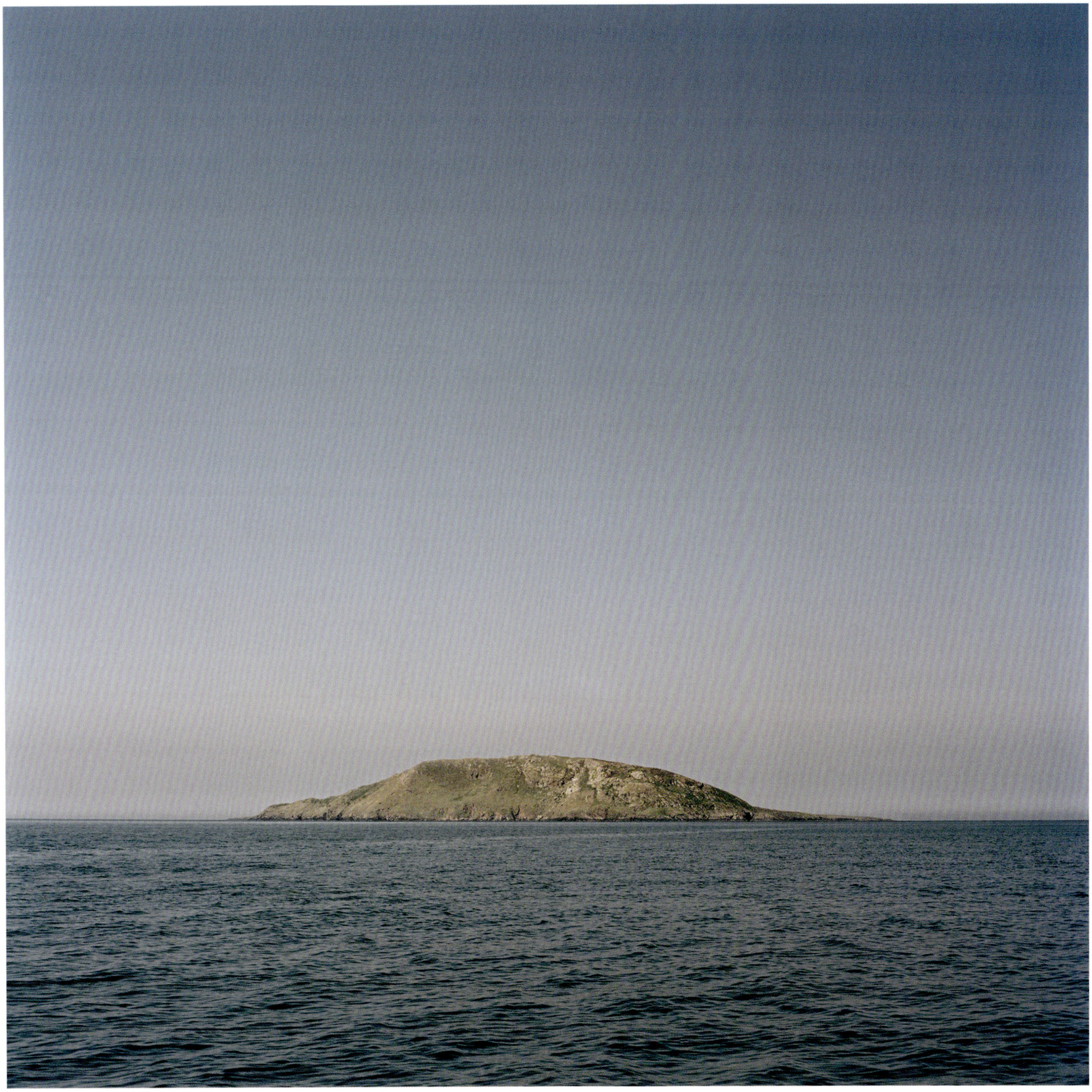

Bardsey Island, Wales, 2018

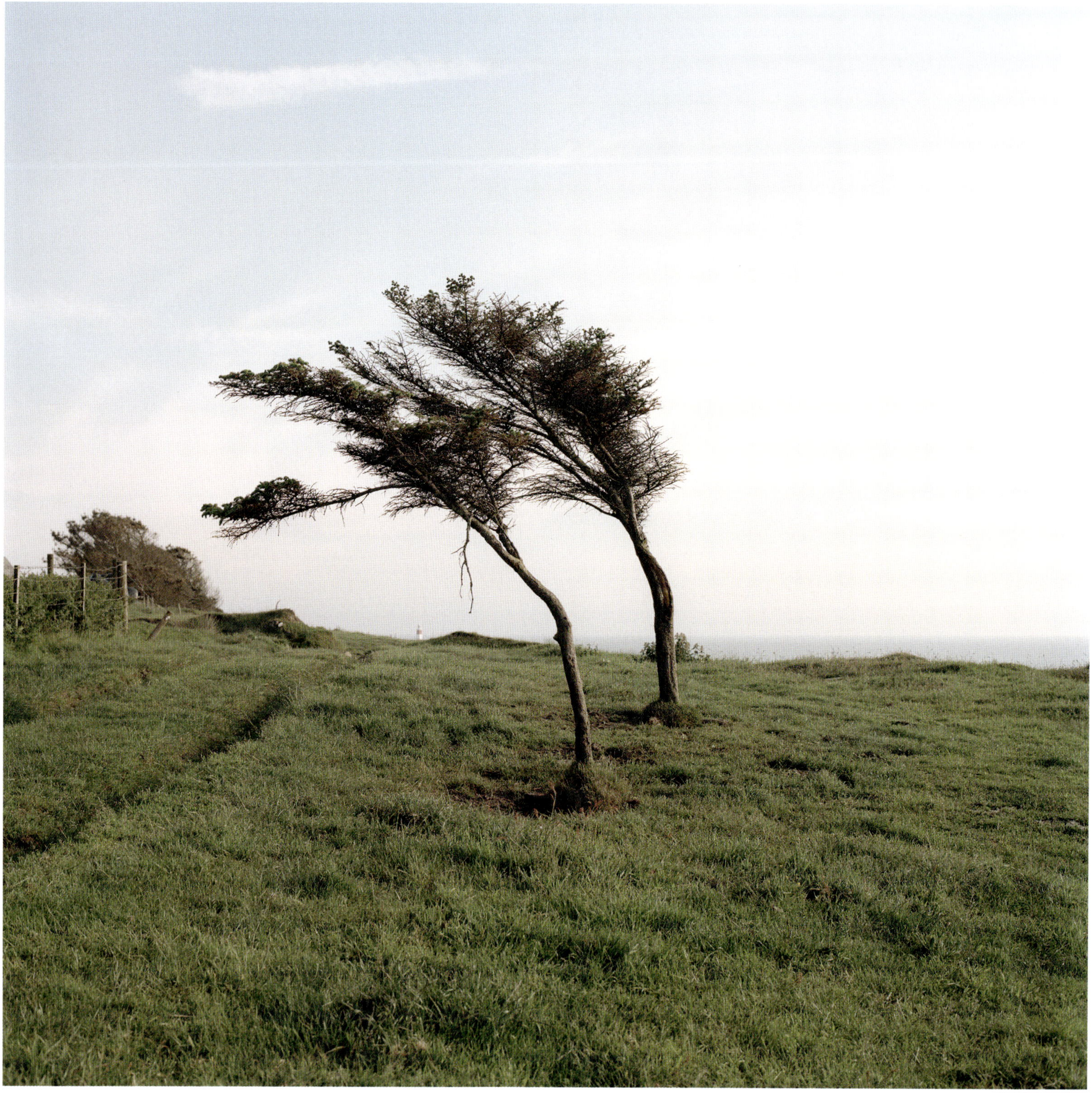

Bardsey Island, Wales, 2018

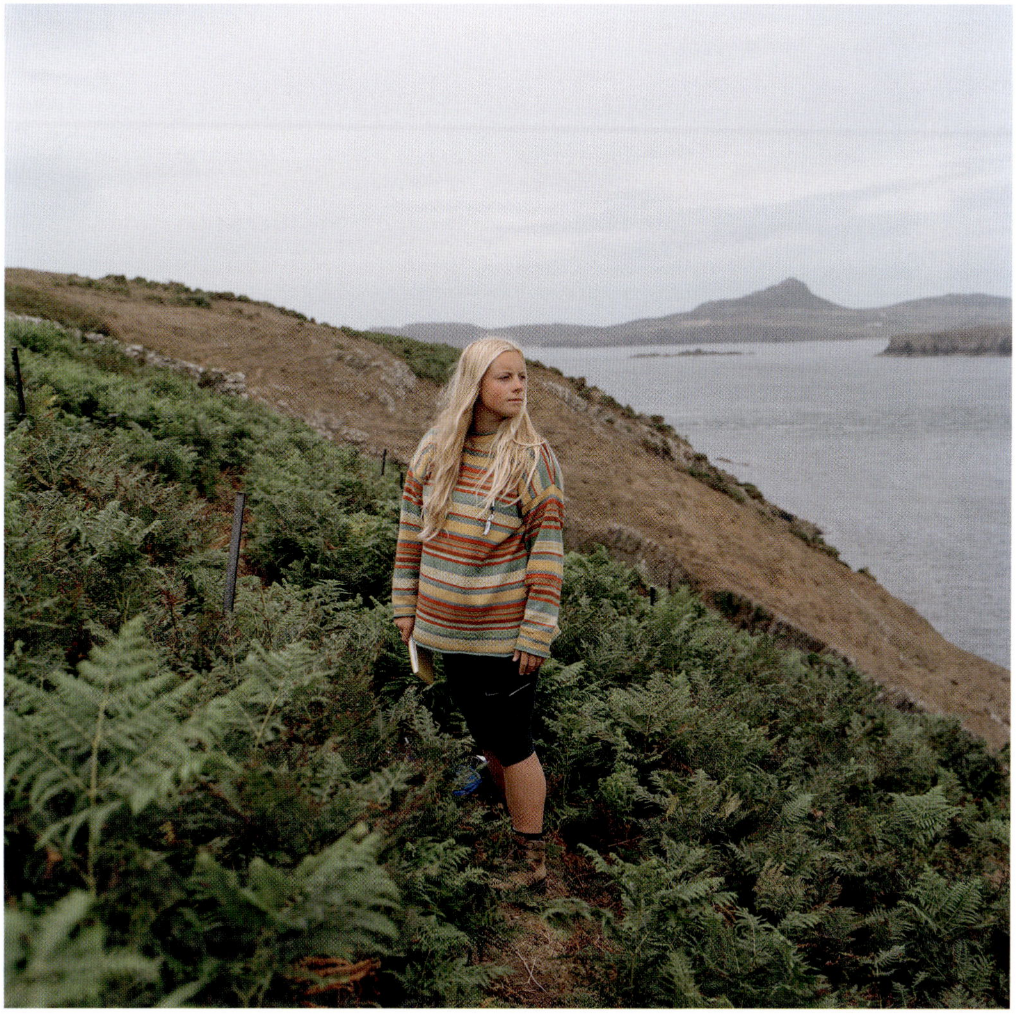

Alys Perry, Ramsey Island, Wales, 2019

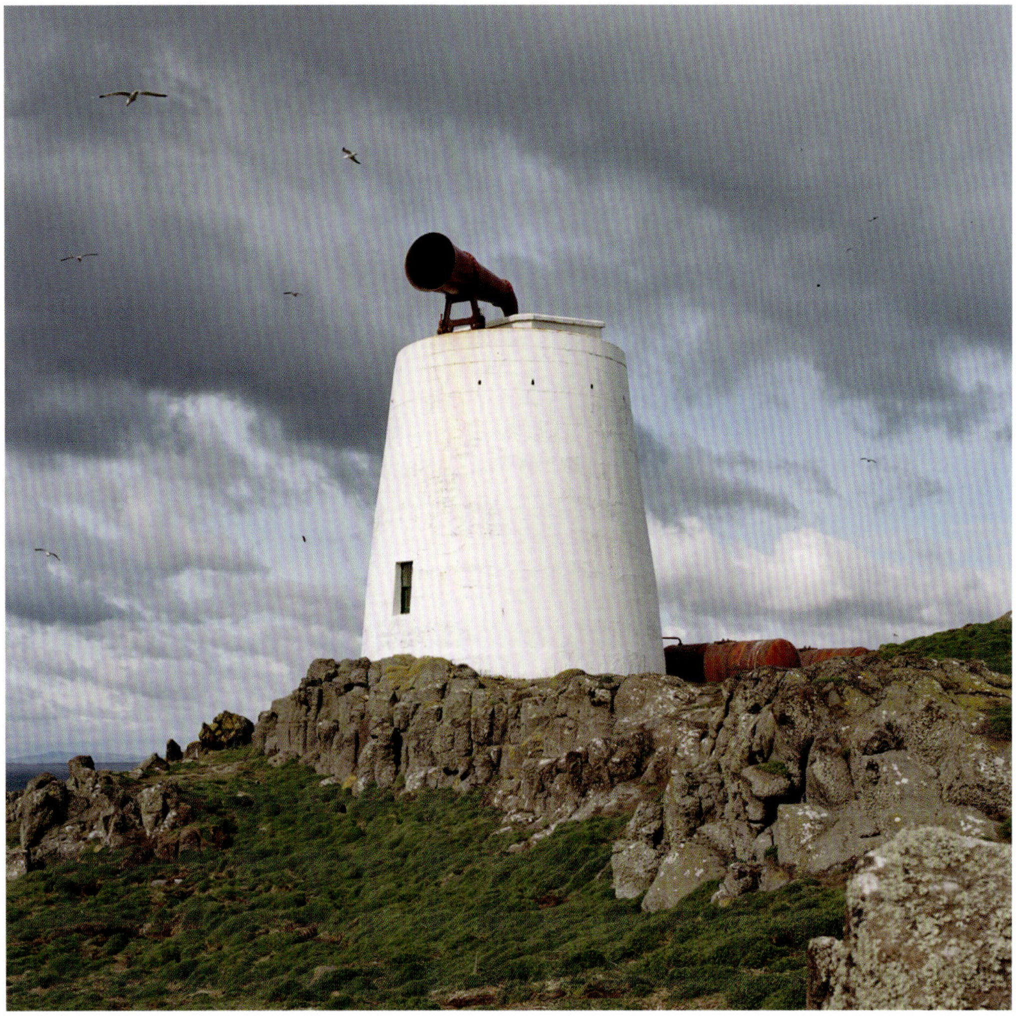

Fog Horn, Isle of May, Scotland, 2022

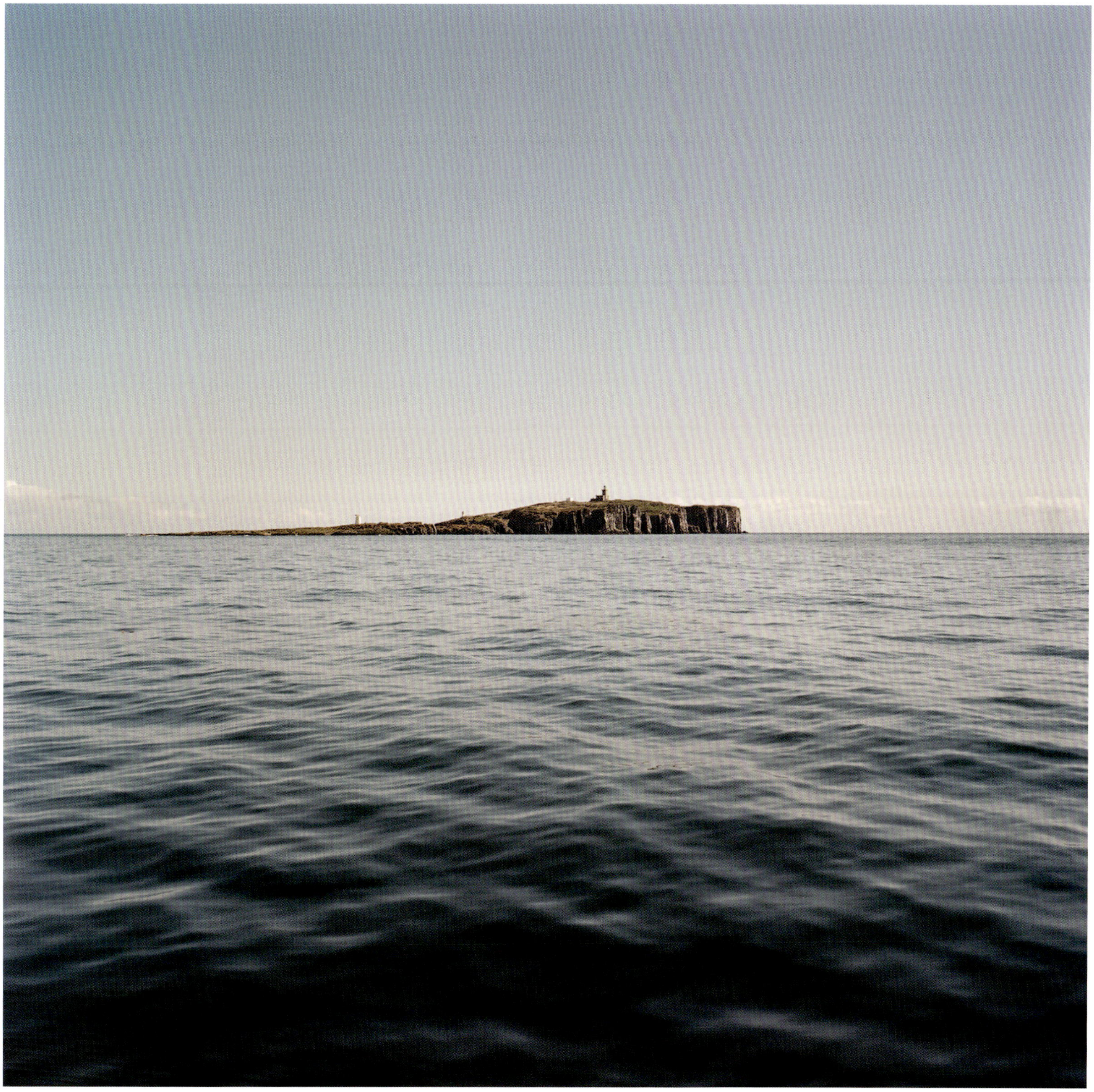

Isle of May, Scotland, 2022

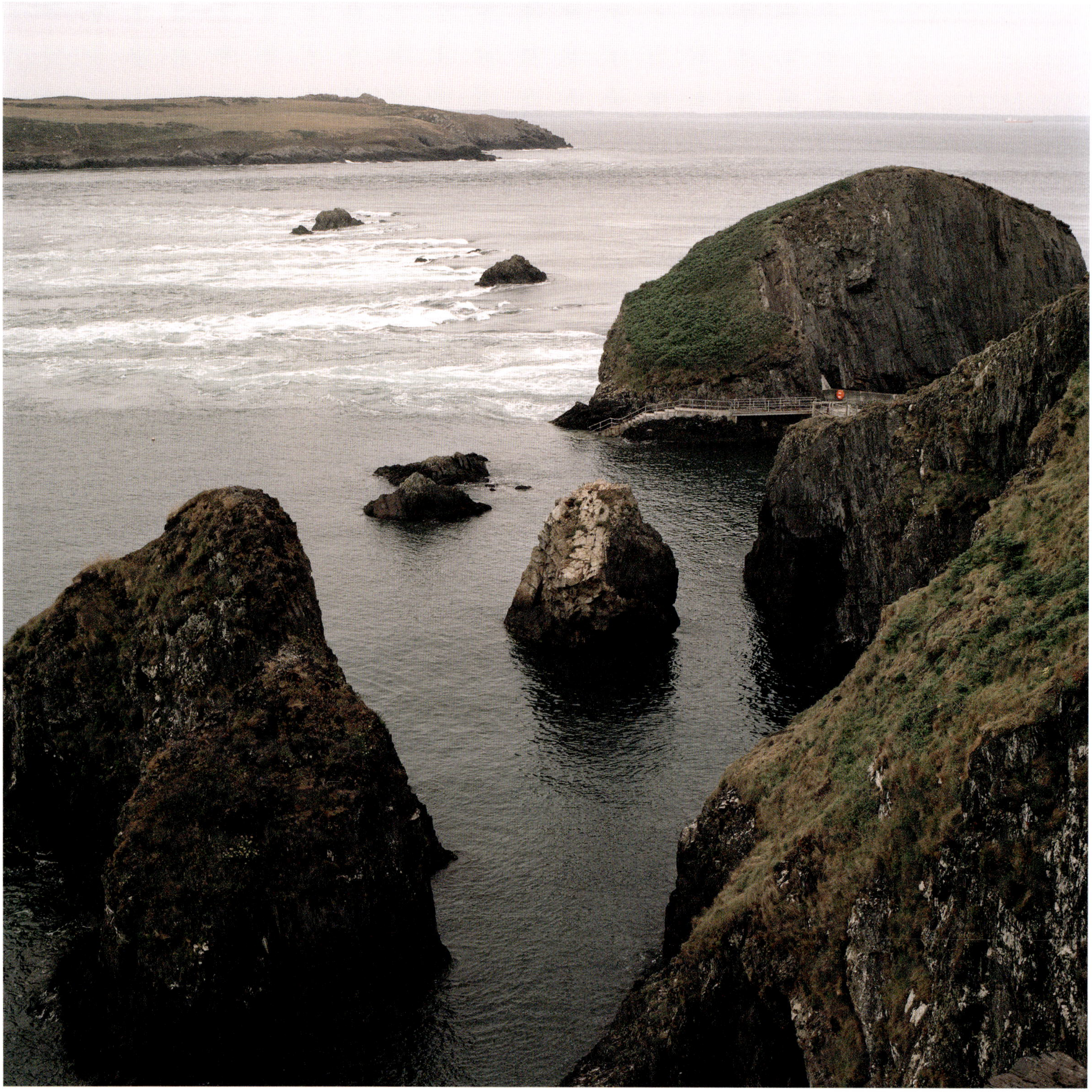

Ramsey Harbour, Ramsey Island, Wales, 2019

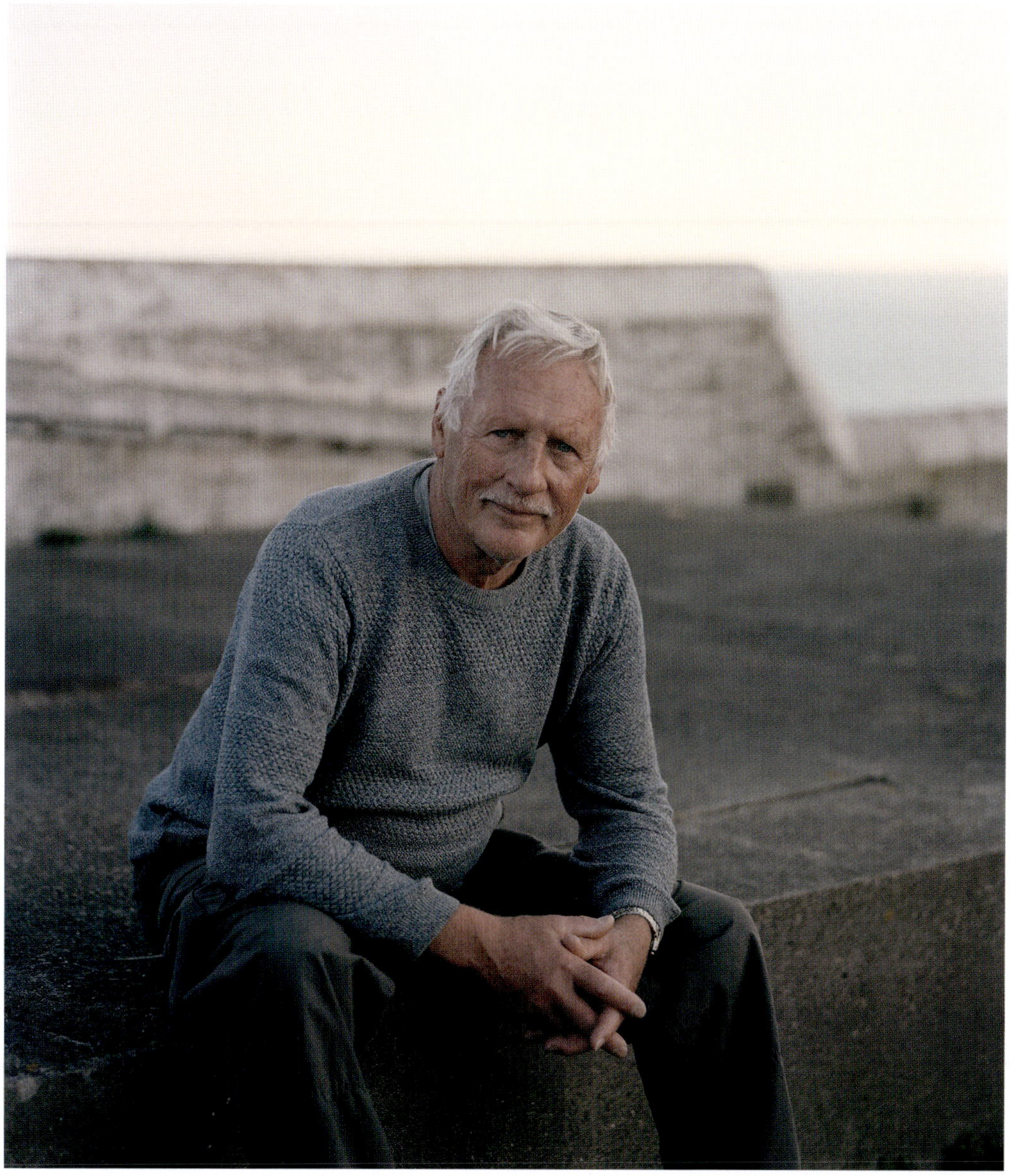

Emyr, Skokholm Island, Wales, 2019

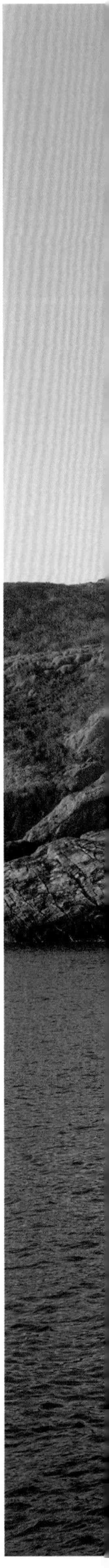

Skokholm Harbour, Skokholm Island, Wales, 2019

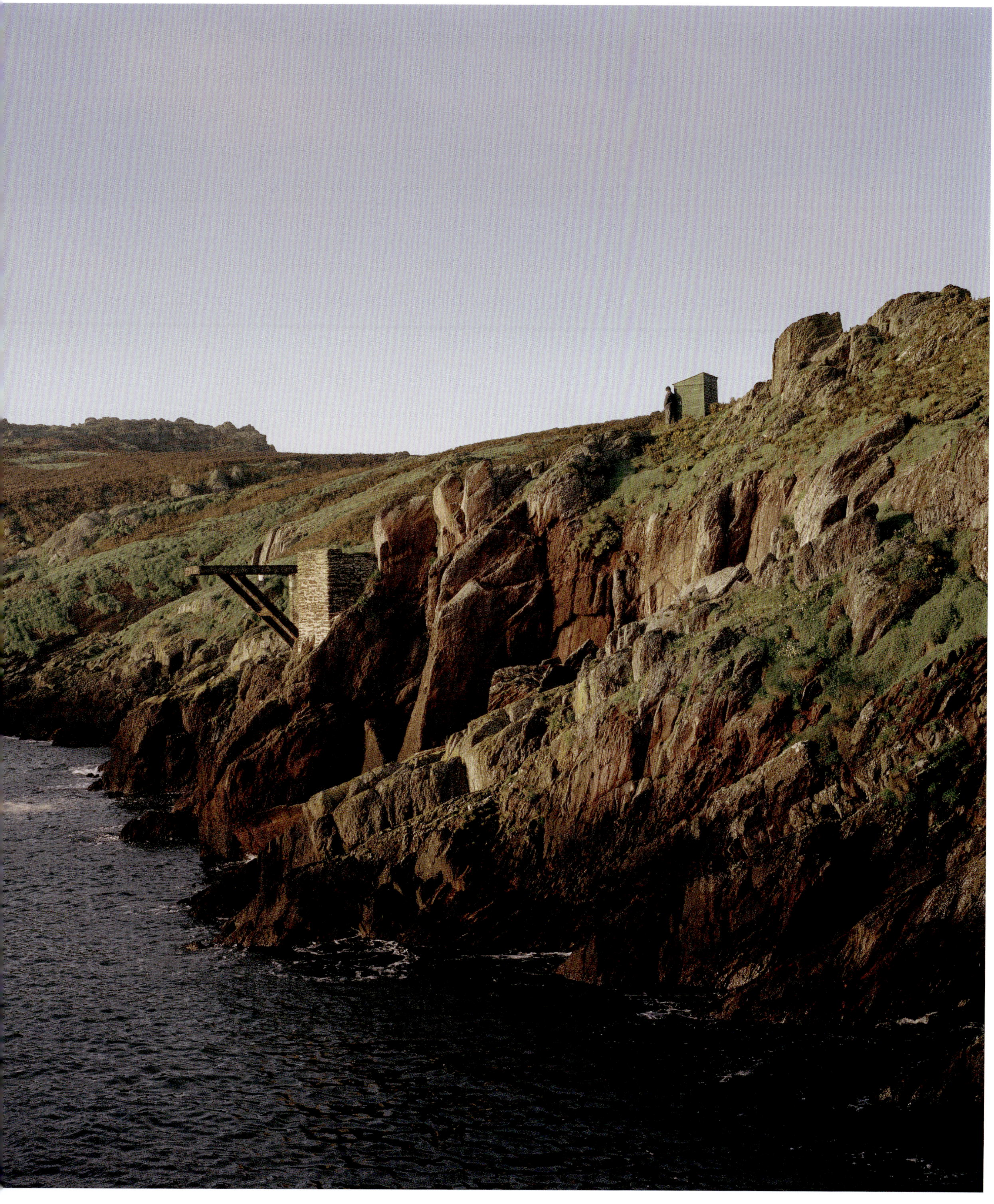

Land Loss

Max Miechowski

'I felt very much on the precipice... [with] this idea of being on a particular piece of land that will not exist in the future. Once it's gone, it's really gone.'

Max Miechowski's *Land Loss* captures a place on the brink. Along the east coast of England, there are homes and businesses at risk of falling into the waves. Norfolk and Yorkshire are especially vulnerable to coastal erosion, as their soft clay cliffs hold little defence against the unrelenting North Sea. *Land Loss* is about the villages and hamlets that suffer sudden, destructive transformation. Here, gardens disappear overnight, as landslides redraw the boundary between ground and water. Facing this ongoing loss of land, Miechowski's work captures a feeling of wavering uncertainty.

Coastal erosion has been happening for thousands of years, but climate change exacerbates the damage as rising sea levels and frequent gales further assail these cliffs. However, Miechowski's photos don't just speak to these unsettling environmental implications. They also say something broader about the nature of impermanence, and the way in which the camera functions as a tool of preservation. Every time he travelled to these coastal areas, often sleeping in his car to catch coppery 5am dawns down on the beach, he found himself in close proximity to the implacable and unstoppable passage of time. At least one of the houses that he photographed has since vanished. Although money is being invested in coastal defence structures, not everywhere can be saved. Even where such defences are built, often they can only slow the inevitable rather than prevent it entirely. There is a melancholy atmosphere to Miechowski's images, an elegy for a disappearing landscape.

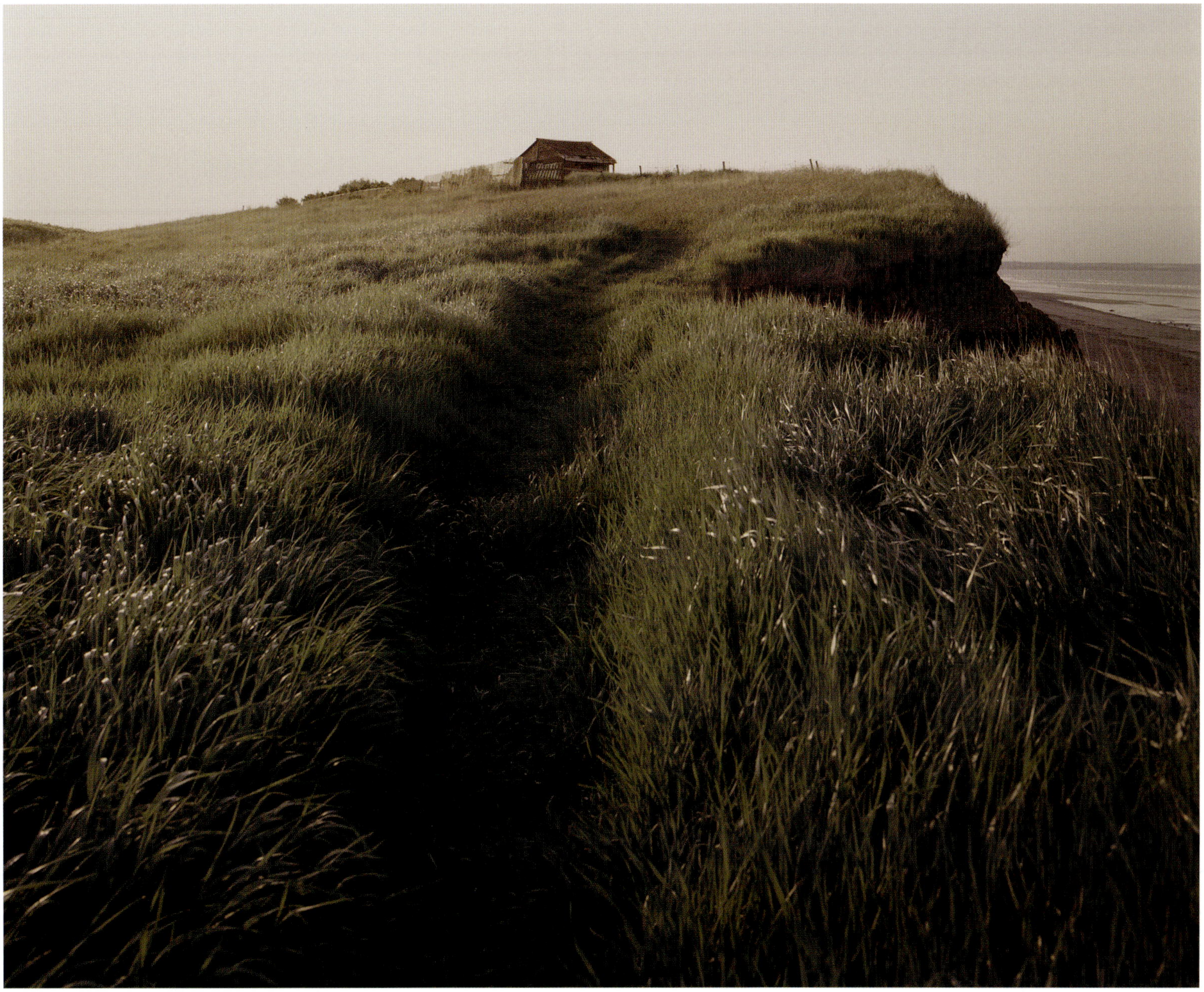

Coastal Path, Skipsea, Yorkshire, England, 2021

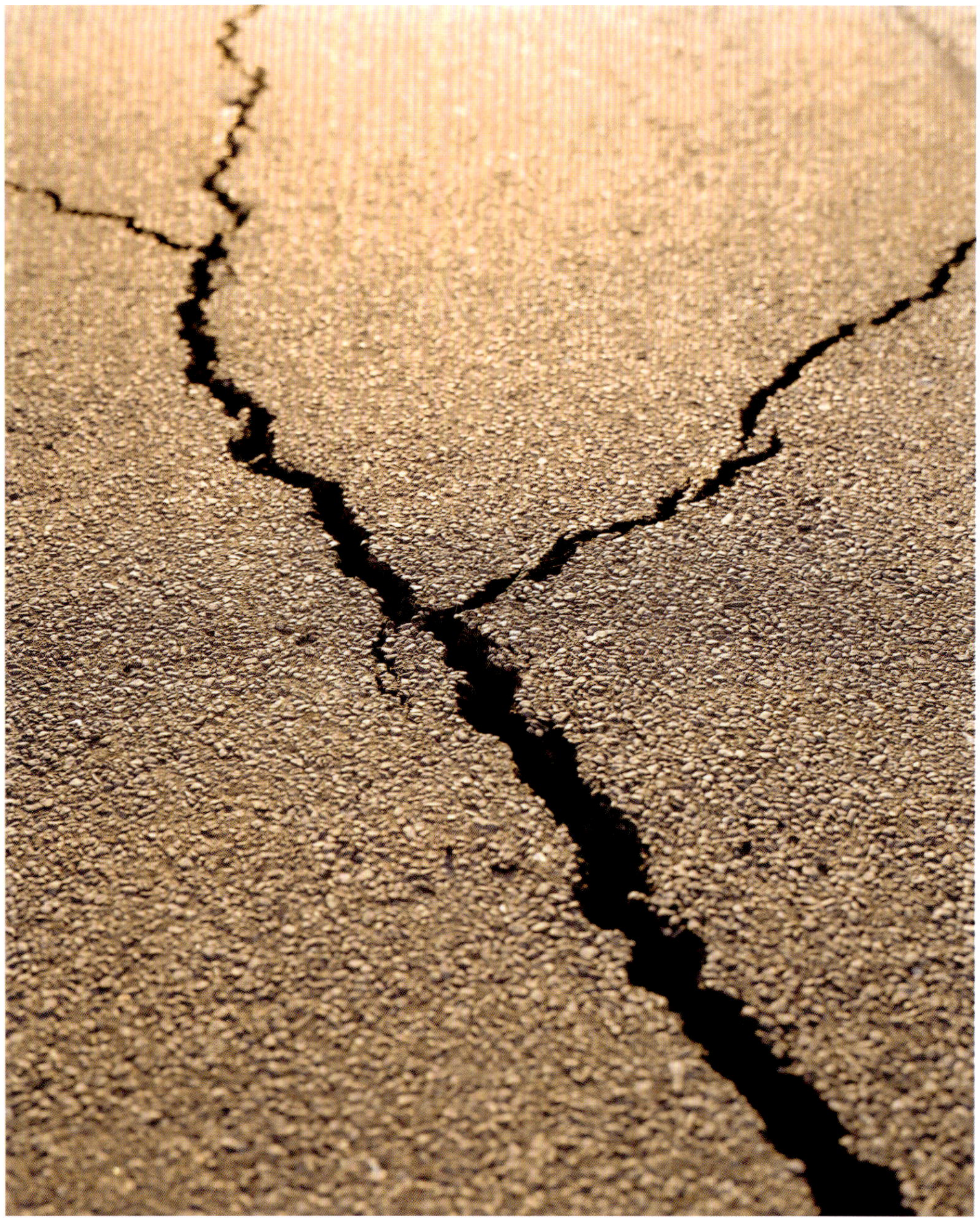

Fissure, Green Lane, Yorkshire, England, 2020

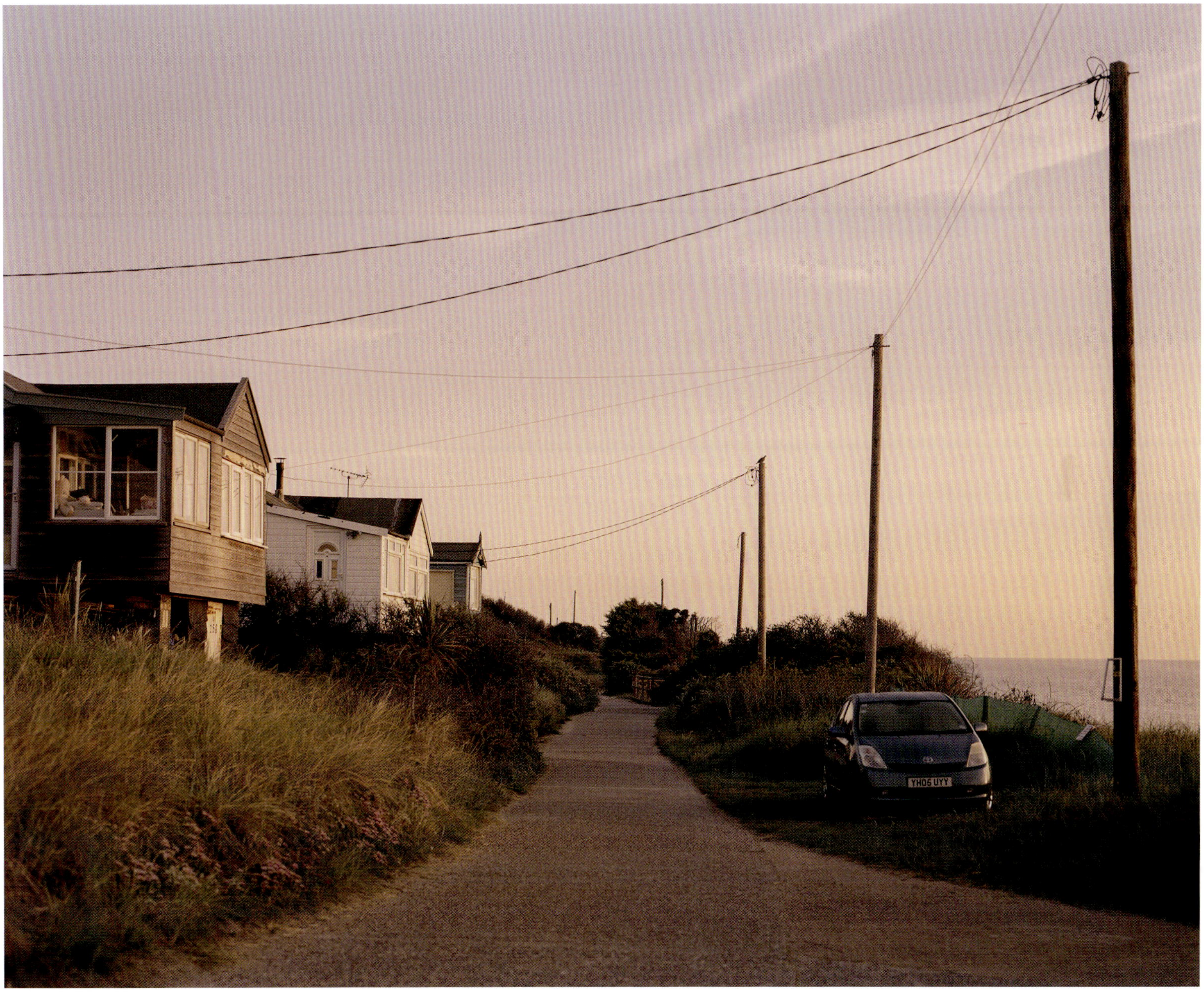

The Marrams, Hemsby, Norfolk, England, 2020

Clifftop Flowers, Covehithe, Suffolk, England, 2020

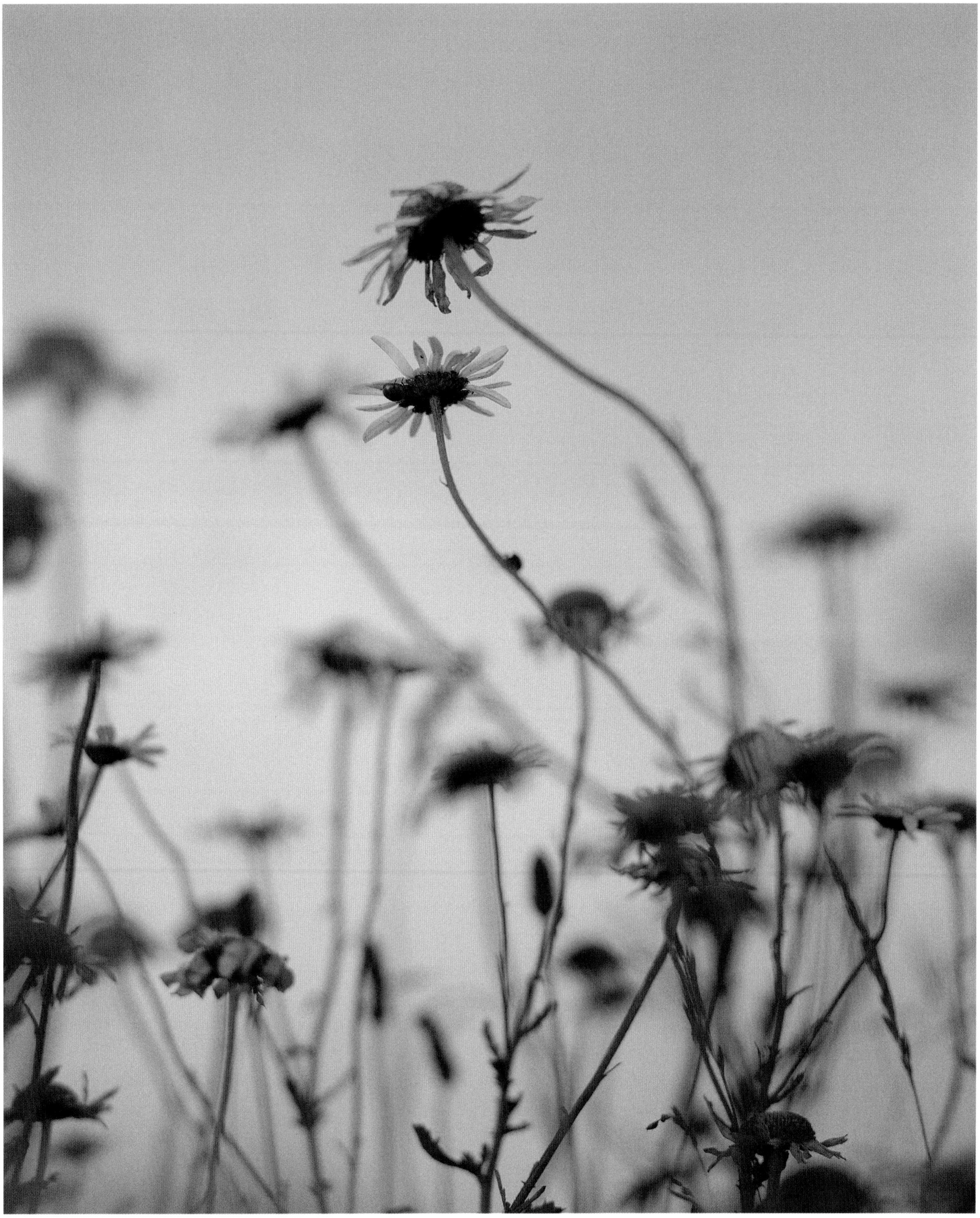

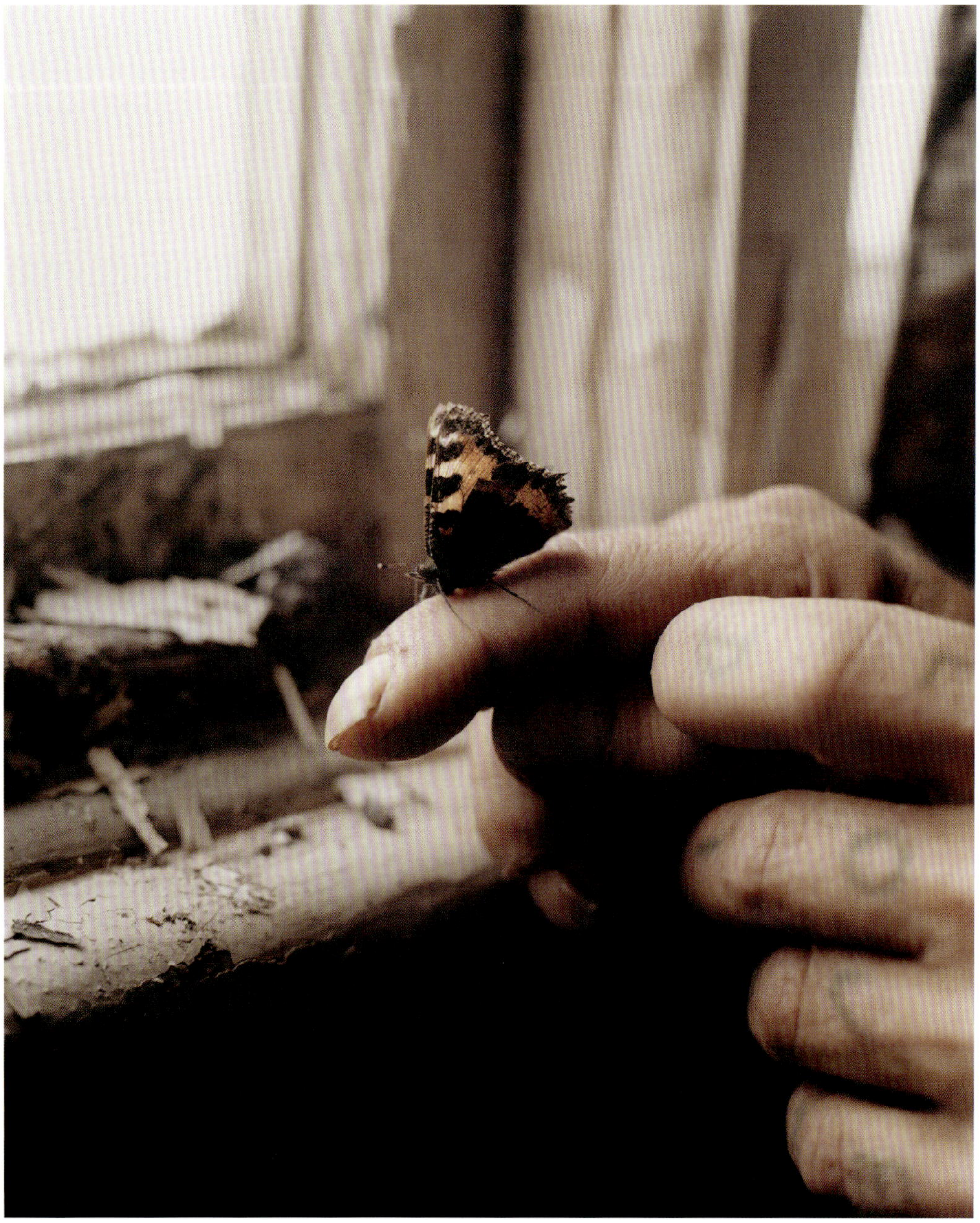

Butterfly, Skipsea, Yorkshire, England, 2020

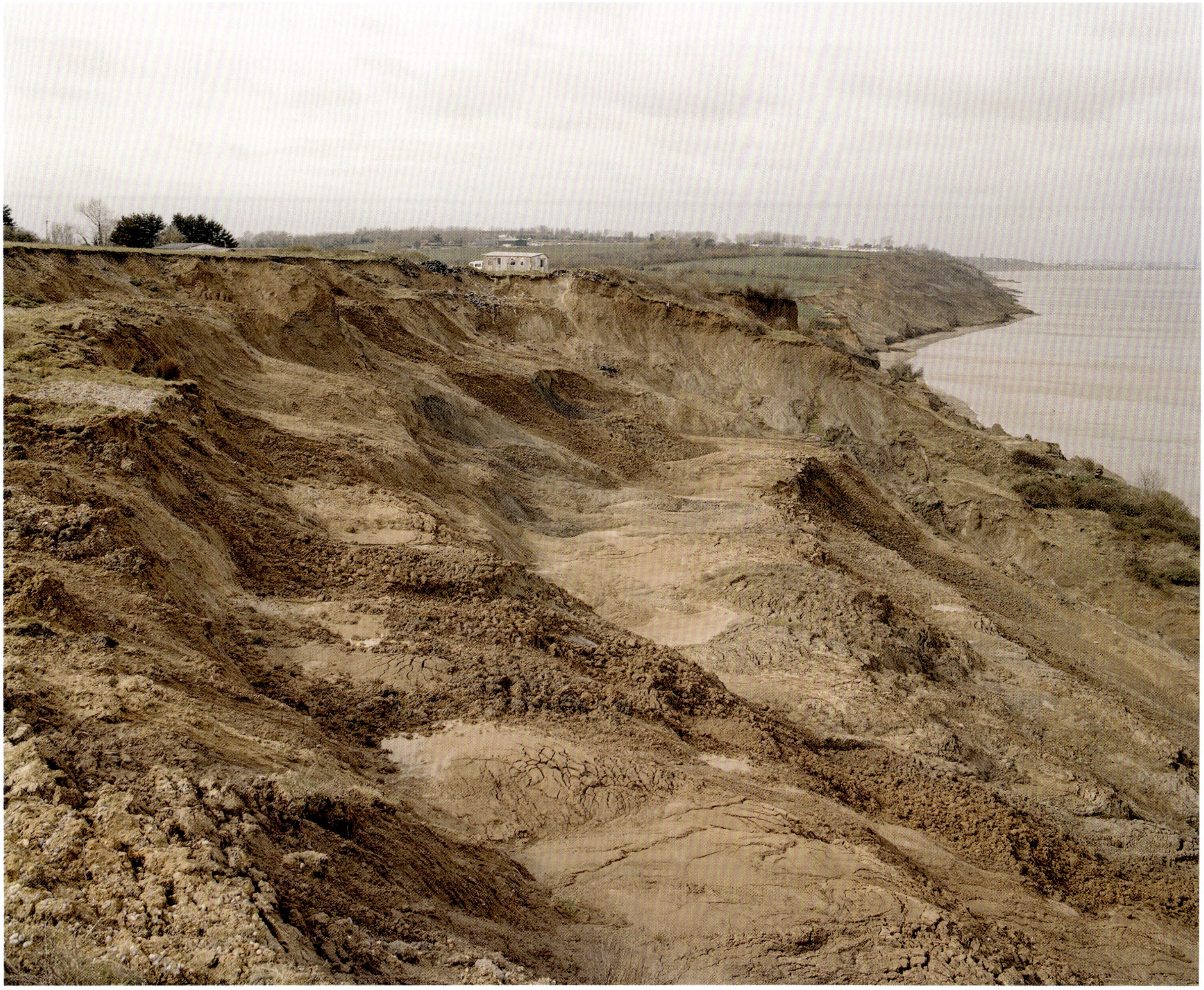

Land fall, Isle of Sheppey, England, 2021

On the Edge

Toby Coulson

'There is definitely humour for me in that landscape, with the people in that very English kind of dress. They come off the tour bus, take their one picture, and go and have fish and chips.'

What is it that drives the human impulse to get a bit too close to the edge? Watch any clifftop, and you'll notice it. Feet tentatively creeping forward, necks craned to peer down at the rocks or water far, far below. Perhaps it's because we like to scare ourselves, adding a shiver of danger in acknowledgement of the drop, edging towards the boundary after which earth gives way to air. Or perhaps it's pure curiosity at what lies just out of sight.

Toby Coulson's photos of people looking out across the English Channel from the Seven Sisters cliffs have a sly edge. Taken at a distance, they allow the photographer to quietly capture those too absorbed by the view to notice that they are also being observed. Often Coulson would sit for hours, waiting to see how a rolling carousel of visitors responded to the cliffs, hoping for moments of visual serendipity.

Much of Coulson's landscape work trades on a sense of playfulness. Another project focuses on the quirks of suburban hedges. Spending time in Derby as a child, where his grandmother lived, Coulson became interested in the repetitive architecture of mid-century housing estates. When every bungalow looks the same, expressions of personality work their way into little details. A hedge can shield a property, creating an additional wall to hide those inside from the world, but it can also boldly assert its presence. The trimmed hedge is its own sort of English cliché, suggesting not only the pleasure taken in outlandishly sculpted greenery but also the petty competition that can prosper in small communities.

Despite their sometimes surreal subject matter, Coulson's photos retain a softness. There is a luminous quality to them, light washing down over these subtly observed scenes, which makes an everyday moment temporarily cinematic.

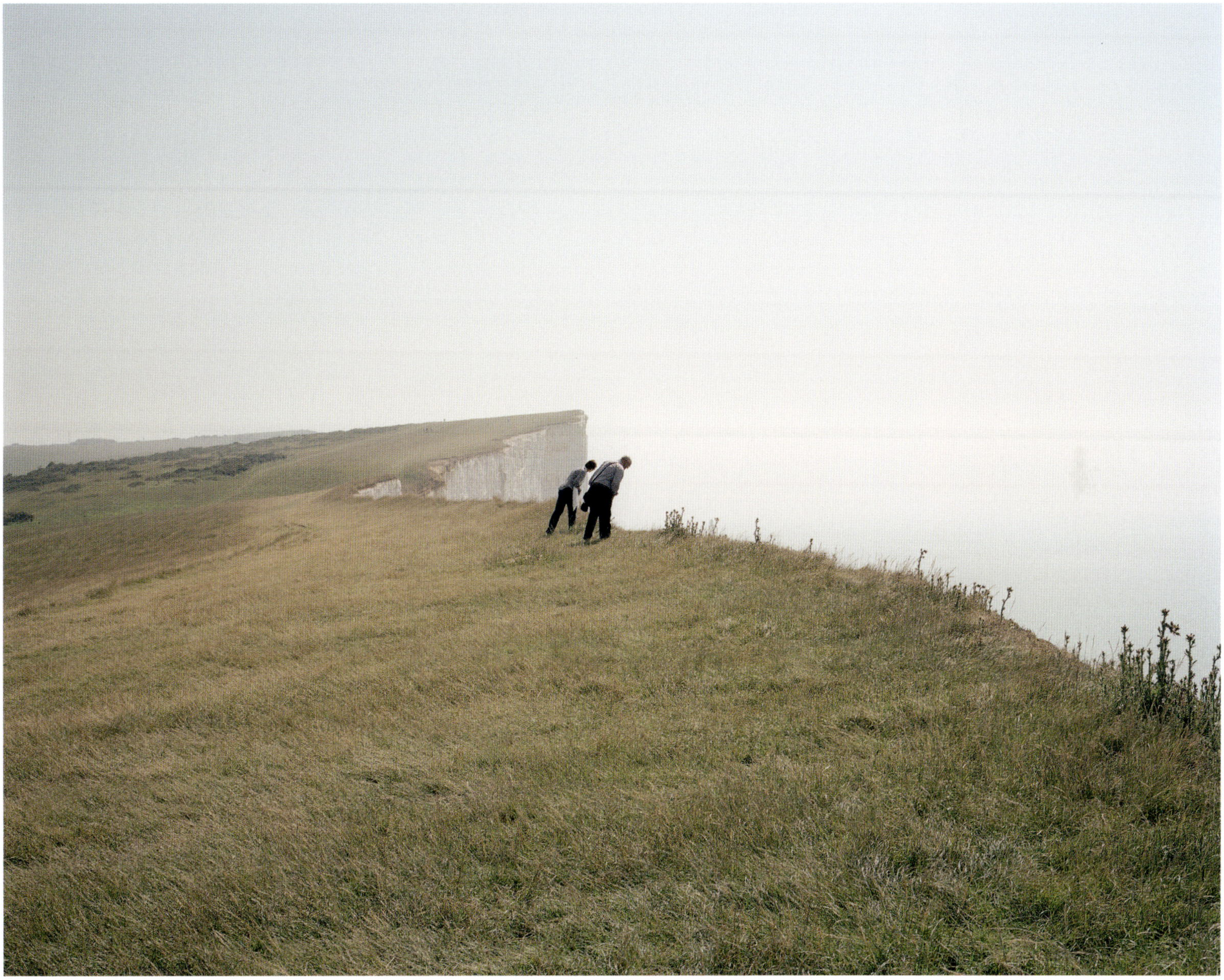

Couple, Places, Seven Sisters, England, 2016

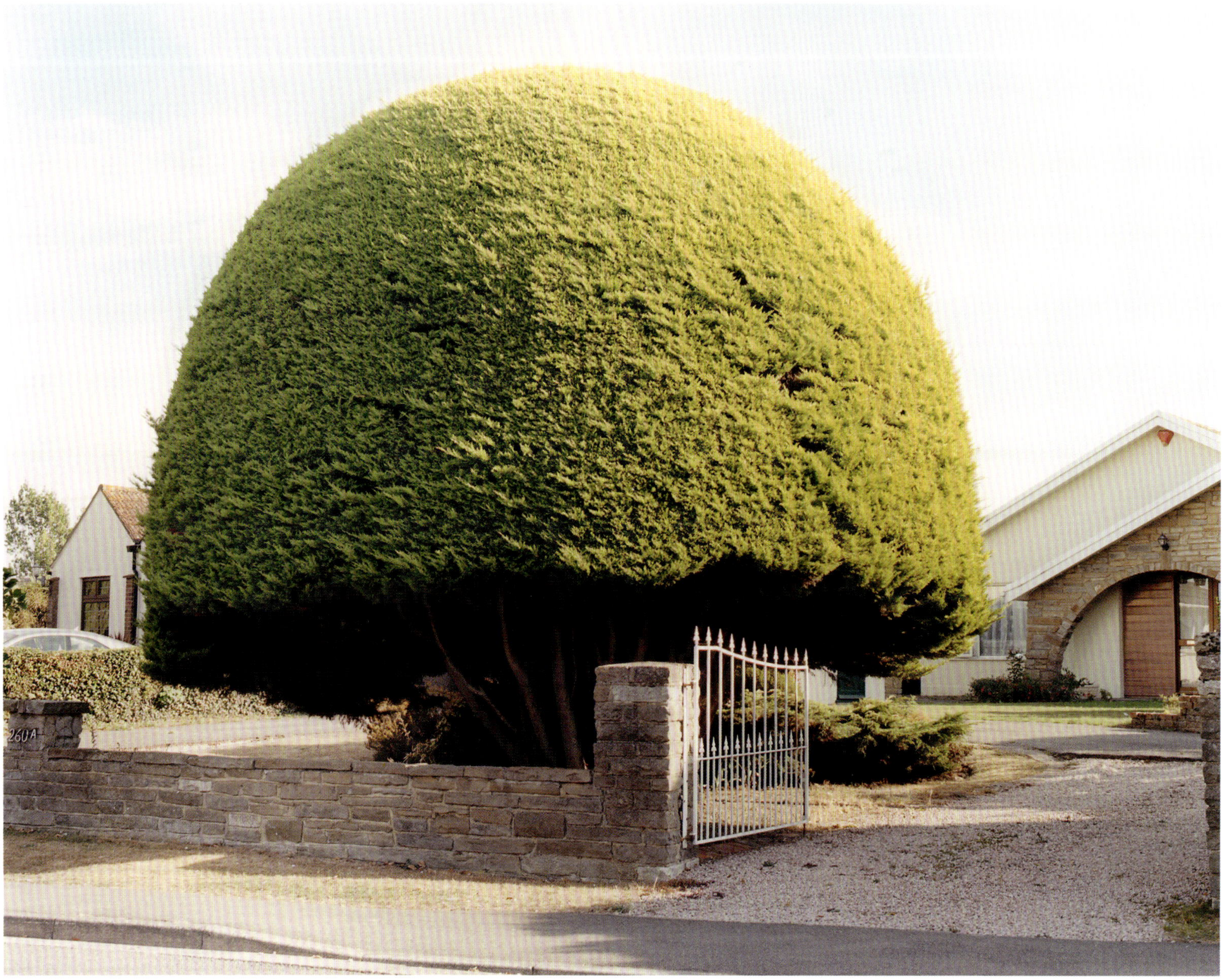

Hedge 1, Suburban Hedging, Margate, England, 2017

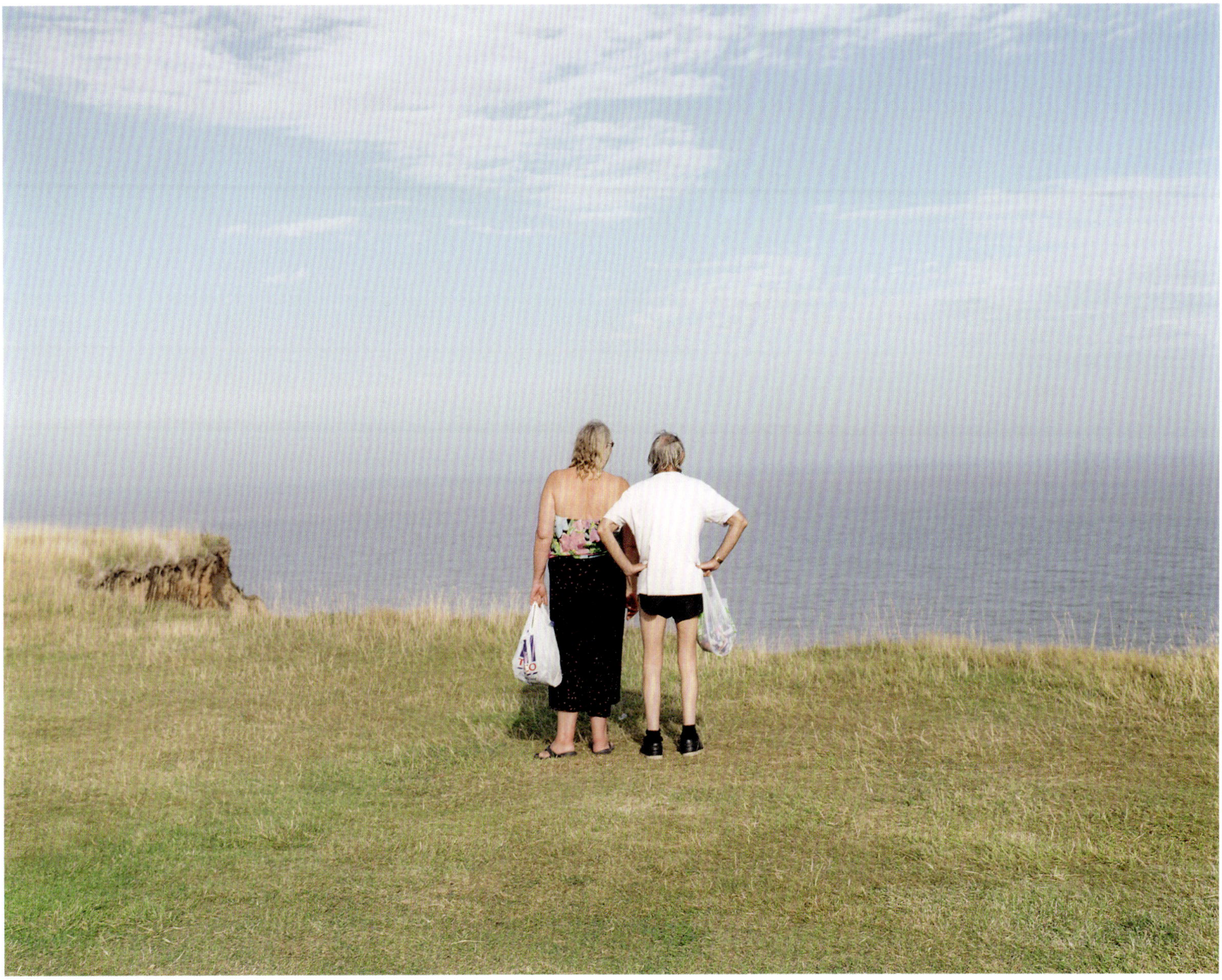

Couple 2, Places, Walton-on-the-Naze, England, 2014

Places, Seven Sisters, England, 2016

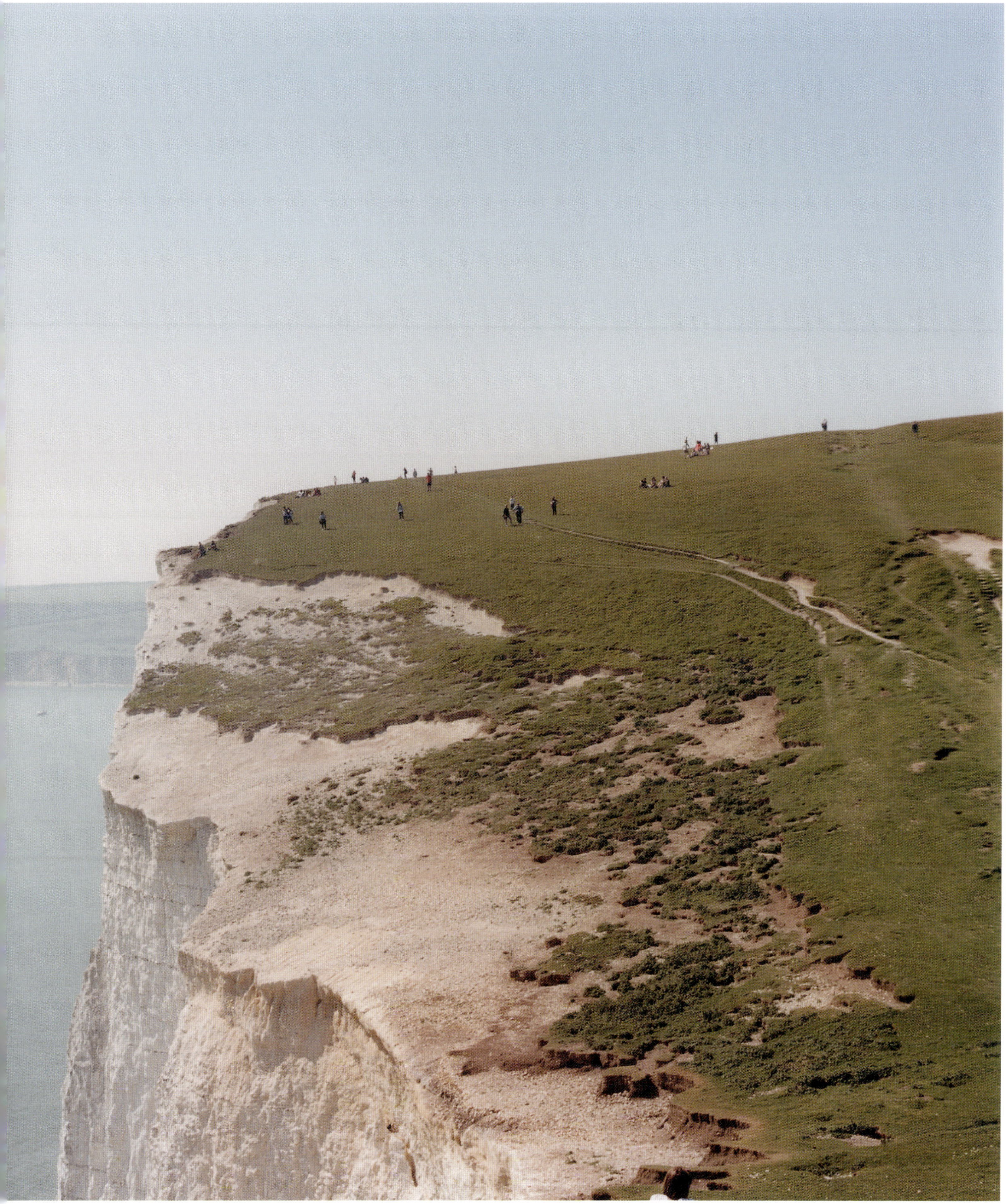

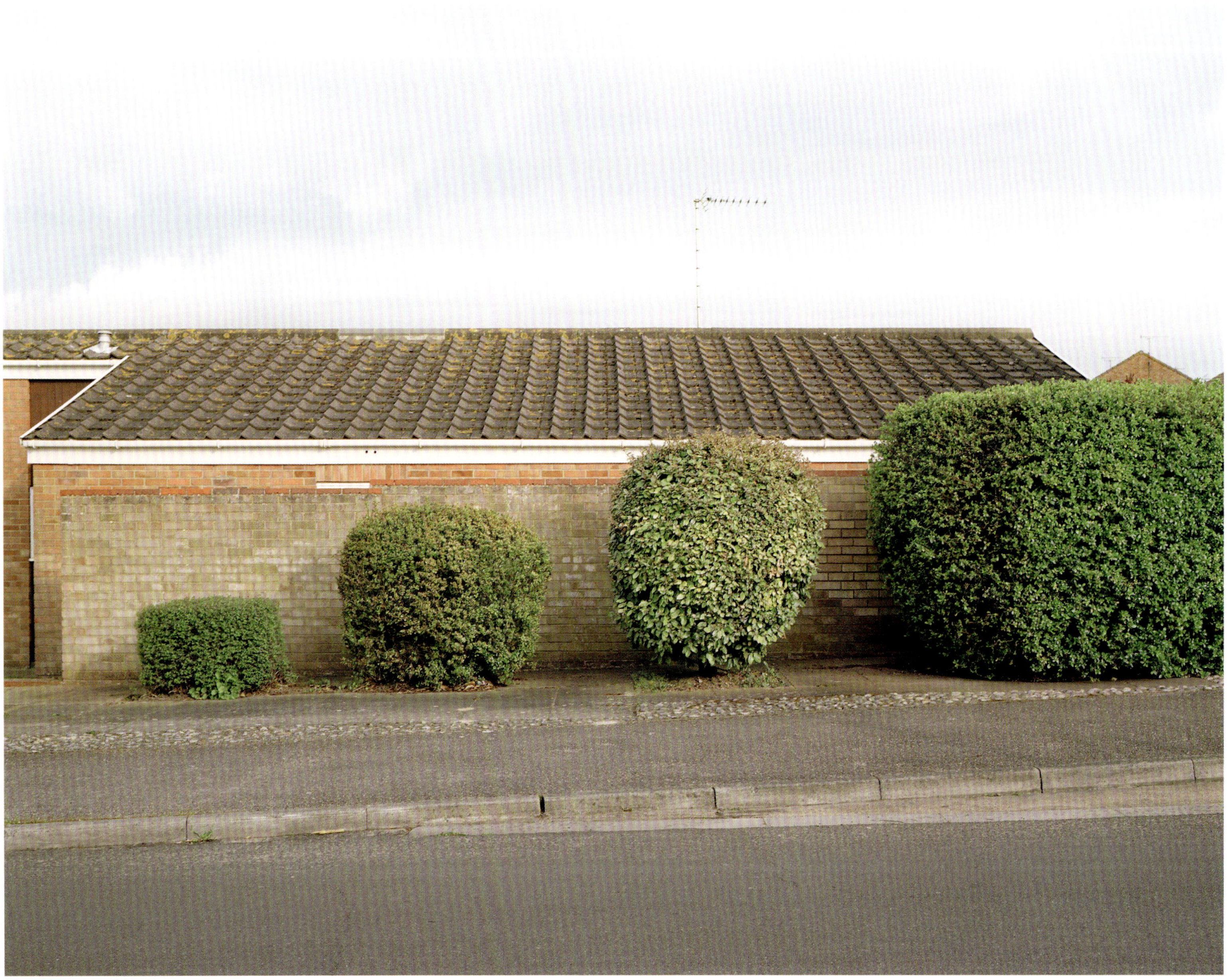

Hedge 3, Suburban Hedging, Margate, England, 2014

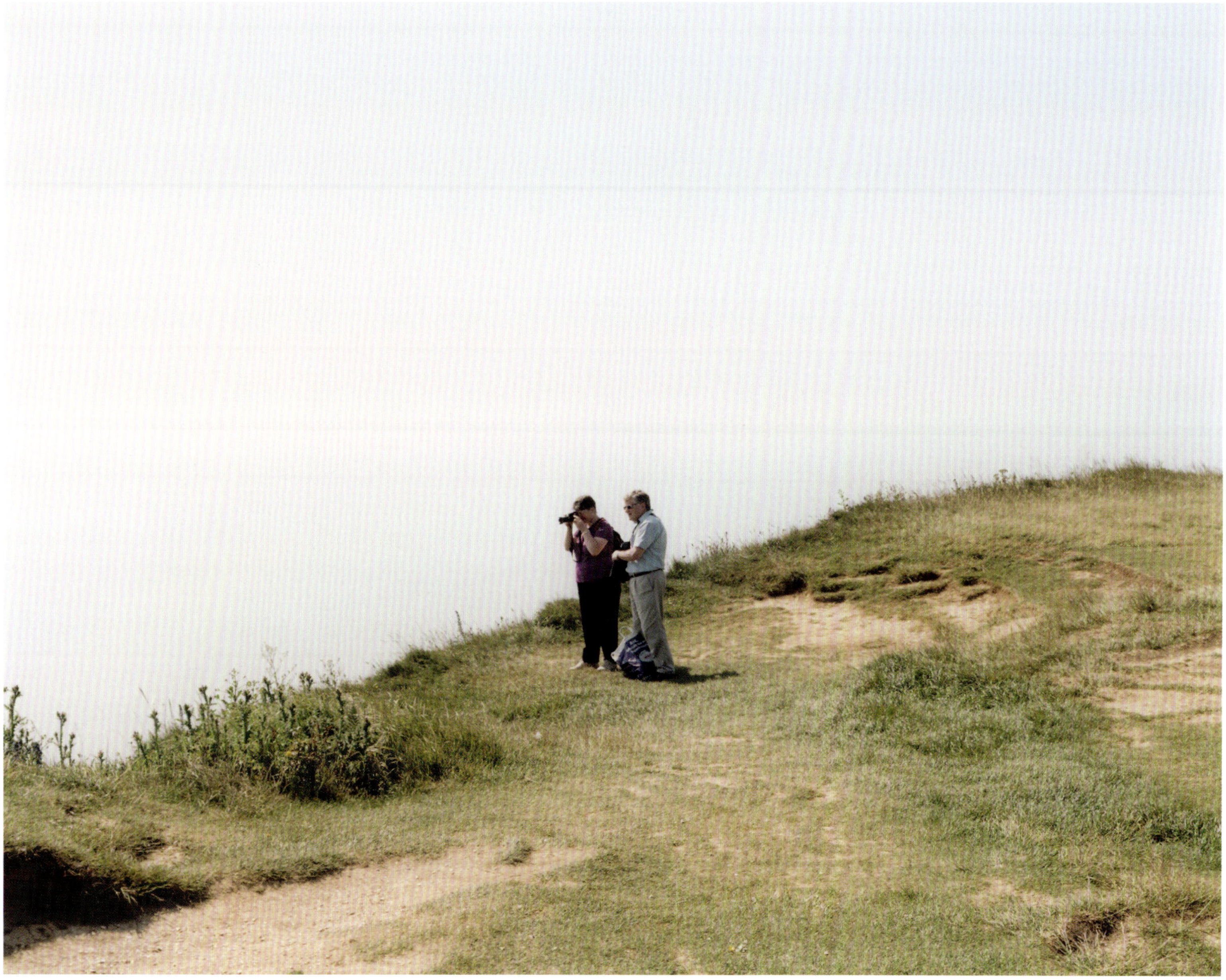

Couple 3, Places, Beachy Head, England, 2014

The Home Front

Melanie Friend

'I remember feeling very sad on one particular beach – just this sense [that] here we are watching these planes as entertainment. In other countries people are terrified by what's in the sky: the bomber, the fighter jet, the drones.'

Air displays are the third most popular form of outdoor spectator activity, after football and horse racing. In 2019 alone, 4.9 million people visited an air show. From the nostalgia of WII-era Spitfires to the aerobatic loops and somersaults of the Red Arrows, these events are often larger (and louder) than parades of military power and ingenuity.

Melanie Friend became interested in these sky-high spectacles after photographing a four-year-old Kosovan refugee called Luarda in 1999. Several months later she caught up with the girl and her parents, who had since been settled in Merseyside. There she heard about how Luarda had screamed and dropped her ice cream when the Red Arrows flew overhead mid-display, the booming noise bringing back traumatic memories. For a photographer whose work often dwells on the far-reaching consequences of conflict, these air shows became an interesting – and disquieting – vehicle to explore the respectable face of war.

Friend spent years travelling around the country to different air shows, from Sussex to Sunderland. The photos she took often require a moment to acclimatise to. In the foreground there might be children splashing in the sea, or families arranged on picnic blankets. But somewhere overhead, there is always a plane: a black cut-out against the blue, white smoke trails etching paths through the clouds. In many of the images, everyone's faces are turned upward, caught in thrilled spectatorship. These are not people who are afraid of what flies above them. It's just another day out, the queue for the ice cream van growing longer as bombers soar through peaceful skies.

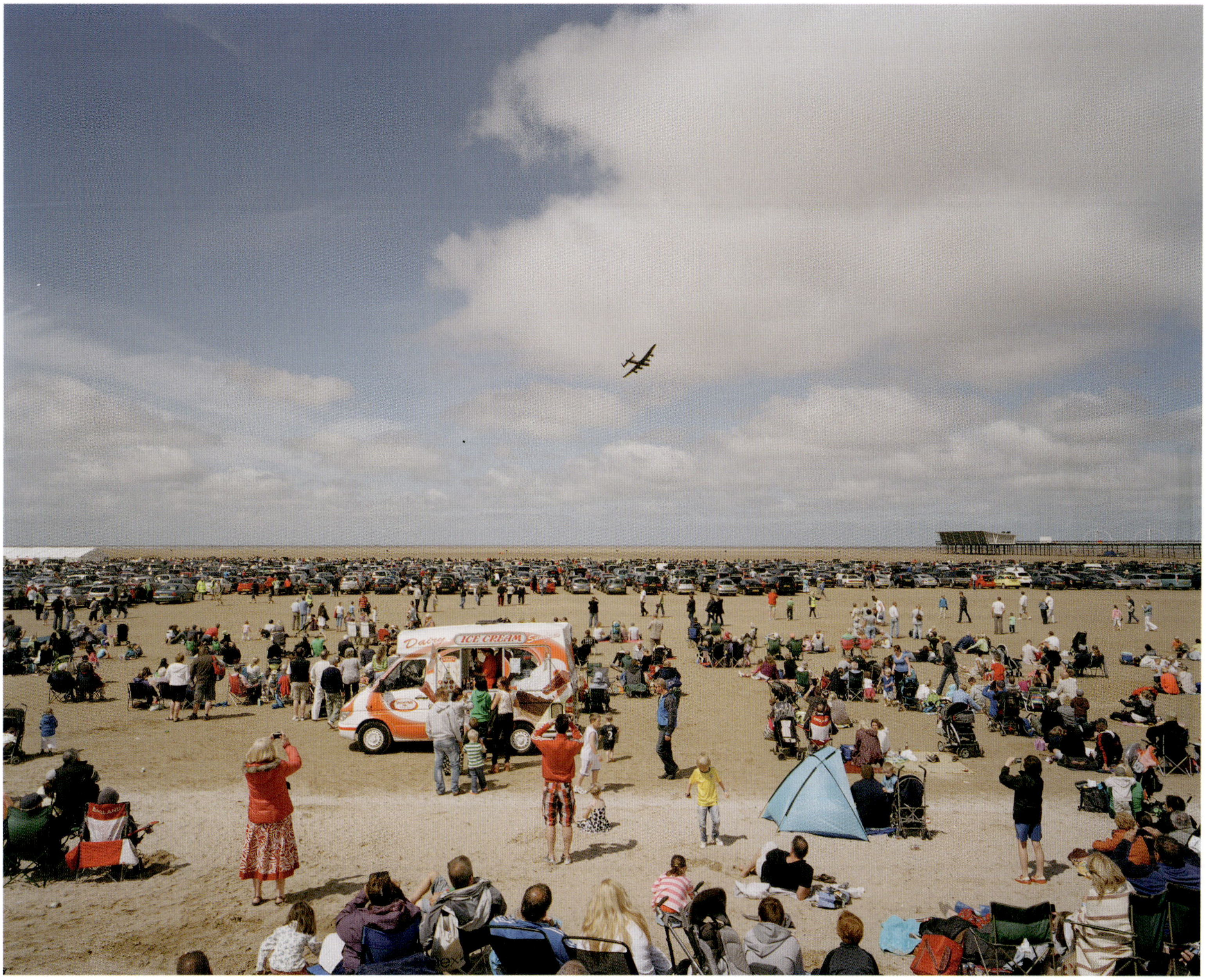

Avro Lancaster bomber (part of a Battle of Britain memorial flight),
Southport Beach, Merseyside, England, 24 July 2011

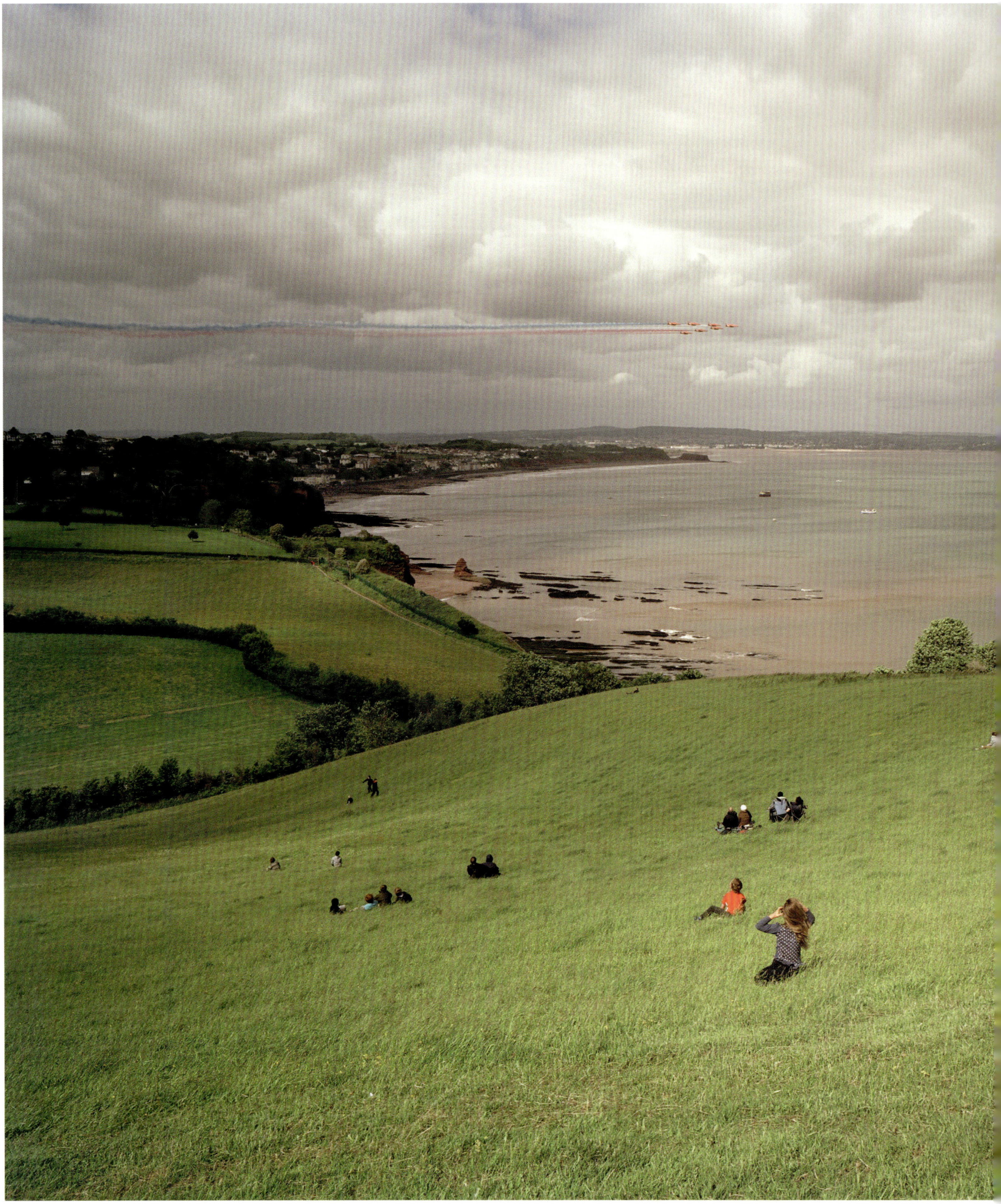

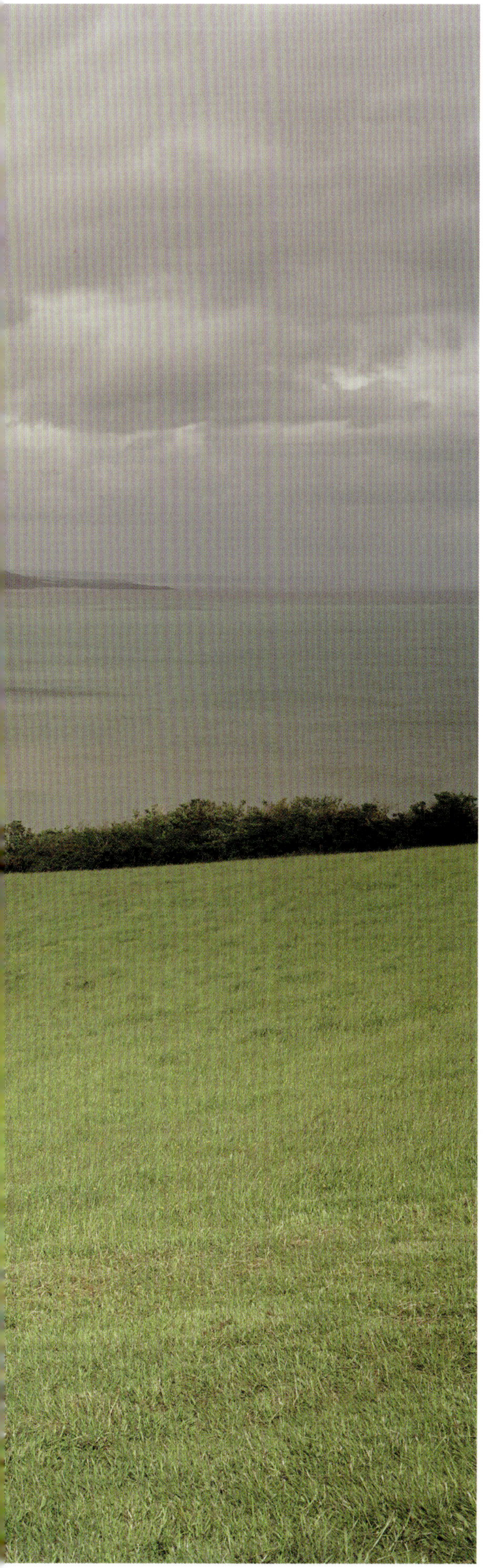

Hawk T1 military trainers (Red Arrows),
Dawlish Air Show, Devon, England, 8 June 2012

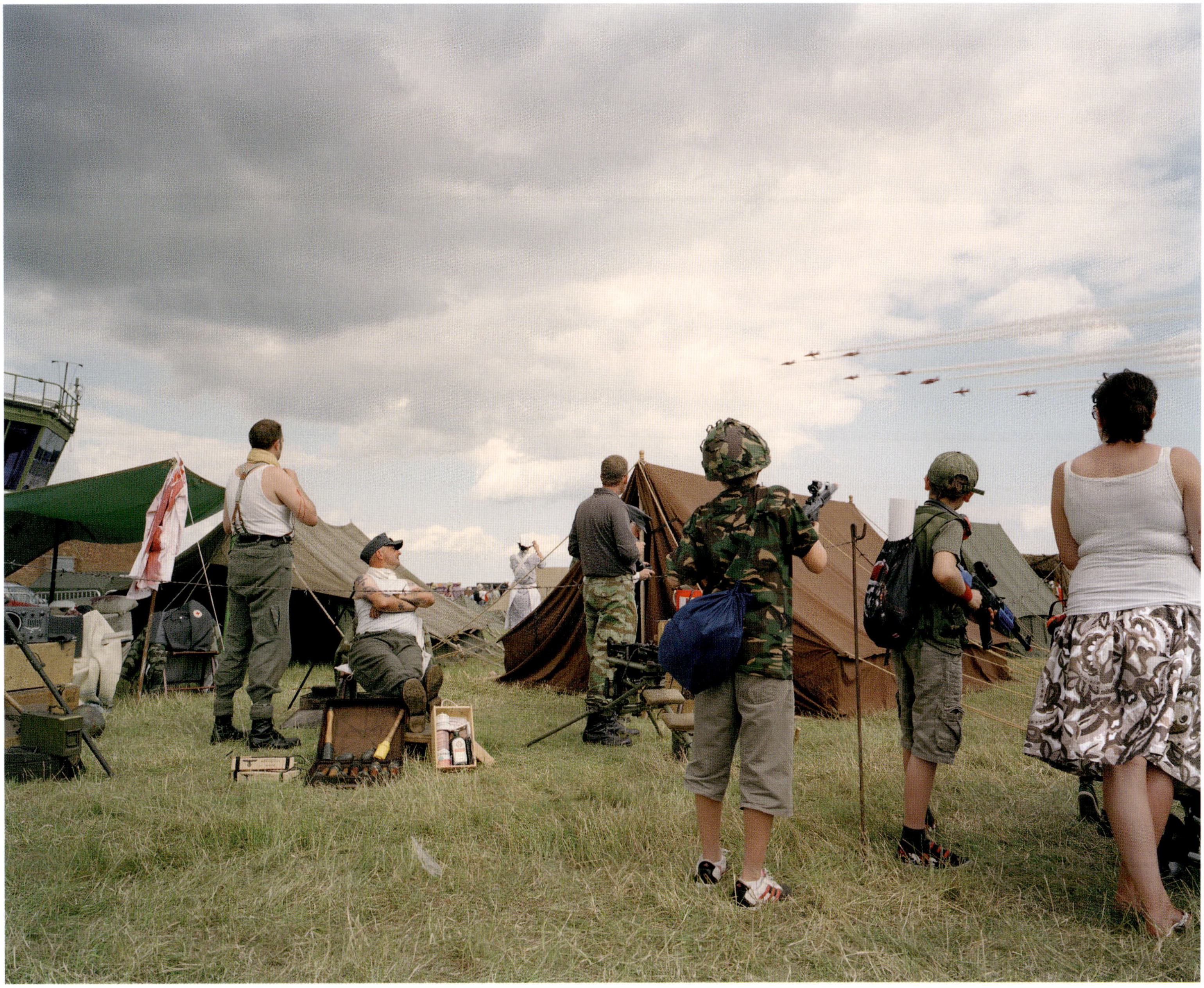

Spectators and Living History reenactors watch display by Hawk T1 military trainers (Red Arrows), RAF Waddington International Air Show, Lincolnshire, England, July 2011

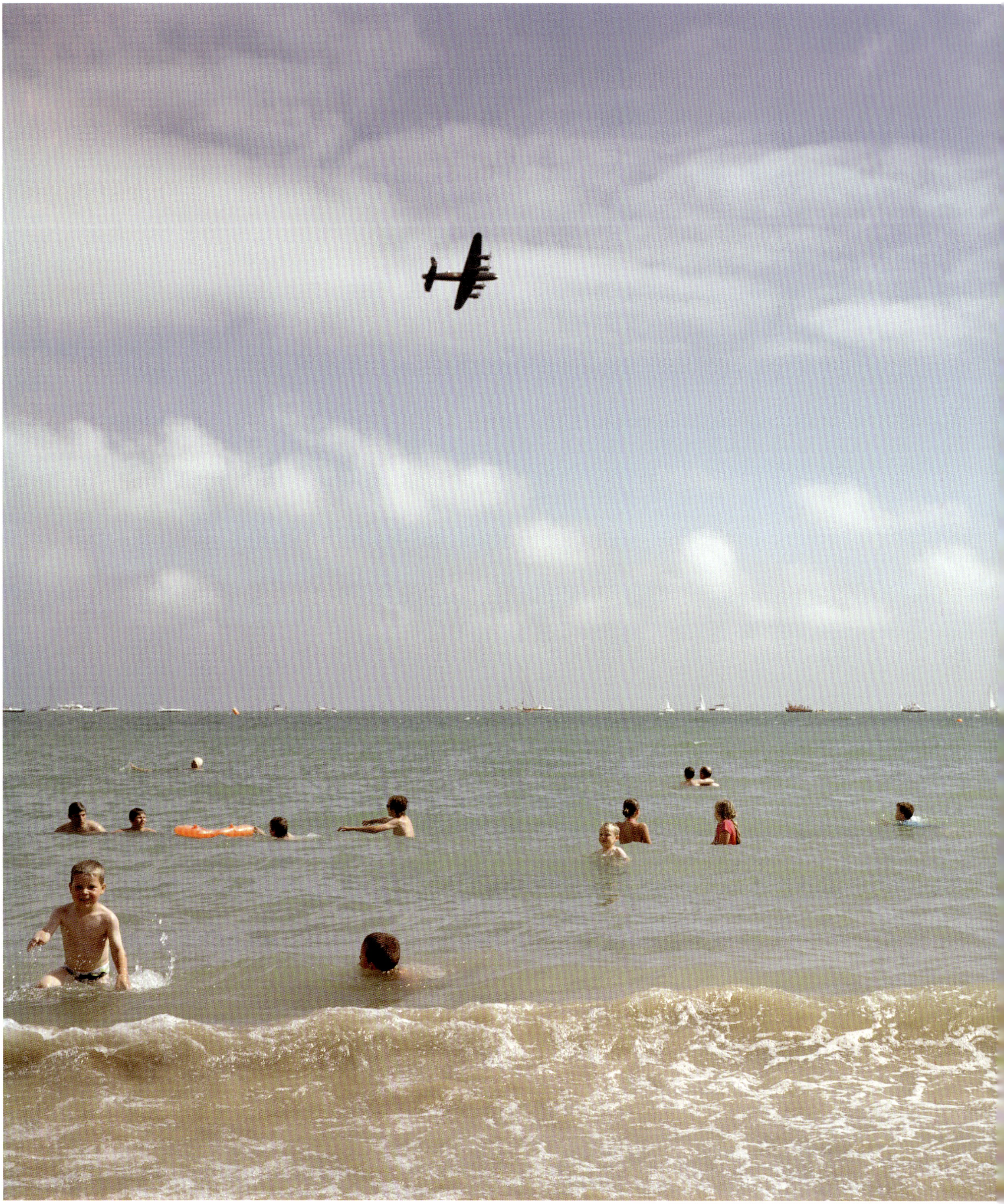

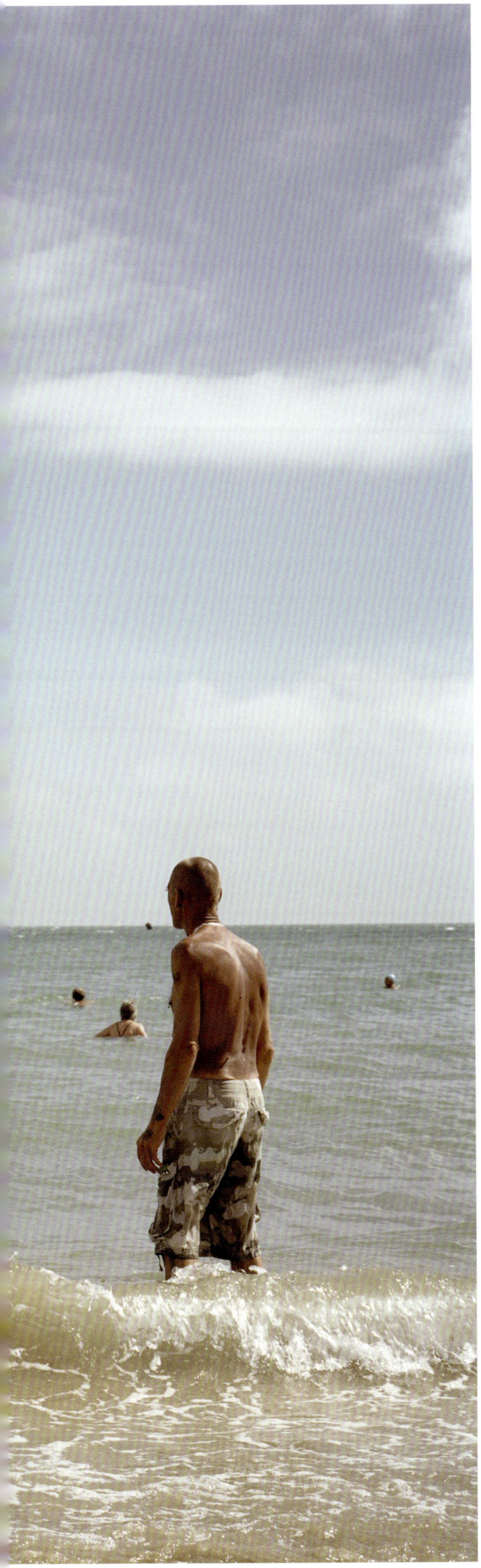

Avro Lancaster bomber (part of a Battle of Britain memorial flight), Eastbourne International Air Show, Sussex, England, 15 August 2009

British Pillboxes

Richard Brine

'Although as objects they look robust, up close you realise that they were built as temporary structures... There's a sense of fragility... Maybe [they will] become protected, visited and loved, like our castles.'

These are strange structures: stocky, nondescript concrete forms built as hardened field defences during WWII. Some hunch low to the ground while others draw attention to their incongruity, perched in between tree trunks or tilted at weird angles. There are still more than 6000 'pillboxes' scattered through the British landscape. This is just a fraction of the initial 30,000 that sprang up when the threat of German invasion seemed imminent in 1940. They were strategically placed around the country, designed to serve as everything from coastal watchtowers to covered sites for machine gunners.

Geography dictated design as their construction was reliant on local materials and labour. In Norfolk, for instance, the concrete was often poured into a temporary mould made of brick, giving the pillboxes a distinct red hue. When the threat subsided again, many were left to stand where they were – brute mementoes of a feared future that never came to pass.

Richard Brine's memories of pillboxes date back to his adolescence, when his school bus would pass one each day. Many now house sheep (or furtive teenagers looking for somewhere to smoke), but others remain pristine and jarring. They appear at odds with their surroundings, interrupting the flat green lines of a field or sitting near medieval castle ruins; layers of history and warfare embedded in concrete and stone. Brine examined satellite imagery and talked to locals to find them. Sometimes he would turn up and find that the pillboxes had already vanished, dismantled by farmers or reclaimed by the sea.

Brine's background in architectural photography is reflected in his large format photos, which are beautifully composed. Despite their utilitarian appearance, there is still something otherworldly about these pillboxes. They conjure a lost world, slowly disappearing beneath the ivy.

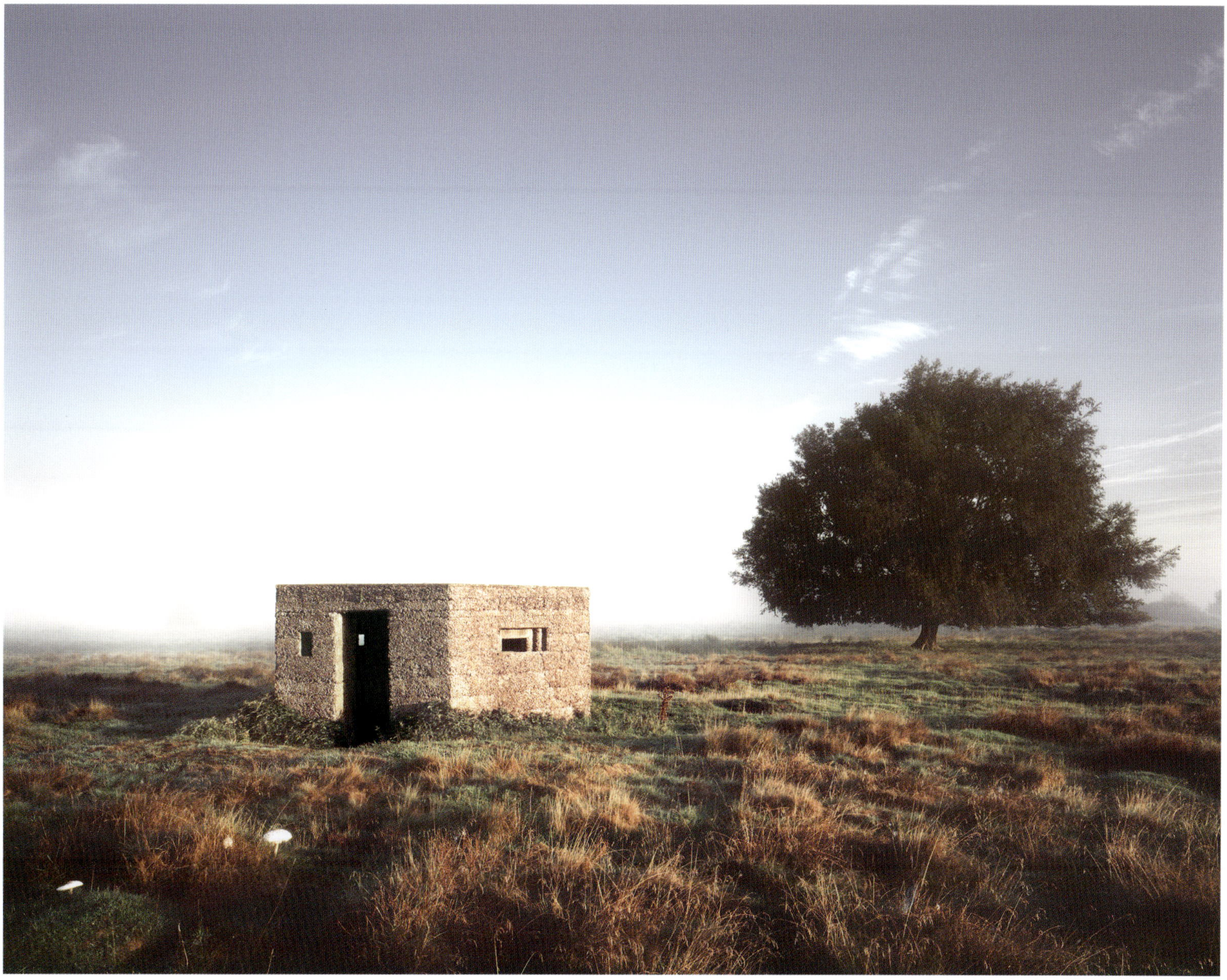

Suffolk, England, 2010

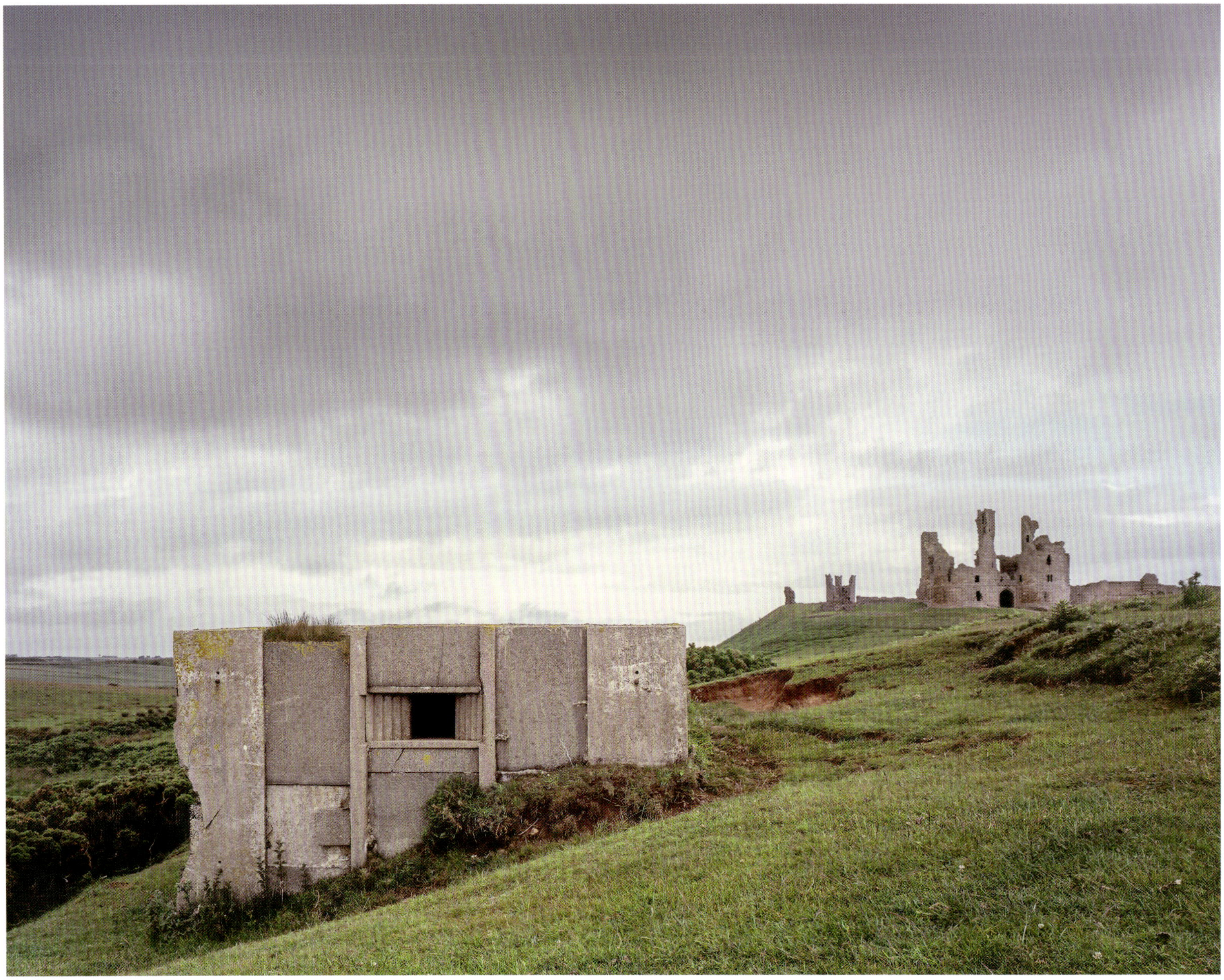

Northumberland, England, 2011

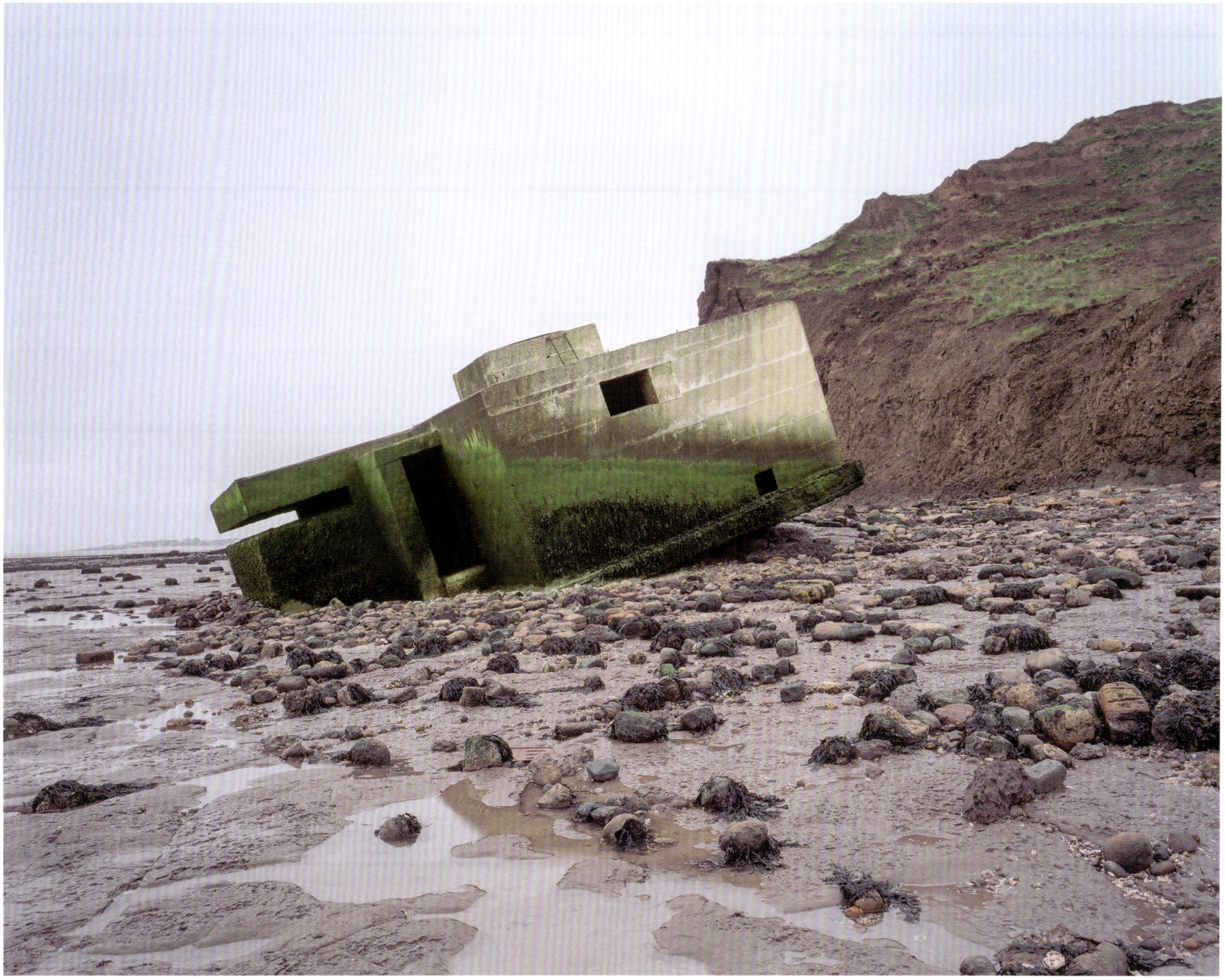

Kent, England, 2011

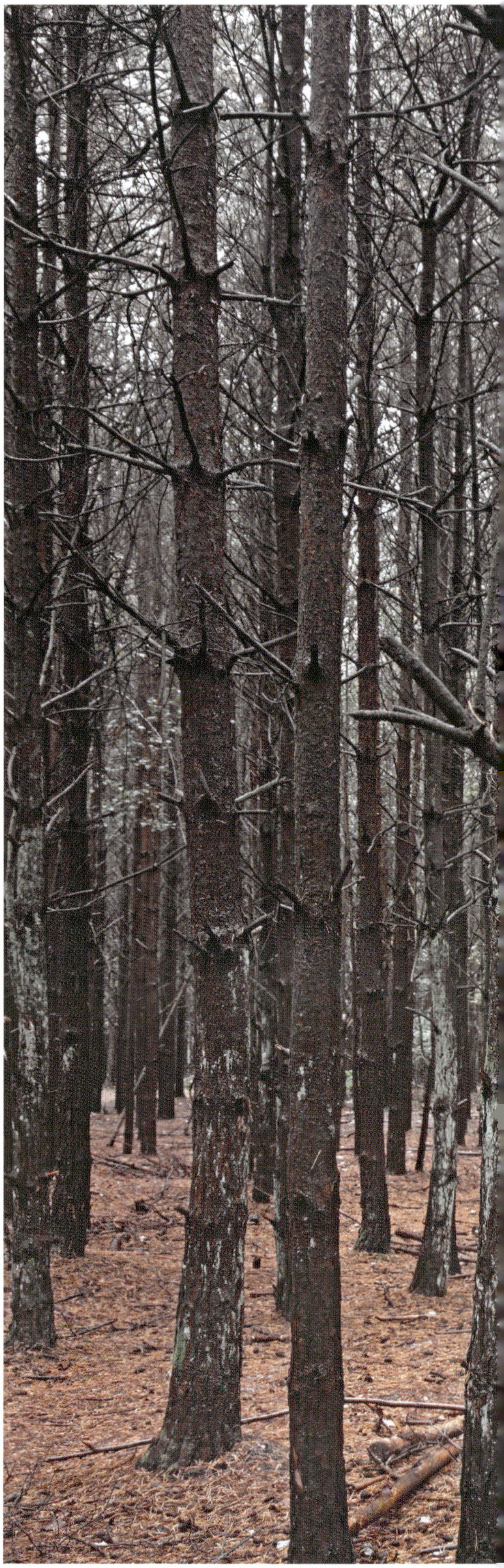

Hampshire, England, 2013

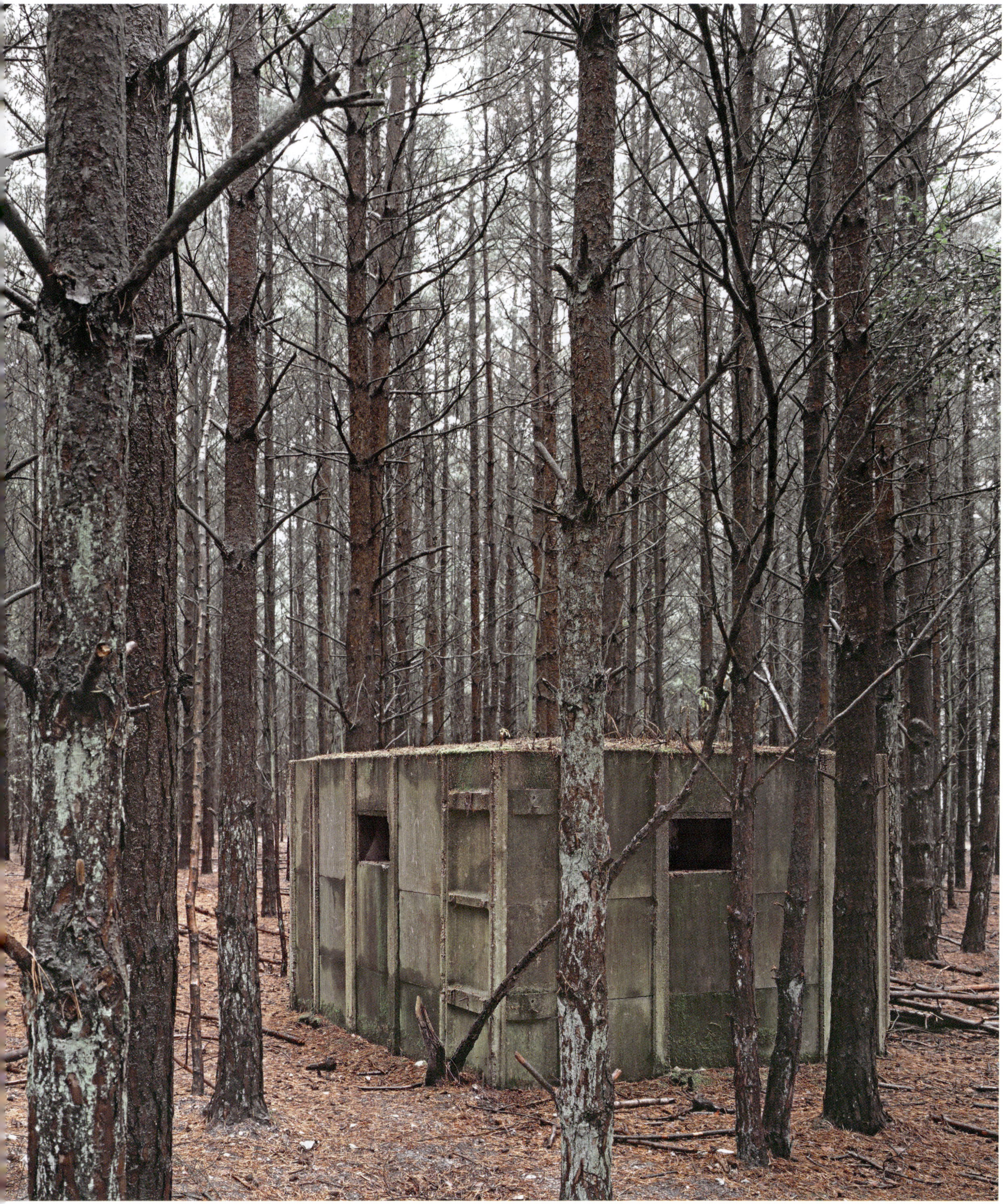

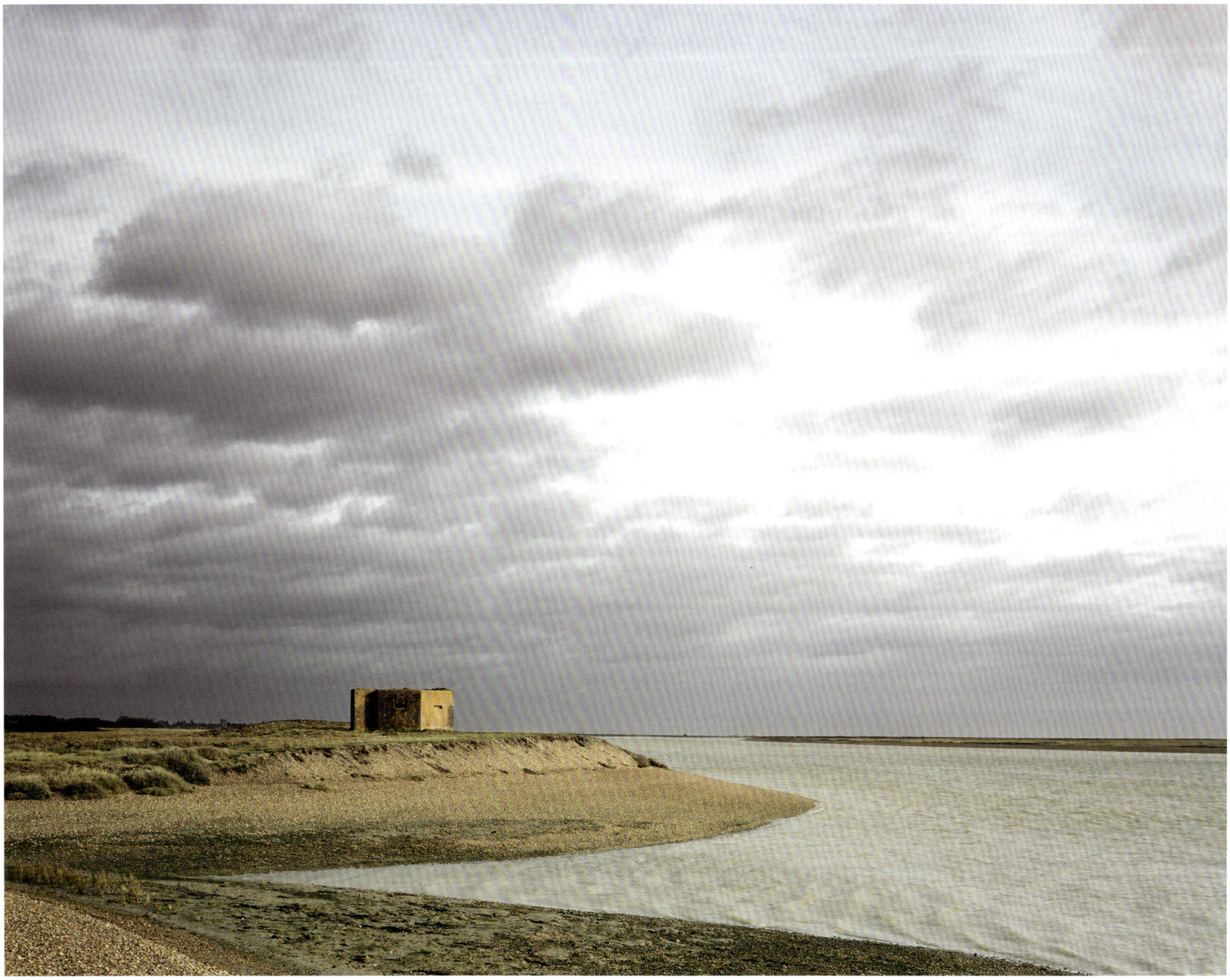

Suffolk, England, 2012

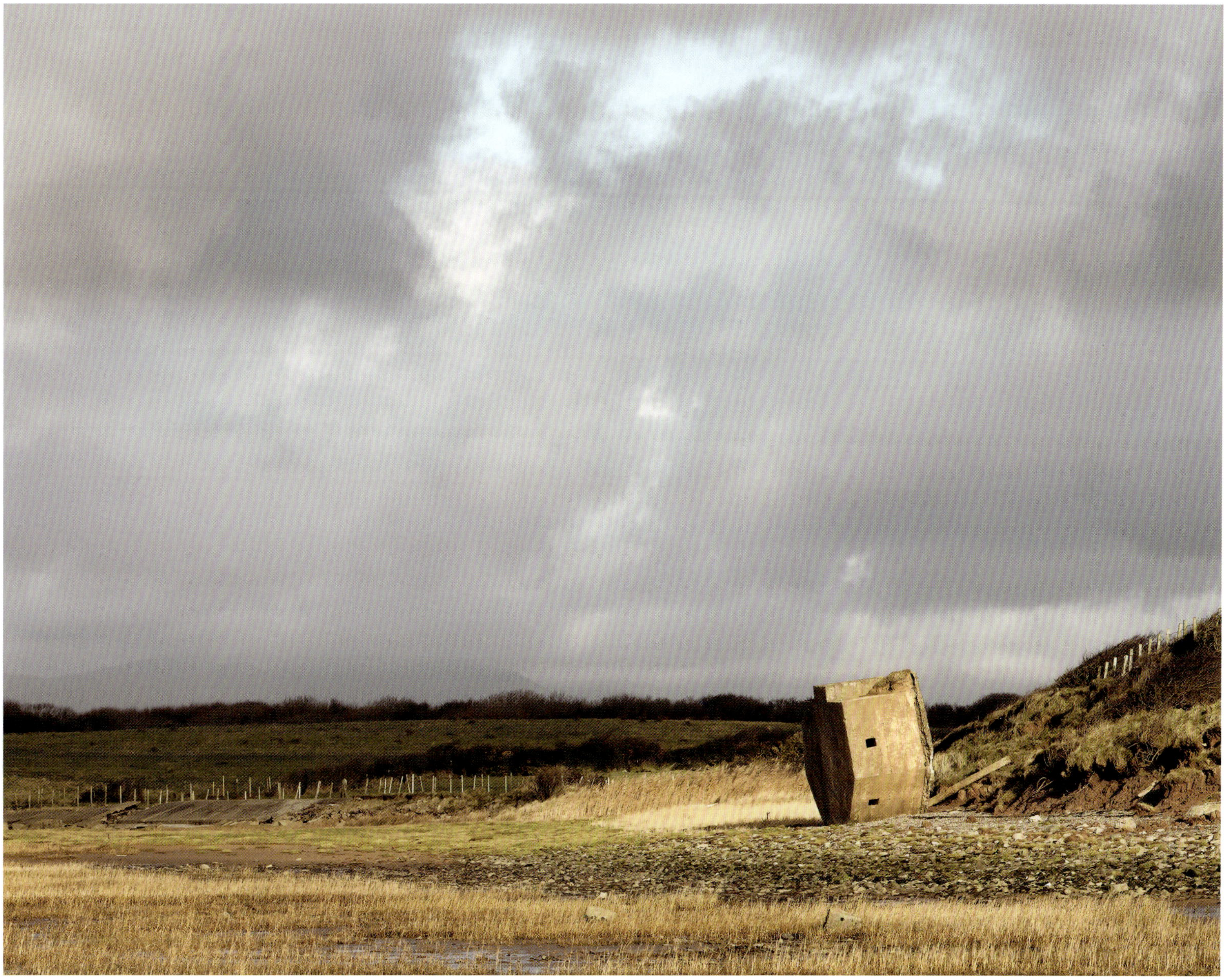

Cumbria, England, 2015

Coastal Brutalism

Jethro Marshall

'All my work is a celebration of manmade participation in the landscape... Those structures or utilities, when juxtaposed with nature, take on a different beauty and a keener visual interest.'

'Anti-bucolic, pro-rural' is Jethro Marshall's motto. His work focuses on the civic aspects of British terrain: its roads and sewage works, sea defences and quarries, the infrastructures that hold the country together. Since returning to the border between Devon and Dorset where he grew up, Marshall's attentions have largely strayed towards intensely local human interventions in the natural world. Familiarity breeds a particular kind of vision, built on accumulated knowledge of the sun's daily movements and how the seasons can clad or strip a landscape.

The images shown here are from two projects, *Coastal Brutalism,* and another project, *Rocky*. The latter is concerned with quarrying, thinking about how the world around us has been built from materials taken from the ground. A quarry is a negative space, a hollow reminder of what has been extracted. Often resembling a lunar terrain, it is a place where nature creeps back over the carved out remains of industrial labour. Often, in the process of taking these photos, Marshall would be asked to leave – threats about health and safety perhaps covering up deeper fears about public observation of these scarred and pockmarked hillsides.

By contrast *Coastal Brutalism* explores places where intervention has been necessary to protect the landscape, ranging over areas where concrete has been used to buttress and protect cliffs and other coastal features. Whether used as military defence or to ward against erosion, there is something powerful in this idea of protection. Marshall's images render these humdrum architectural features newly remarkable: anti-tank cubes scattered across the beach like giant children's toys, sea walls curving voluptuously overhead. His trademark monochrome imagery is sparing but unafraid of drama. It is attentive to scale, both compositionally and in its understanding of the extent and force of human toil and endeavour.

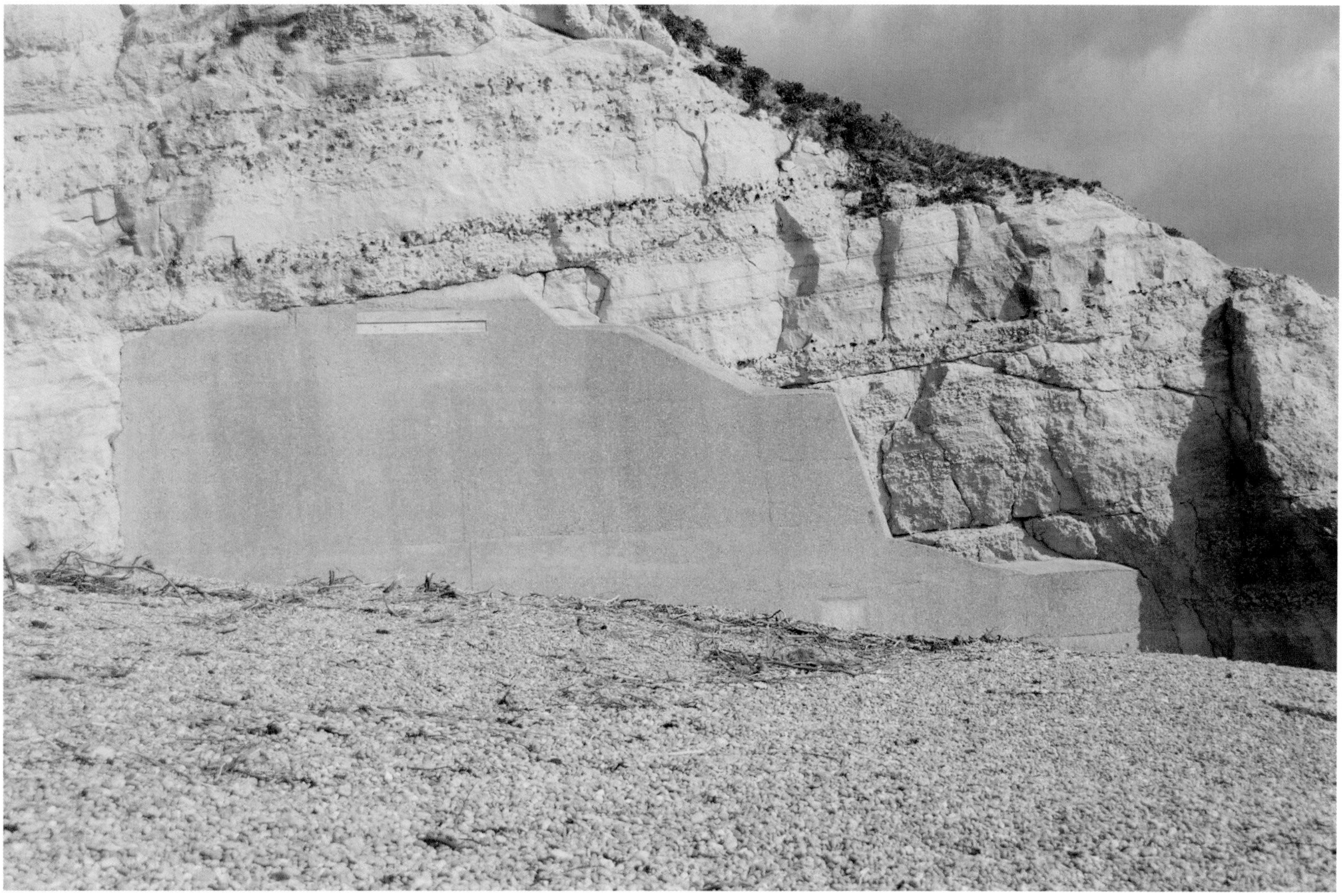

Cliff Stabilisation, Coastal Brutalism, Beer, England, 2018

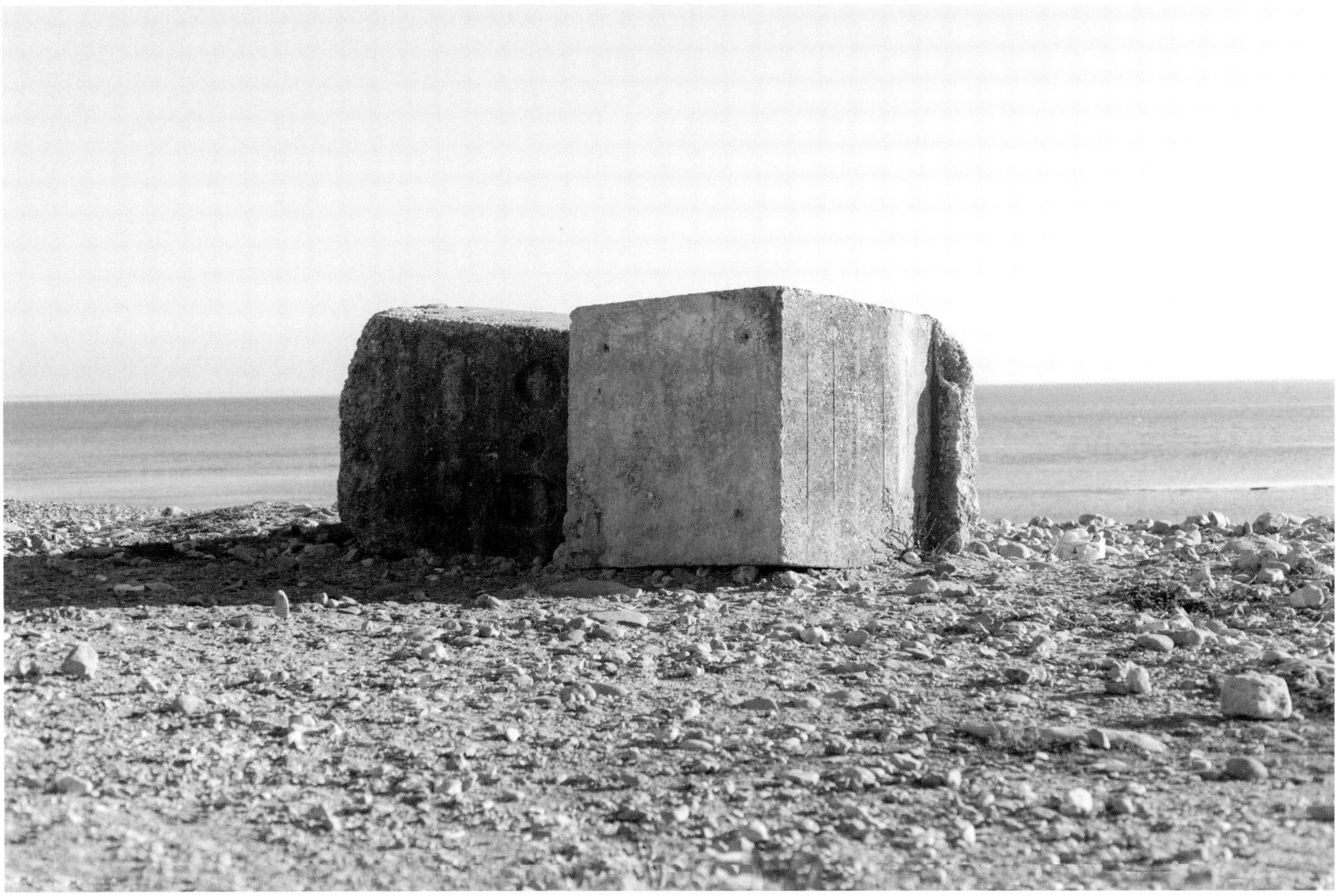

Parking Prevention, Coastal Brutalism, Lyme Regis, England, 2017

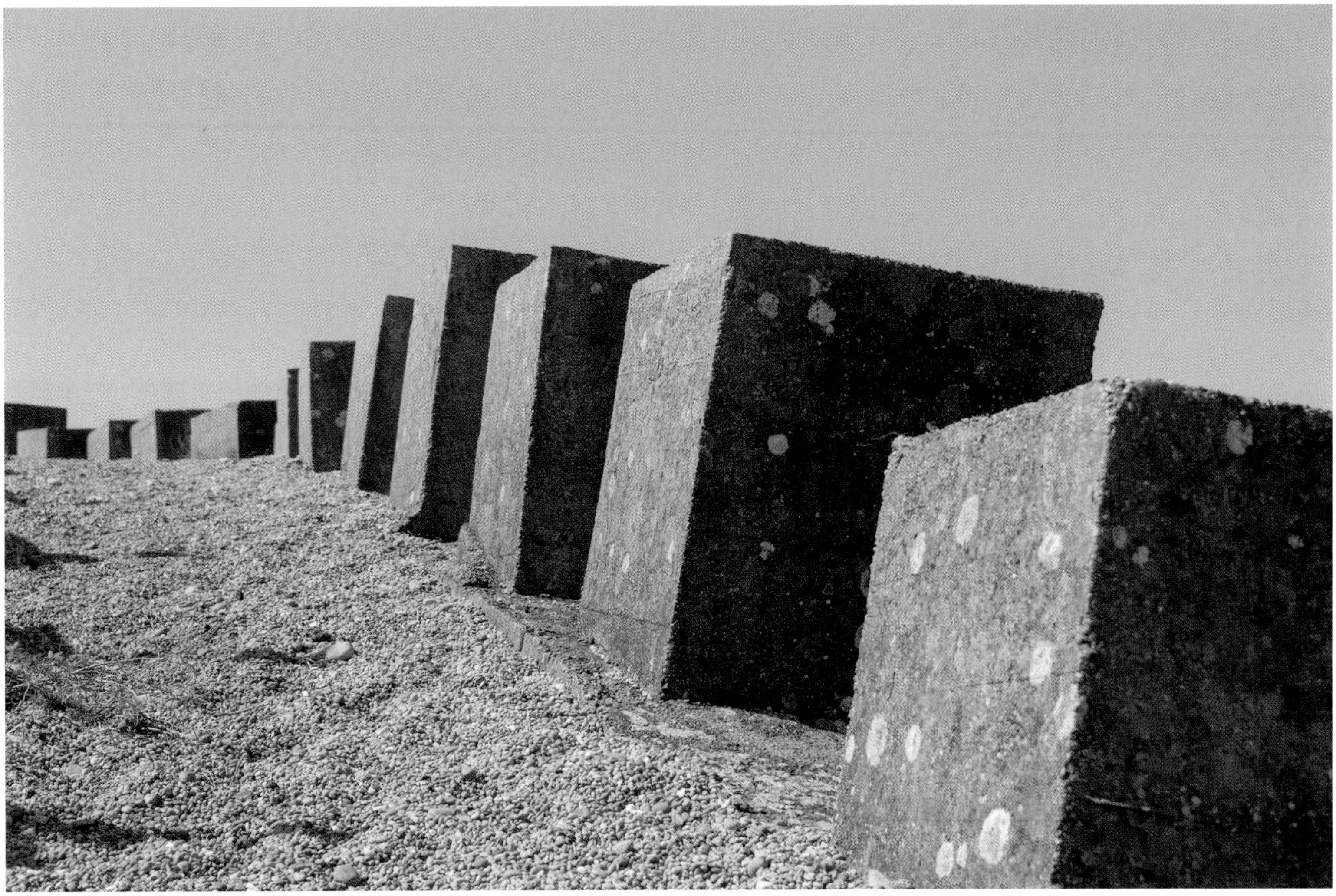

Anti-tank Cubes, Coastal Brutalism, Abbotsbury, England, 2018

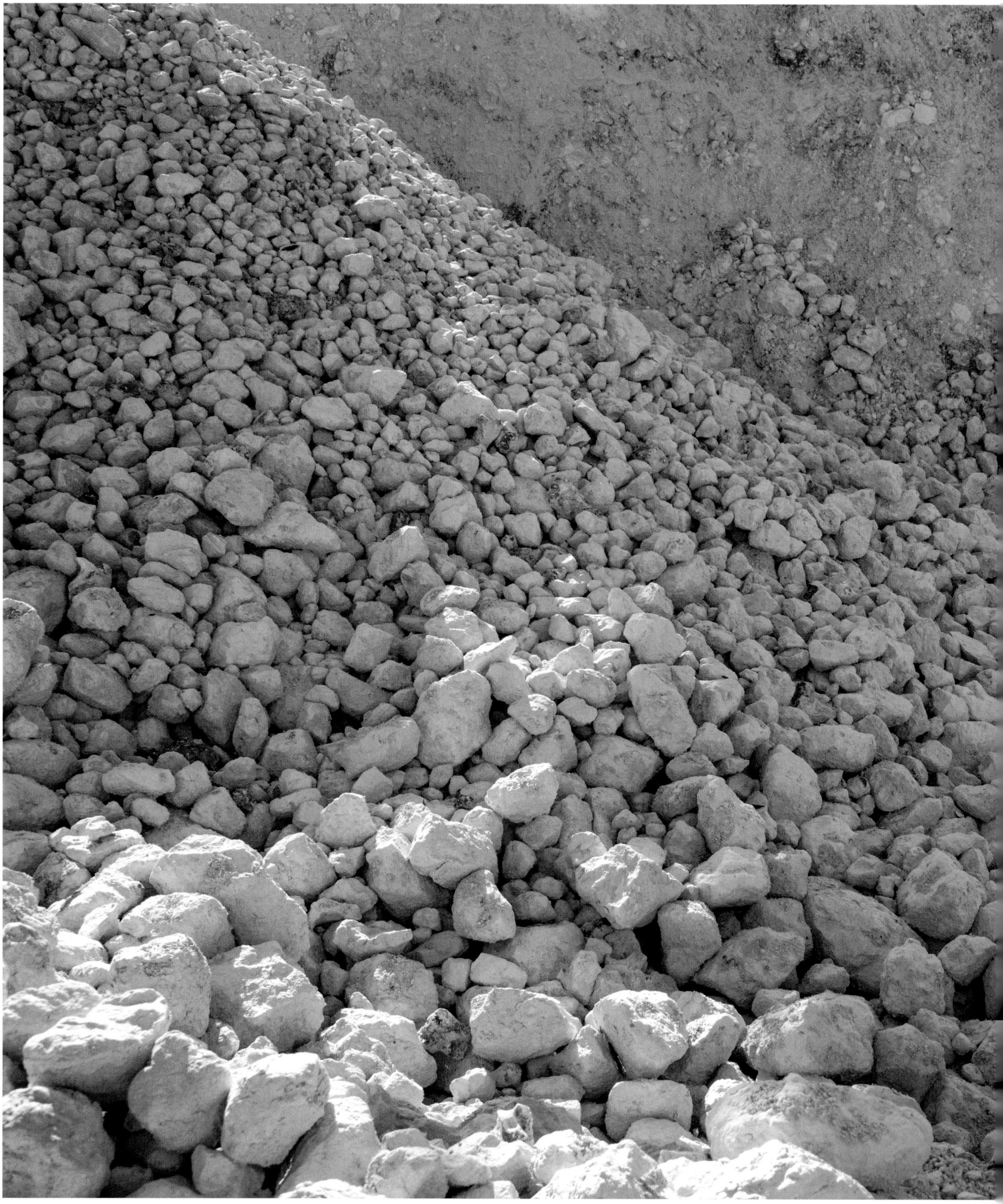

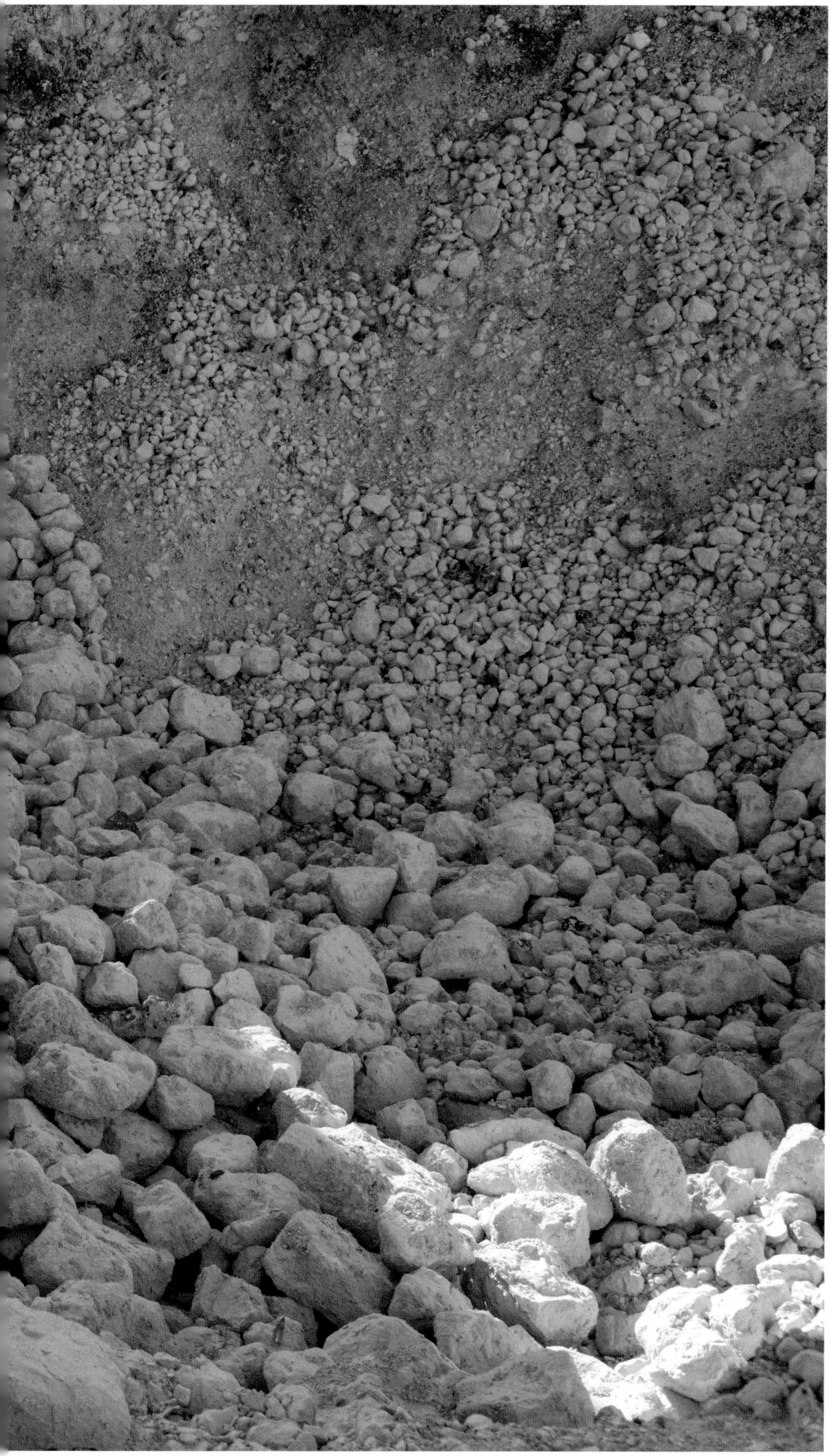

Chalk Quarry, Rocky,
Shapwick, England, 2019

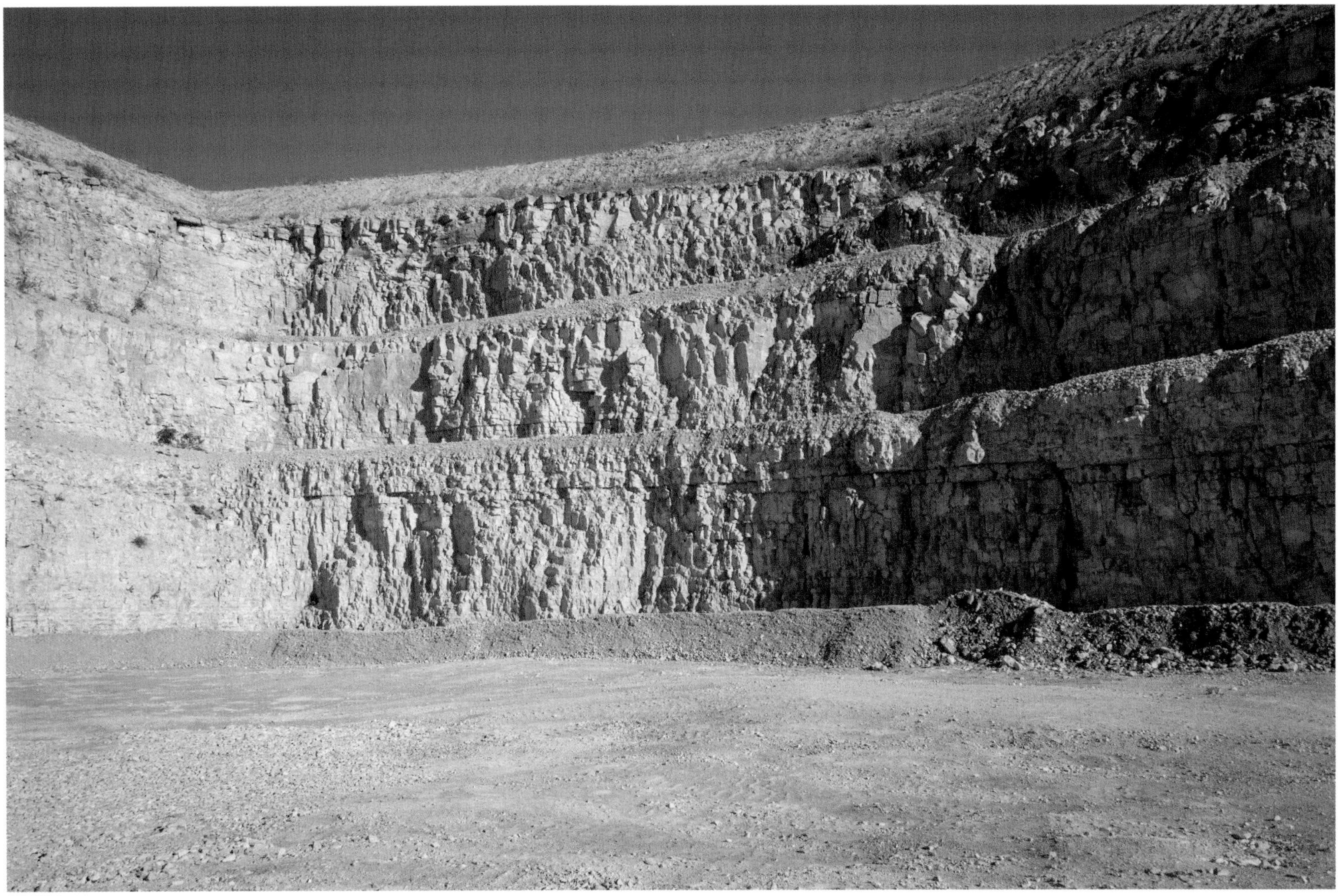

Gravel Quarry, Rocky, Worth Matravers, England, 2018

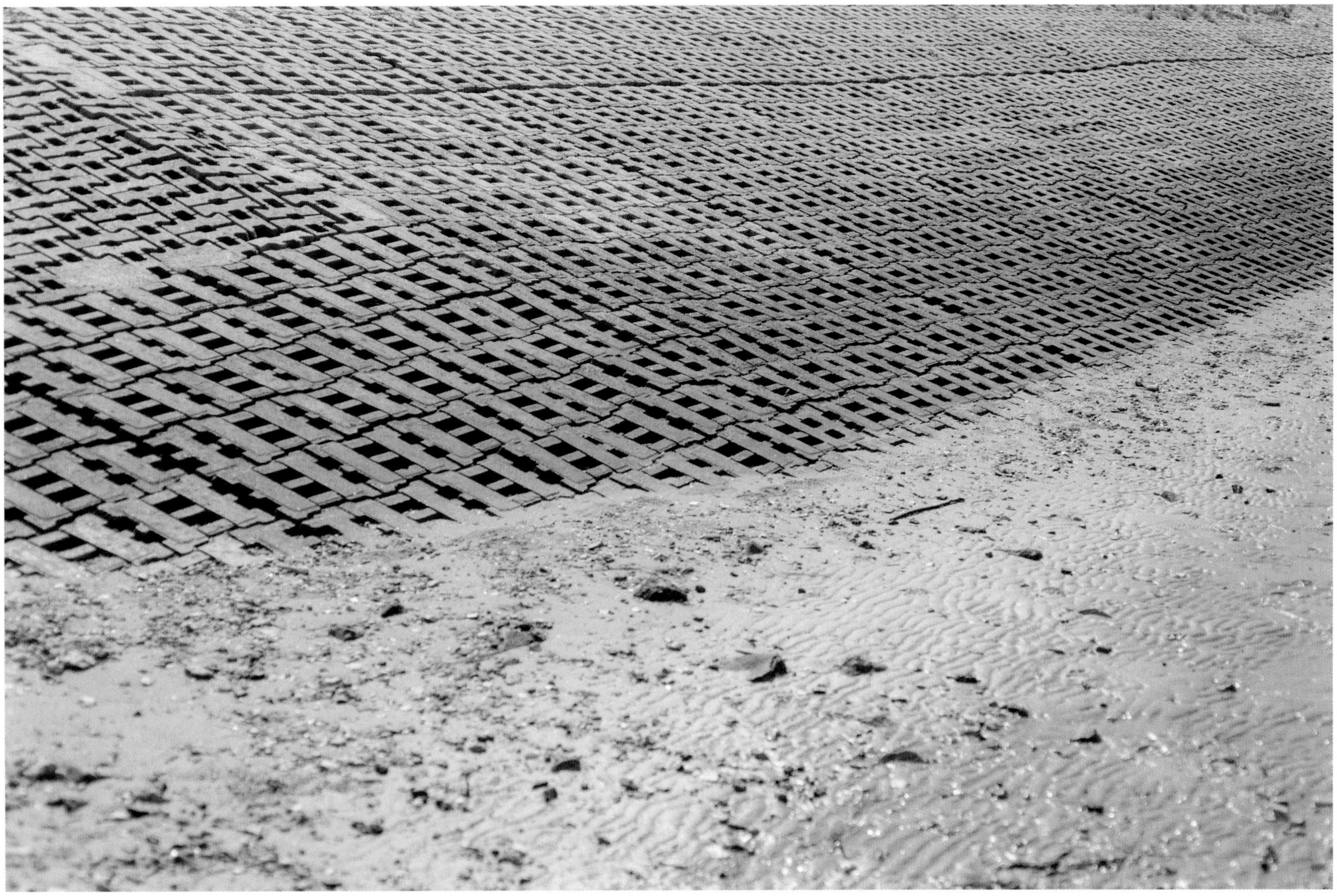

Revetments, Coastal Brutalism, Exmouth, England, 2017

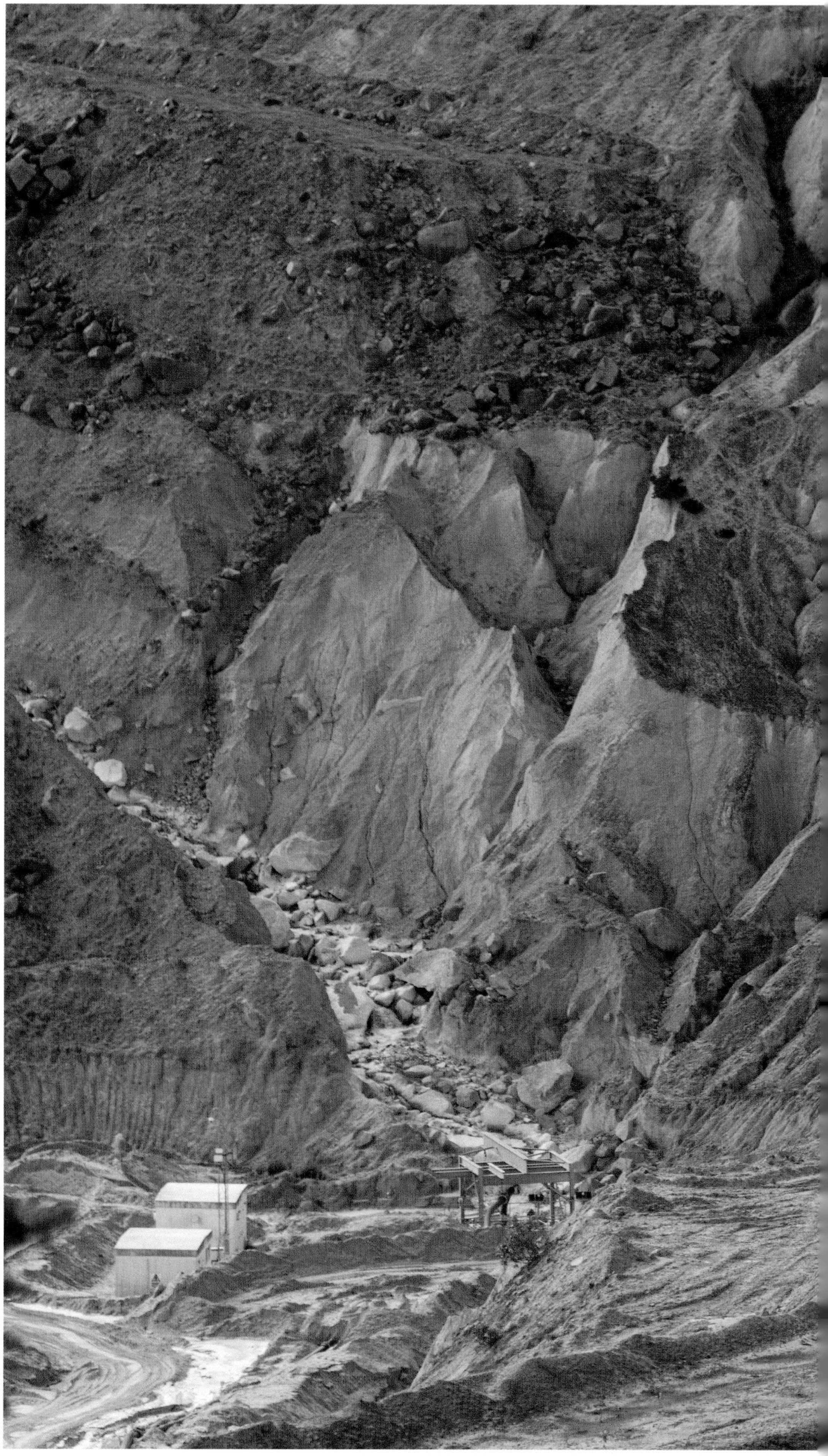

China Clay Pit, Rocky,
Ivybridge, England, 2018

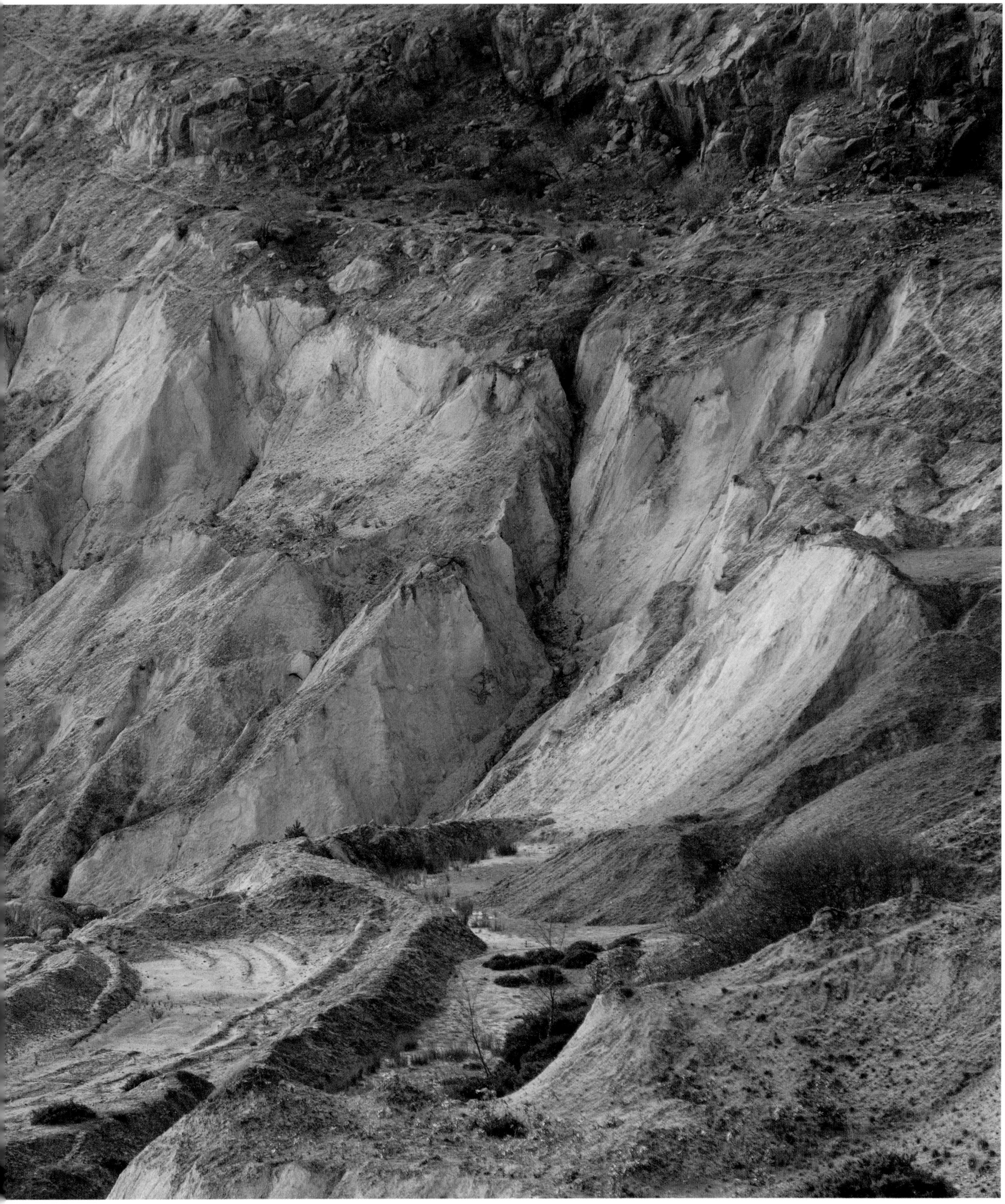

The Tides

Toby Trueman

‘The images wear away until you’re left with nothing but that line, the horizon where there’s nothing left. But ironically, everything is left because you’ve got sea, sky and land. That’s all there is.’

As a child, a horizon can be a challenging thing to understand. It is a lesson in perception, a demonstration of how much the eye can hold. On the coast it is especially perplexing. How to comprehend that the line right out there on the edge of the sea is not, in fact, the end of the world?

In Toby Trueman’s *The Tides*, the line rules the image. Regardless of what’s happening in the foreground – glassy reflections in a rockpool, mist shrouding weathered stone – there sits a horizon in the distance. Sometimes it is crisp. At other times, softened. In a continually altering landscape, moulded by weather, time and human action, that line is eternal.

Trueman’s work holds a tension between transformation and endurance. It is at once a document of something in flux (the tide) and something constant (the horizon). *The Tides* takes place near the photographer’s home in East Lothian, about 25 miles east of Edinburgh. Rather than carefully tracking the tides, Trueman embraced the element of surprise: turning up at different points in the day, curious to see what the shore would reveal. Often relying on long exposures to smooth the sea, the process of making each image became almost meditative: providing a unit of time between the shutter being pressed and released for the photographer to wait and watch. The photos reveal a certain uniformity of colour and light, leaning on a muted palette of greys and washed-out blues, while the horizon bisects the image into a series of panels to be filled with rocks, boats, lighthouses and cloud formations. They are also a portrait of the North Sea’s changeability, and as the oceans rise and the coast crumbles away, that change will continue. The horizon will endure though: always there, always hovering just beyond reach.

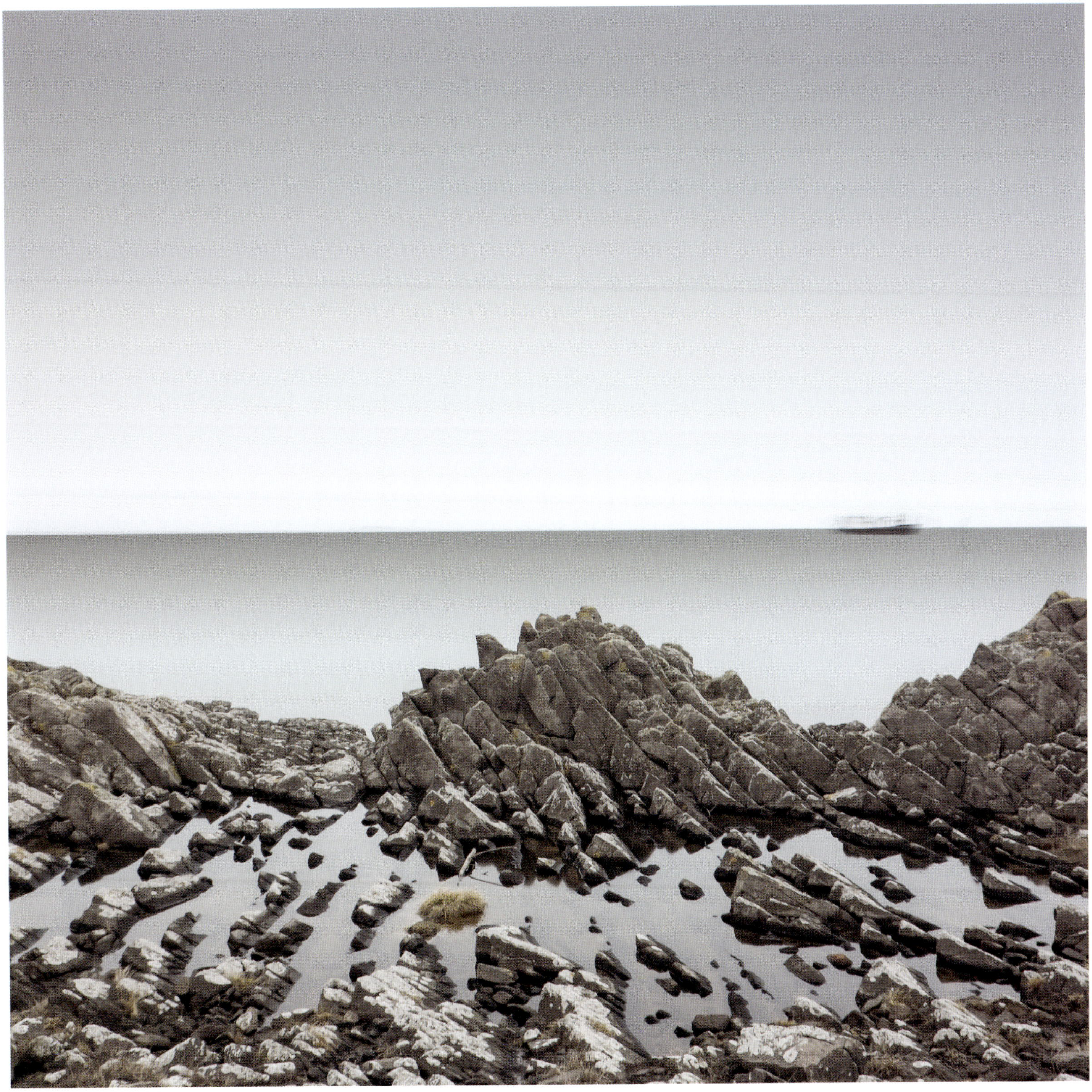

The Tides #1, Ravensheugh, East Lothian, Scotland, 2015

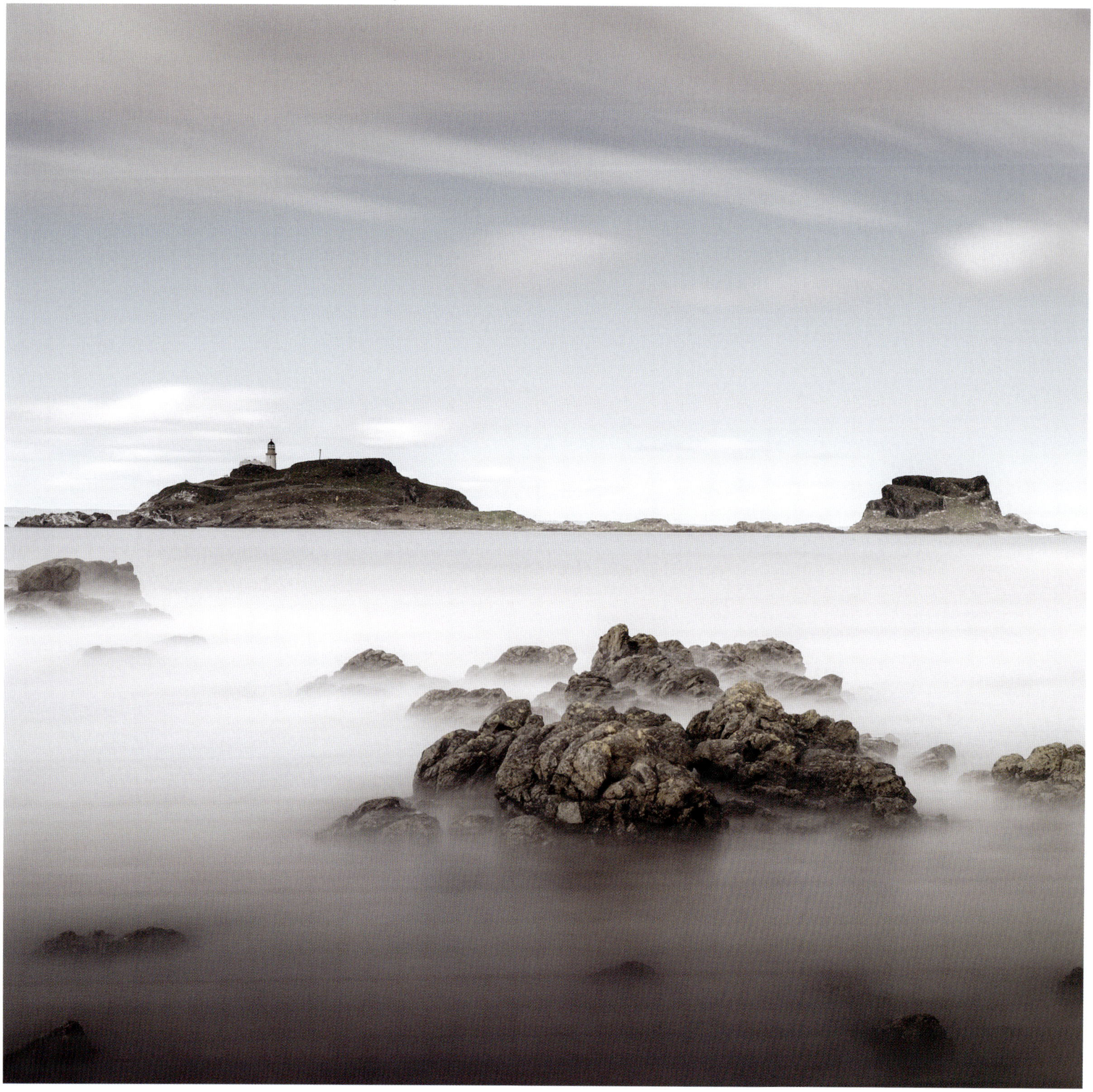

The Tides #5, Yellowcraig, East Lothian, Scotland, 2015

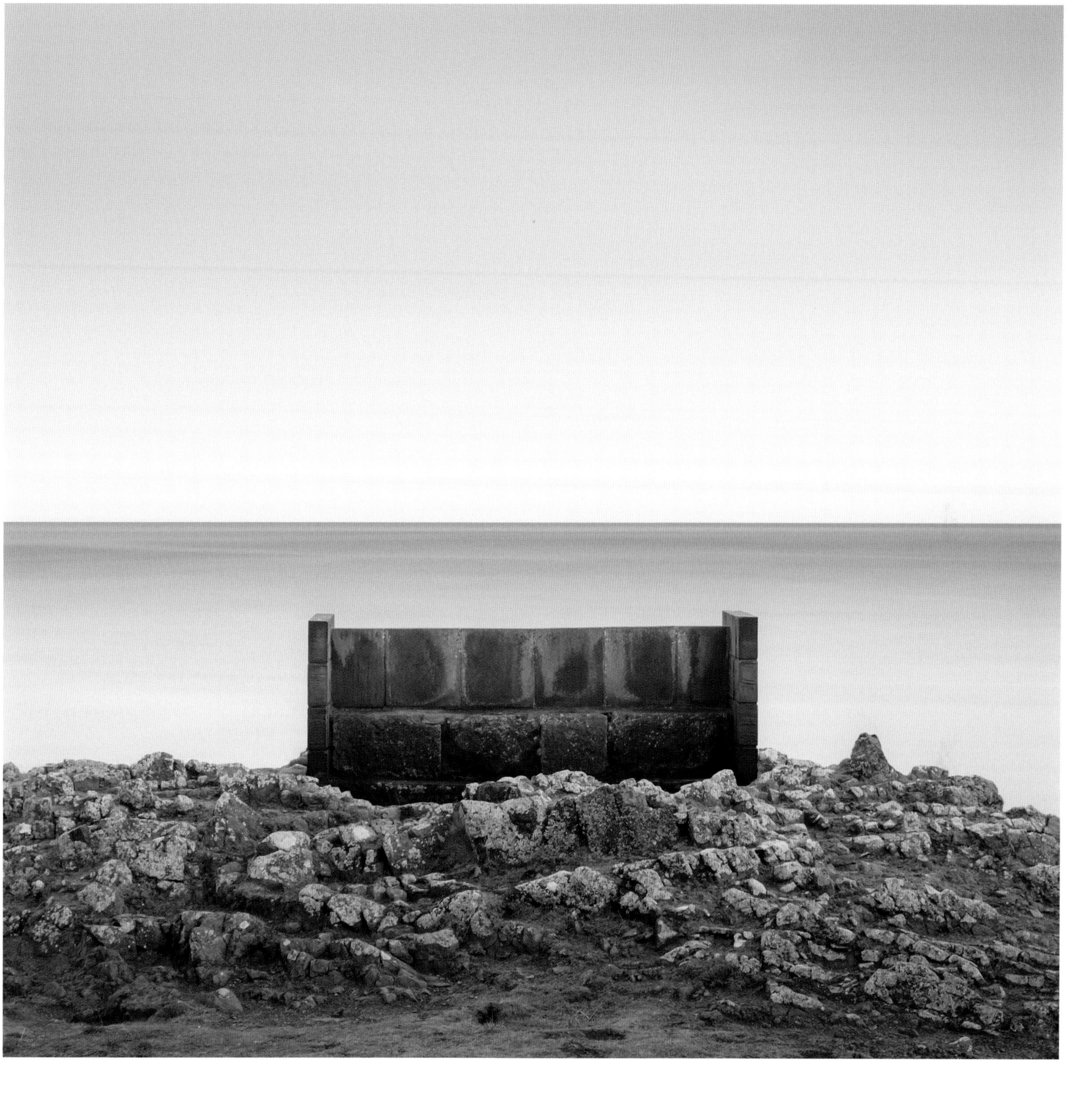

The Tides #4, Ravensheugh, East Lothian, Scotland, 2015

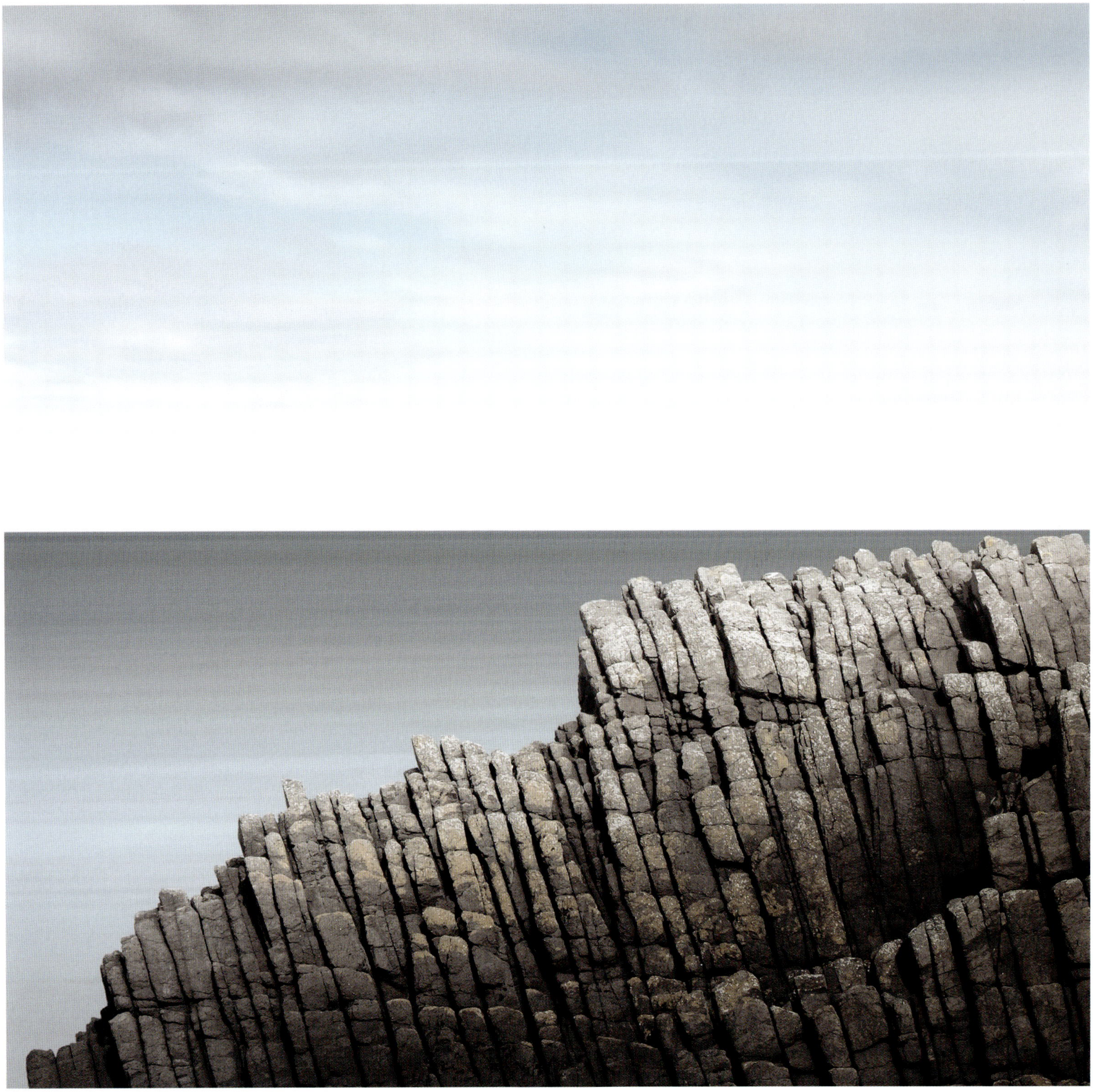

The Tides #3, Ravensheugh, East Lothian, Scotland, 2015

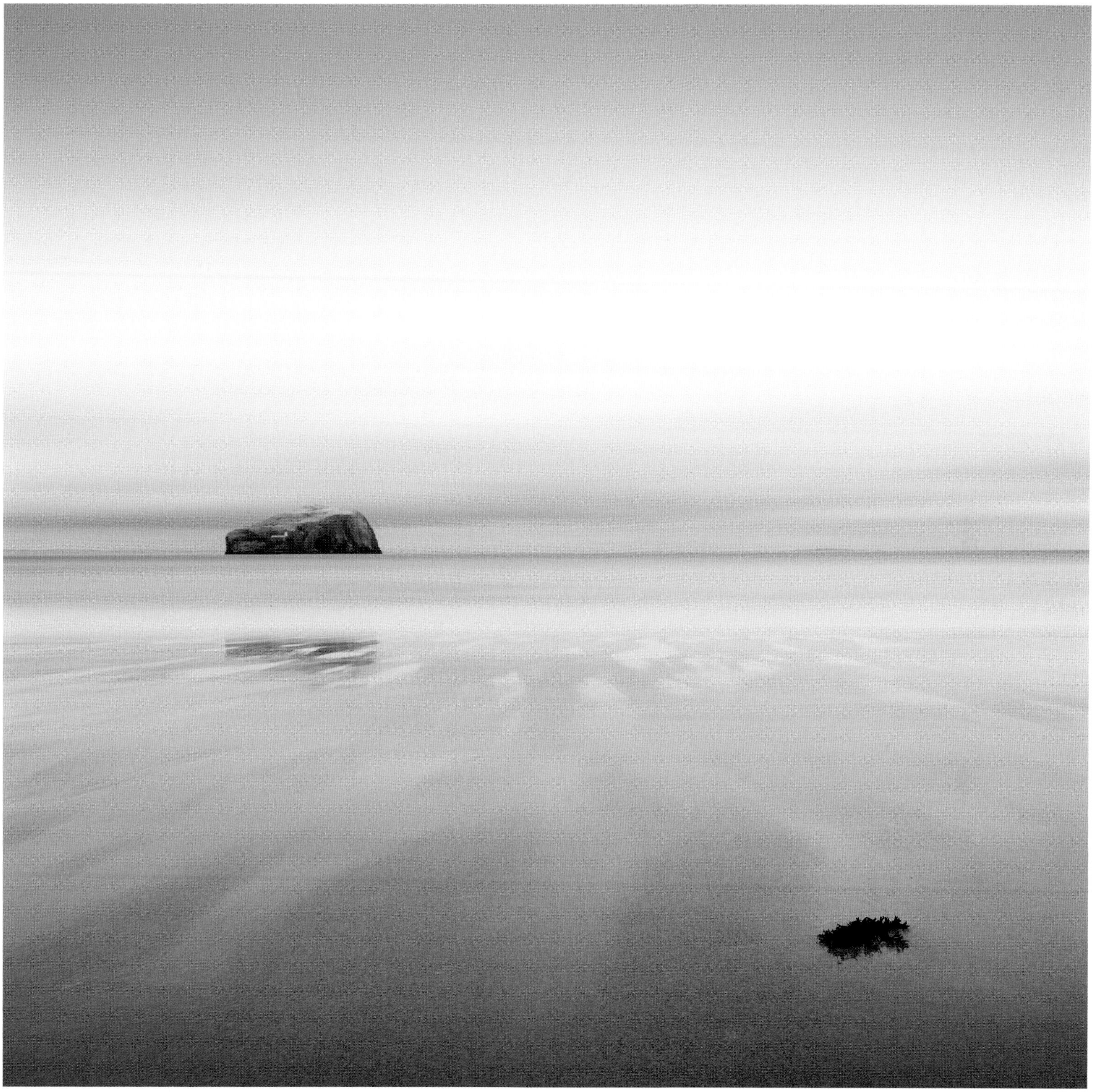

The Tides #9, Seacliff, East Lothian, Scotland, 2015

Close to Home

Iain Sarjeant

'I use my camera to take visual notes, using it to explore [my] environment… I find it quite meditative, a process of getting in the zone. The walk is part of it because it's repetitive.'

In taking one step and then another, we map the world with our feet. Author and academic Lauren Elkin writes in her meditation on city strolling, 'I walk because it confers – or restores – a sense of placeness.' In motion, we learn something new about our surroundings and create physical maps for ourselves of locales both familiar and fresh. Iain Sarjeant's work is largely concerned with how we see and situate ourselves within ordinary places: the routine backdrops to our comings and goings, the environments we interact with just by existing in them.

Close to Home is a project that takes an even closer look at familiar territory. The Scottish photographer is based near the village of Strathpeffer in the Highlands and has lived in the region for the last thirty years. The images were all captured within a two-mile radius of the village, usually during his daily walks. Like a basket into which one might place conkers or feathers found on morning strolls, Sarjeant kept a folder on his desktop where he could collect these locally taken images. Over time, he began to enjoy the limitations imposed by this sense of proximity. Unlike the novelty of an unknown location, the appeal was in the intimacy – in recurring visits that yielded new sights or tiny shifts in the known landscape. Snow descended. Trees fell. There was always something worth looking at.

Sarjeant's style of photography replicates the experience of walking. He shoots on an 'old, old SLR' that is light enough to carry around and raise immediately. He does not spend long swathes of time composing his photos. Like a single moment glimpsed while on the move, his photos are taken quickly – spontaneous and responsive, preserving the swing of seasons and temperatures as the scenery slowly rearranges itself.

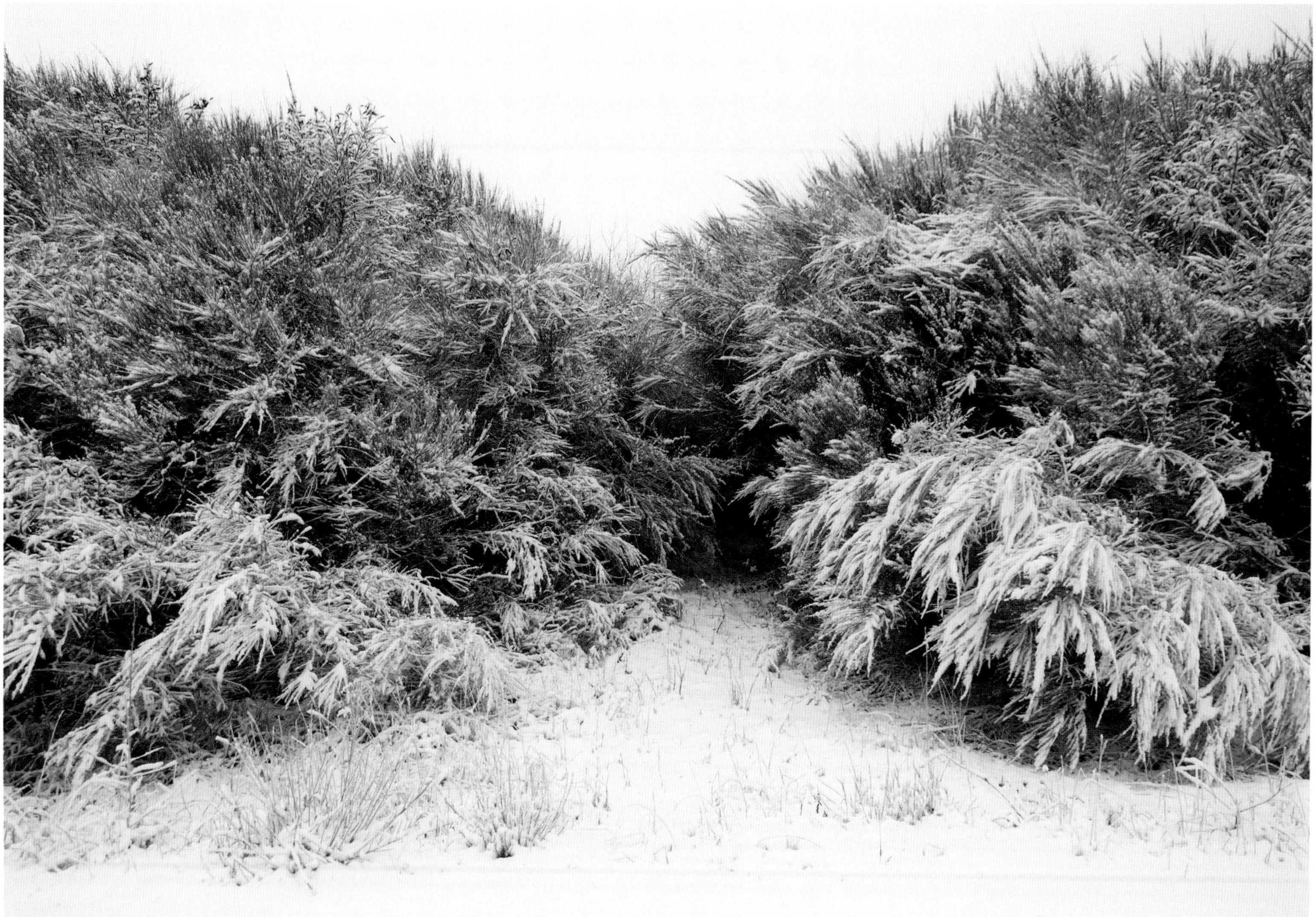

Near Strathpeffer, Ross-shire, Scotland, December 2015

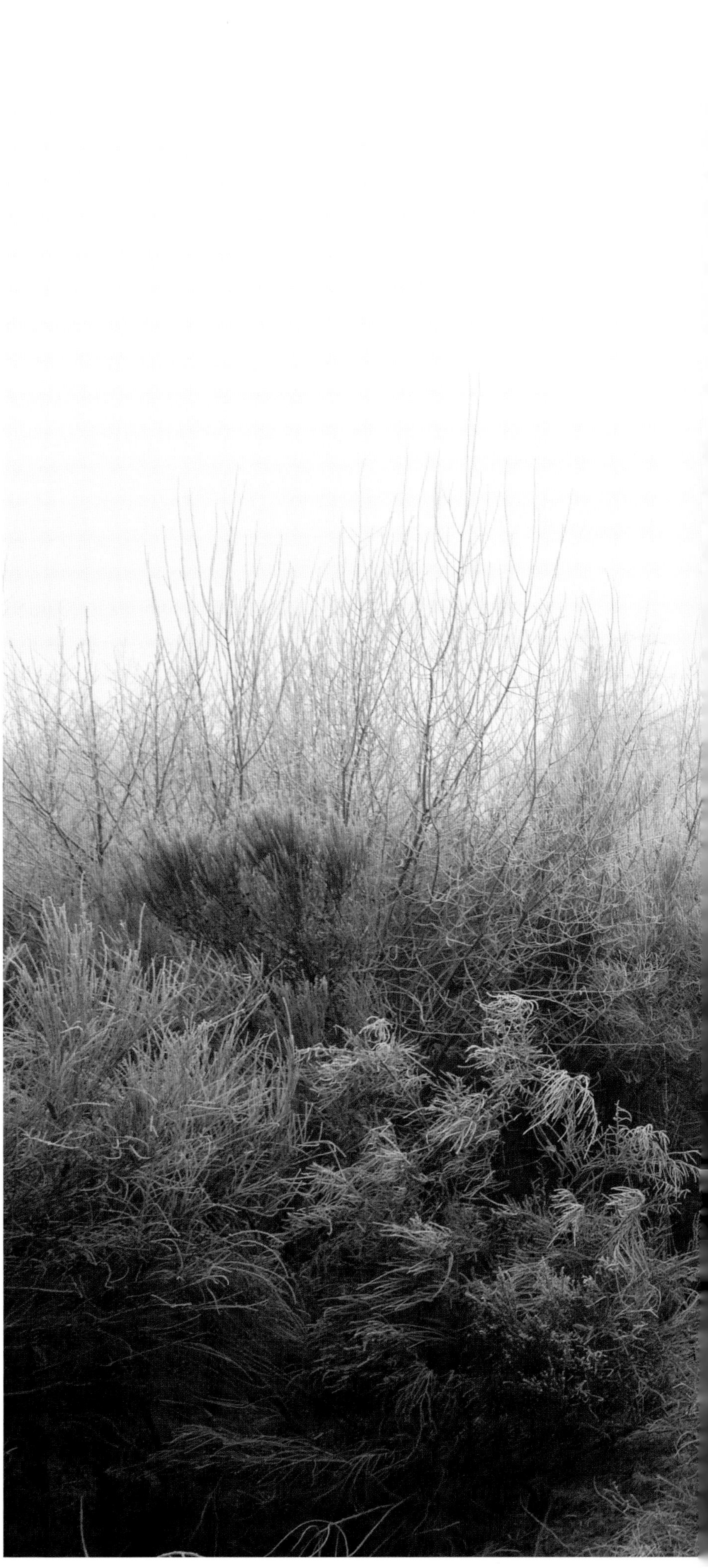

Near Strathpeffer, Ross-shire, Scotland, January 2017

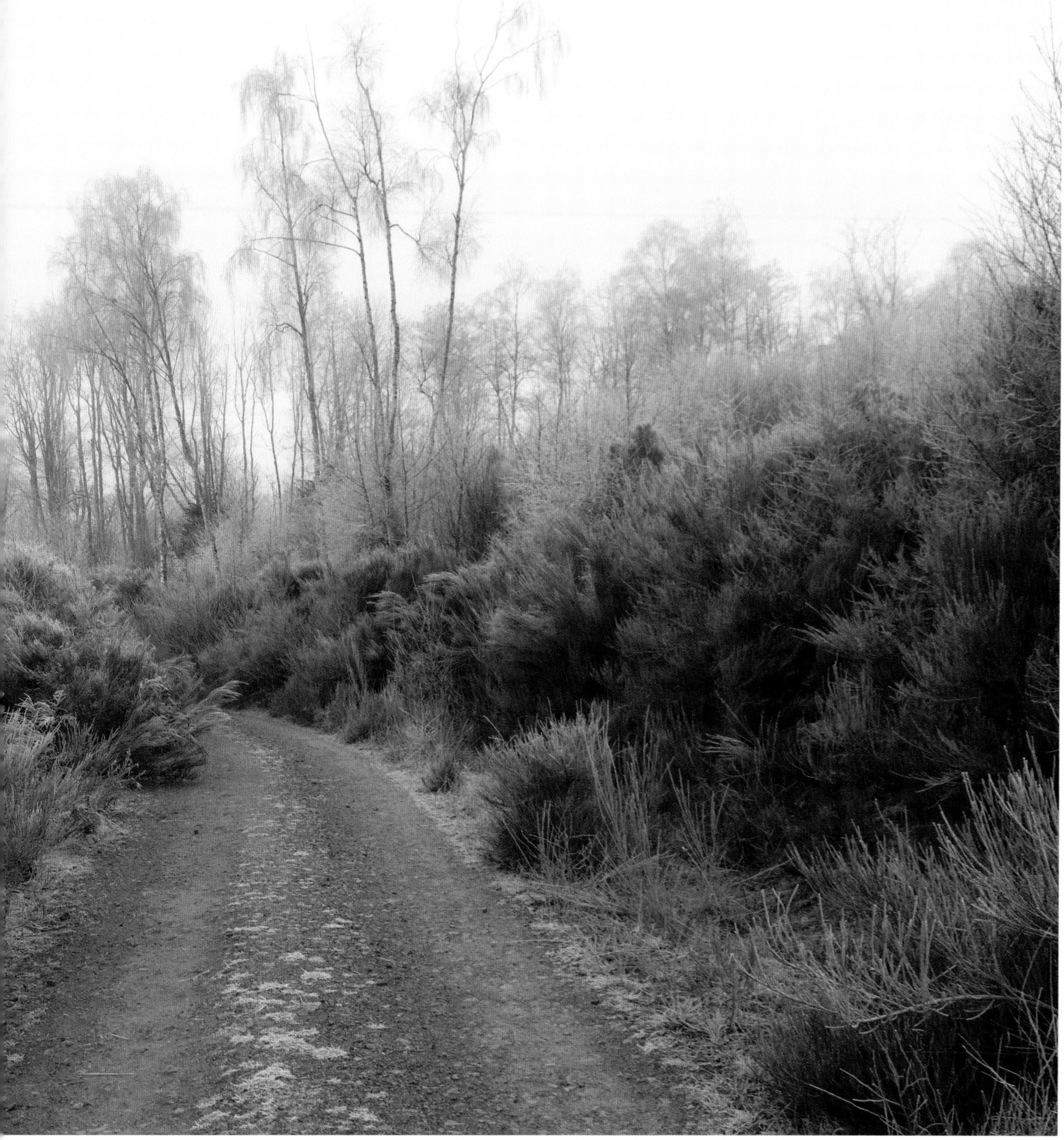

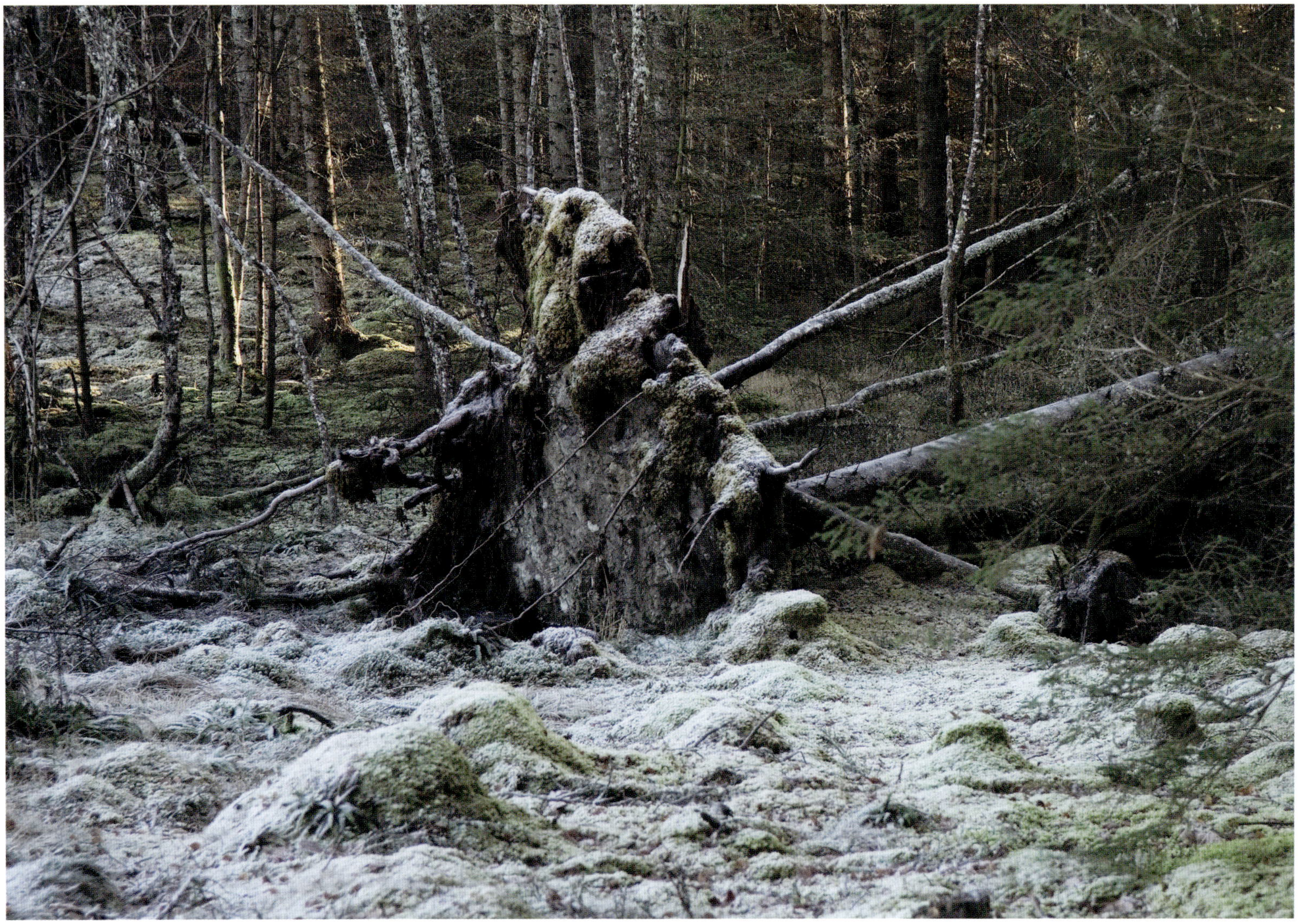

Near Strathpeffer, Ross-shire, Scotland, December 2014

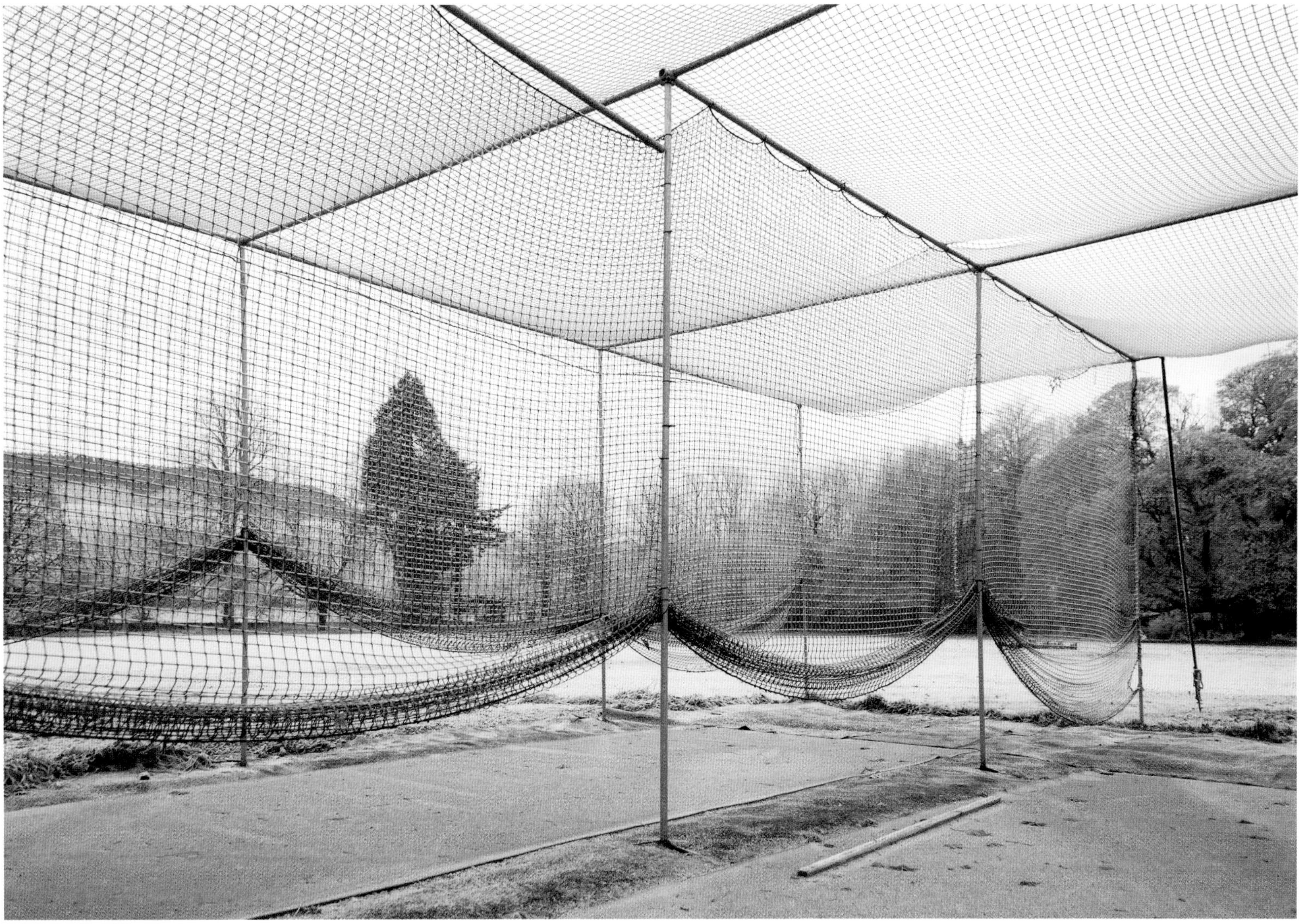

Near Strathpeffer, Ross-shire, Scotland, December 2016

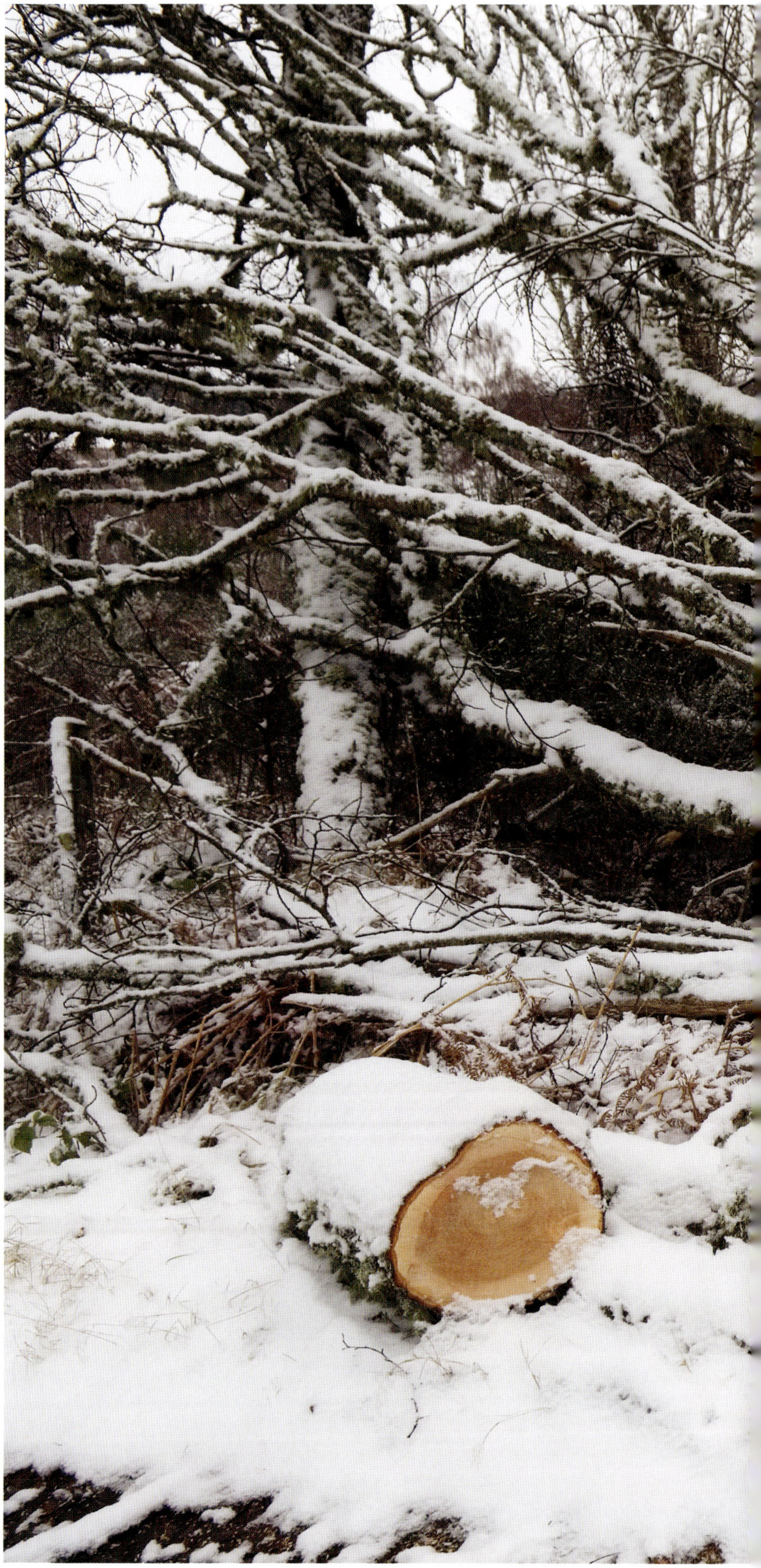

Near Strathpeffer, Ross-shire, Scotland, December 2013

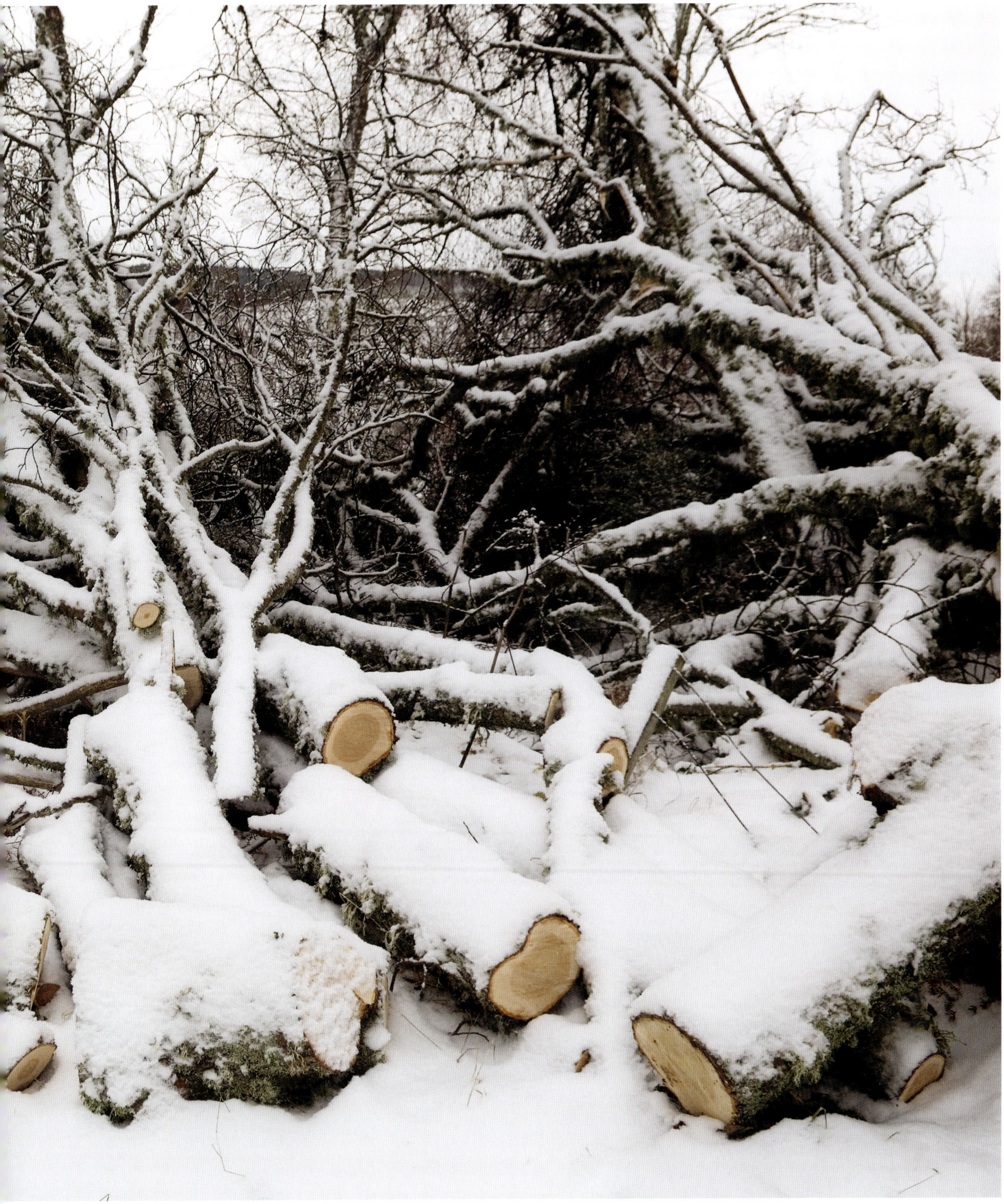

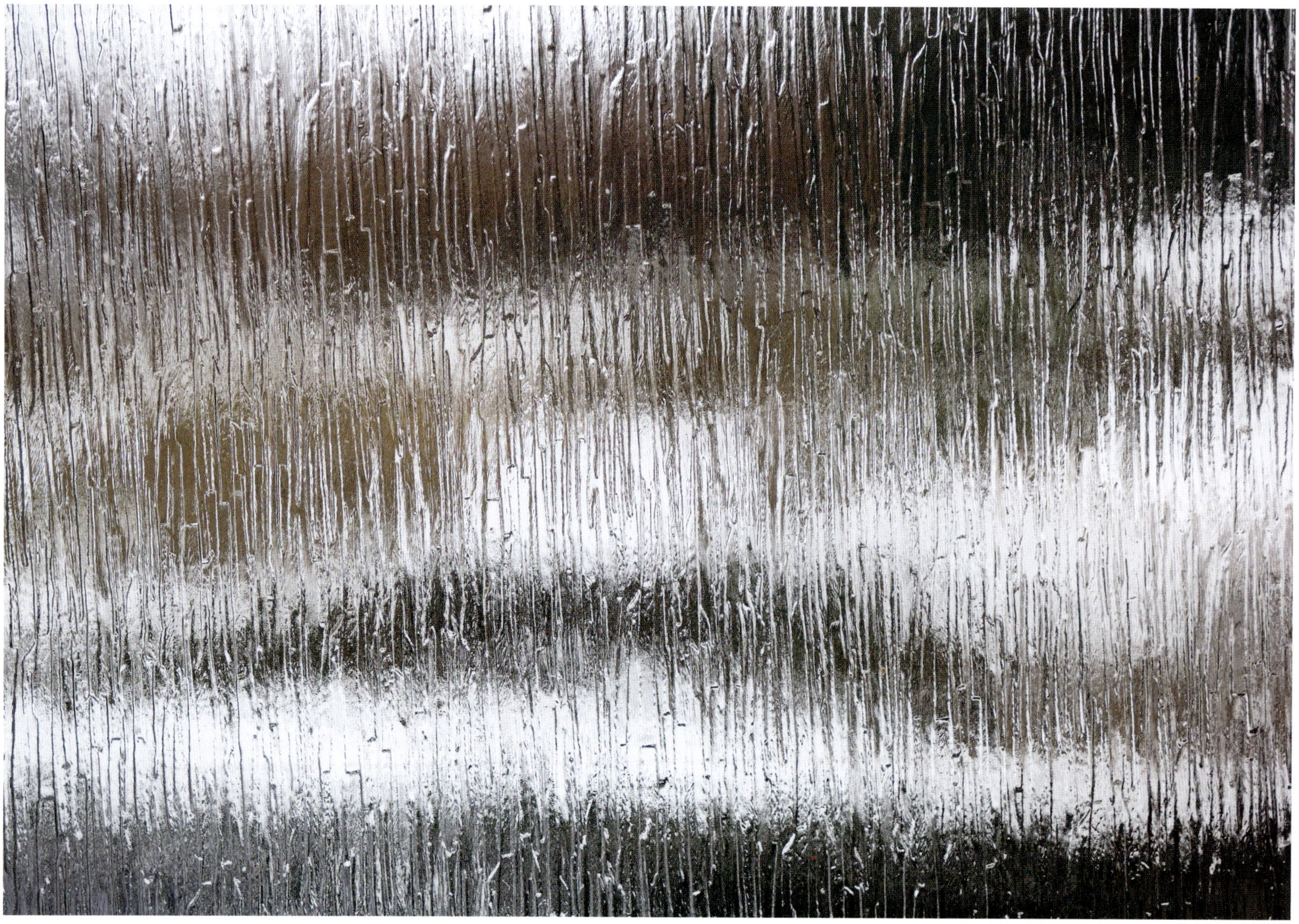

Near Strathpeffer, Ross-shire, Scotland, May 2014

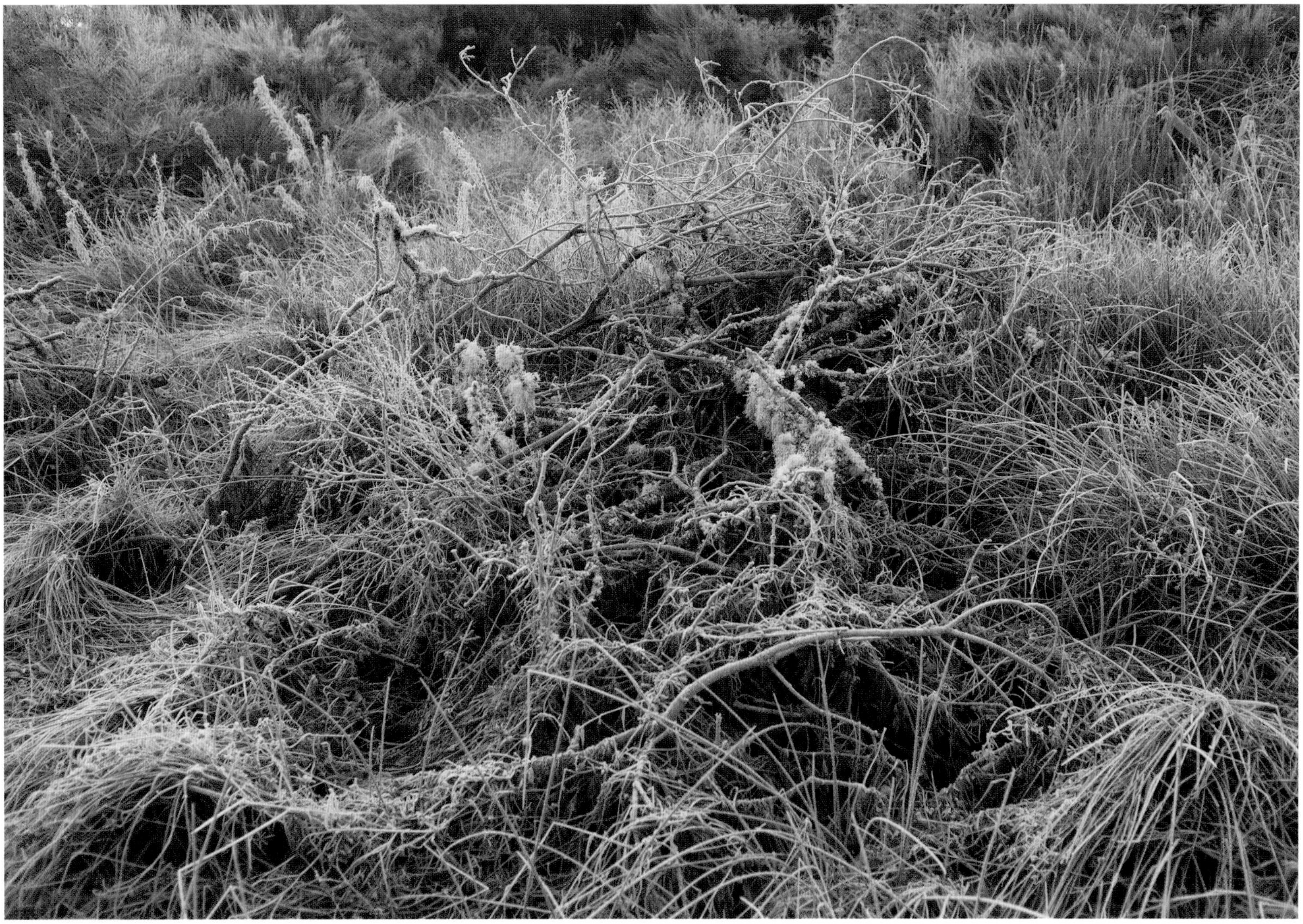

Near Strathpeffer, Ross-shire, Scotland, February 2017

Explosions

Sarah Pickering

'There's this sense of an explosion suspended permanently... You can't tell the trajectory. They're set on the ground, but some look like they've been dropped from the sky.'

Smoke Burst. Landmine. Electric Thunderflash. Large Maroon. These are all the names of fake bombs manufactured by the simulation pyrotechnic industry. Used by police and military instructors in training exercises, they are meant to prepare their forces physically and psychologically for worst-case scenarios. Some emit plumes of fire or send sparks high into the air. Others float just above the tarmac like lost clouds. Many of them were created by people who work in special effects. Landmine was designed by a man who also creates explosive devices for James Bond movies.

Sarah Pickering's *Explosions* is a project about the distorted lines between entertainment and violence, as well as documentary and fiction. The explosions she photographs are real, but they are a dress rehearsal for much bigger, more traumatic events.

These bursts of flame and smoke happen under tightly controlled circumstances, usually on nondescript patches of land or army bases. They are mostly commercial displays. Standing out of shot are not only the pyrotechnic specialists but also small groups of spectators from the military and police making shopping lists, choosing which bangs and blasts they want to buy this time.

There is something stunning in these photos, especially if we take that word to also mean 'startling' or 'dazing'. Even though these scenes are intended to mimic dangerous situations, through Pickering's lens they acquire a surreal grandeur that demands you don't look away. Against the flat skies and dull green scrub, they flare incongruously, hovering forever in the moment of eruption. They are a magic trick: a moment of illumination that conjures catastrophe until the smoke fades away.

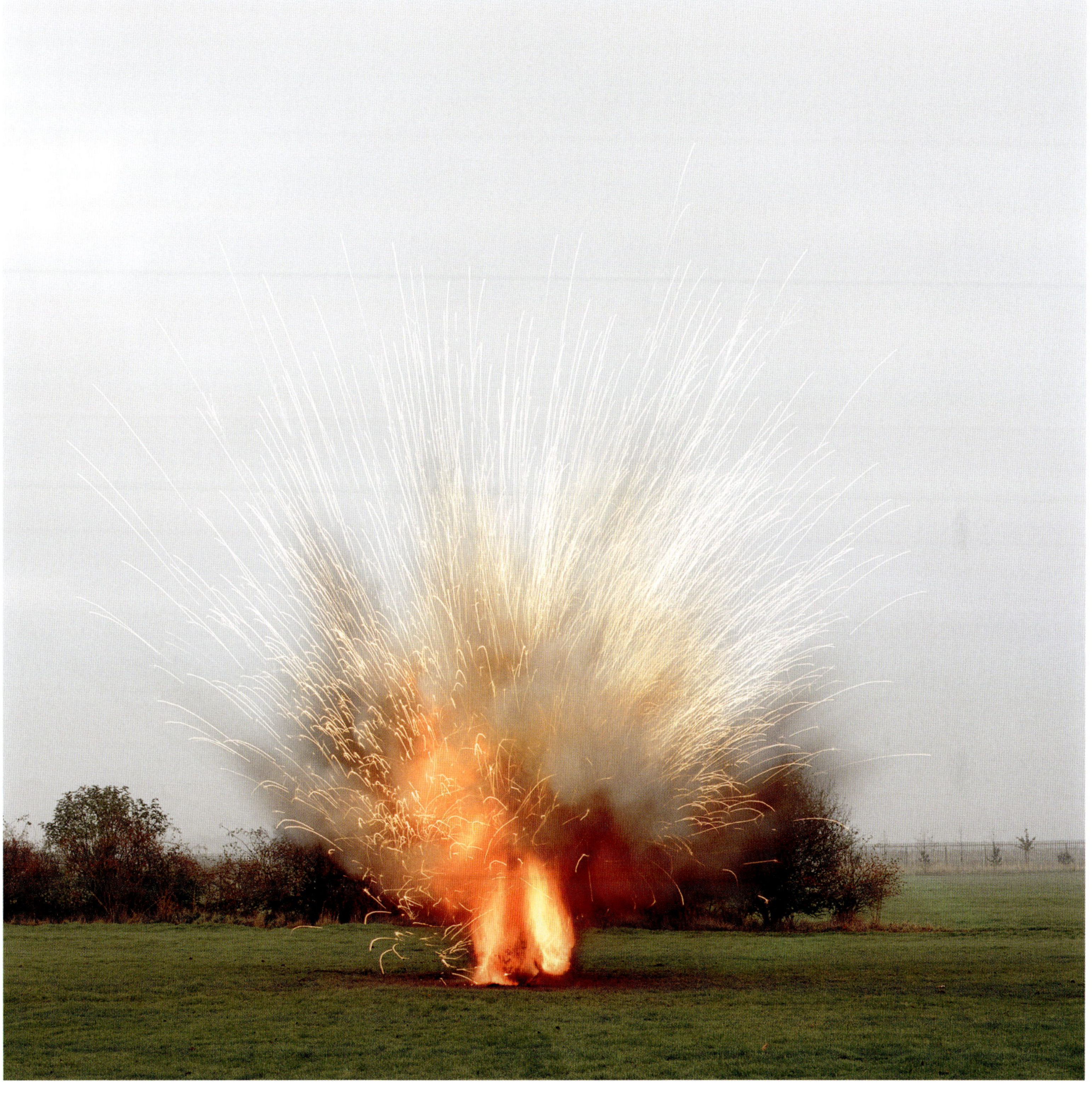

Landmine, Lincolnshire, England, 2005

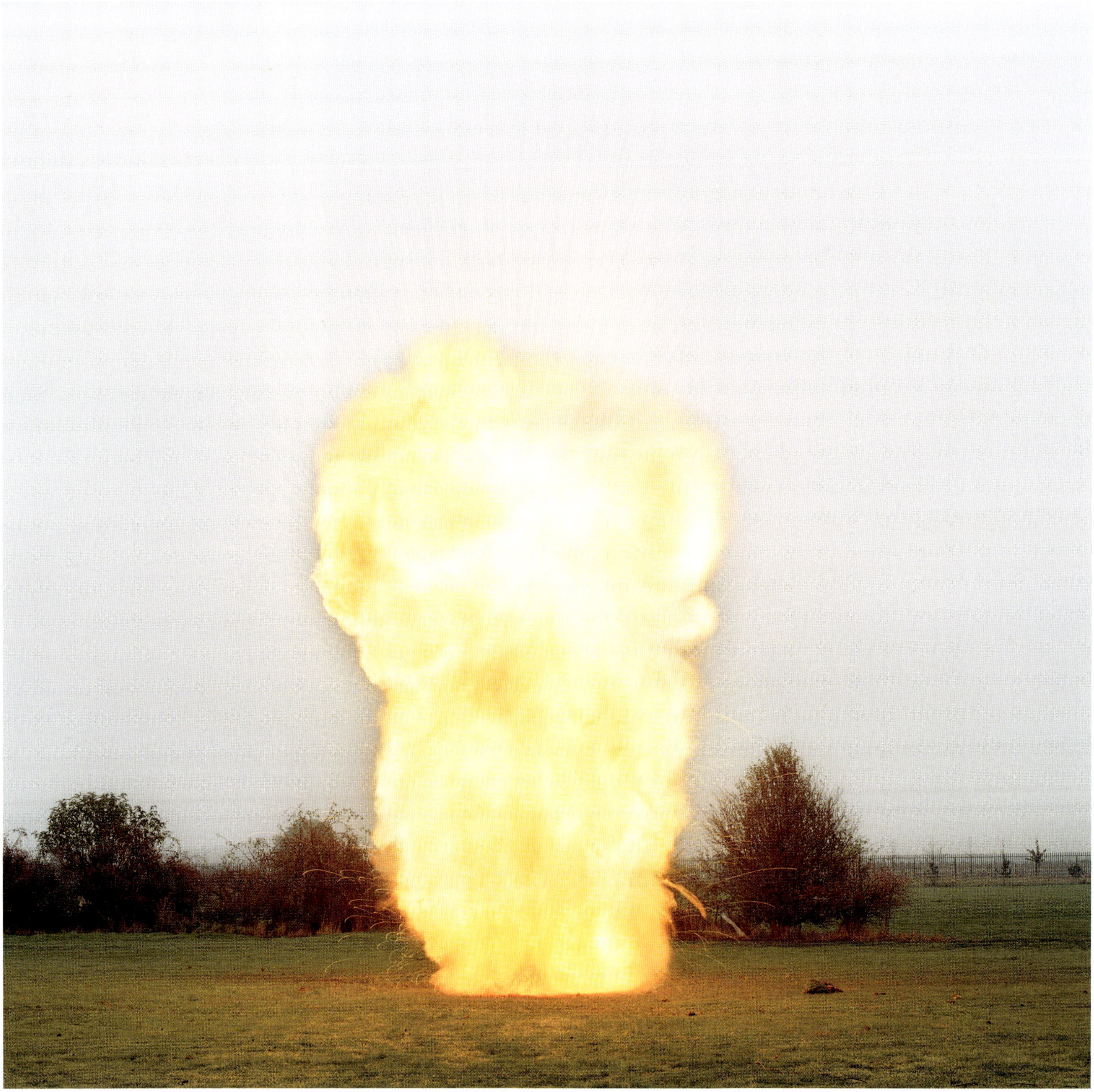

Fuel Air Explosion, Lincolnshire, England, 2005

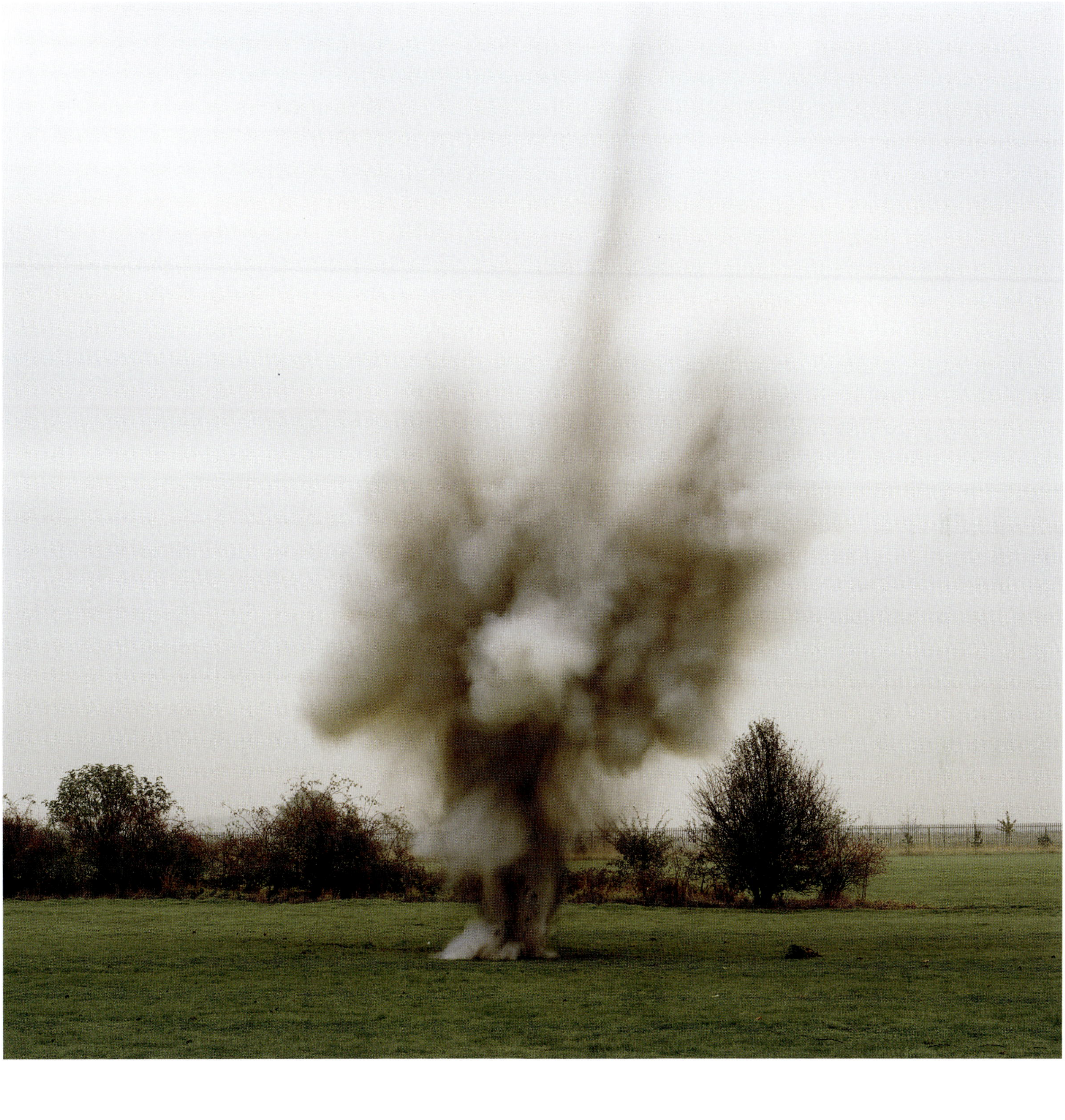

Artillery, Lincolnshire, England, 2005

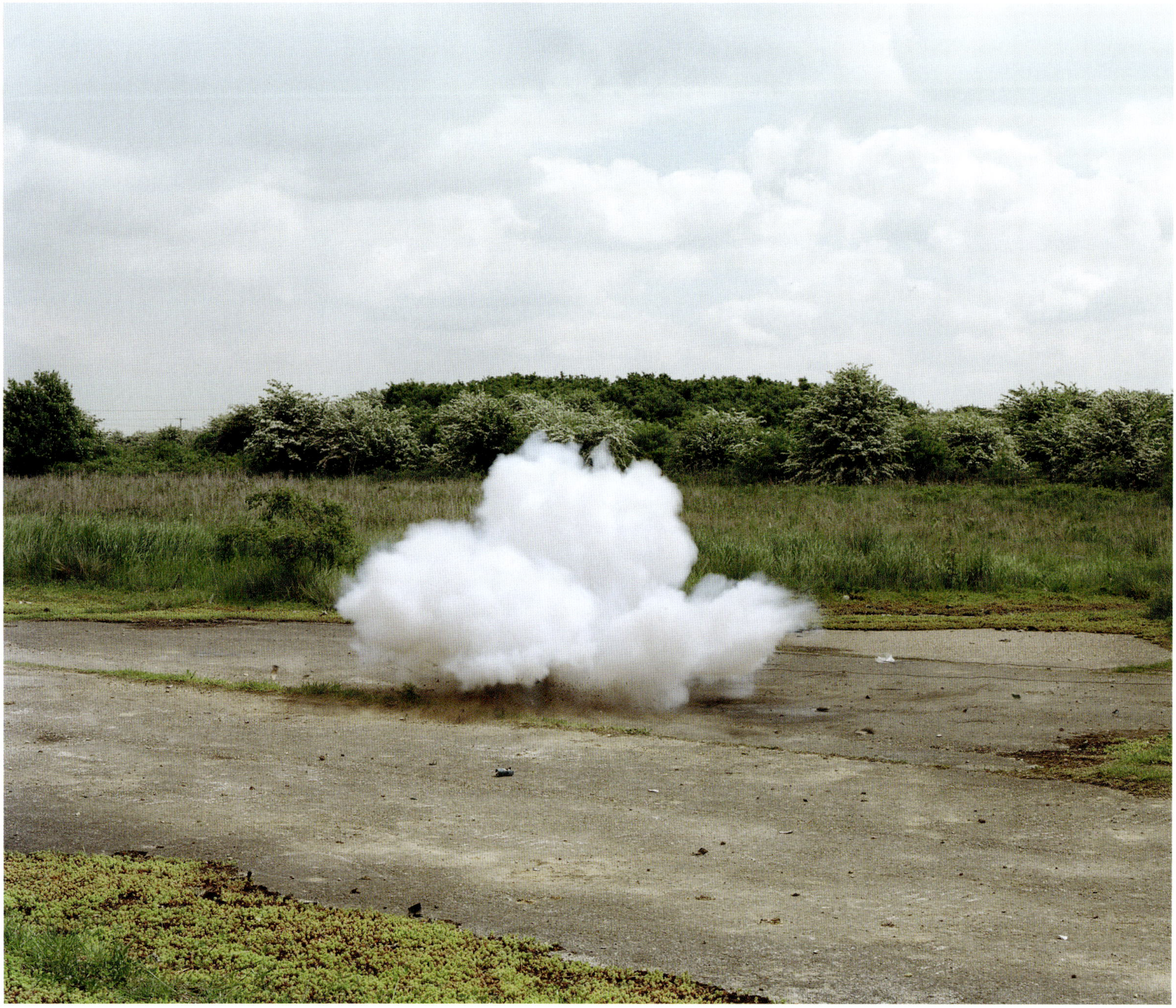

Electric Thunderflash, Lincolnshire, England, 2004

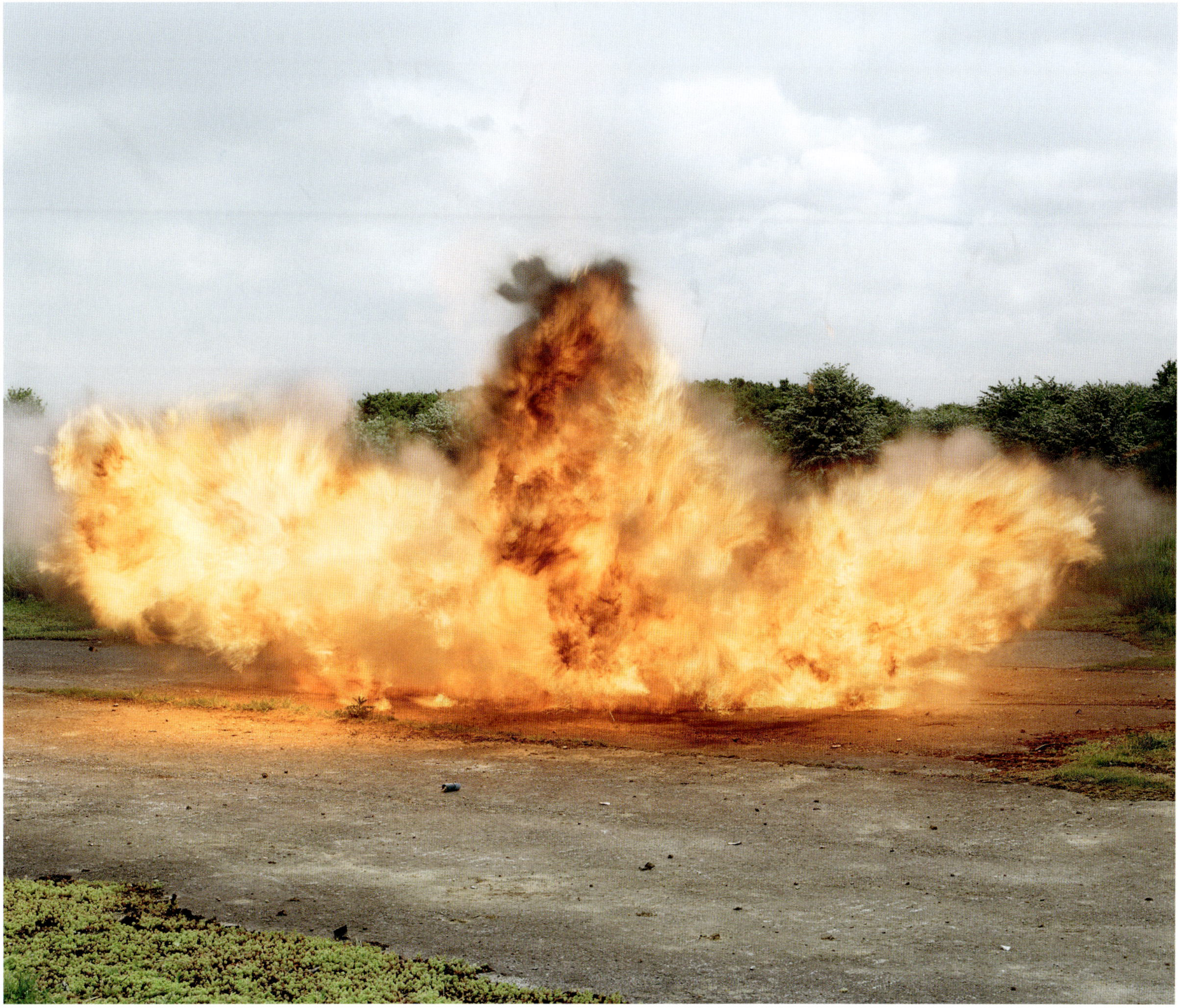

Fire Burst, Lincolnshire, England, 2004

Exposed by the Sun, Washed Out by the Sea

Miriam Nabarro

'The speed at which you have to work makes it a rough alchemy... You're building up these tones and scraping away and layering on again. It's a very dynamic process.'

There is a fantastic simplicity to the cyanotype. It is one of the oldest forms of photographic image-making, requiring only paper and a mix of two chemicals (ferric ammonium citrate and potassium ferricyanide). When paper brushed with this solution is exposed to light, it immediately reacts and turns a watery Prussian blue, while anything that blocks the light casts down a reverse shadow in white, leaving a ghostly outline behind.

Miriam Nabarro has used cyanotypes in a number of contexts, including community workshops. In Calais she worked with refugees to document their phone chargers, transforming these practical lifelines into spectral silhouettes. In *Exposed by the Sun*, Nabarro turns her attentions to the coast. Building on her preoccupation with borders and forced migration, these cyanotypes were created in 2018 as a response to Brexit and the migration crisis. They were made in Carrick Shore in Dumfriesshire, a remote part of southwest Scotland where the land meets the Irish Sea, right on the edge of Britain.

Each cyanotype must be carefully prepared, the paper carried down to the shore in blankets. Once sun hits the solution, there are only two or three minutes before the final image sets. These cyanotypes are living portraits of the elements, submerged in layers of sand, shells and salt water before being washed clean again by the sea. Nabarro calls the results 'imaginary maps'. With their abstracted shapes and pale splotches resembling countries, they come to symbolise unknown journeys towards a hoped-for, yet often inaccessible, destination. The photographic process itself, exposed to sun and sea, mirrors these arduous journeys.

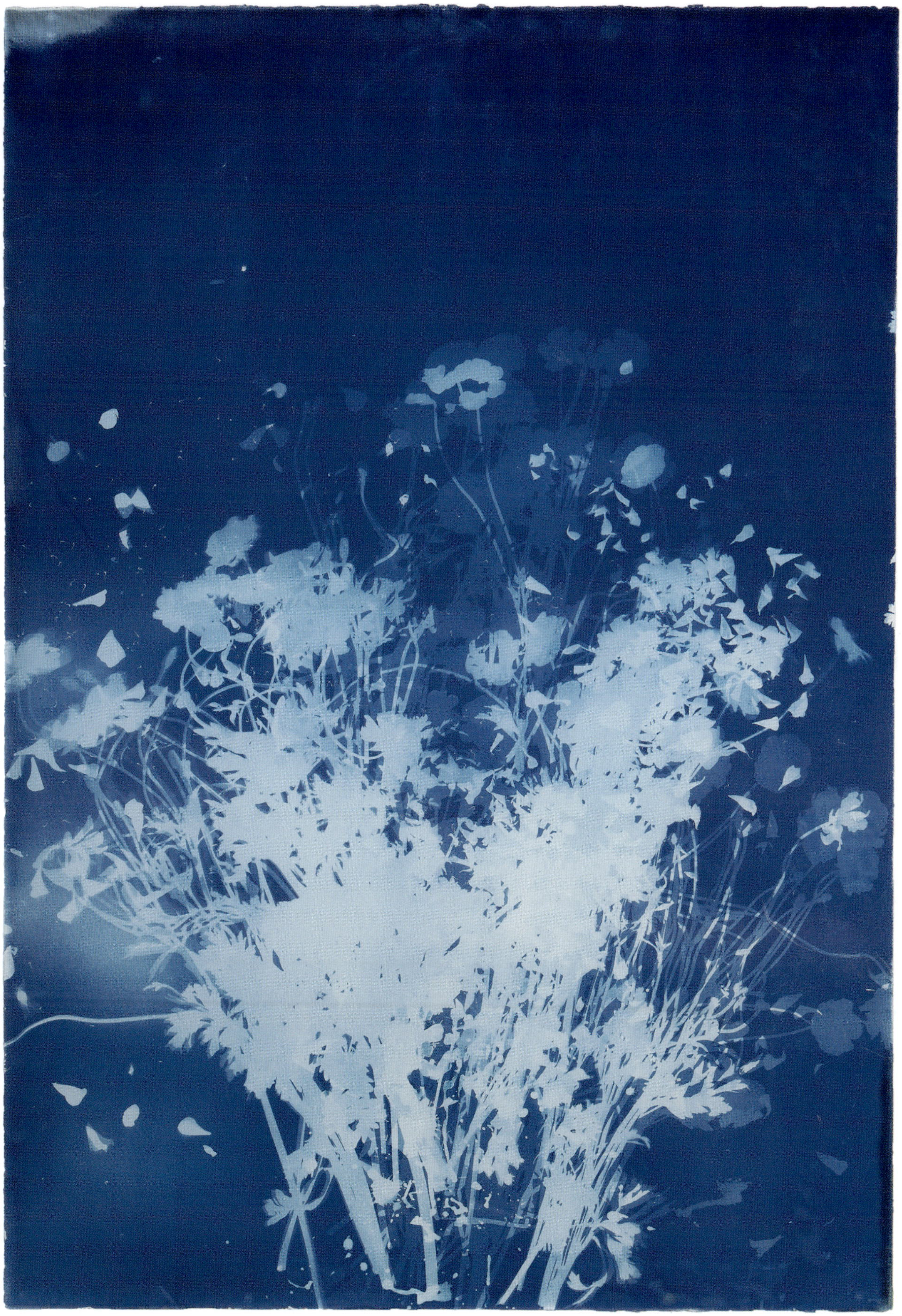

Exploded Geum I, Botanicals, Quidhampton, Hampshire, England, 2020

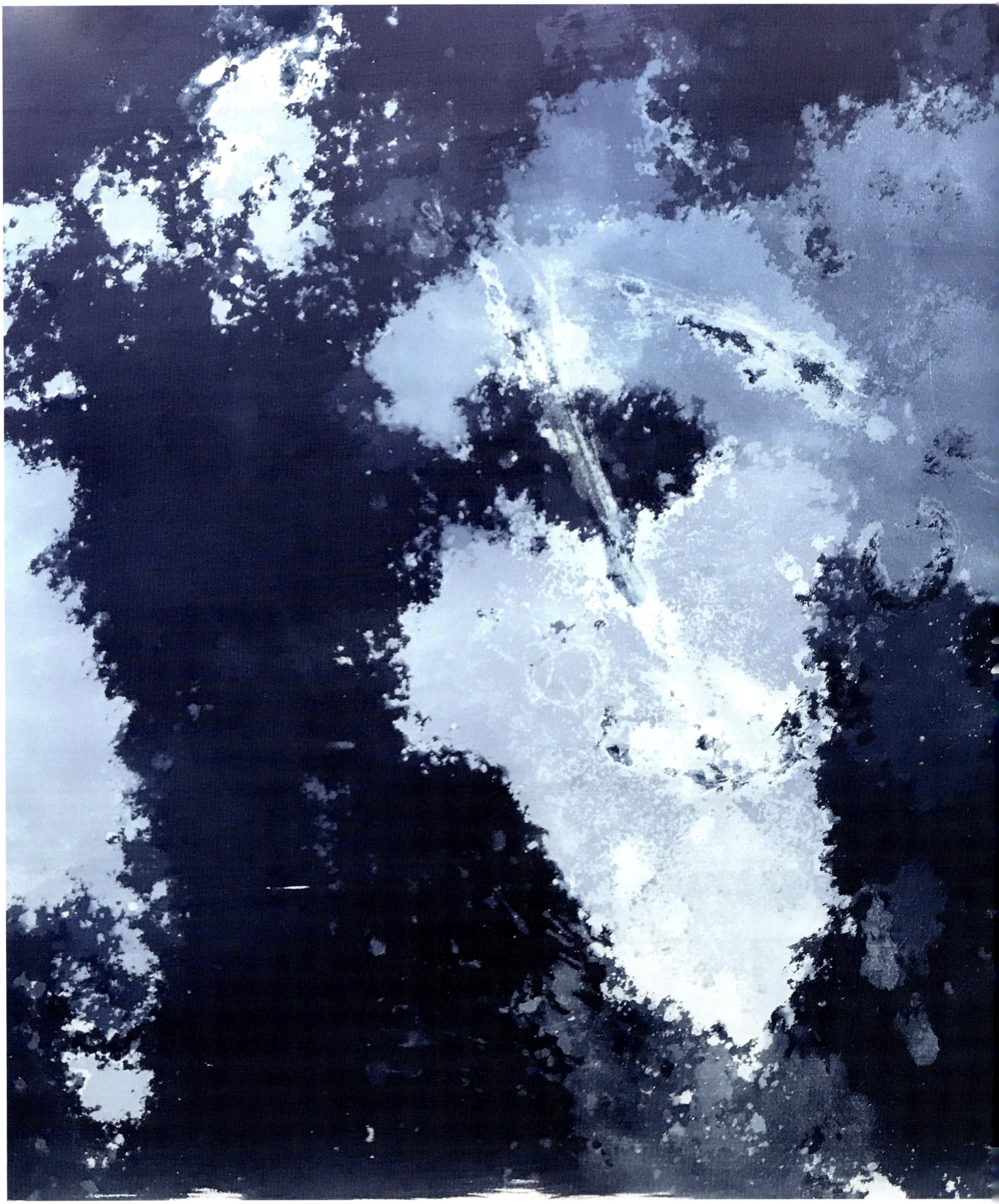

Precarious States, Imaginary Maps, Carrick, Scotland, 2018

Precarious World, Imaginary Maps,
Carrick, Scotland, 2018

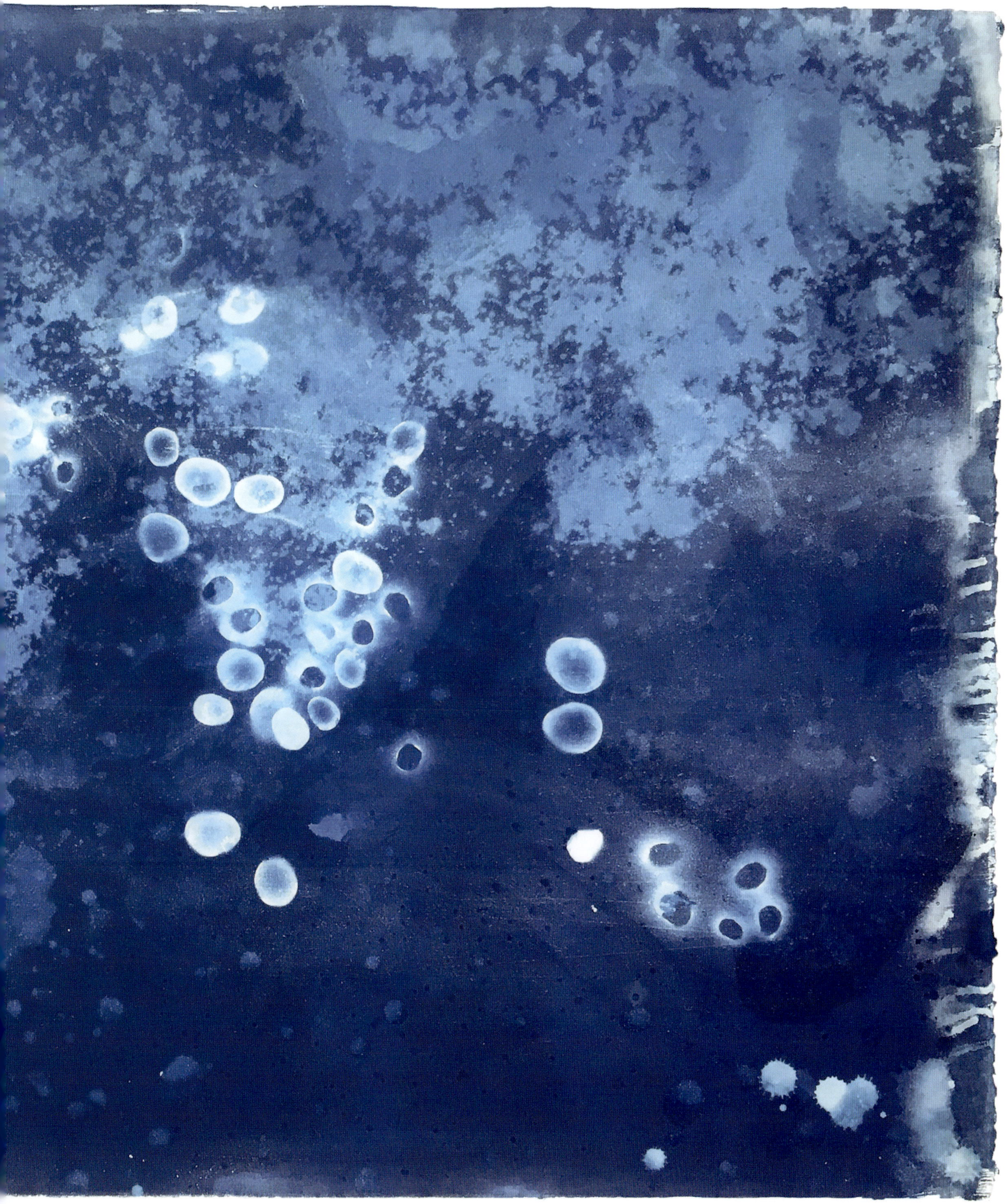

Funland

Rob Ball

'When you look a little bit closer, you can see the cracks, and the broken bits of pavement. You can see the paint is perhaps not as vibrant as it once was. The British coast is inherently honest.'

Familiar sounds drift out across the sand: twinkling music, the clatter of pennies and slot machines. Overhead the gulls scream in concert with rollercoaster goers. Welcome to Funland, to the Mirage, to Golden Palm. Enjoy your Happy Dayz. For more than a decade, Margate-based photographer Rob Ball has been documenting coastal resorts across the country. From Ramsgate to Skegness, his work focuses on the piers, bingo halls, rides, amusement arcades and food kiosks that announce their presence between the sea and the town in a brash fanfare of colour and noise. There is something unreal about these spaces. As typically British as they feel, in truth they are pure Americana with many of the designs – from bowling alleys to big dippers – bought 'off the rack' from expos in Las Vegas. This accounts for the uncanny repetitions and similarities found in different resorts, their names invoking the same dreams and pleasures of another land.

No paradise can be perfect. Ball focuses on evidence of ageing and decay, as well as the seasonal renewal that occurs when sun-bleached surfaces are touched up, ready for the summer crowds. Since the Victorian era, the British seaside has been a hub for leisure seekers. In more recent decades, constantly in battle with the draw of cheap flights and package holidays, these venues now often hold a slightly dilapidated, nostalgic air: all retro signs and pastel colours. Ball warns against the lure of too much sentimentality though. His photos capture the realities of coastal tourism, from the neon lights to the rubbish in the gutters. After all, this is not another world. It is the unvarnished, ever-shifting, ever-garish British seaside – welcoming a bustling cross-section of visitors when the days are long, then hibernating each winter as they await another year of fun.

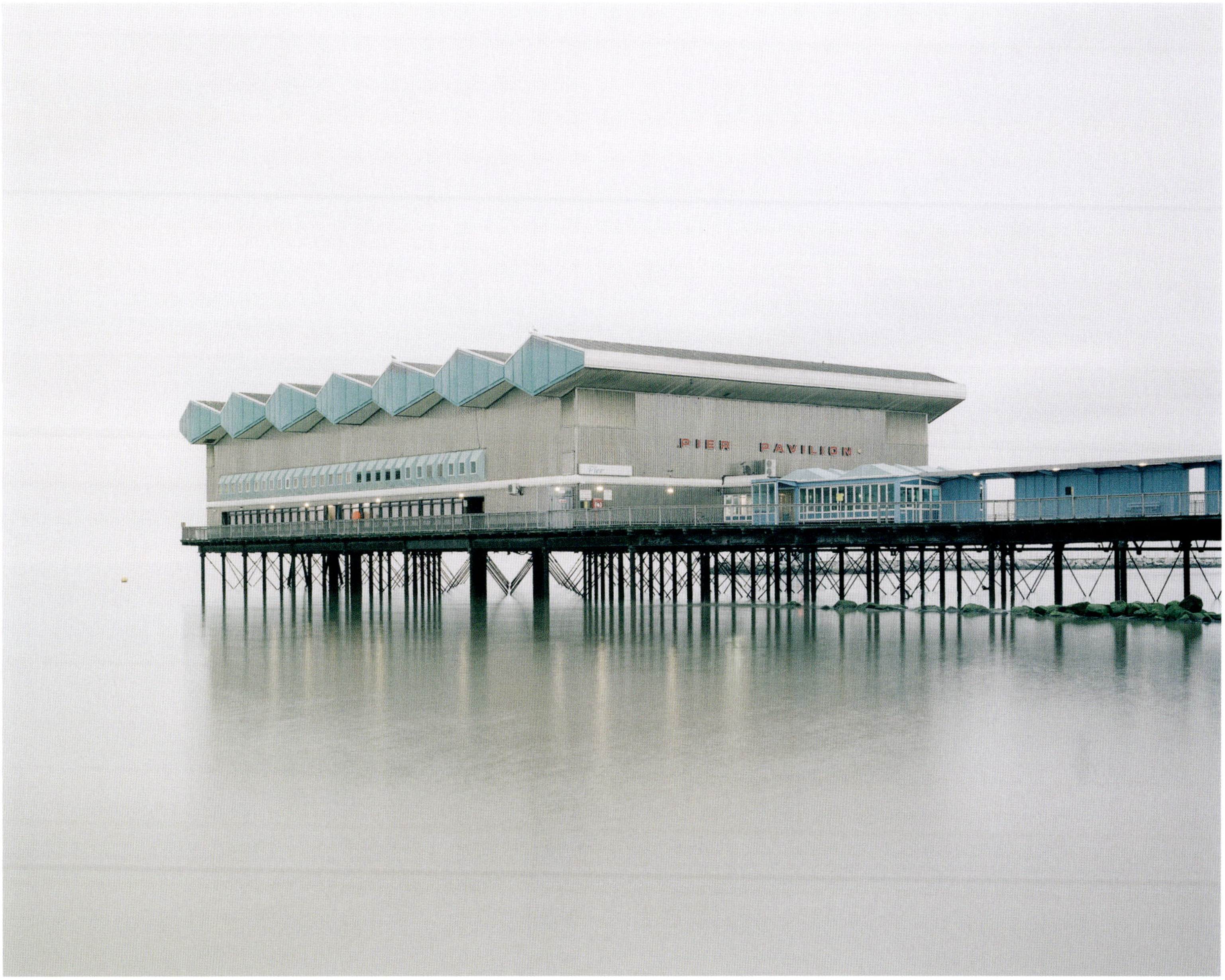

Herne Bay Pier, Herne Bay, England, 2011

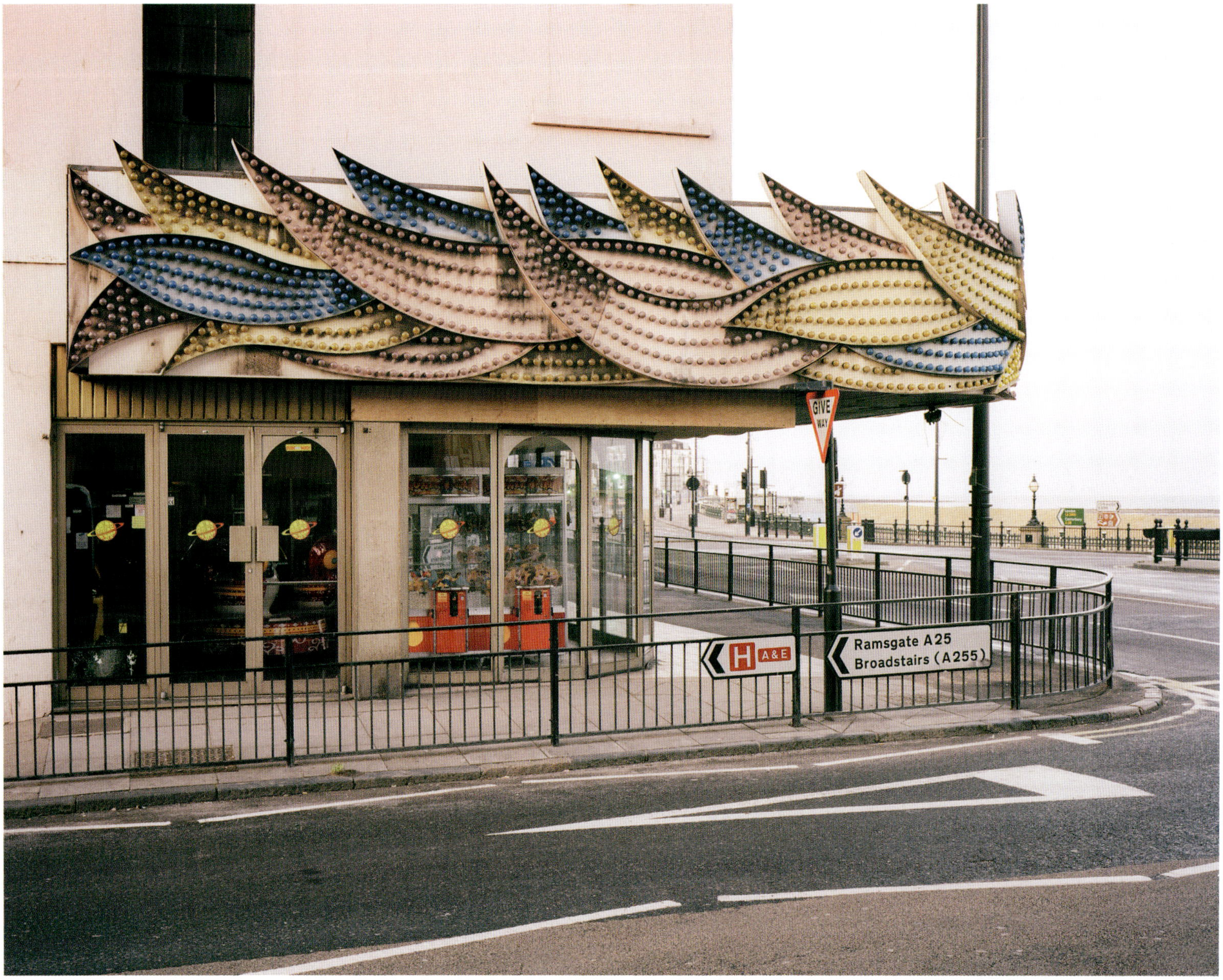

Belgrave Road, Margate, England, 2014

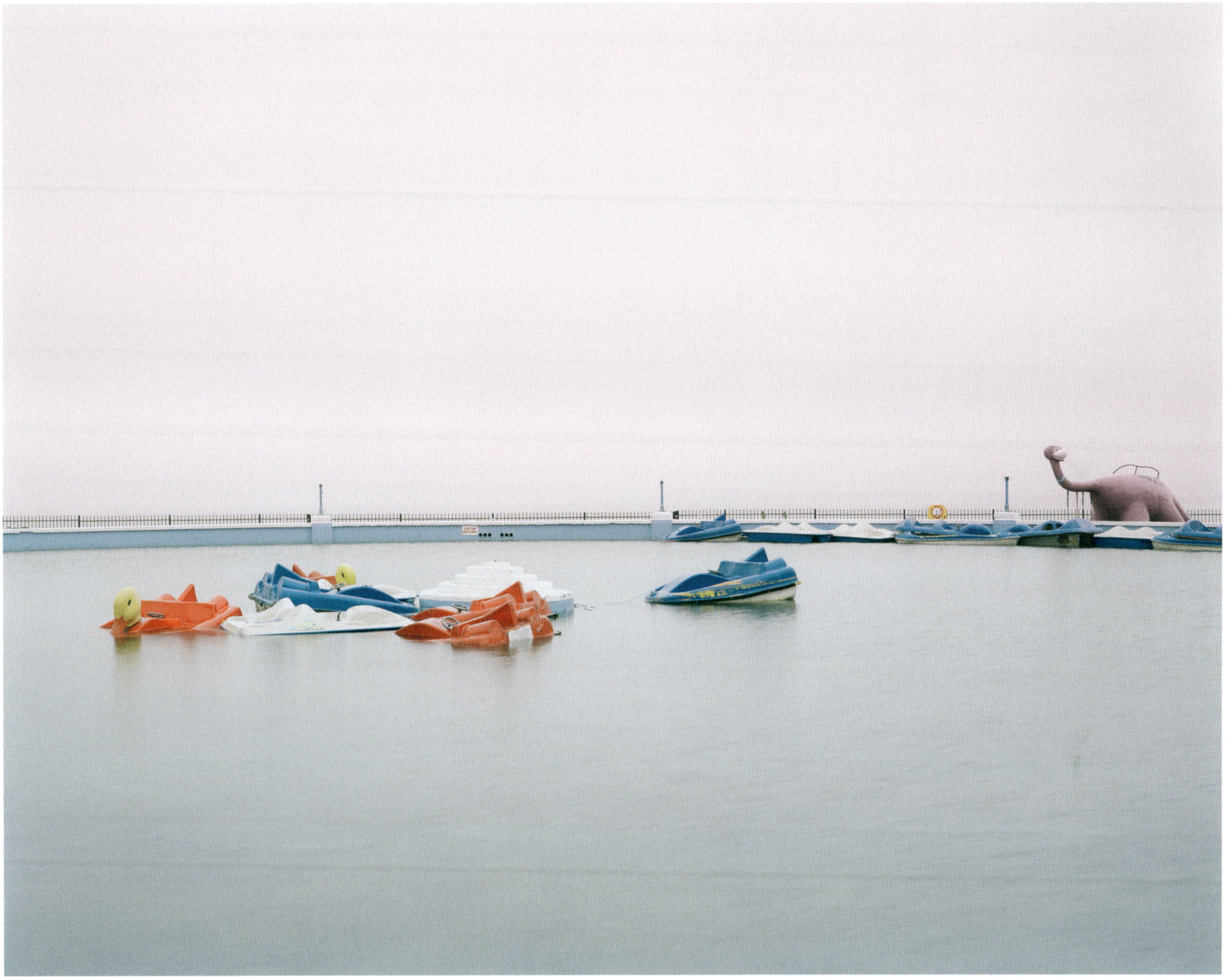

Westcliff Boating Lake, Ramsgate, England, 2010

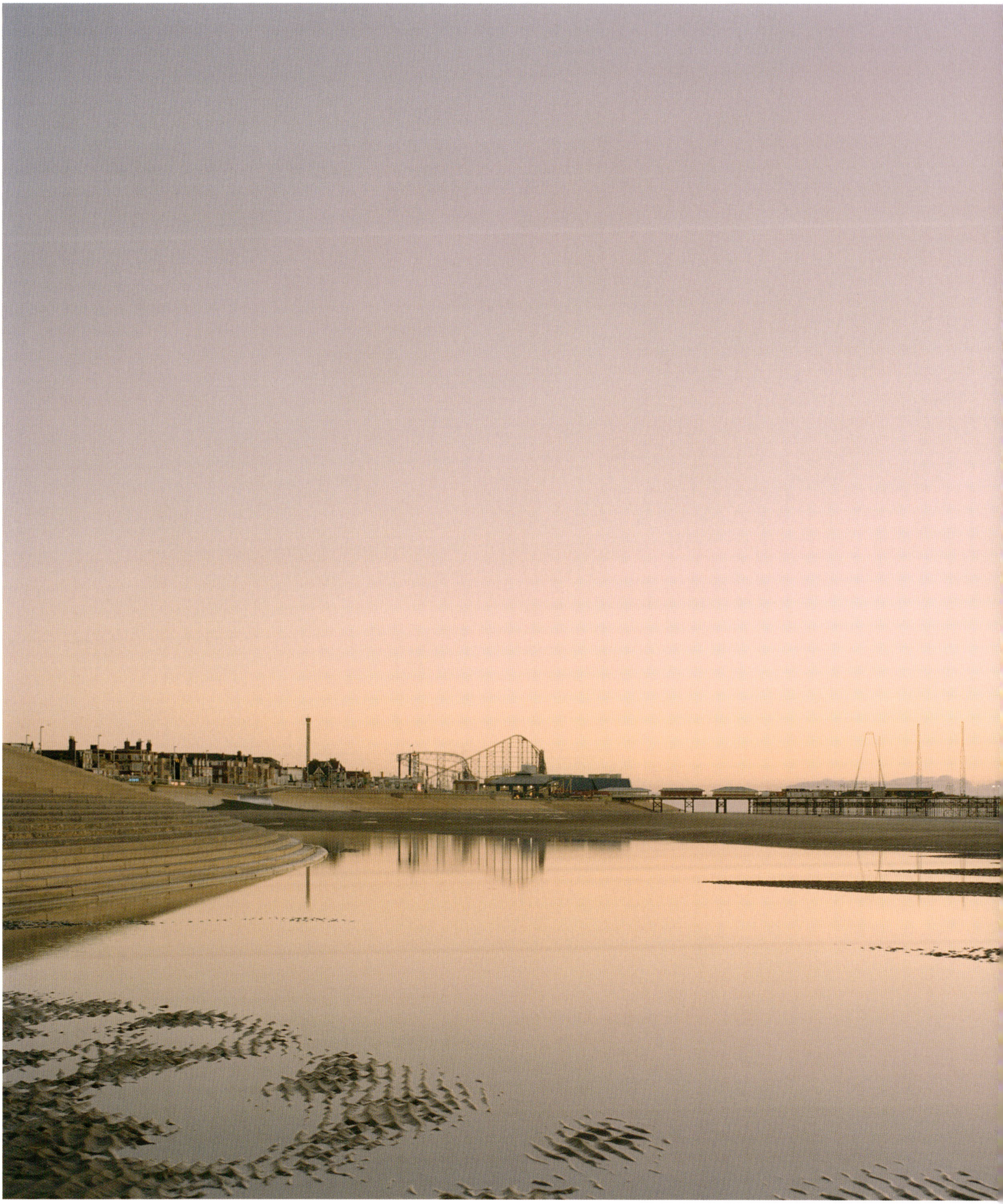

South Pier, Blackpool, England, 2018

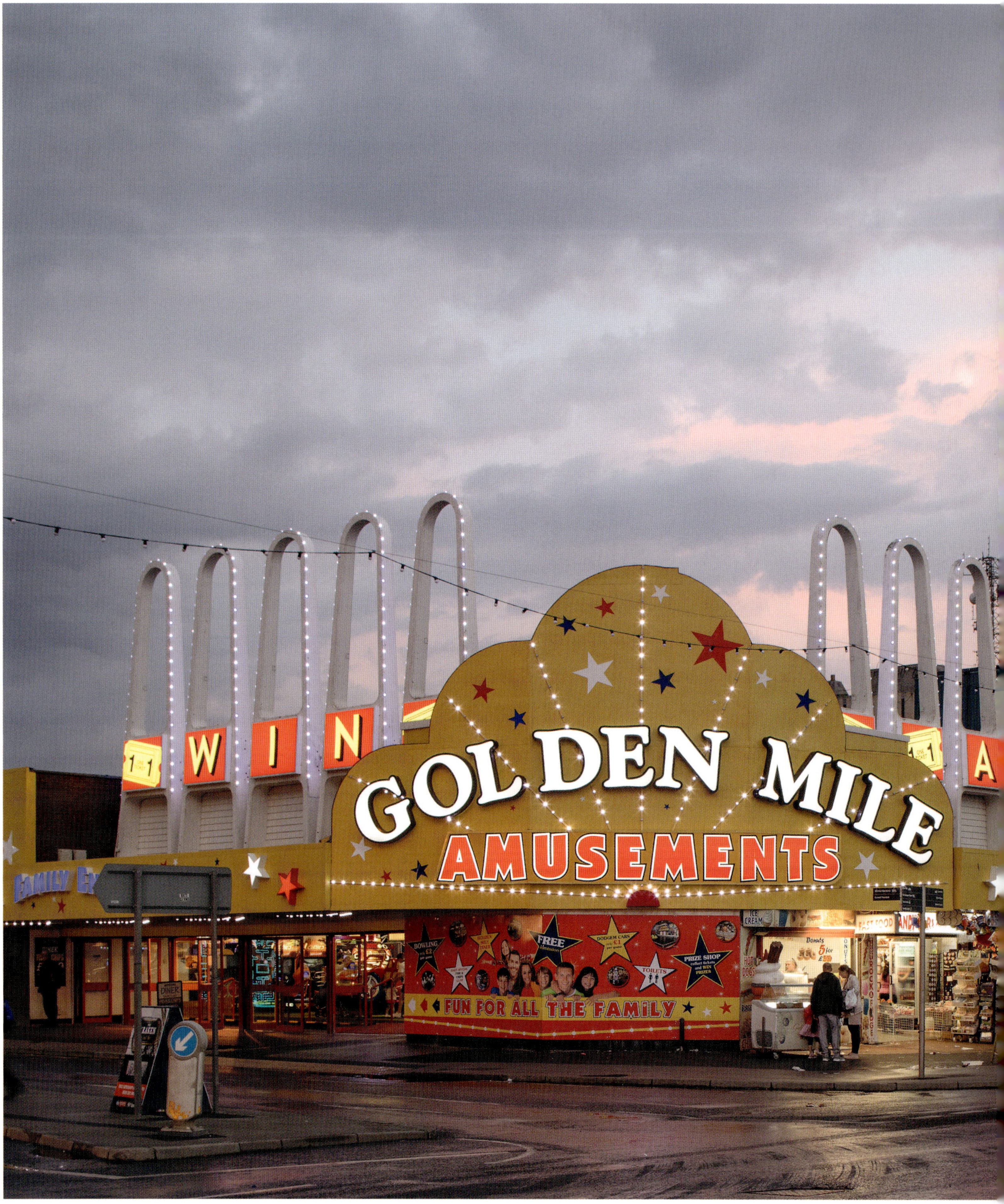
WIN
GOLDEN MILE
AMUSEMENTS
FREE
FUN FOR ALL THE FAMILY

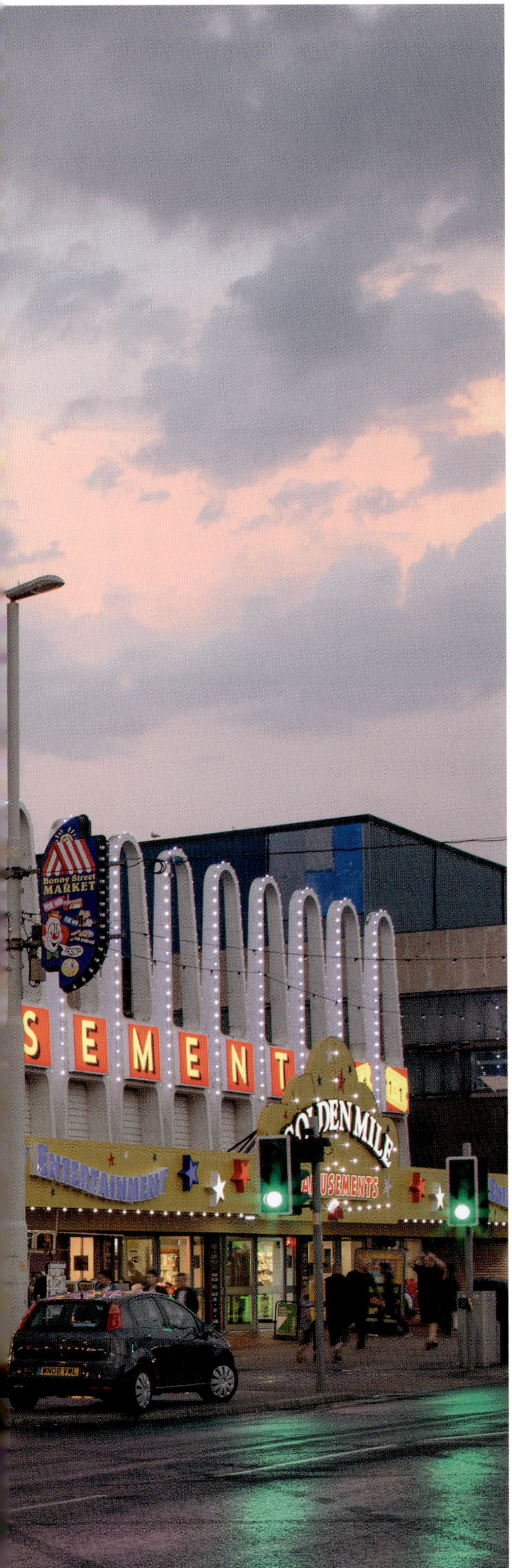

Golden Mile, Blackpool, England, 2018

Landscape Studies of a Small Island

Simon Roberts

'I'm interested in making work that understands the landscape as an active process, shaped over time as much by politics and economic as by geological and environmental forces.'

Simon Roberts' photos are usually shot from slightly above. Only slightly. There are no cranes or drones here. Instead, the photographer will often stand on the top of the camper van that he drives around the country, documenting British public life. The effect is subtle, but almost omniscient. It gives Roberts greater control as narrator of the scene – that slight elevation shifting the viewer's perspective.

The landscapes that Roberts gravitates towards all have something to say about national character. *We English*, one of two projects in this book, began in 2007 when he returned from a year in Russia. He wanted to transfer his interest in the complexity of belonging and collective identity to his own country, particularly focusing on the English at leisure. Picnicking, shooting, holidaying and playing sports are ways of considering the habits and social strata that make up a nation. Leisure is interesting because it asks a series of deceptively simple question. What do we care about when we are not working? What kinds of pleasure do we seek? And where do we go to find it?

The more explicitly political *Merrie Albion* is a decade-long survey of a changing country. In 2010, Roberts was appointed as the official British Election Artist – tasked with creating a historic record of the General Election that resulted in a coalition government. From the grim effects of austerity to the 2012 Olympics, various royal ceremonies and, finally, Brexit, it is a portrait of an anxious nation: divided, unsure of itself, desperately seeking moments of collectivity. Roberts' photographs hold a strong element of record-keeping. They bear witness. 'I want to make work that provides some sense of historical significance,' he says. 'What exactly is happening at the moment? Who should be accountable?'

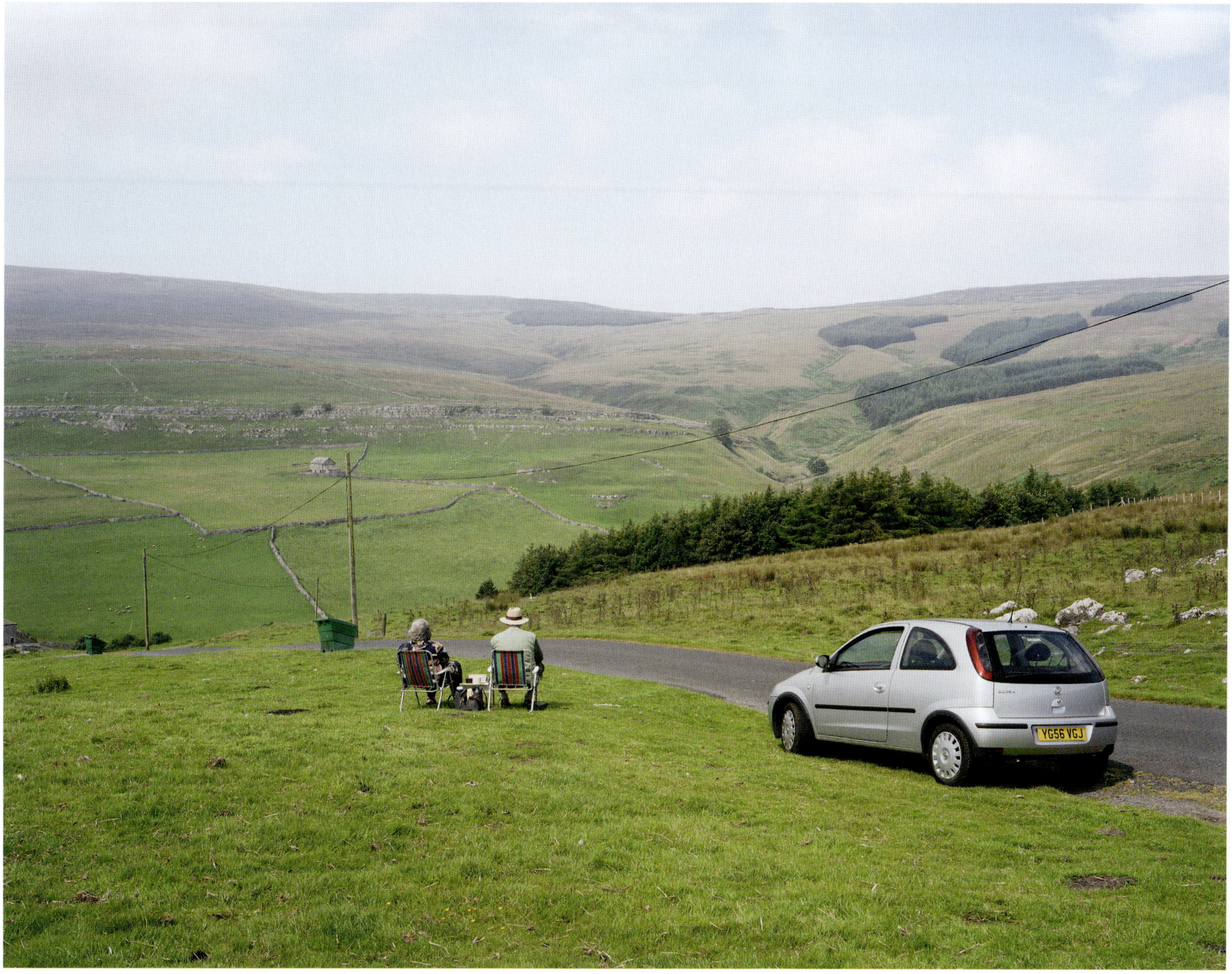

Fountains Fell, We English, Yorkshire Dales, England, 3 August 2008

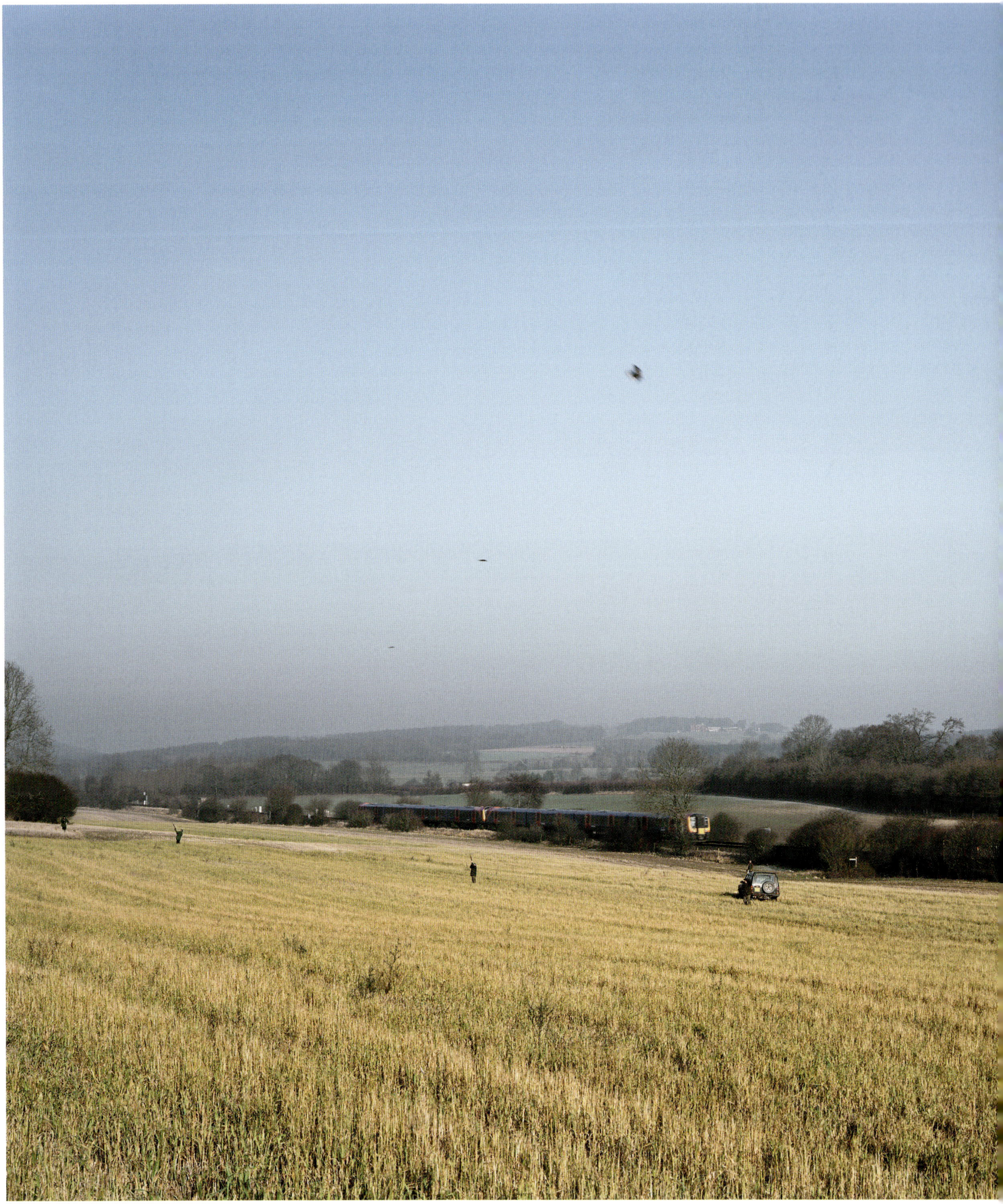

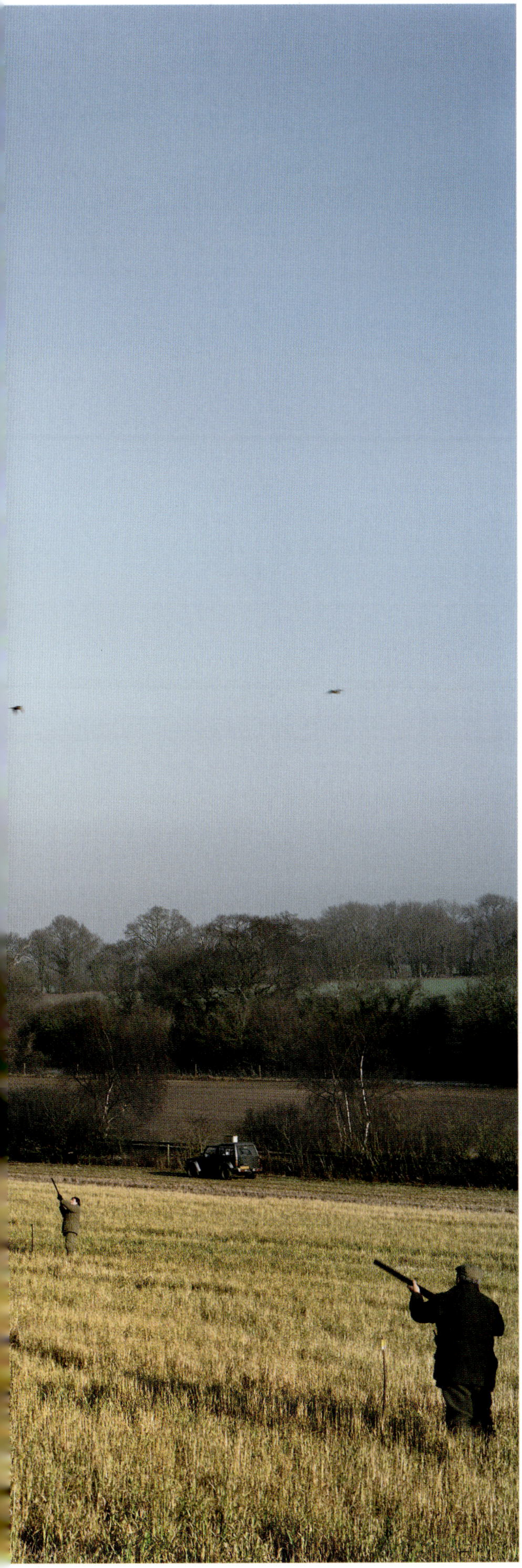

Heberdens Farm, We English, Hampshire, England, 20 December 2007

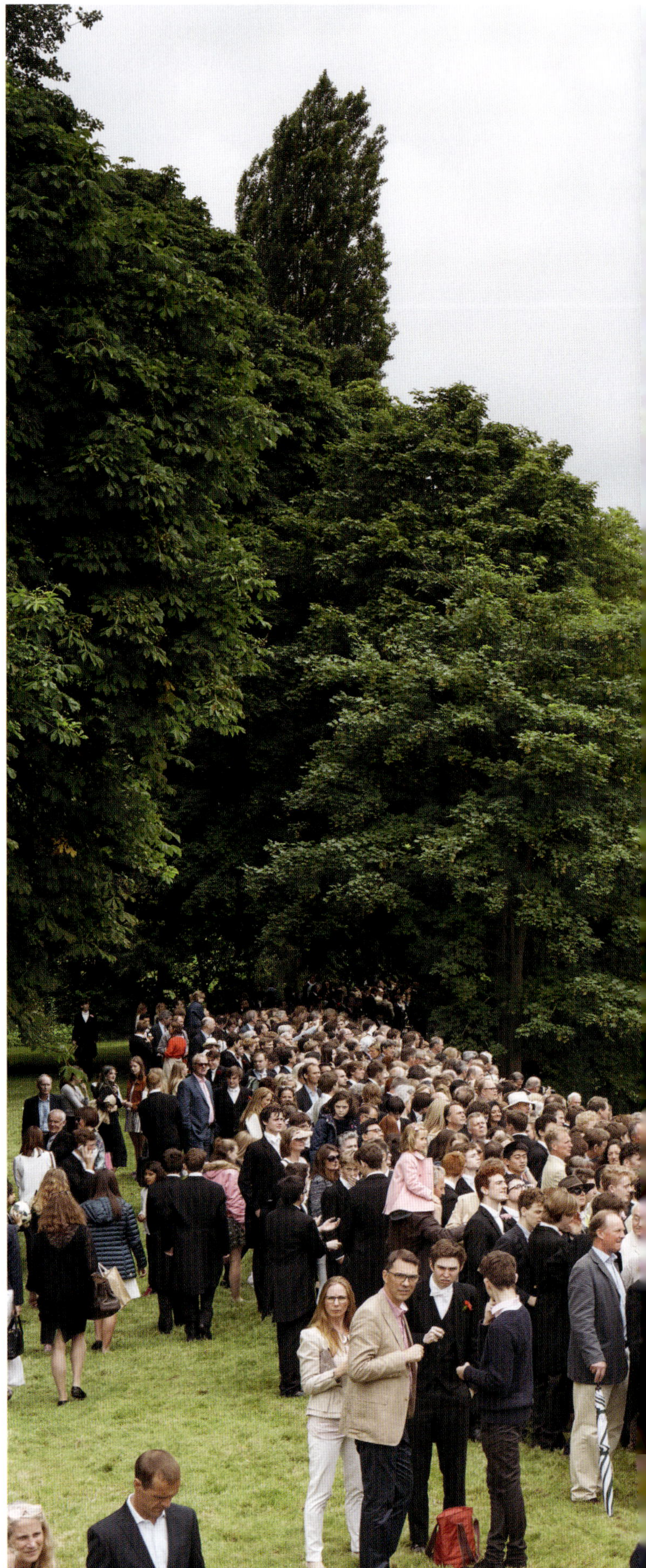

Annual Eton College Procession of Boats,
Merrie Albion, Berkshire, England, 17 June 2016

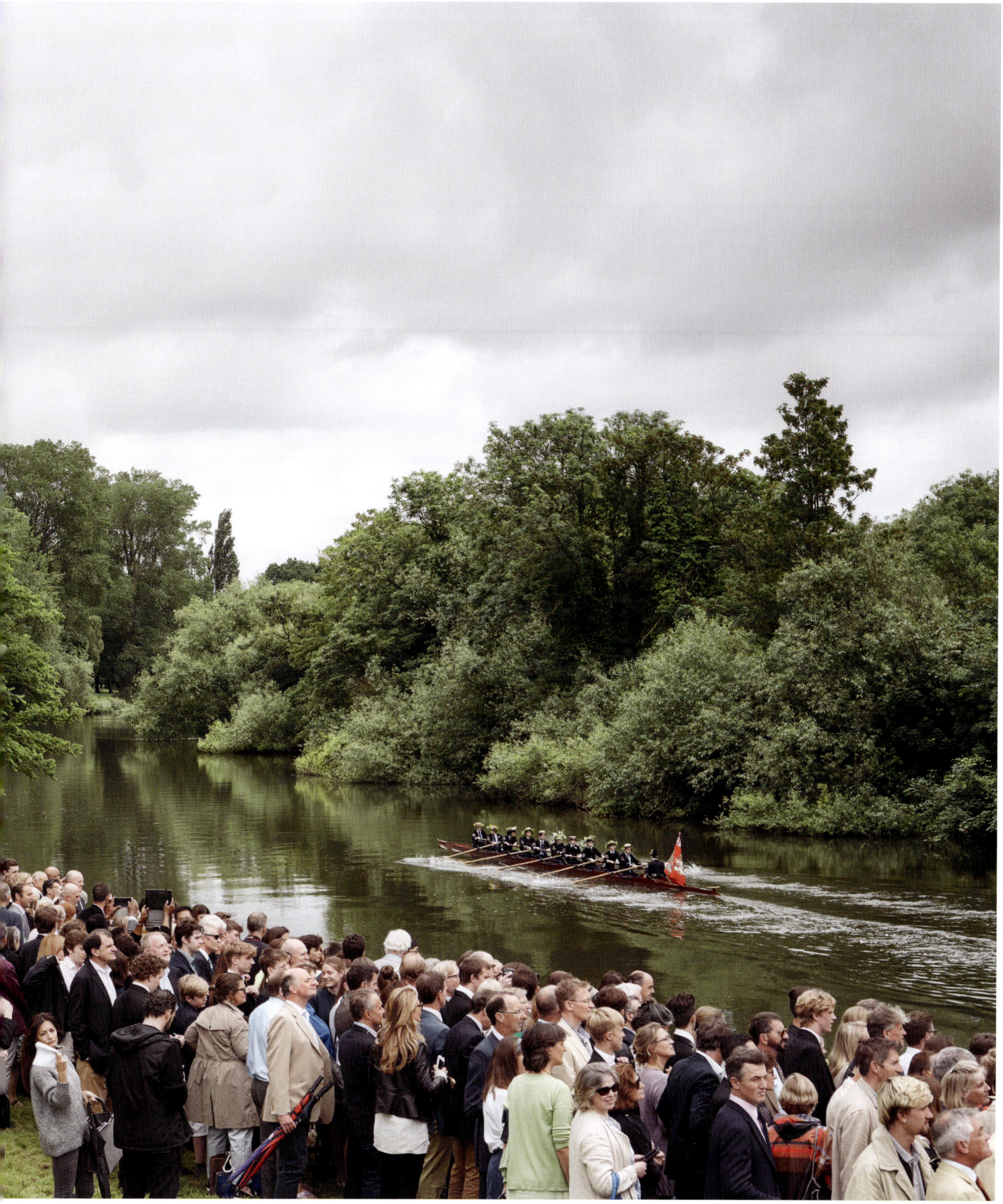

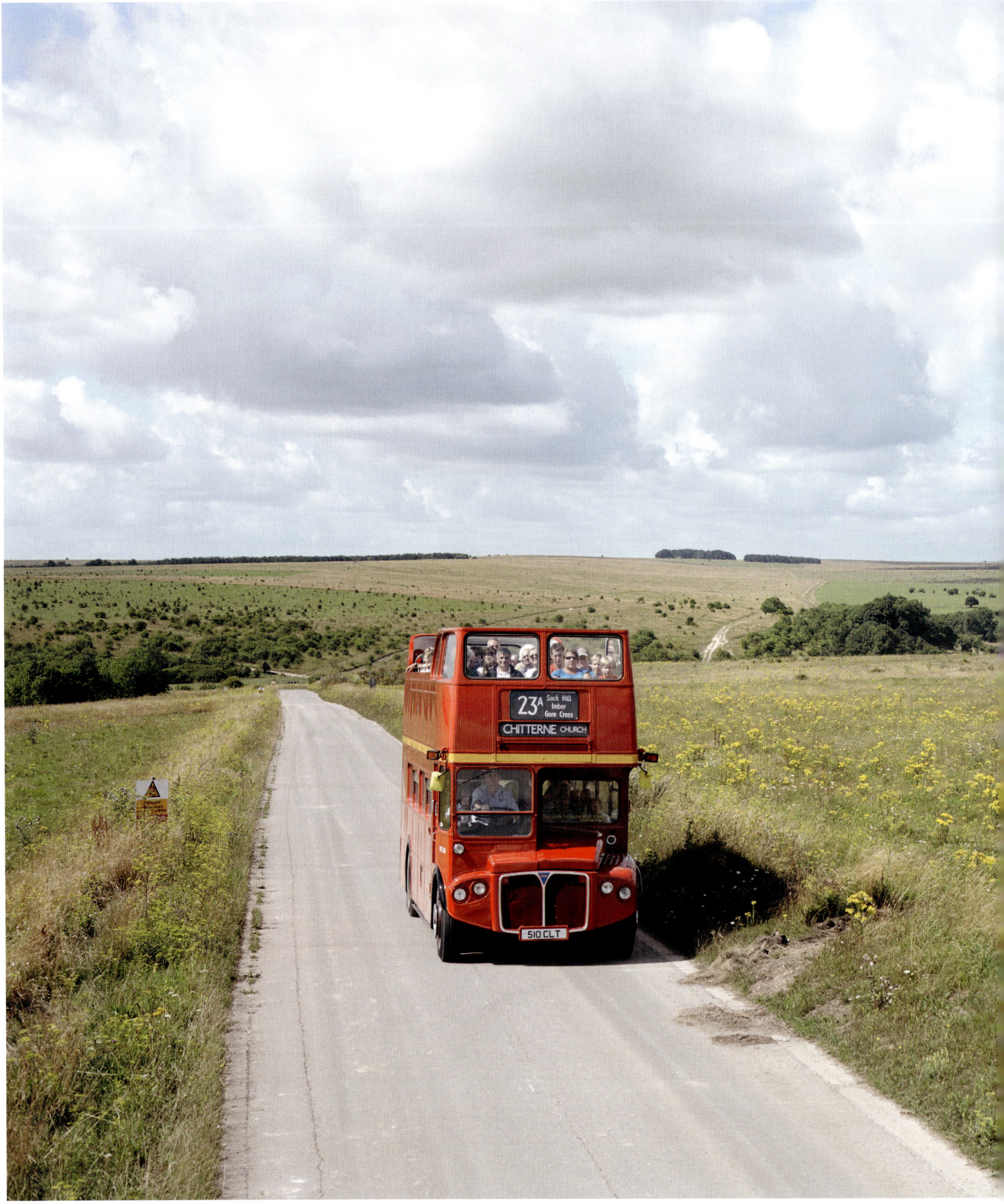
23A
Sack Hill
Imber
Gore Cross
CHITTERNE CHURCH
510 CLT

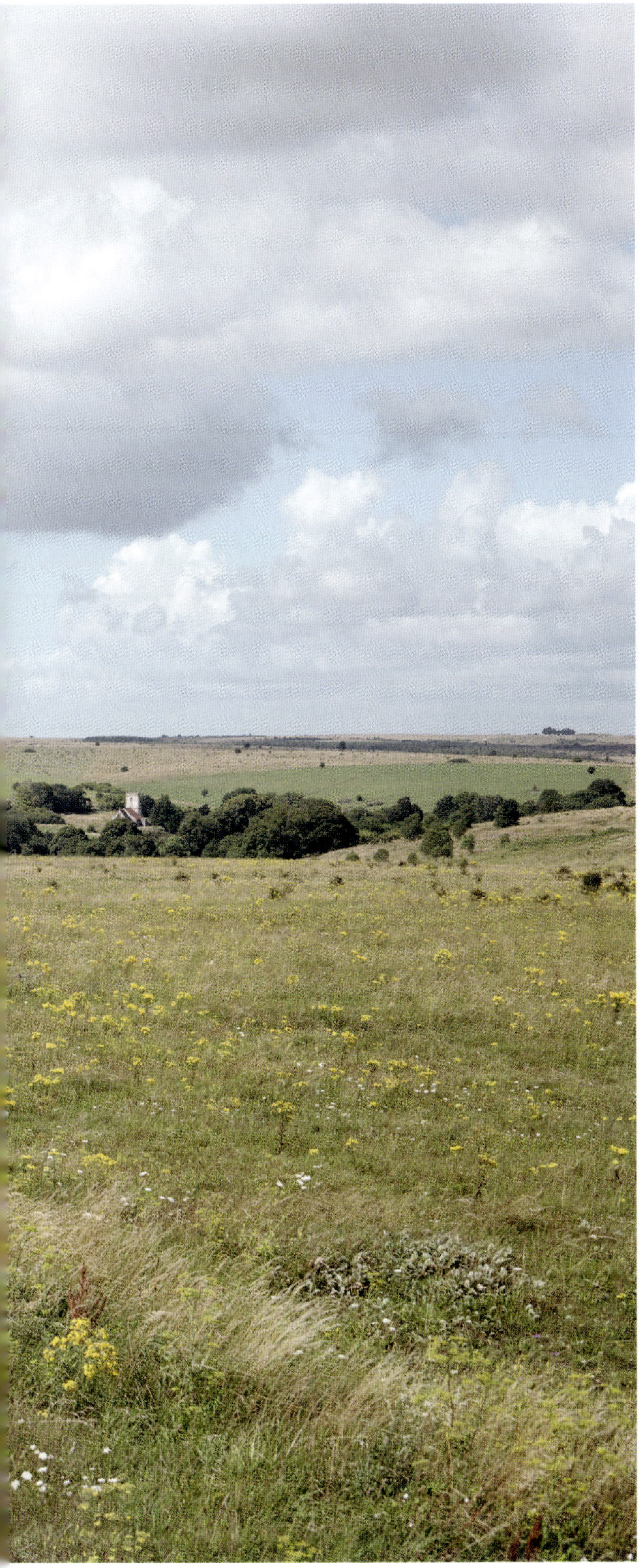

Imber Village Open Day, Merrie Albion,
Wiltshire, England, 3 August 2013

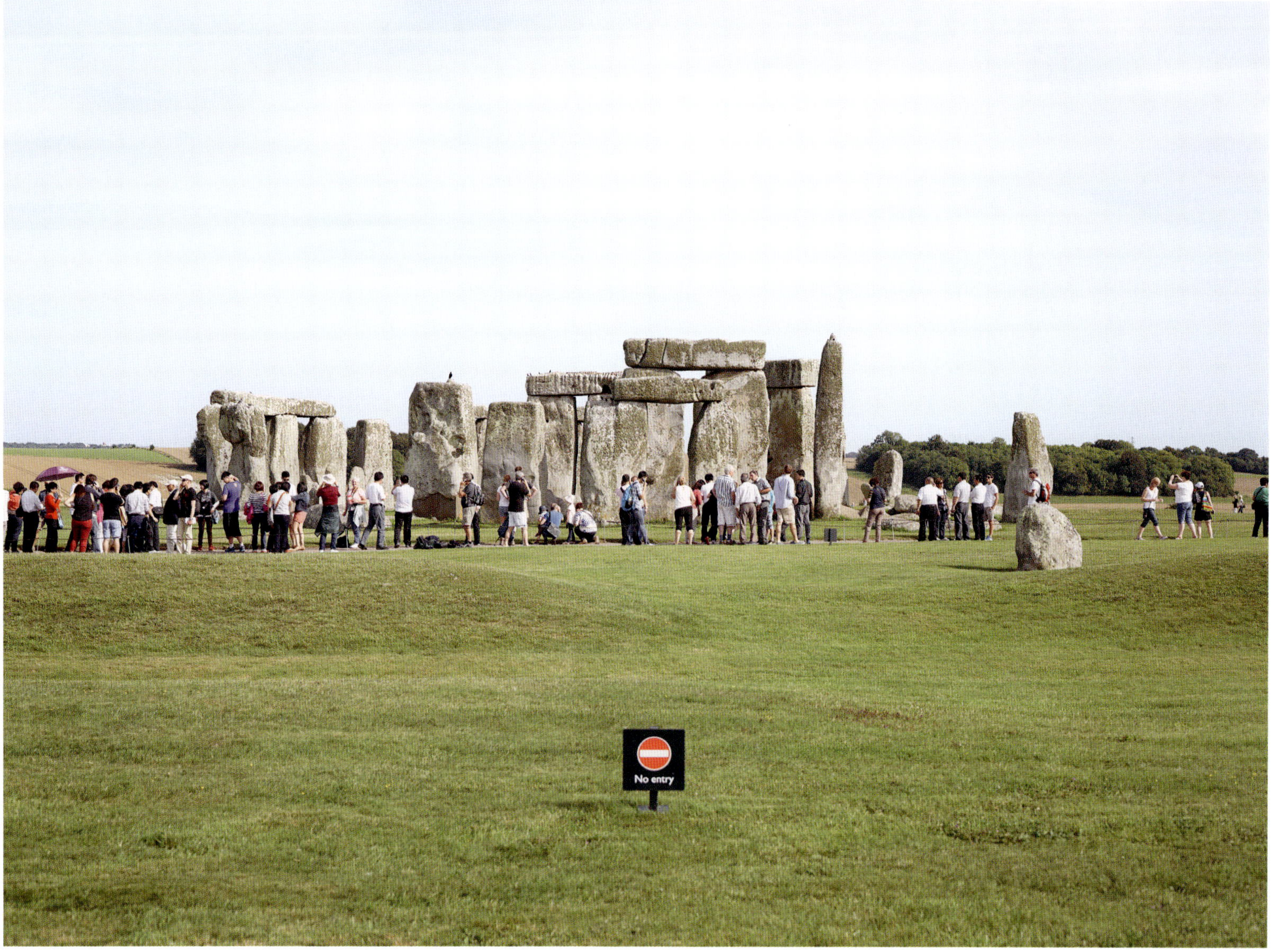

Stonehenge, Merrie Albion, Wiltshire, England, 3 August 2013

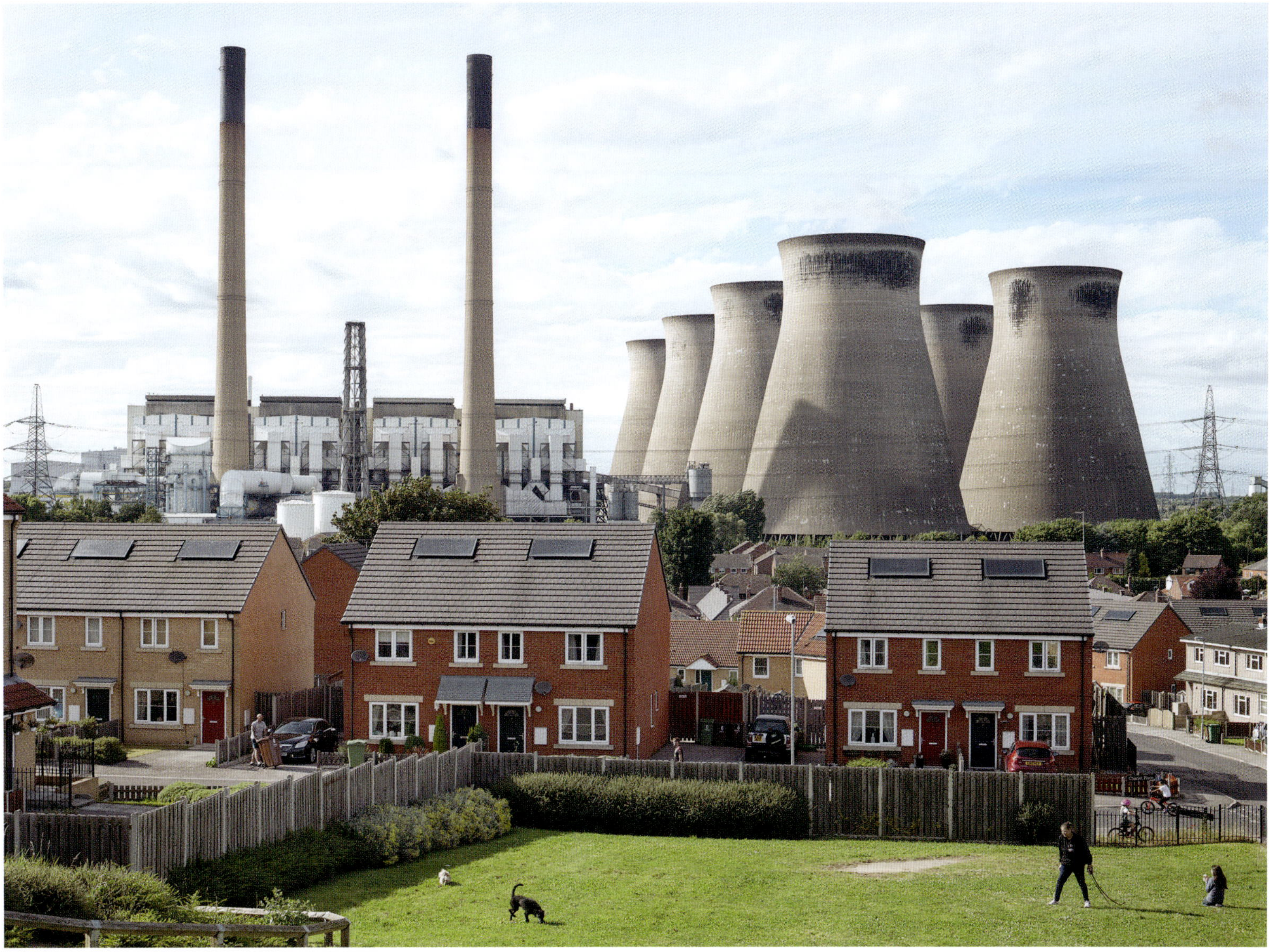

Ferrybridge Power Station, Merrie Albion, Knottingley, West Yorkshire, England, 5 July 2016

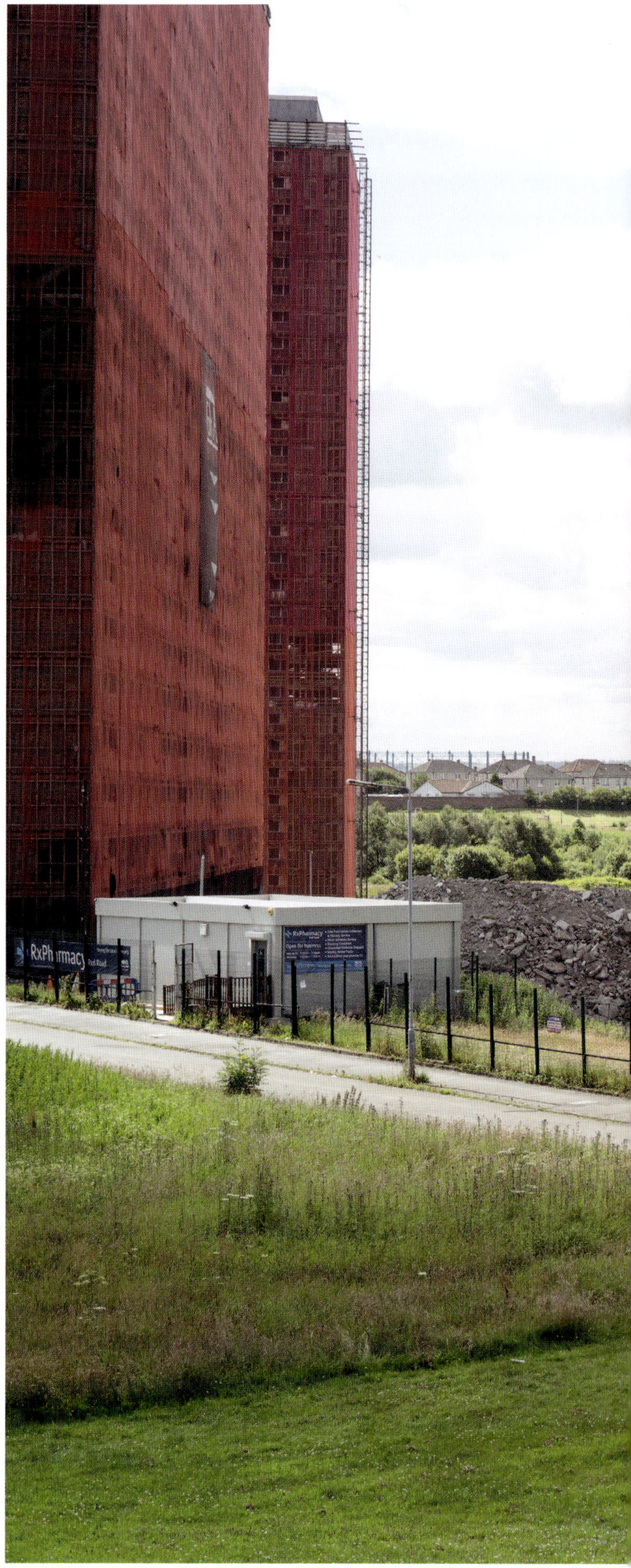

Red Roads Flats, Merrie Albion, Glasgow, Scotland, 30 June 2014

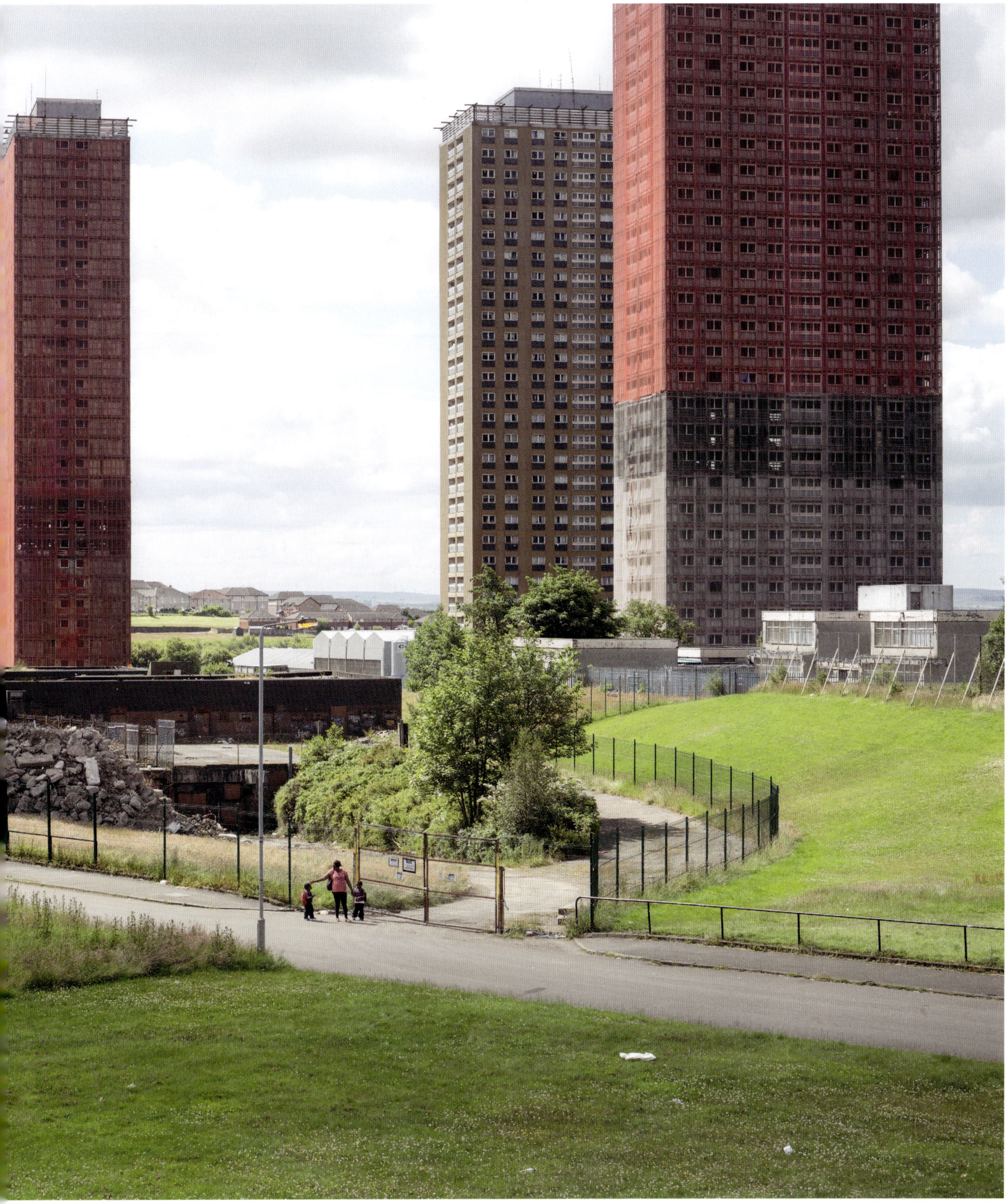

British Watchtowers

Donovan Wylie

'They represented a fragility, in so far as they were these strange objects on hilltops: very isolated, lonely beacons. Yet at the same time, they were militaristic and brutal and colonial.'

In Donovan Wylie's *British Watchtowers*, the tools of surveillance come under scrutiny. During the mid-1980s, a series of watchtowers sprung up along the Irish border, predominantly in South Armagh. An ominous symbol of the Troubles, they were manned by British soldiers whose presence served as a reminder of not just the ongoing conflict, but also the inescapable glare of occupation. These structures had a strange, almost futuristic look, reminiscent of medieval hill forts but rendered like space stations, their struts and squat buildings overlooking swathes of green.

After the Good Friday Agreement was signed in 1998, Northern Ireland went through a period of demilitarization. Between 2000 and 2007, these watchtowers were decommissioned and subsequently demolished. Wylie caught them on the brink of obsolescence: relics of the past that had to be destroyed to make way for a new future.

In order to photograph them, Wylie needed an even higher vantage point than the watchtowers. The Ministry of Defence allowed him access to a series of helicopter rides, so he could capture the towers from the sky. He saw the project as a necessary taxonomy, a systematic document of a chapter in Northern Ireland's history. 'History' is a word that comes up frequently for Wylie. He expresses a desire to be 'in' history, as though reaching for the right place on a map.

Home wasn't the first place he wished to photograph. In fact, it was somewhere that the Northern Irish photographer wanted to escape. But in returning to a history that was also his own, in looking at what he wanted to ignore, he found something revelatory. Later work took him to similar towers in the Kandahar province of Afghanistan, where NATO observation posts rose from the dusty landscape, conflict playing out yet again under watchful eyes.

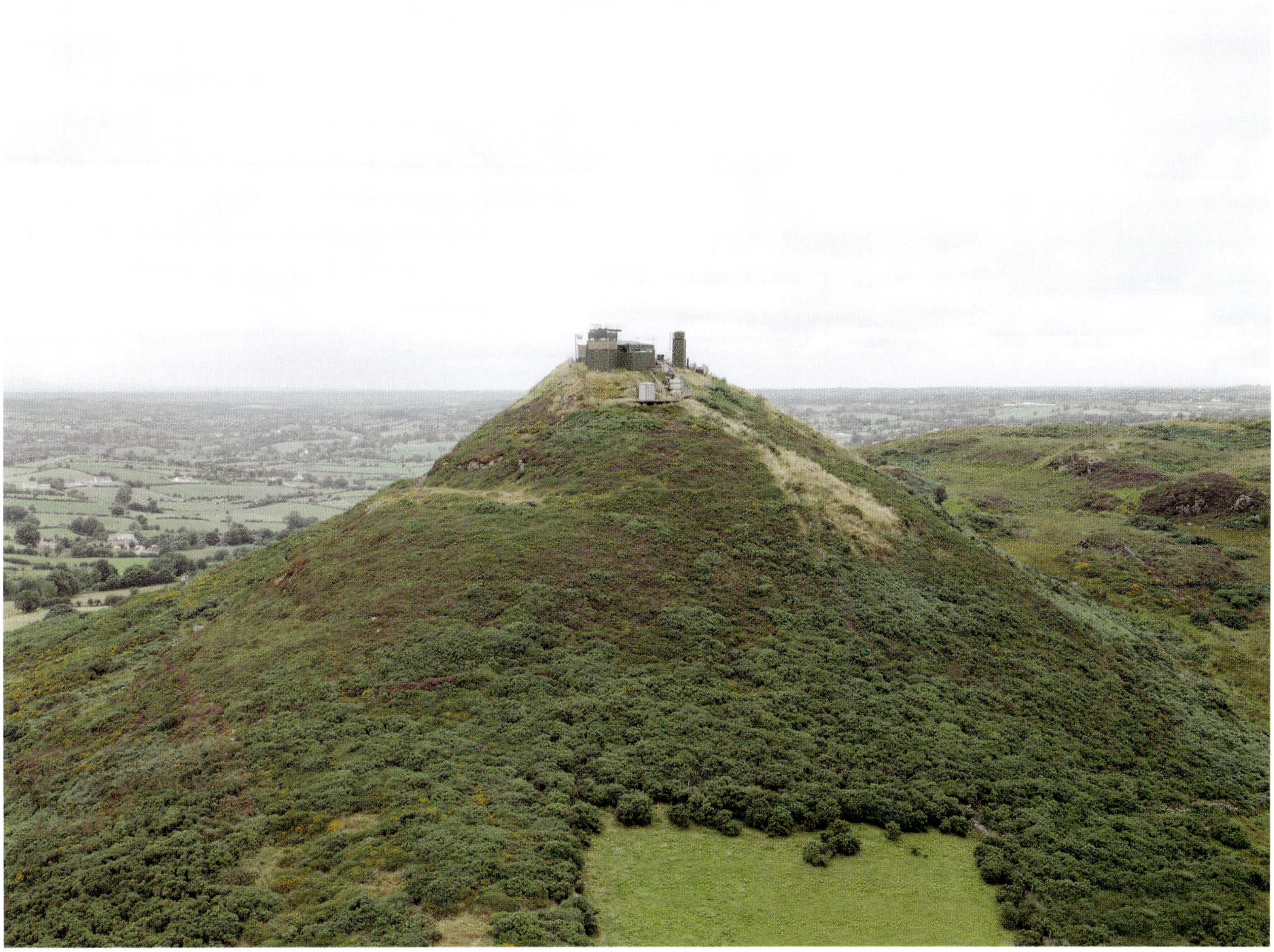

Romeo 12, South Armagh, Northern Ireland, 2005

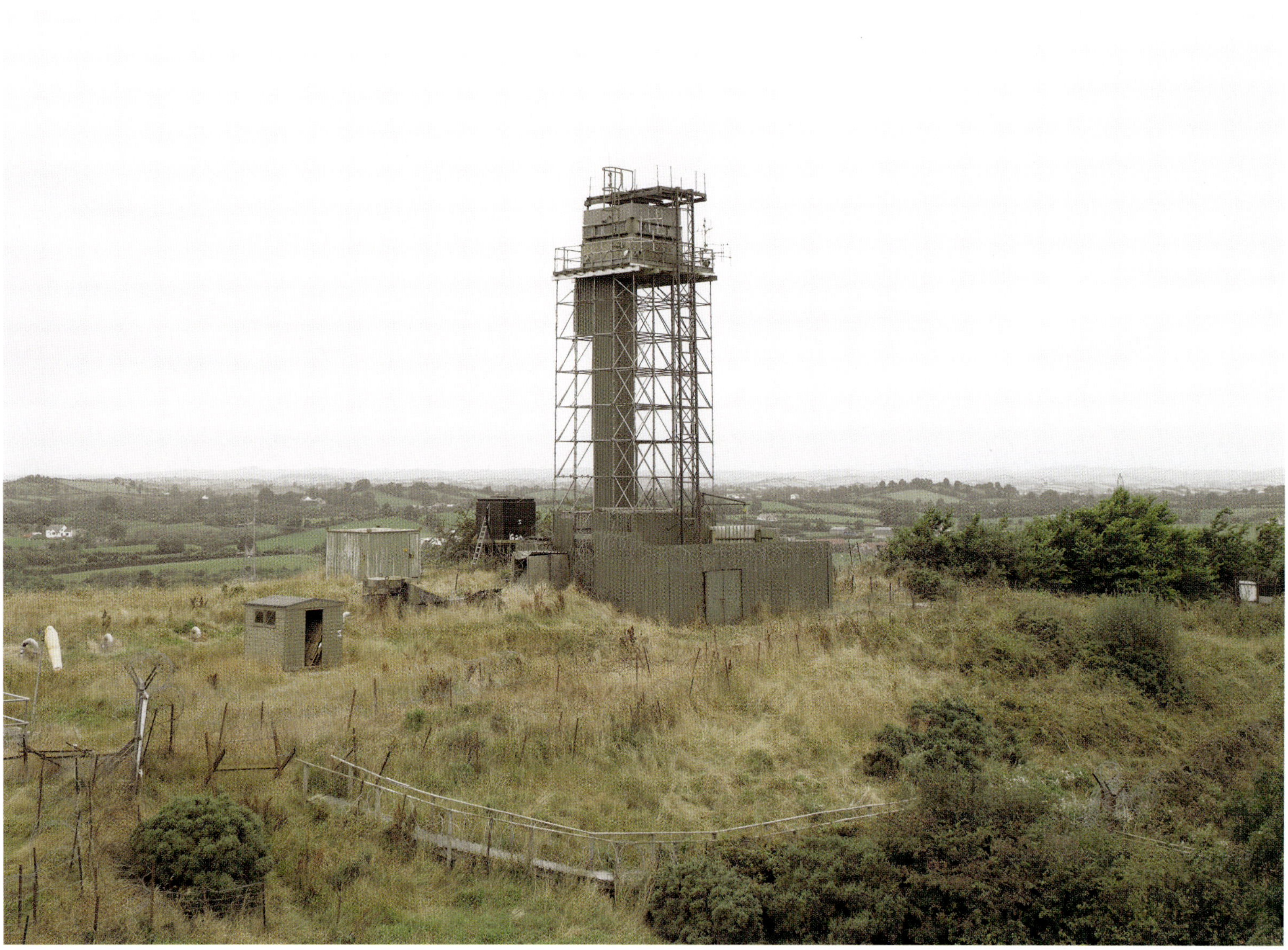

Golf 20, South Armagh, Northern Ireland, 2005

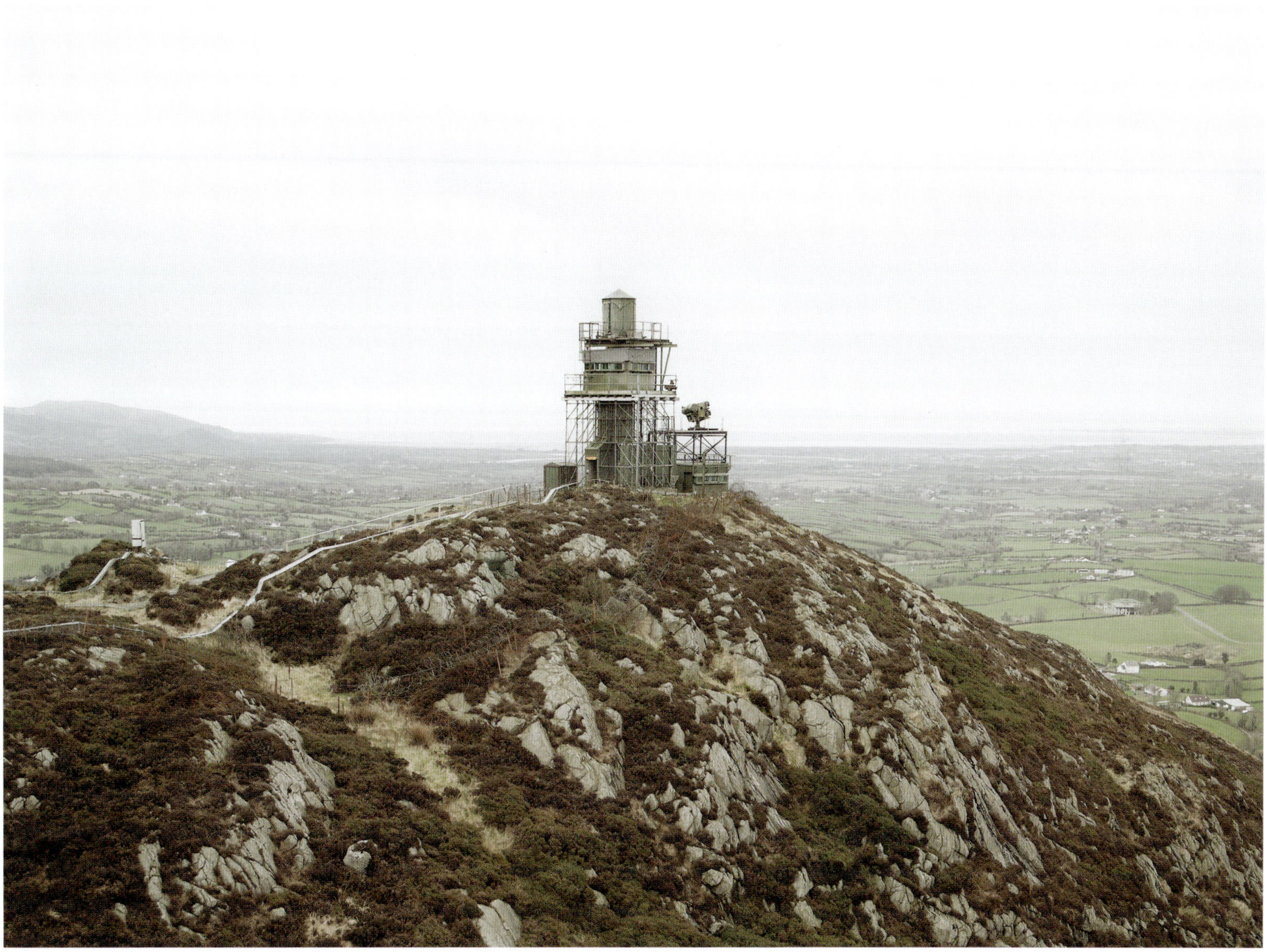

Golf 40, South Armagh, Northern Ireland, 2006

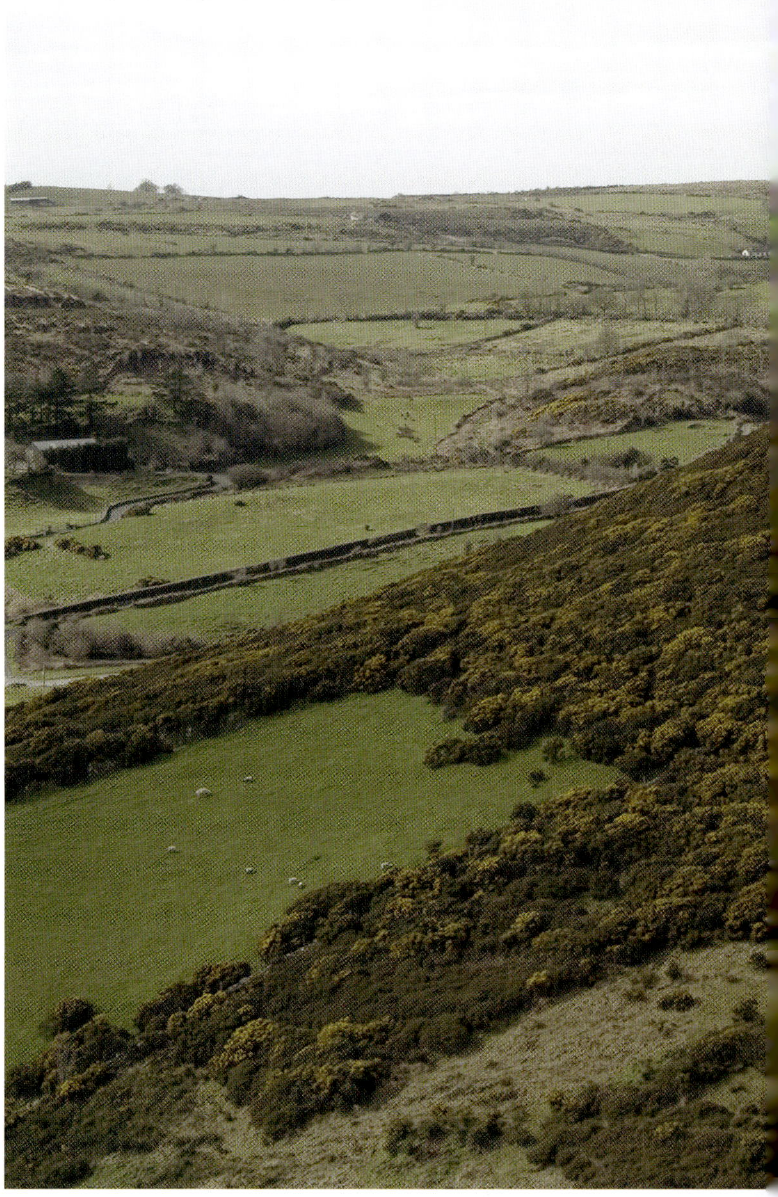

Romeo 12, South Armagh, Northern Ireland, 2006

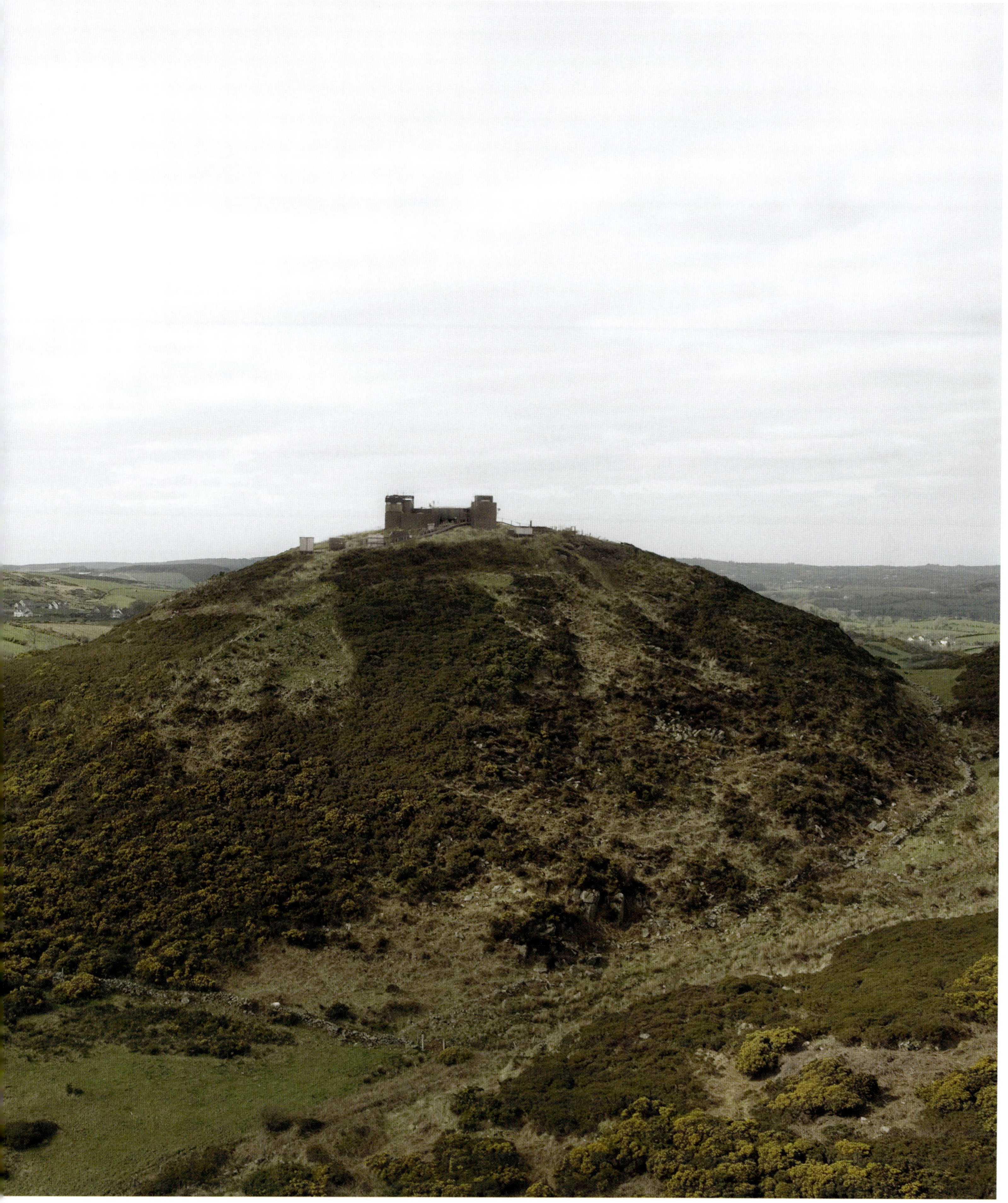

Farmed, Drained, Reclaimed

Paul Hart

'It's dead space, in a way. There's a lack of scale... I think I concentrated on objects and little things I found that grounded it, rather than on large views of nothing.'

The Fens in East Anglia are fertile territory for writers: flat, wet, domed by an unrelenting sky. From Graham Swift's *Waterland,* with its descriptions of 'the wide empty space of reality', to Daisy Johnson's magic-realist *Fen,* filled with tales of women who transform into eels, this region of marshland and drained fields is damply atmospheric. Largely nutrient-rich working land, the Fens stretch out across four counties, yielding everything from wheat to potatoes and sugar beet.

Paul Hart spent a decade documenting the Fens. In a triptych of projects titled *Farmed, Drained* and *Reclaimed,* he observes the layers of change and manmade intervention that have shaped this region. In doing so, he also records the area's profound uncanniness. Although it is a place where plants and livestock thrive, it is also a monoculture, defined by open expanses carved out by large-scale agribusiness. Many of Hart's images have a ghostly feel, full of misted horizons and bare trees. They often feature lines vanishing into the distance: electrical cables, narrow lanes, silver waterways, the hard ridges of tilled fields. The scale and distance are unmooring, making it hard to distinguish one view from another. After a while one begins to feel lost, or maybe lulled, drifting through an illimitable landscape.

Hart works using wide format film cameras. Many of these monochrome images were created with a Hasselblad, so that each frame of the Fens is held within a neat square. Like Graham Swift, Hart likes to dwell on emptiness. Even if the photo was taken on the side of a busy road with trucks thundering in the background, the resulting image yawns wide and unoccupied. The only human incursions are distant and blurred: a car sliding by with the headlights on, a solitary walker reduced to matchstick height against the clouds.

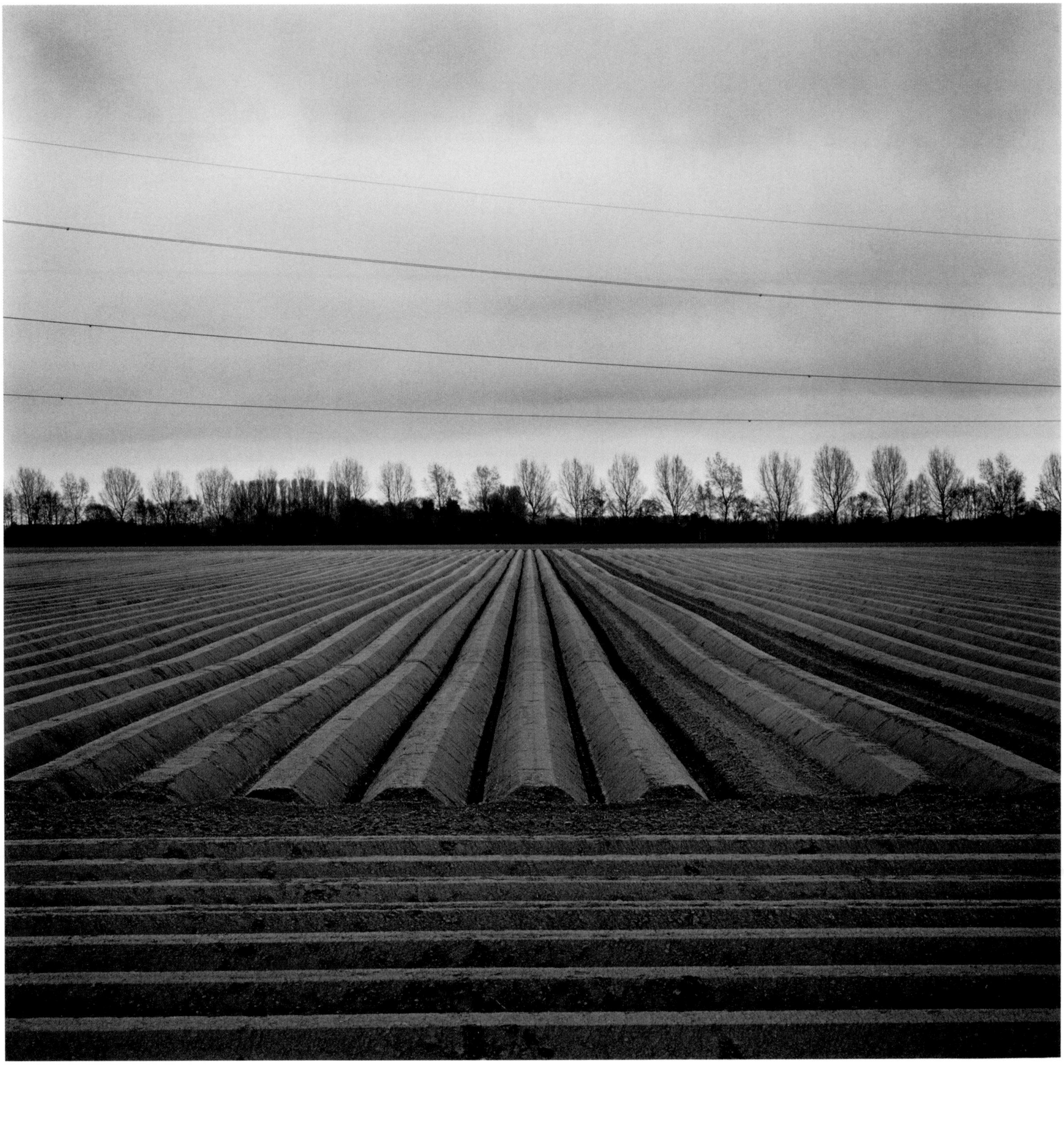

Walpole St. Andrew, Reclaimed, England, 2019

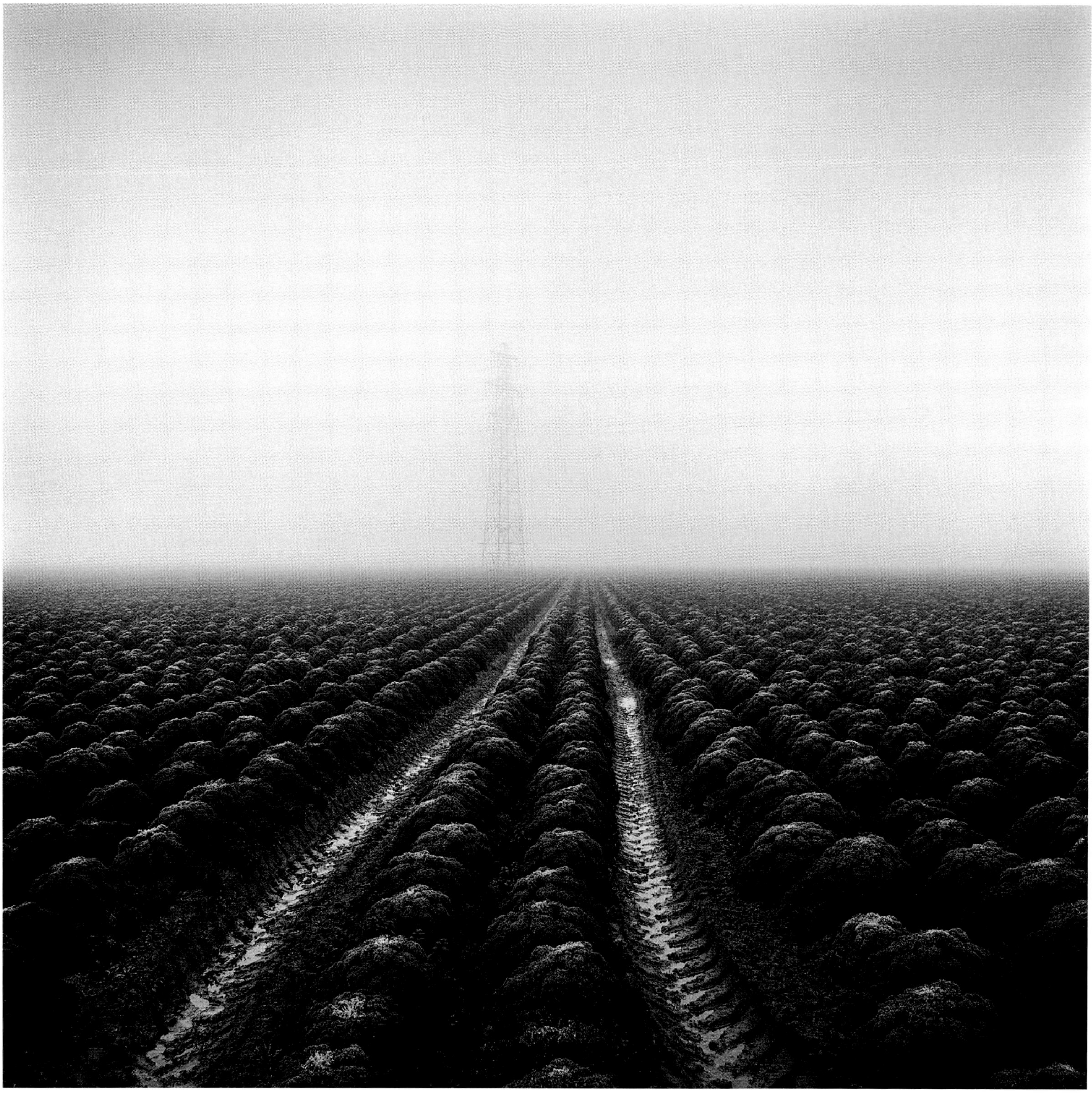

Station Farm, Drained, England, 2017

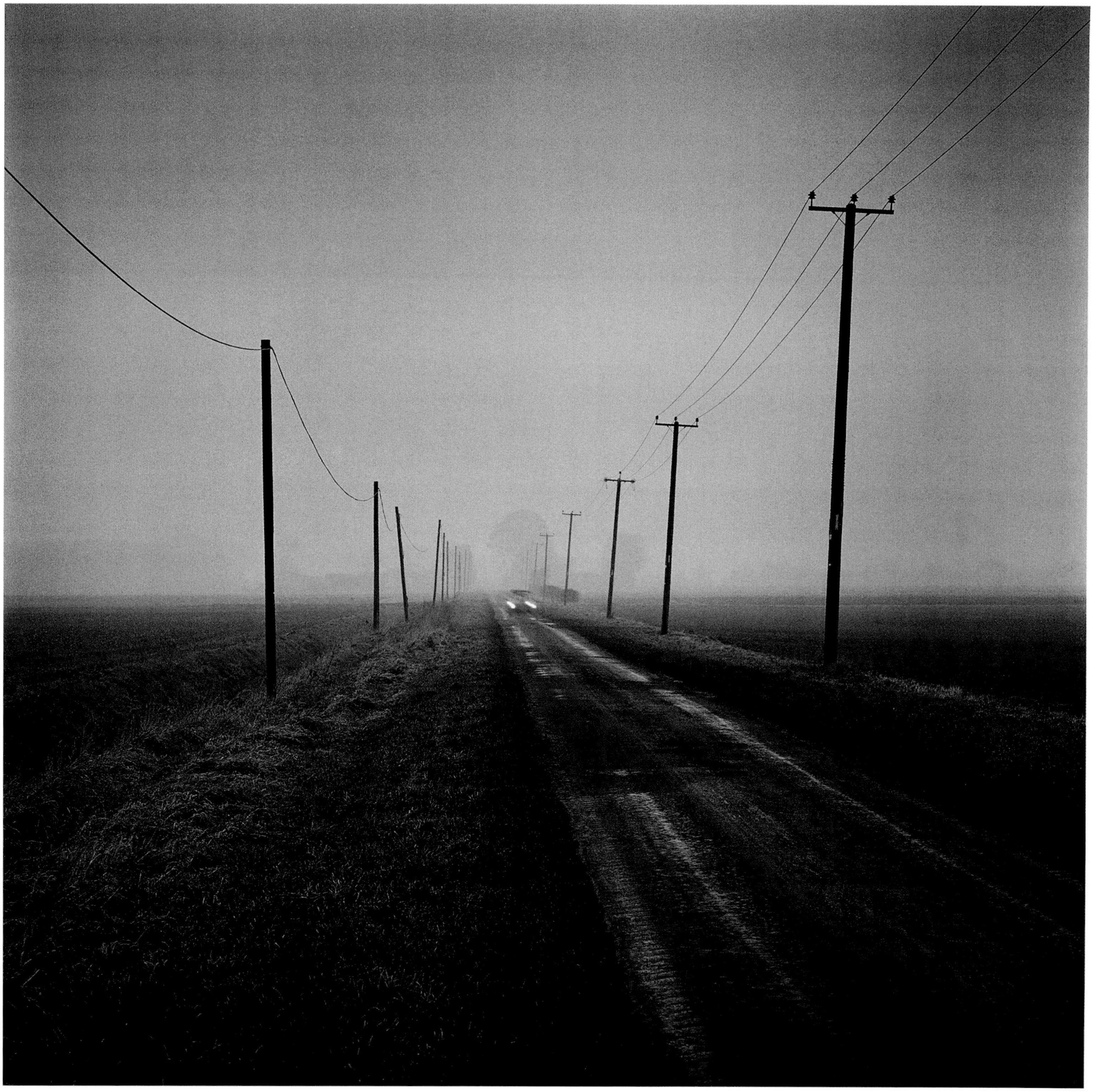

Staunt Road, Drained, England, 2017

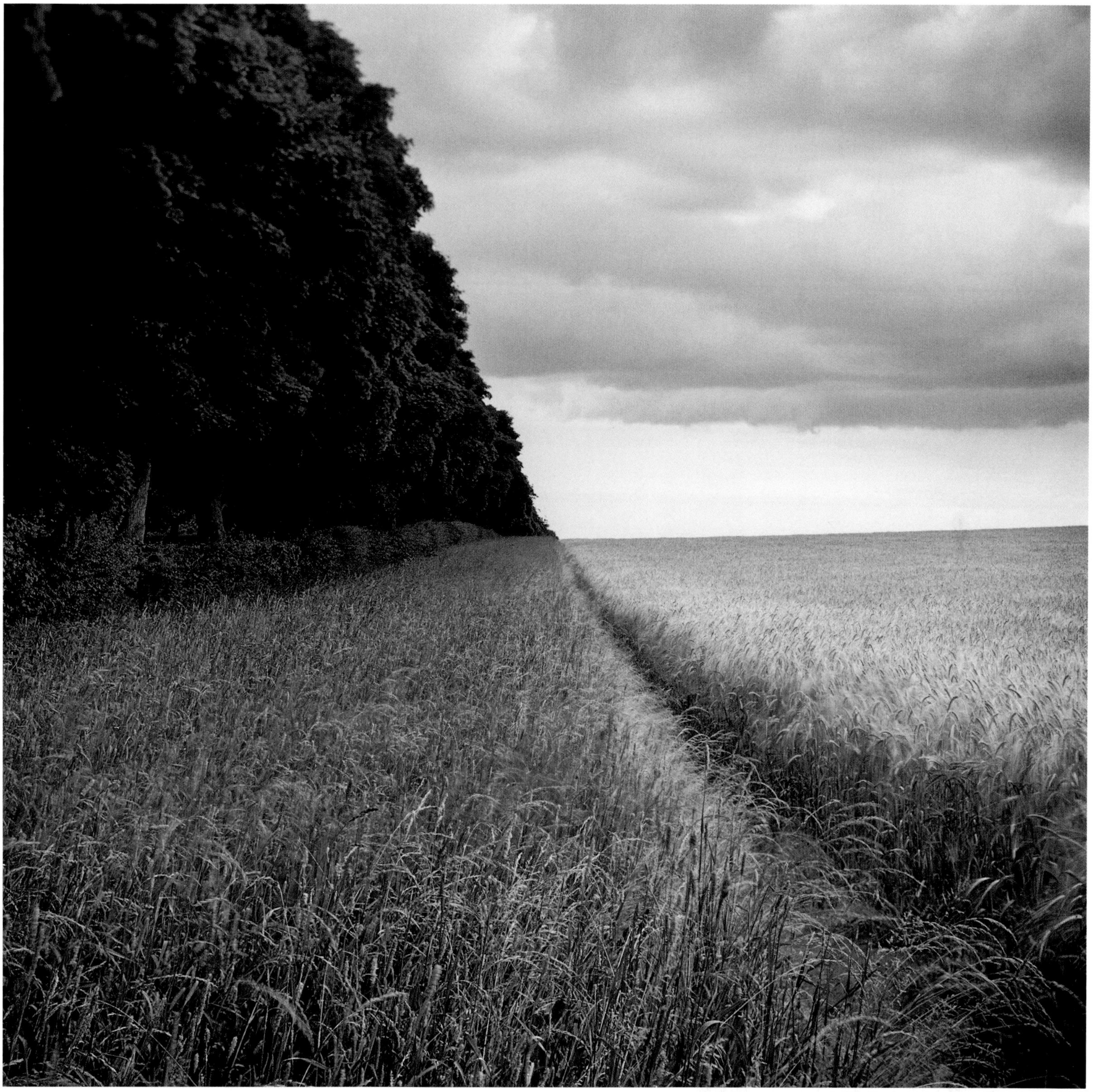

Anmer, Farmed, England, 2009

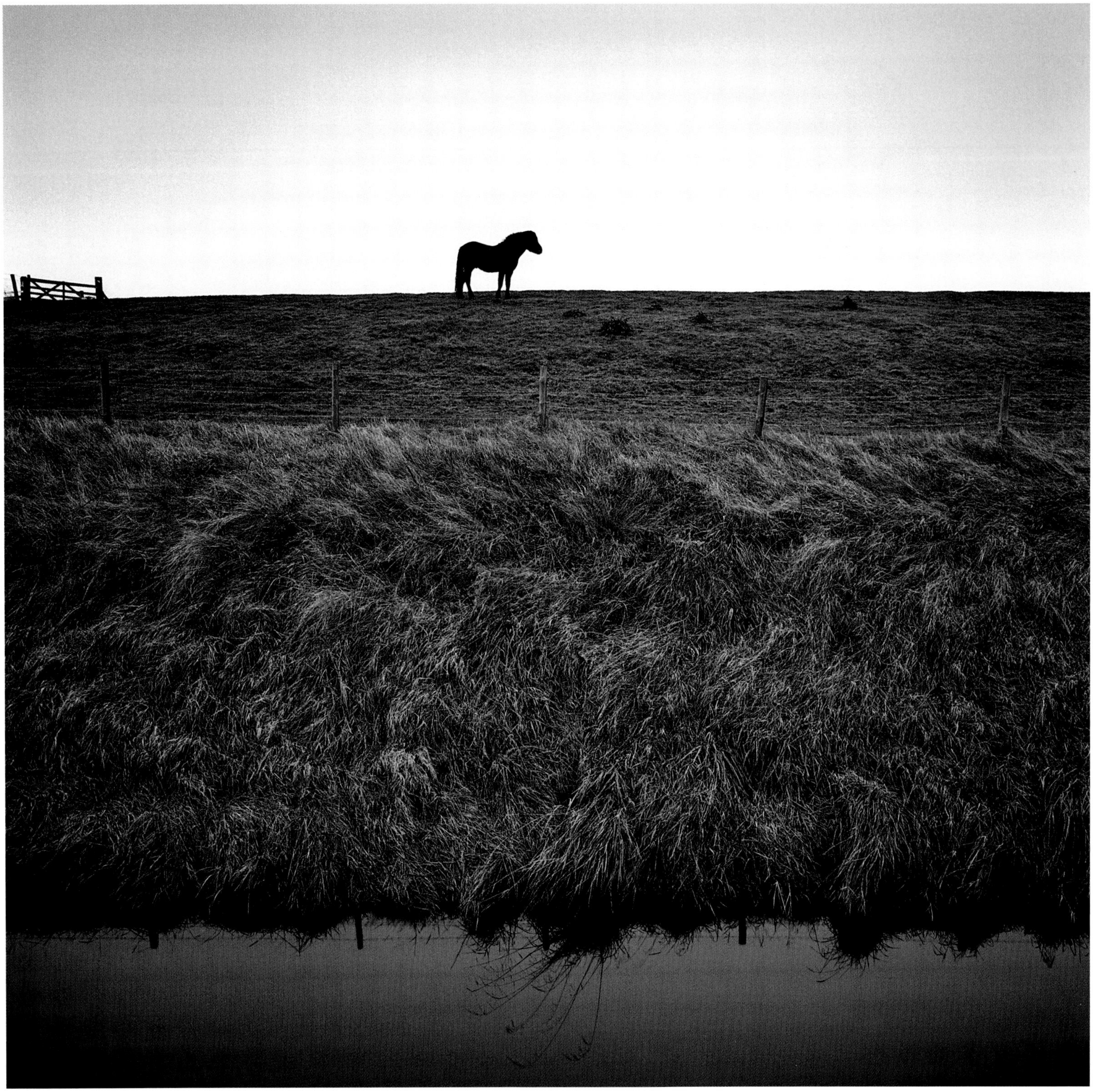

Sea Bank, Drained, England, 2016

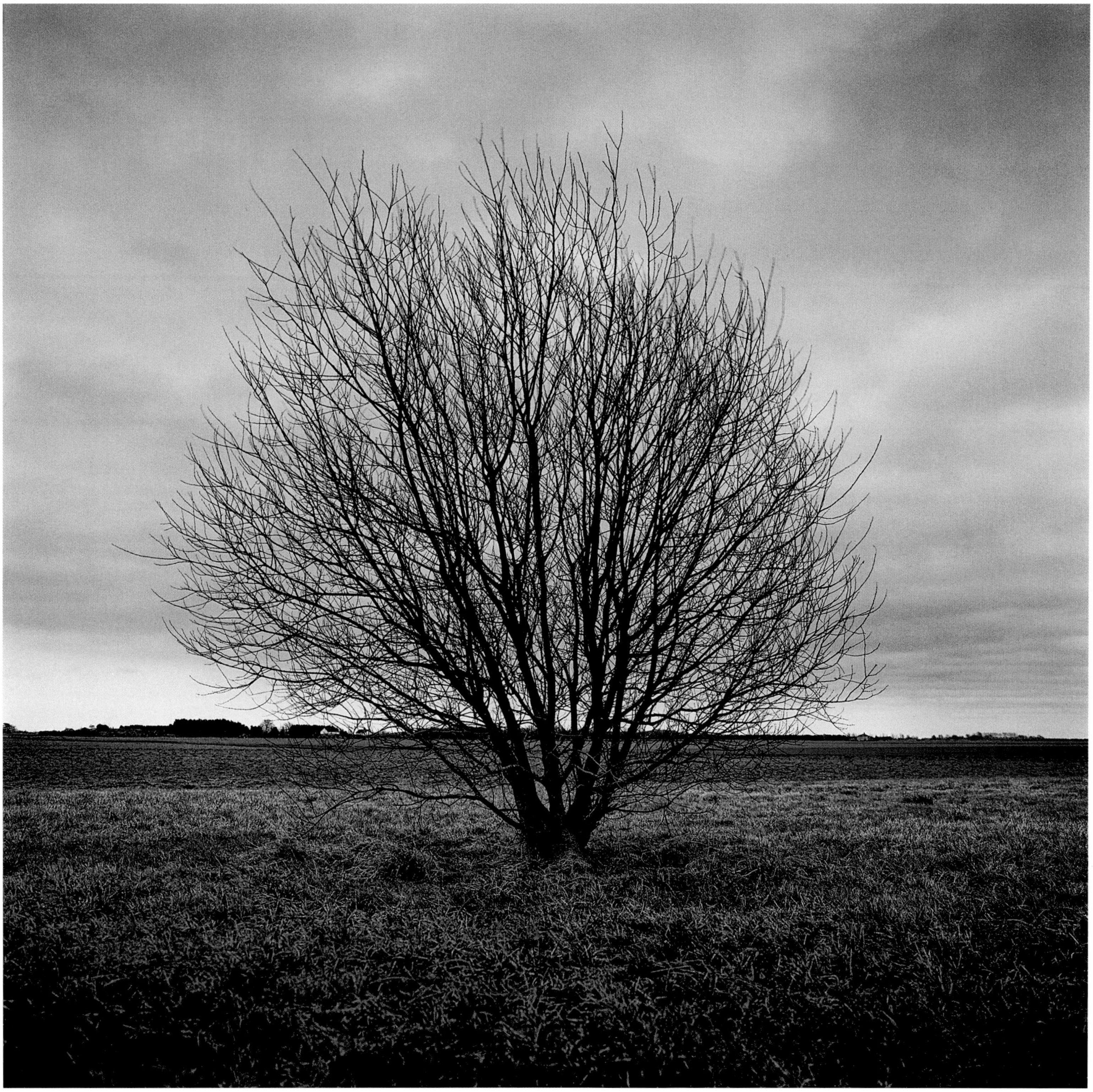

Fishtoft, Drained, England, 2017

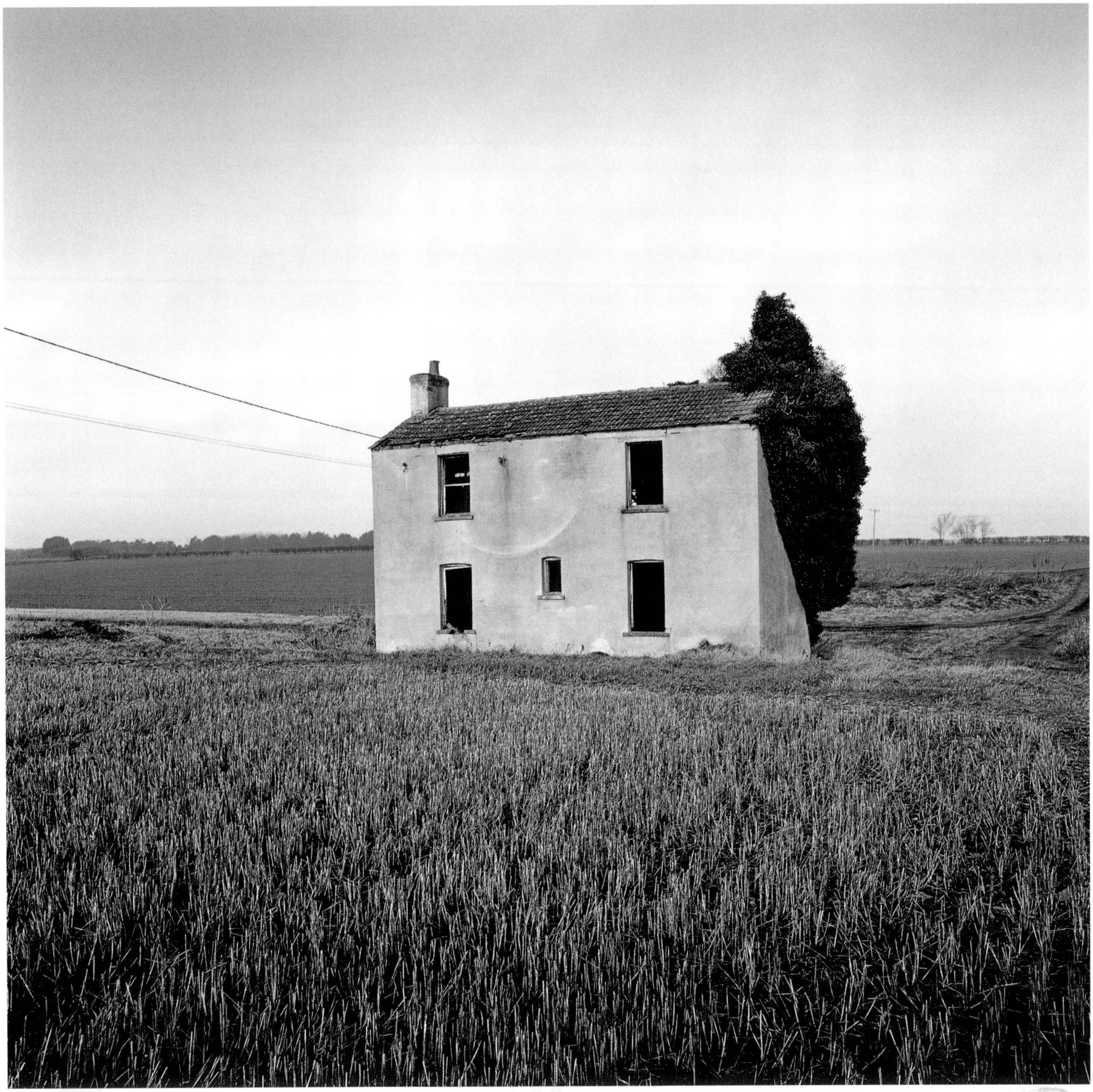

Metheringham Heath, Farmed, England, 2015

Beyond Me, Beside Me

Ian Potter

'I've always been one of these people that likes to turn the extra corner and go the extra [mile], just to see what's around the next bend.'

Beyond me. Beside me. The names of Ian Potter's projects sound almost incantatory when repeated one after the other. They suggest an impulse to situate, to locate. For the former fashion photographer, the natural world is a grounding sphere. Many of Potter's photos are concerned with the shifting perspectives suggested by those titles, inviting the onlooker to cast their eyes in all directions – to look beyond, above and beside. They also encourage an appreciation of those overlooked patches of land we might otherwise ignore: hedgerows, verges, scrub, the strips that edge fields of crops. They are rich tracts, their weeds and wildflowers hosting vast communities both animal and vegetal. You never know what you might find in these unremarkable between-spaces. Some house rare insects. Others reveal poisons, like hemlock or deadly nightshade. It can be wise to glance at what's right beside you, or just beyond you.

Many of Potter's photos retain echoes of landscape painters such as John Nash or Eric Ravilious, and are similarly immersive. They are often muted, almost sepia-toned: soft blocks of green against equally soft browns and greys. Looking at them in sequence, the edges of each frame become more apparent. They reveal a series of striated layers, moving from textured cow parsley to blustering skies or shaded strips of cropped grass. These landscapes appear unadorned, aside from leaves and petals. They are calmly, almost flatly composed, suggesting an atmosphere of a breath being held, of something still and waiting.

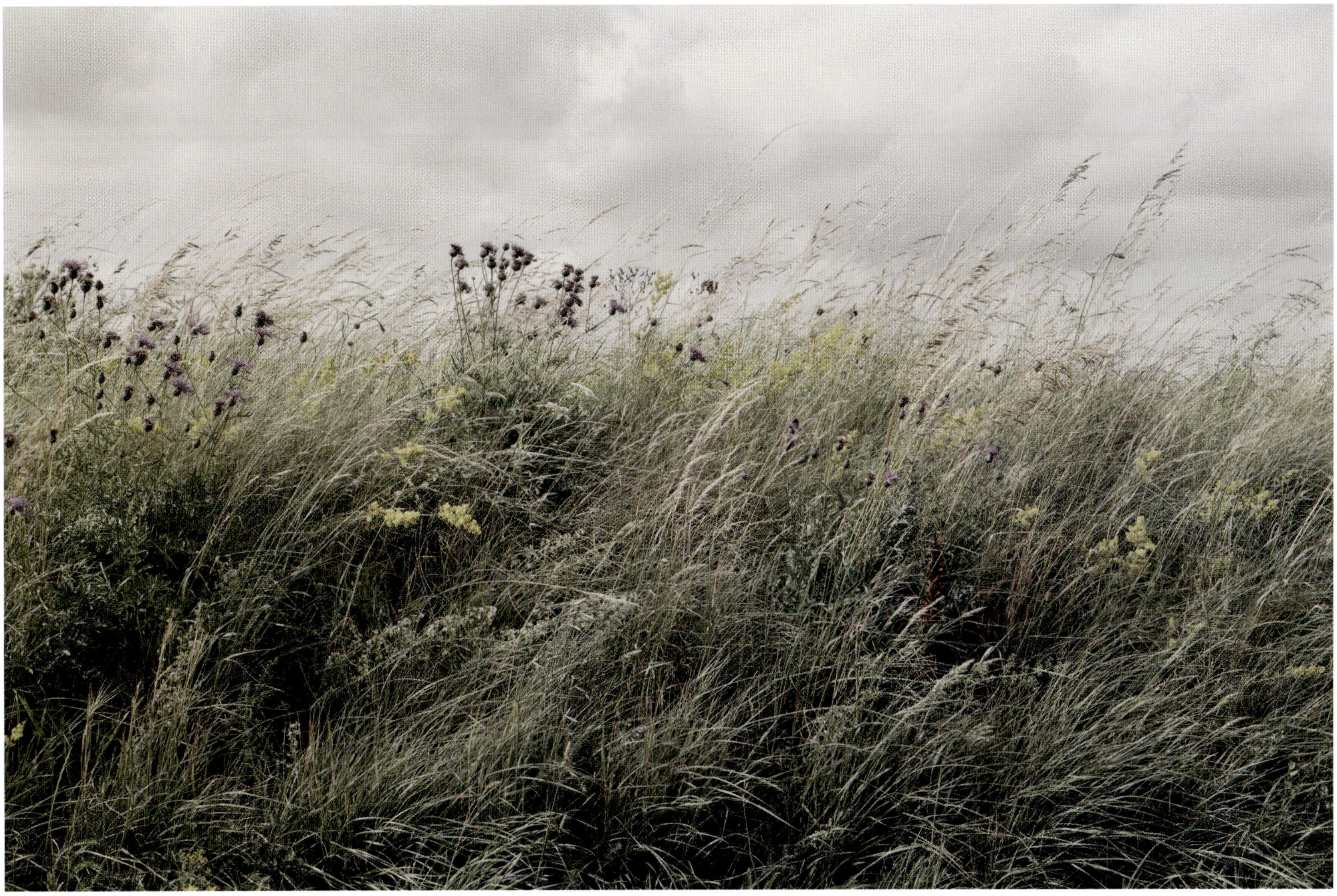

51.550132, -1.119292, 2020

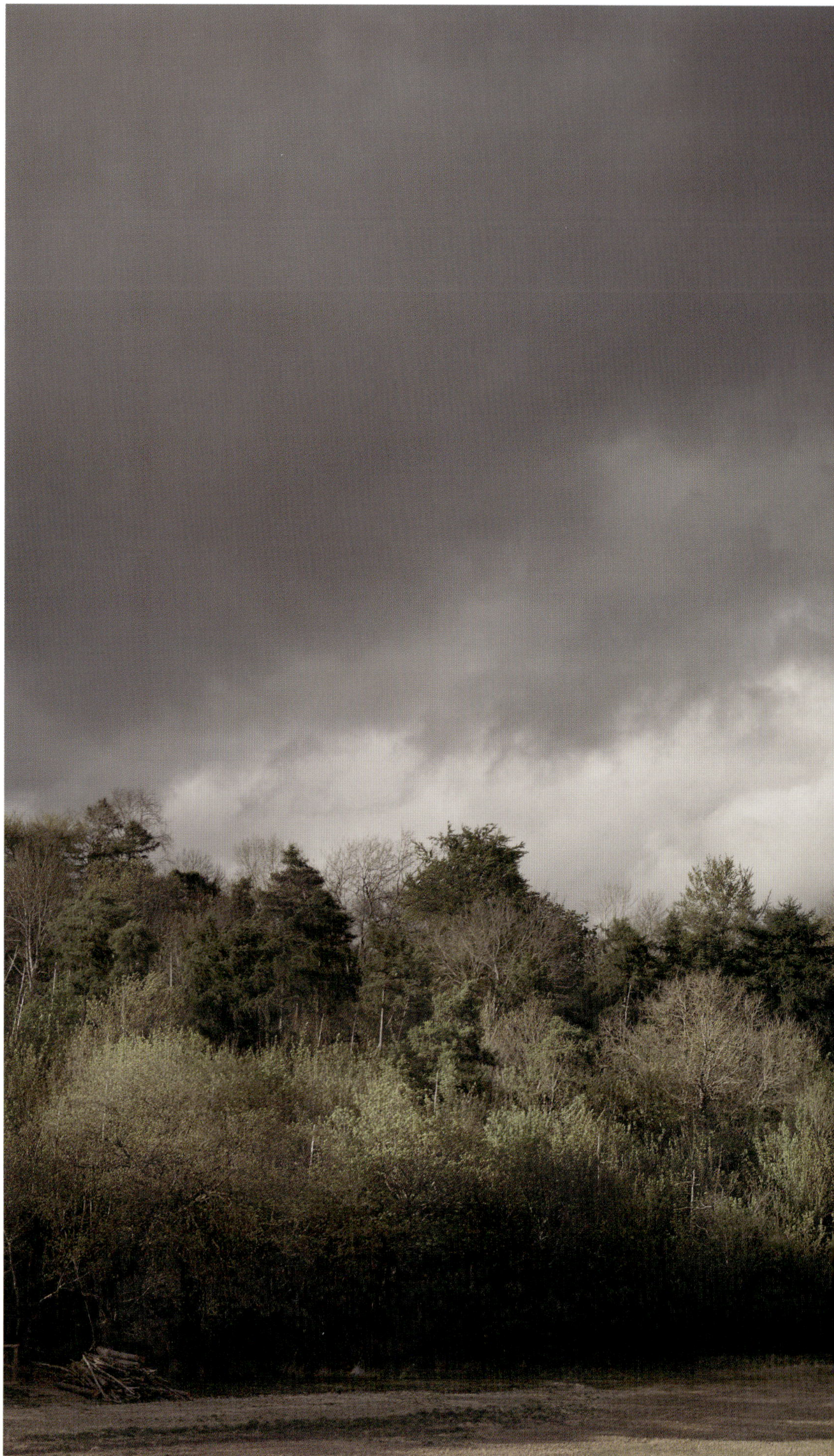

51.507667, -1.137182, 2019

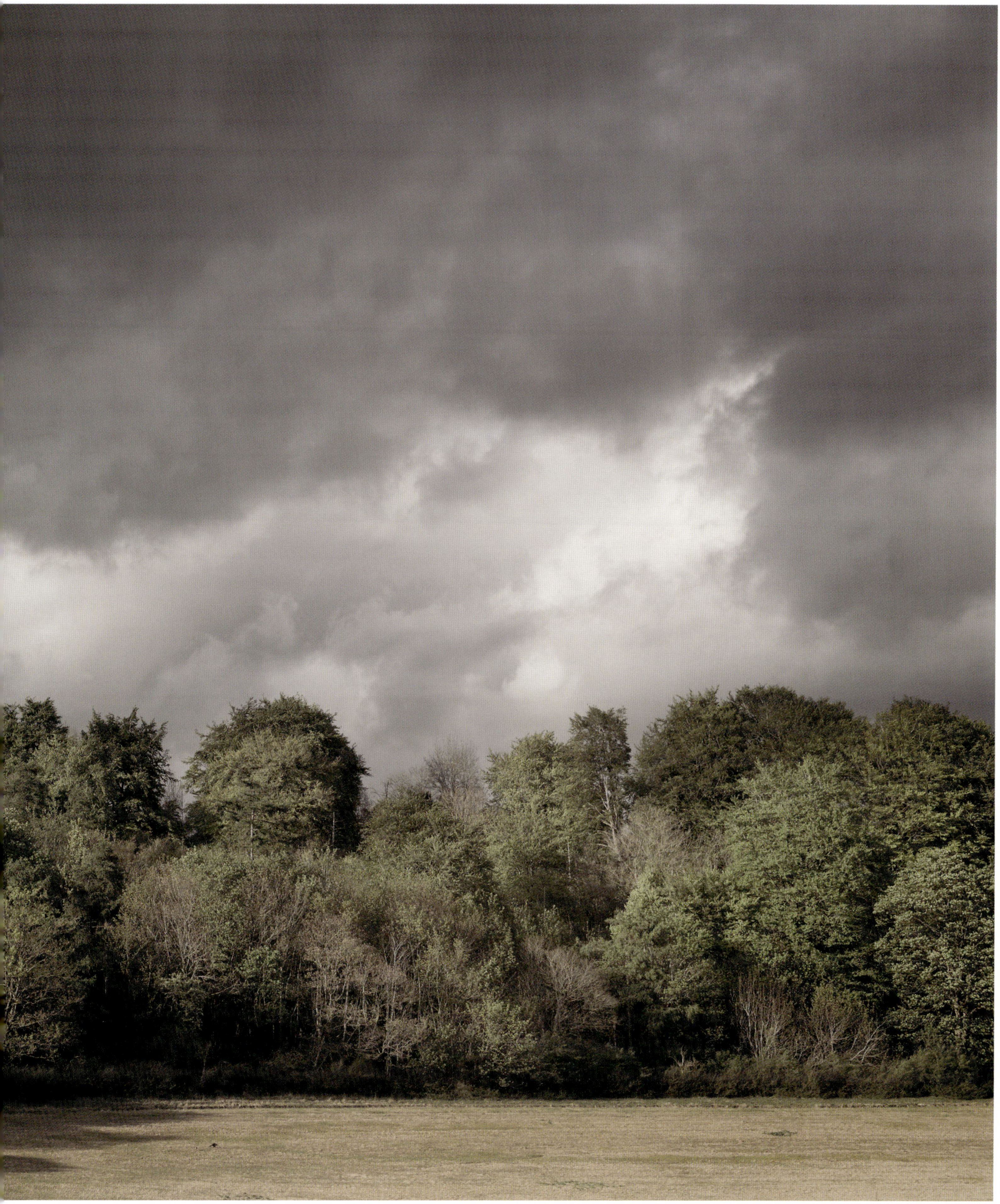

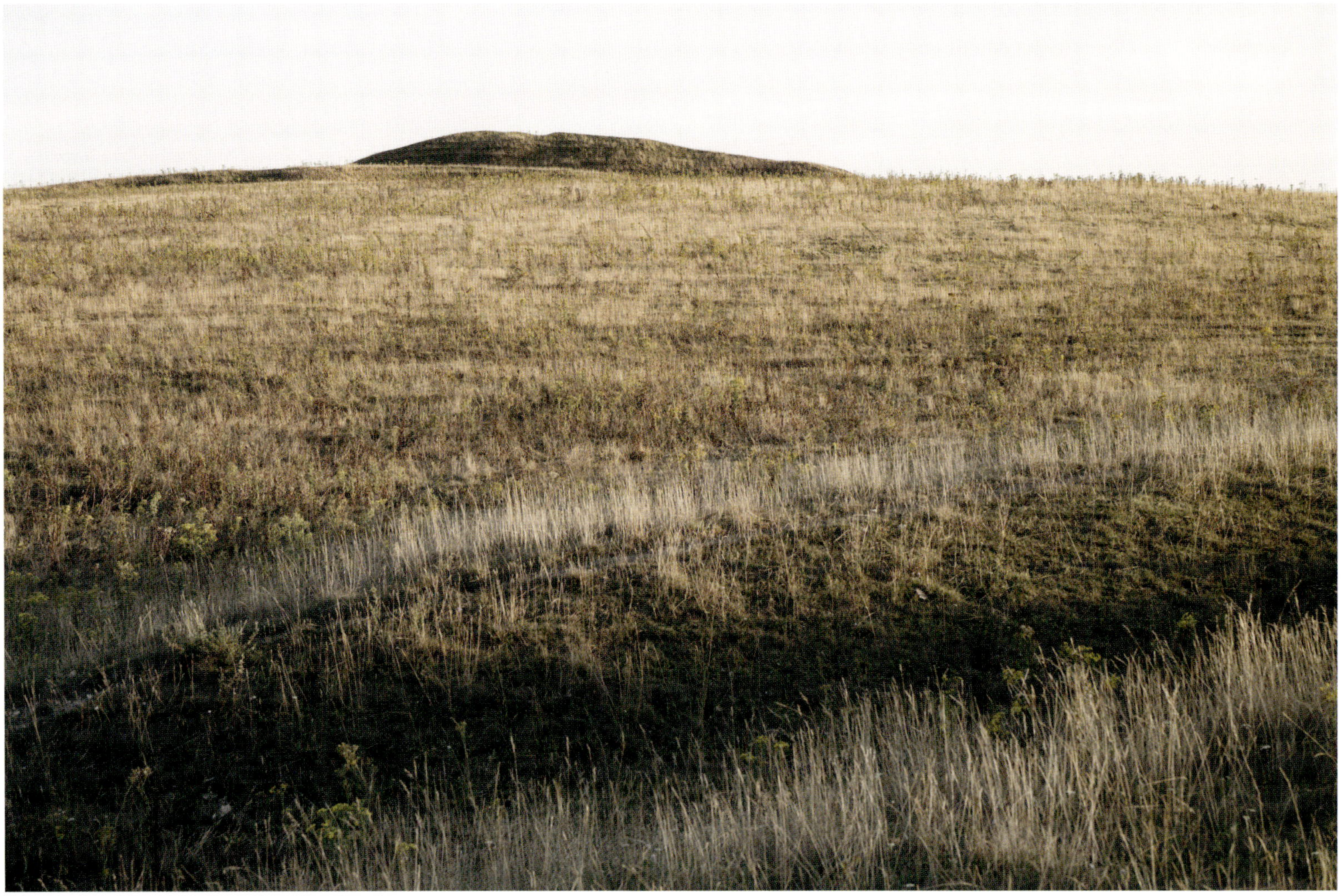

51.371205, -1.839559, 2022

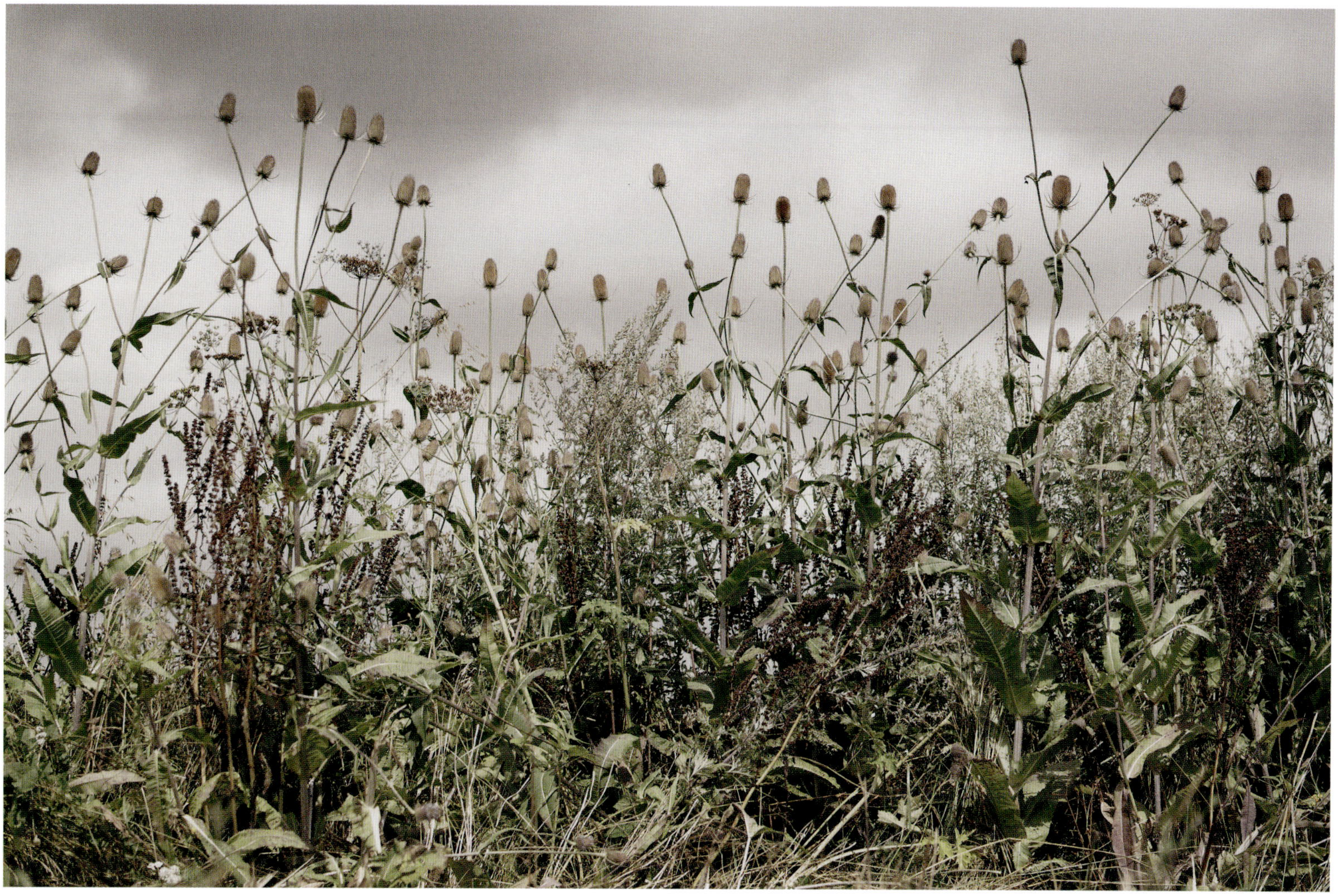

51.641256, -1.199991, 2021

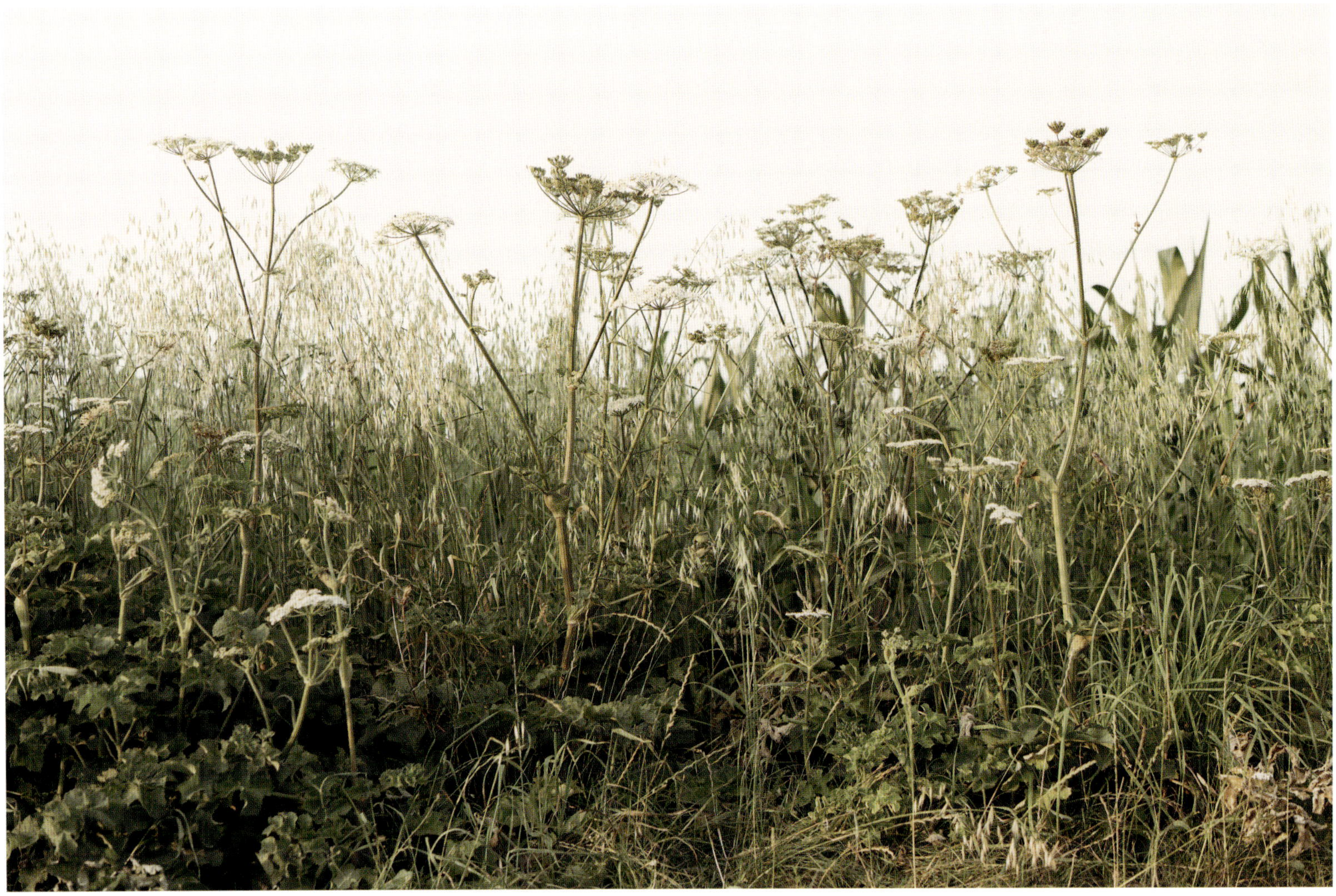

51.627157, 1-080672, 2021

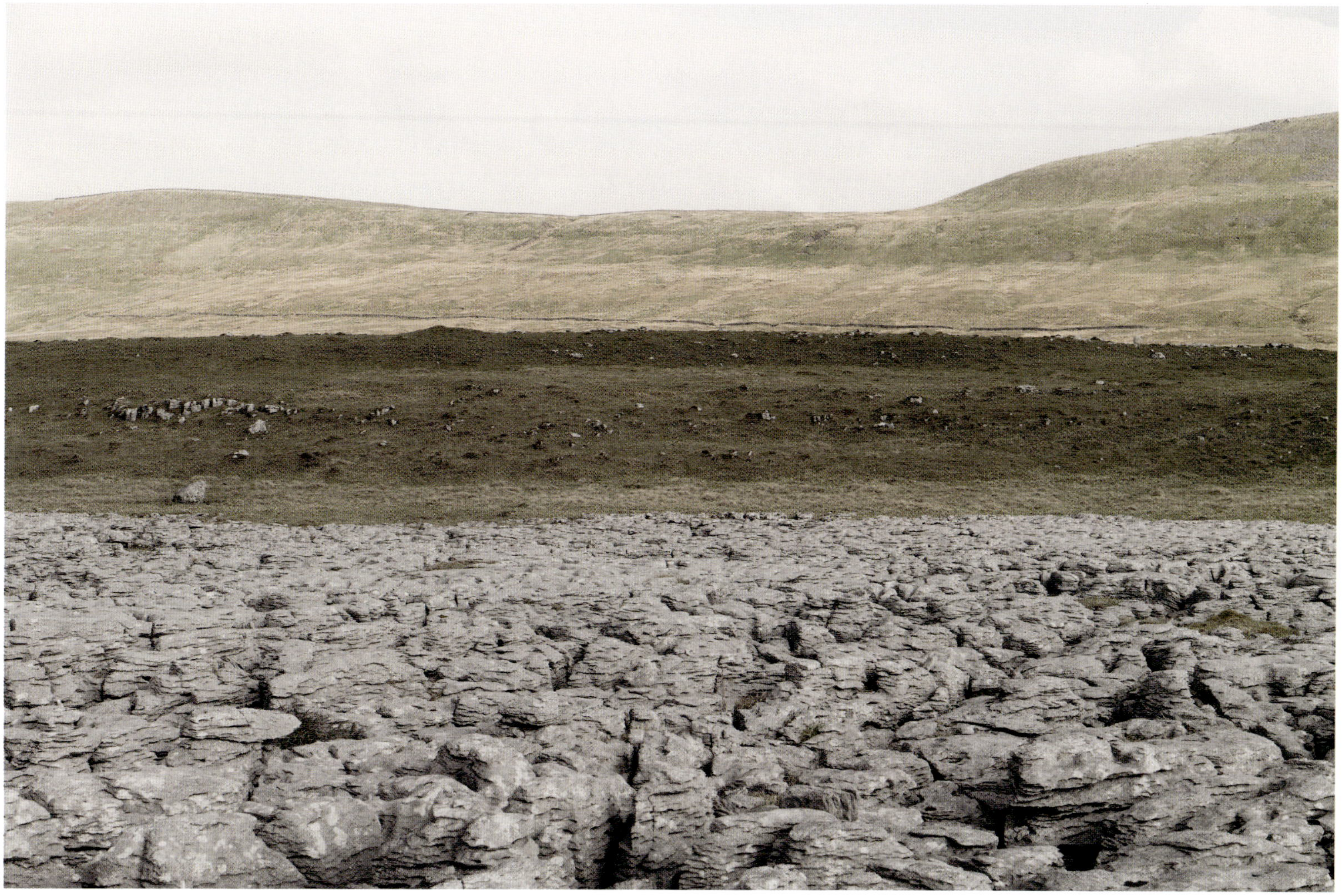

54.187531, -2.392275, 2022

At the Valley's End

Kaveh Rostamkhani

'There is a memory buried in the landscape... You see all these signs hinting at stories, at the history... You see the power of nature taking back these places.'

Landscapes frequently hint at former lives. The decommissioned quarry welcomes a fuzz of grass over its grey belly. Abandoned cottages subside back into the ground, stone walls now open to the sky. Kaveh Rostamkhani's *At the Valley's End* traces the contours of the formerly thriving mining industry in coal-rich South Wales. When the photographer was given a grant to study in Wales for a year, Rostamkhani chose to make his focus local. He moved to Newport and embarked on a study of the surrounding area, taking coaches to different towns and villages to observe the decades-long decline after Margaret Thatcher crushed the miners' strike in the mid-1980s.

Coal tells a particular story of Britain: one of industrial advancement, hard labour, global expansion and colonialism. It also tells a story of the lack and loss felt in places that haven't recovered since the closure of the pits. In the decade following the end of the strike, 25,000 Welsh miners lost their jobs. Unemployment rates have remained high ever since. Now, memories are retained not only in the landscape – the capped mine shafts, the stilled machinery – but also by the ageing communities left behind while younger people are forced to move elsewhere for work. Rostamkhani's photography is sensitive to the ways in which a post-industrial landscape shapes its people. In a mixture of colour and black and white photography he explores the starkness and subtle beauty of this setting; observing quiet, pebble-dashed houses, slag heaps, social clubs and railway tracks once used to ferry Welsh coal to the rest of the world. In many of these images, wilderness has crept back into the frame, carpeting abandoned infrastructure in green.

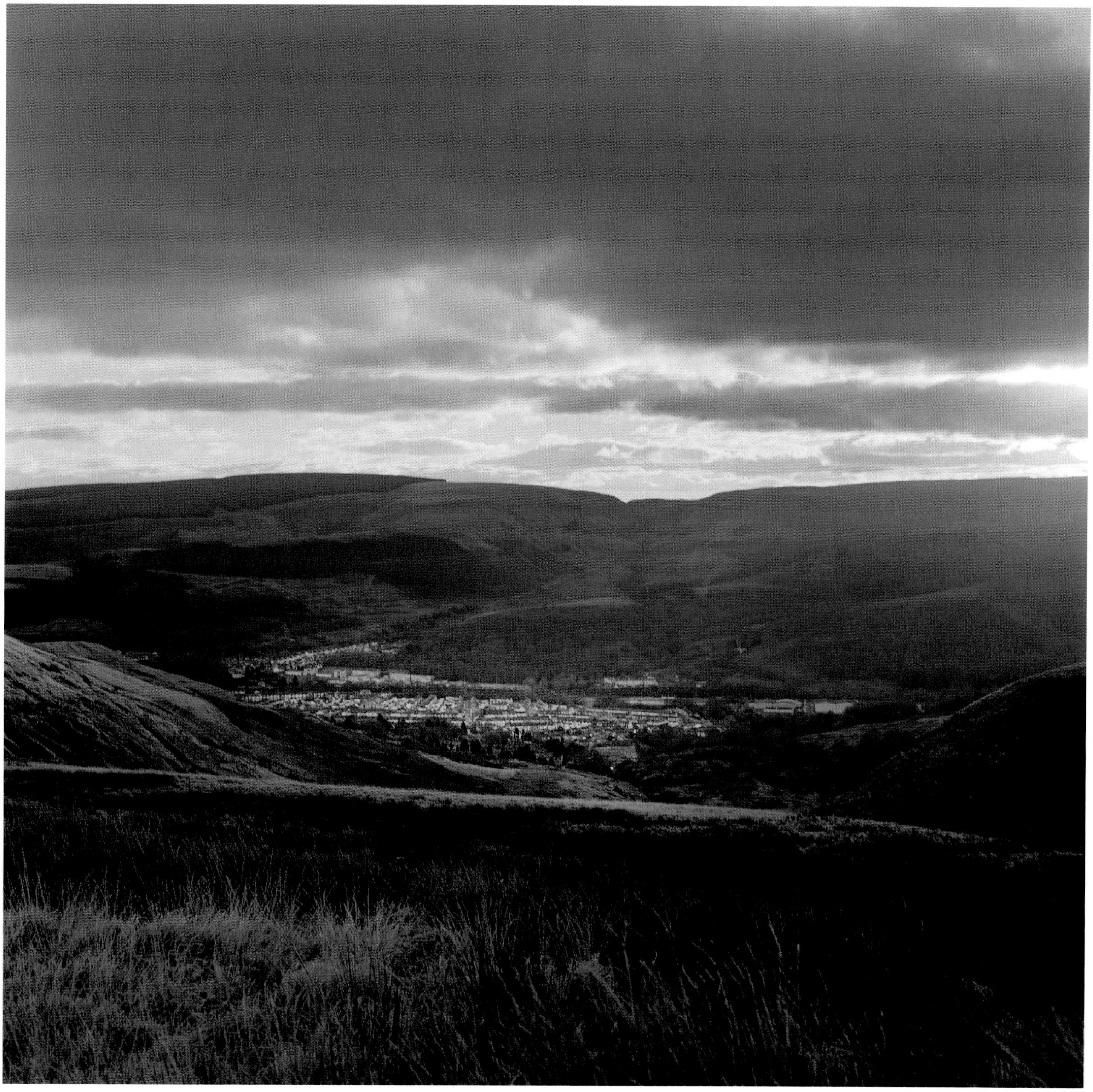

Treorchy, Rhondda Valley, Wales, 2012

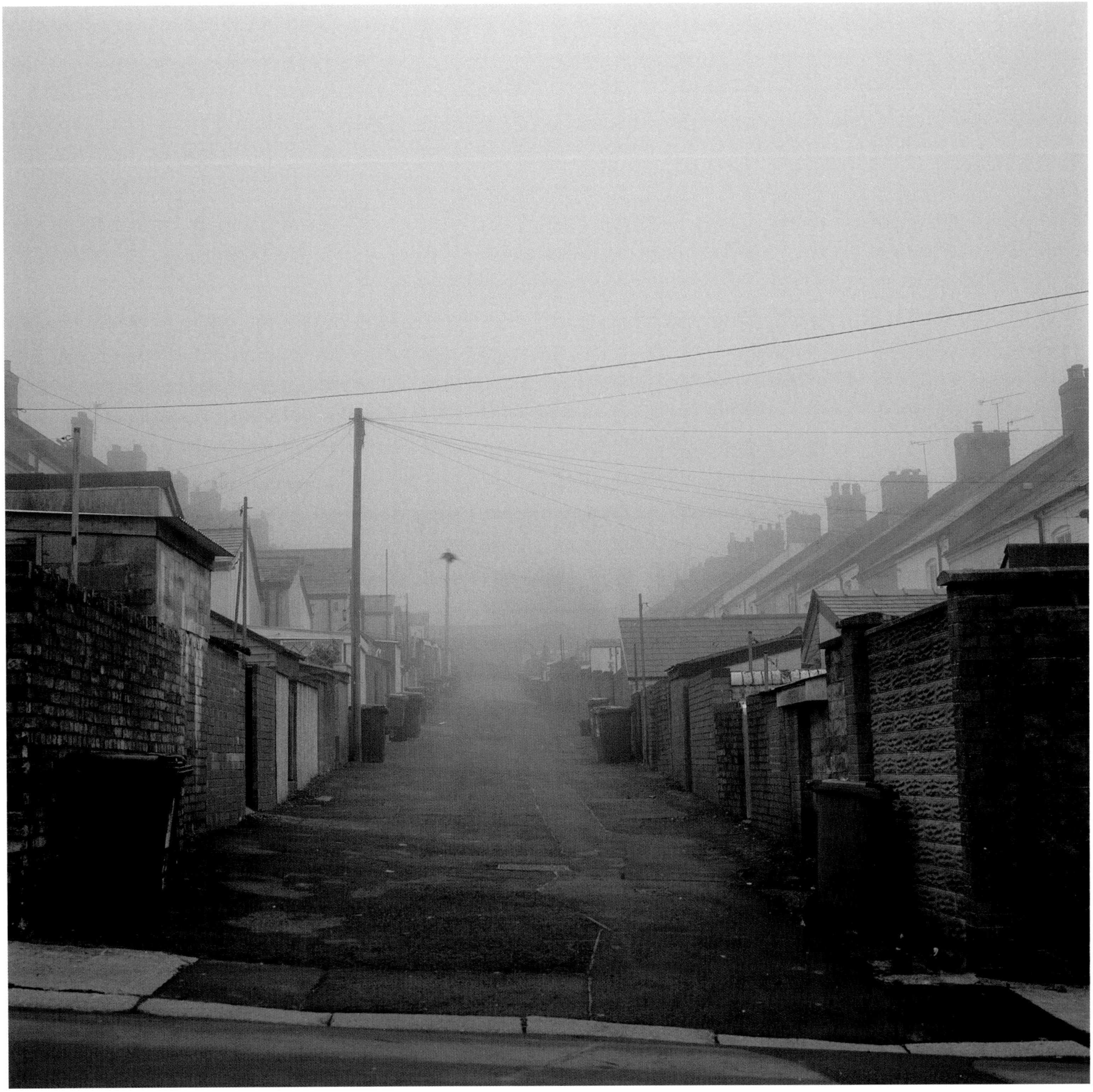

Terraced houses in Blaenavon, South Wales, 2012

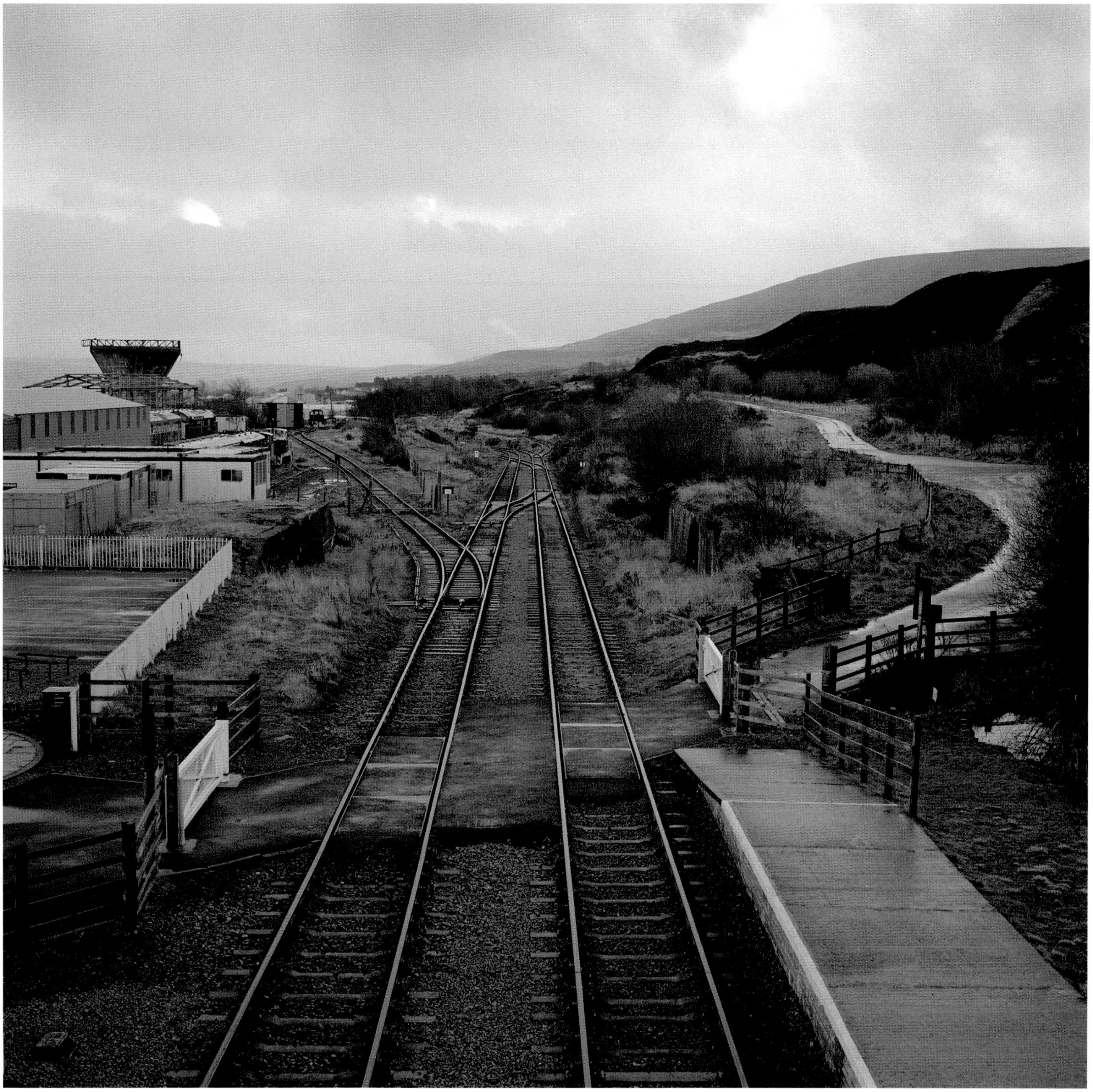

Pontypool and Blaenavon railway, once used to transport mined coal to surrounding areas, South Wales, 2012

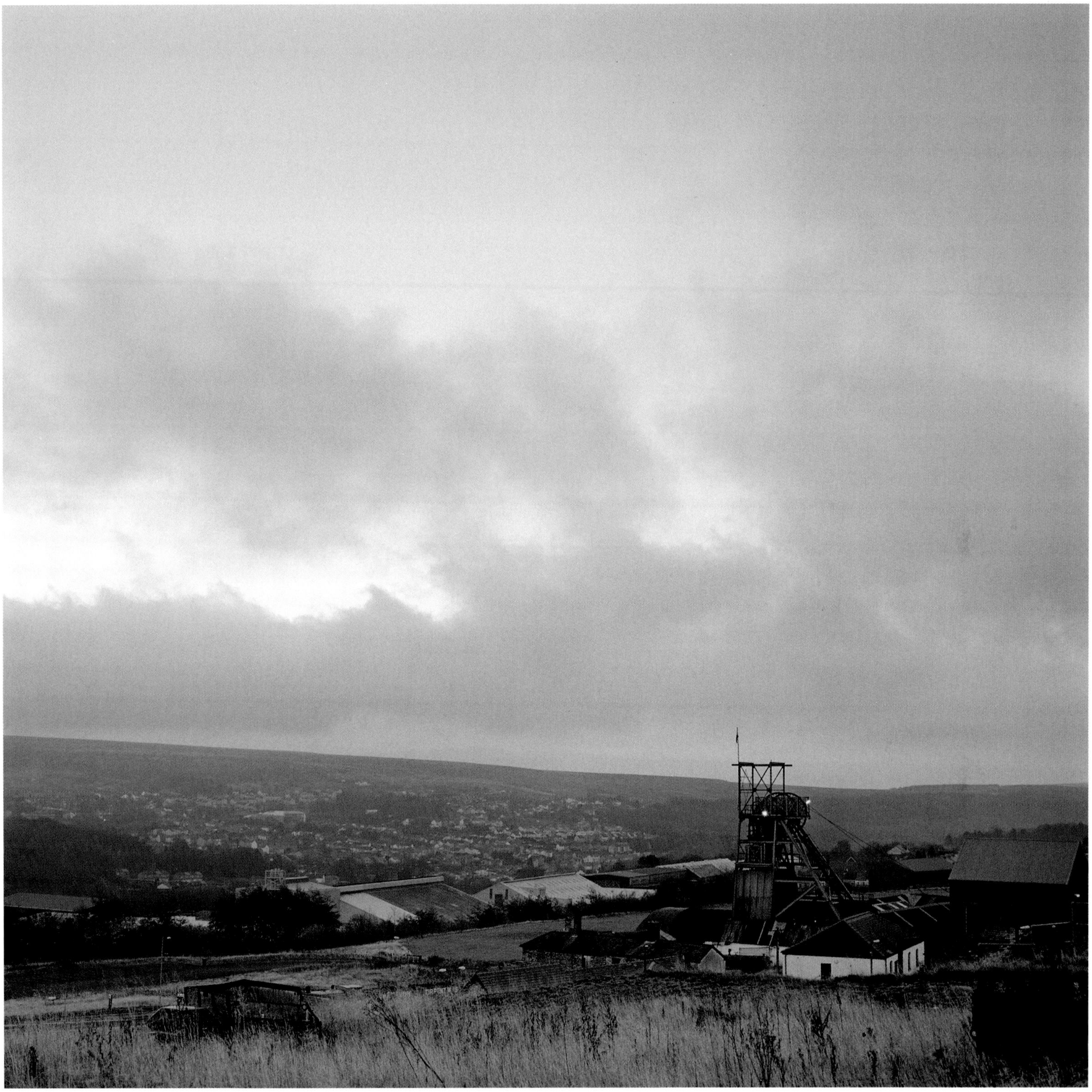

Winding mill marking former colliery Big Pit, now the National Coal Mining Museum, Blaenavon, Wales, 2012

Drawn to the Land

Sophie Gerrard

'Those who talk of our landscape have always been quite male. I felt there was a female voice to explore... It was just what I needed: travelling the country and spending time with women who knew the land.'

There are many reasons to run a farm. It might be a family business, part of a working tradition handed down through the generations. It might be an individually chosen path, built on a desire to nurture a complex ecosystem. While working on *Drawn to the Land*, Sophie Gerrard encountered numerous stories about agricultural life. From small-scale tenant farmers to vast inheritances, she met with women whose days are spent dealing with livestock, crops, weather, business and conservation.

Gerrard embarked on the project when she returned to Scotland after nearly a decade of living and working abroad. This homecoming was shaded by reflections on national identity in the lead up to the 2014 Scottish independence referendum. This developed into a meditation on who owns and tends to the land. Rural working life is still highly gendered. By choosing to focus on female farmers, Gerrard felt that she could tell a new story about Scotland.

The resulting body of work is a beautiful but unsentimental reflection of farming life. Portraits of six hill farmers from across Scotland are interspersed with domestic interludes and the terrain they work on. Although many of these images offer an atmosphere of grandeur, this is no romanticised pastoral. It is a place where life and death rub shoulders, and a place of great political significance. Engaging with the realities of these farmers' lives means engaging with the daily questions and tensions embedded in the Scottish landscape: from controversies around renewable energy to second homes and agricultural landlordism. However, the project also alights on something deeper. Overlooked and underrepresented, these women are the custodians of some of the most inhospitable and isolated parts of Scotland. The dedication and emotional connection that these women show to their land is unrelenting. Like soil beneath one's nails, it accumulates photo by photo, a quiet reminder of the earth's constant presence.

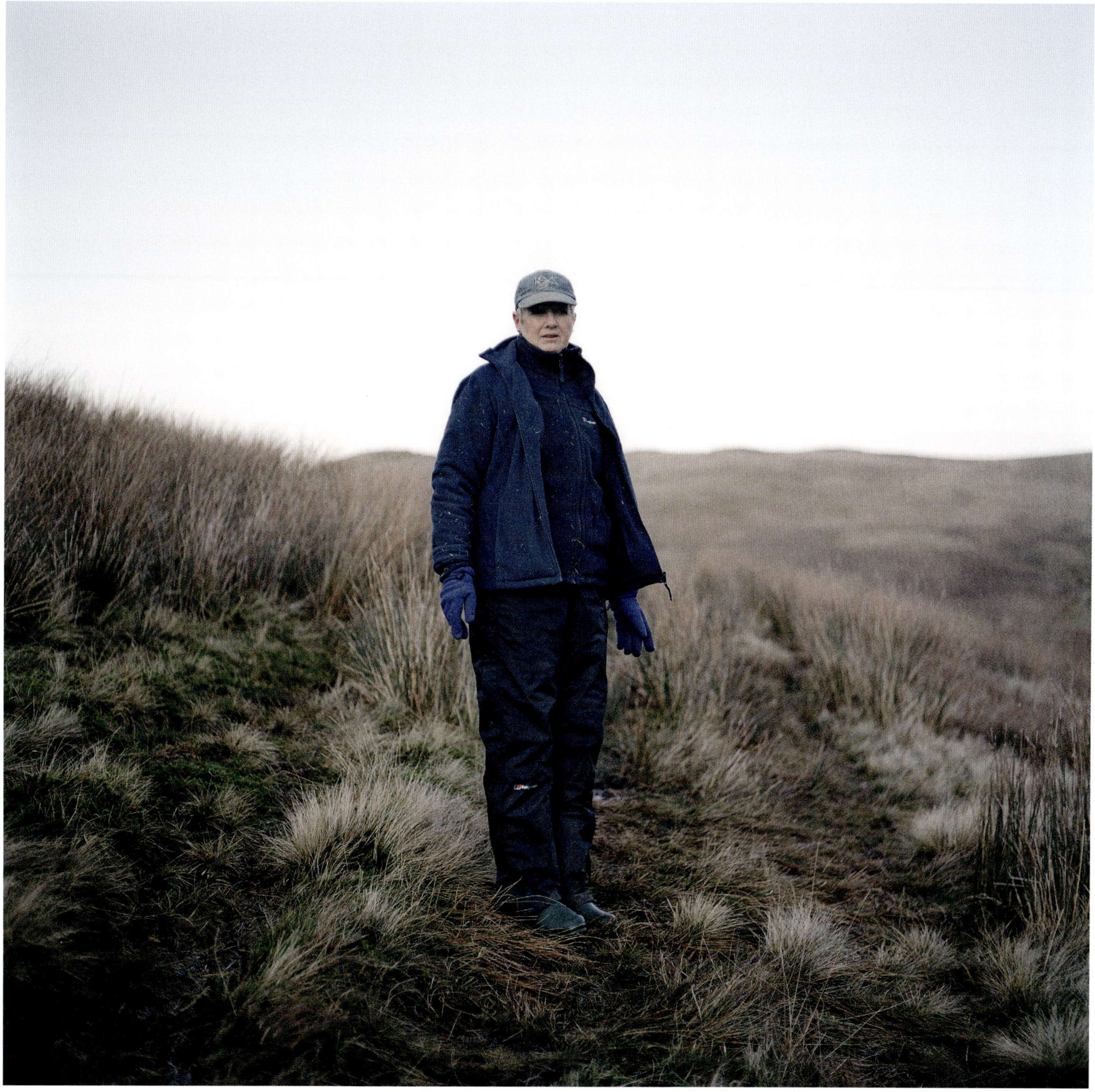

Lorraine on her hill farm, Megdale, Langholm, Scottish Borders, January 2014

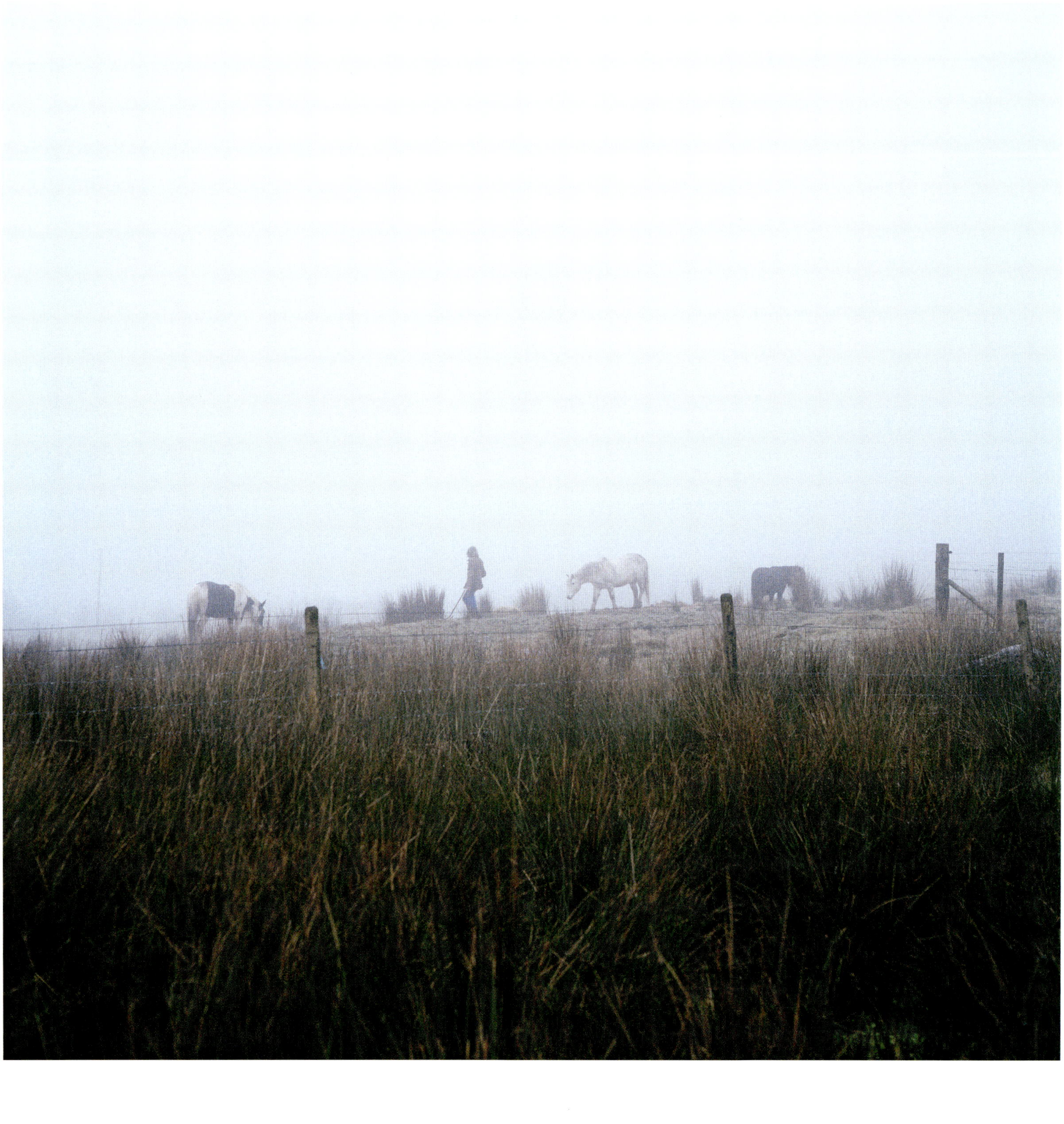

Minty feeding the ponies, High Lee Croft, Isle of Mull, Scotland, March 2014

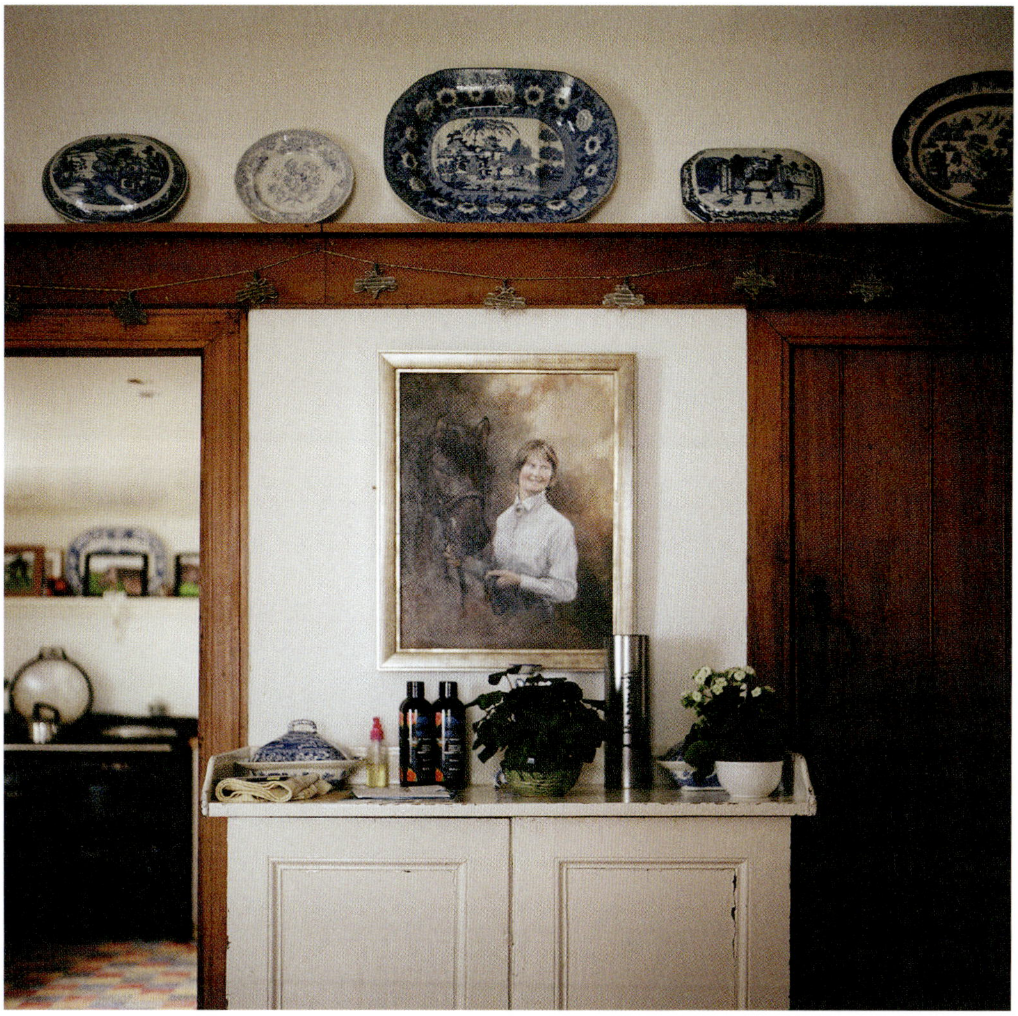

Mary's home, Connachan Farm, Perthshire, Scotland, March 2013

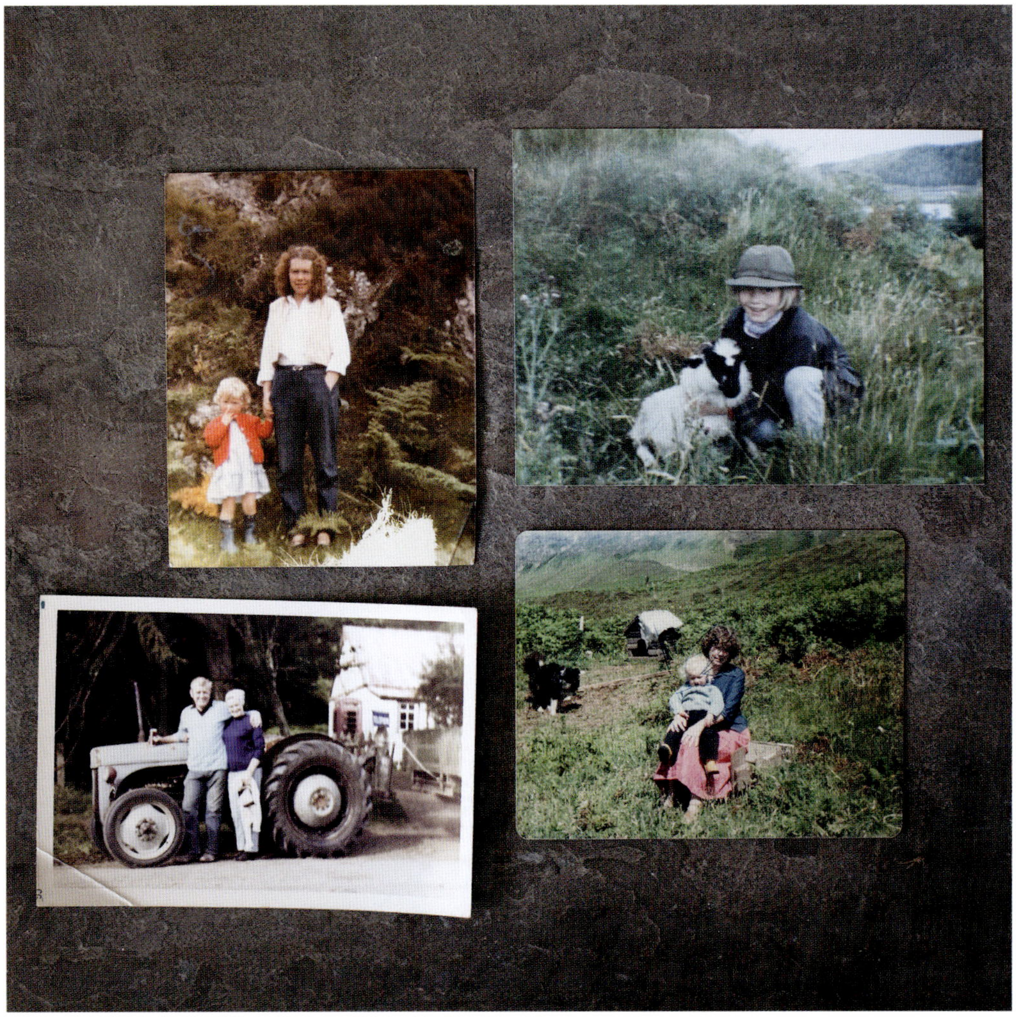

Photographs from Sarah's childhood, Isle of Eigg, Scotland, 2015

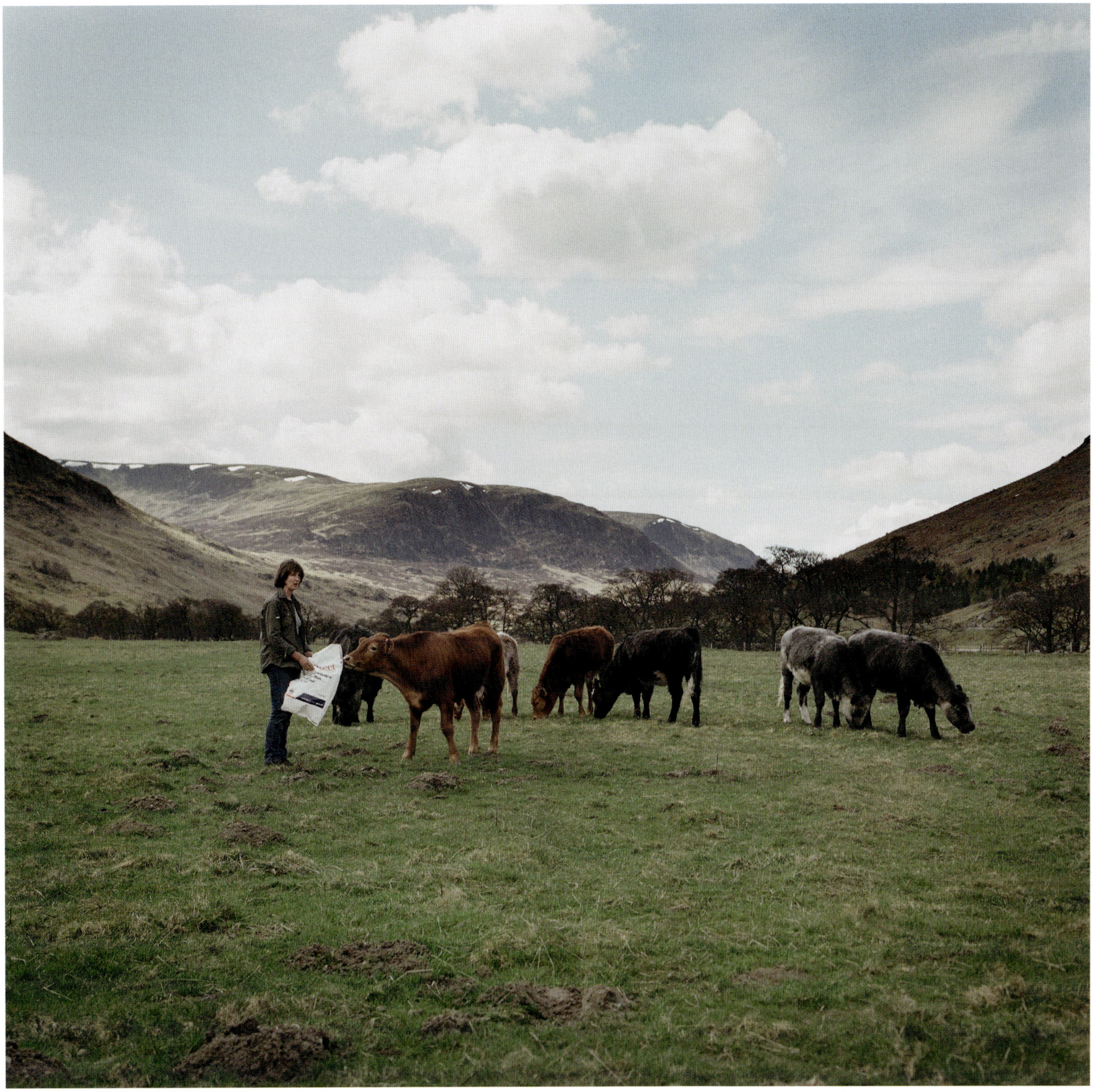

Mary on her hill farm, Connachan Farm, Perthshire, Scotland, April 2015

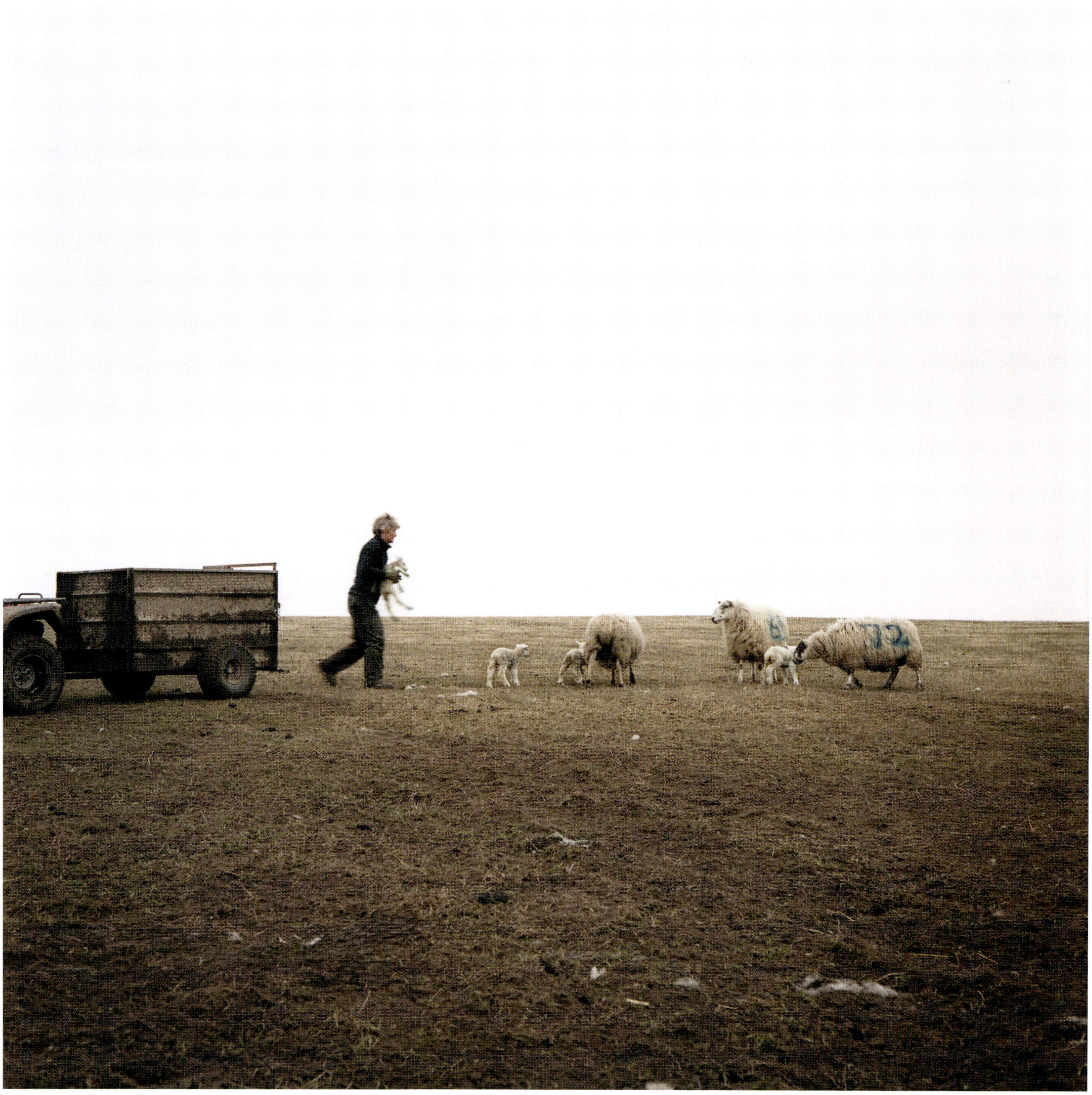

Patricia during lambing, Threeburnford farm, Scottish Borders, April 2013

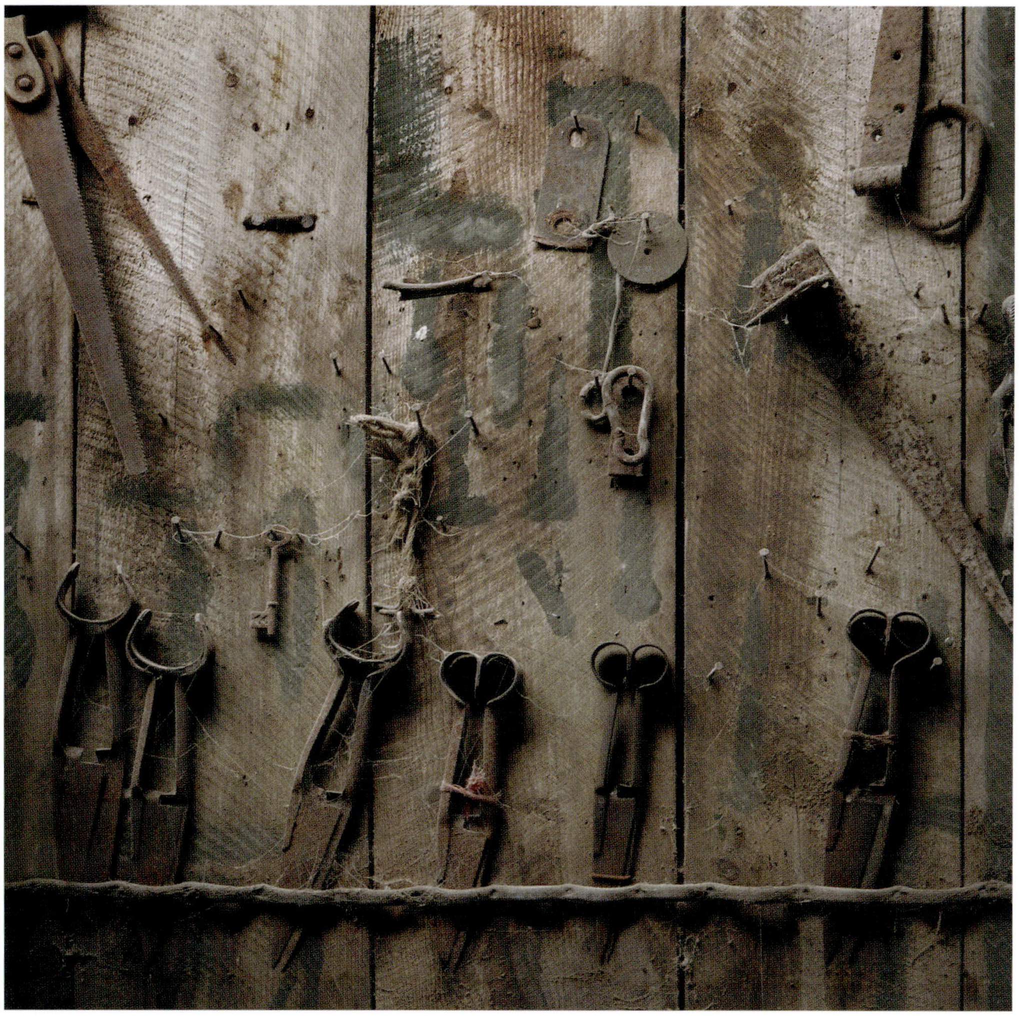

Shears, Brackley farm, Dalmally, Argyll and Bute, Scotland, March 2013

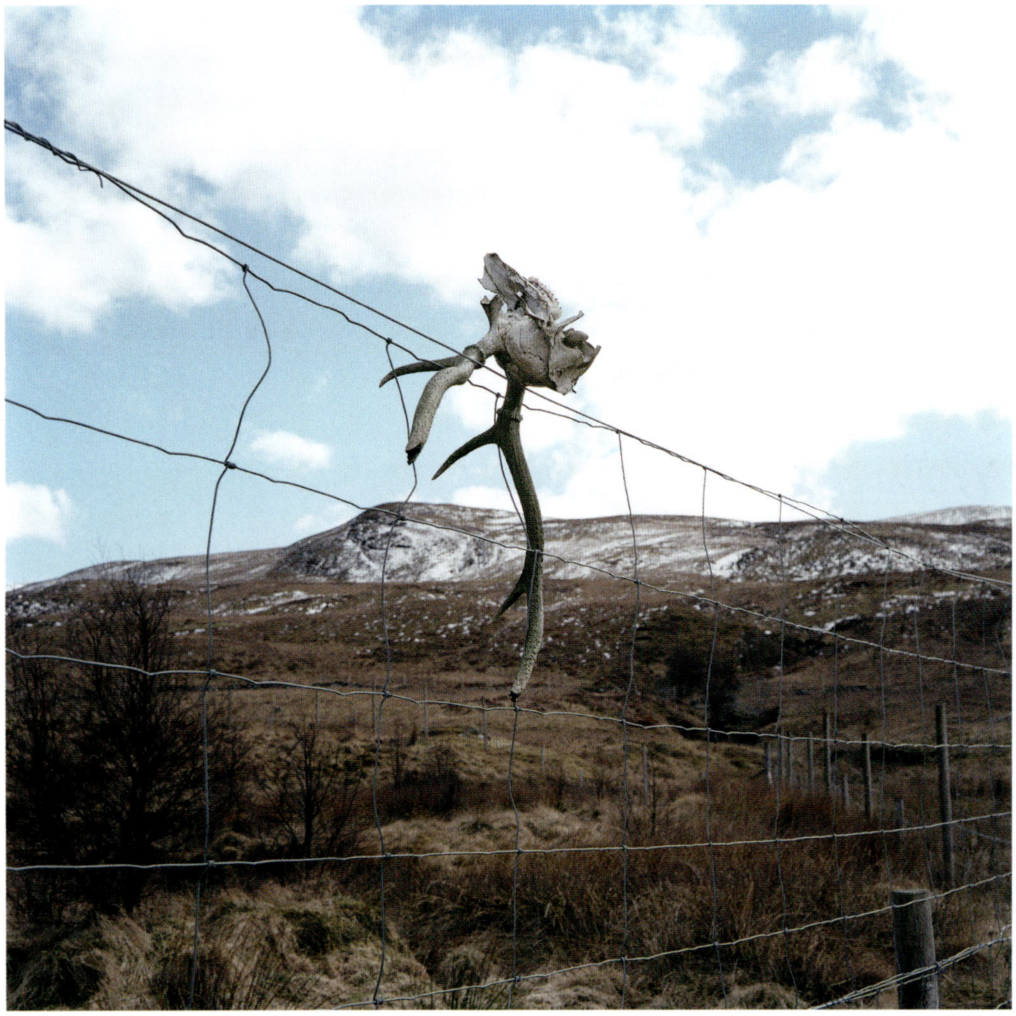

Deer skull on Sybil's hill farm, Brackley farm,
Dalmally, Argyll and Bute, Scotland, March 2013

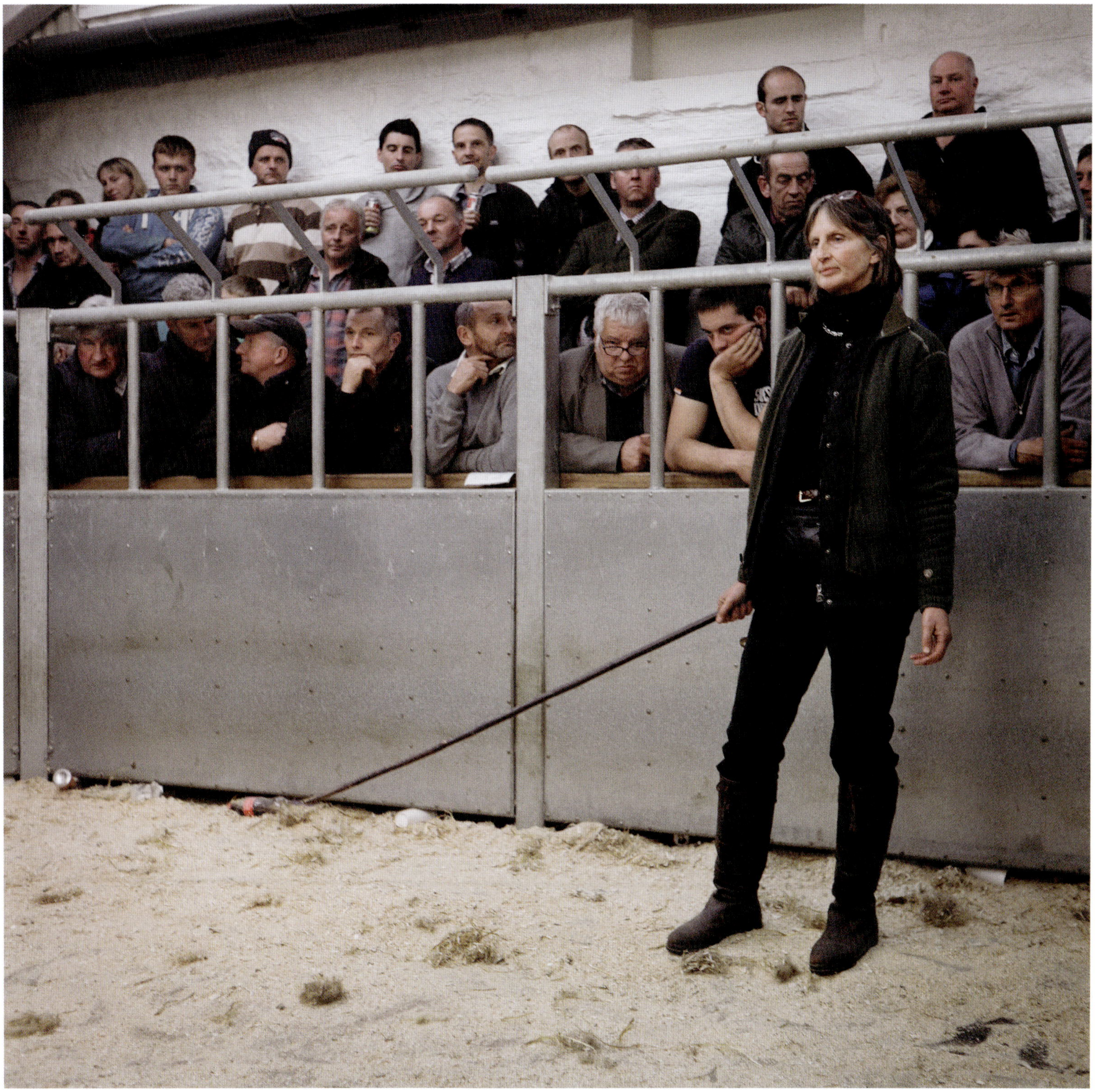

Mary at the Dalmally Tup Sales, Dalmally, Argyll and Bute, Scotland, October 2013

This Bitter Earth

Spencer Murphy

'I didn't want it to be a strict documentary of a devasted landscape... It sounds horrible to say, but there is a weird beauty in it... Not like the surface of the moon, but maybe another planet.'

In 2022, the NFCC (National Fire Chiefs Council) estimated that there were over 500 wildfires in England and Wales, more than double the year before. As temperatures rise year on year, hot weather and dry conditions will continue to create a perfect tinderbox – and these fires will be increasingly common. Spencer Murphy spent a summer documenting the wildfires that hit Britain back in 2018. That year Saddleworth Moor became the site of a seven-square-mile conflagration, which took three weeks and hundreds of firefighters to extinguish. It was hard to fully overpower the flames as the fire smouldered in peat bogs beneath the surface, reigniting again and again. Murphy photographed the charred aftermath of this destructive event, as well as London's largest ever grass fire in Wanstead Flats, a historic green space which forms the southern-most part of Epping Forest.

Murphy's medium format images are not just atmospheric, they're unsettling. Like any wound, a burn is a rupture in the order of normal things. Here much of the greenery is gone. The earth is blackened. Singed plants still stand, some reduced to little more than charcoal skeletons. While documenting these scenes of natural devastation, Murphy began to have nightmares about burnt trees – these living landmarks, rings in their trunks often revealing their great age, felled by the unstoppable progress of flames.

Climate change is reshaping our landscapes, whether via winter floods waterlogging fields and destroying homes or the soaring heat of high summer that sparks a wildfire. Water and flames both threaten not only human life, but also the delicately balanced ecosystems they rip through. Murphy's photos in *This Bitter Earth* are a sober reminder of this fact. The places he photographs are not quite barren, but they are in an advanced state of injury. Firefighters walk over ground that has become a dark crust. The air remains hazy with smoke, thick enough that you can imagine it catching at the back of your throat.

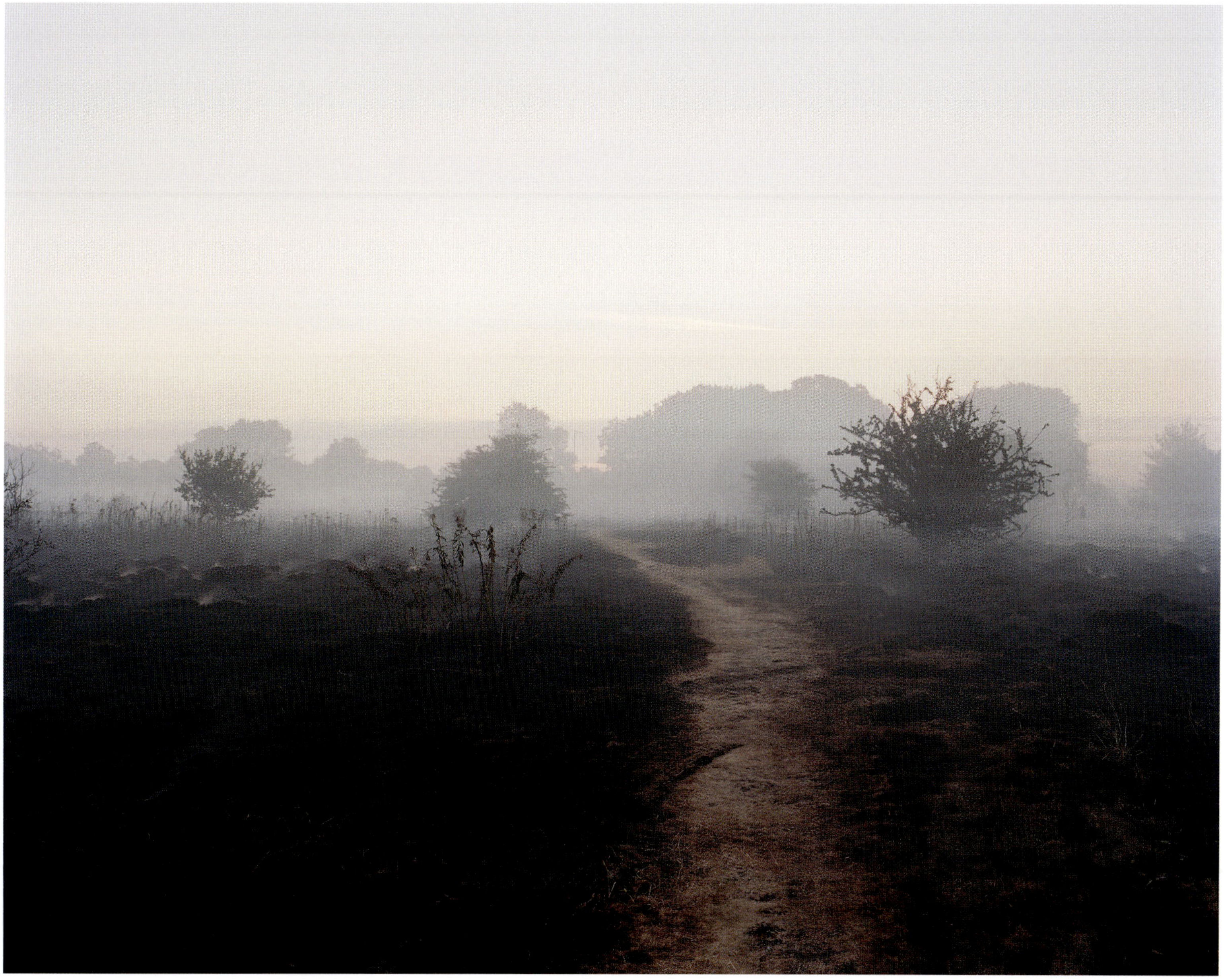

Wanstead Flats, England, July 2018

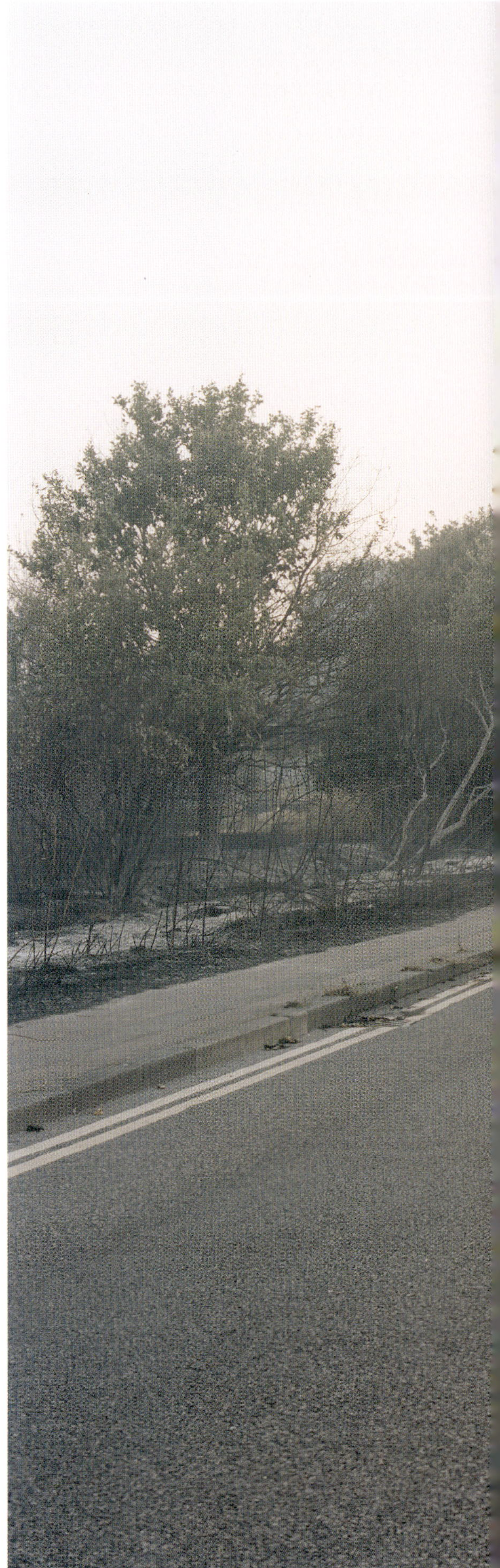

Wanstead Flats, England, July 2018

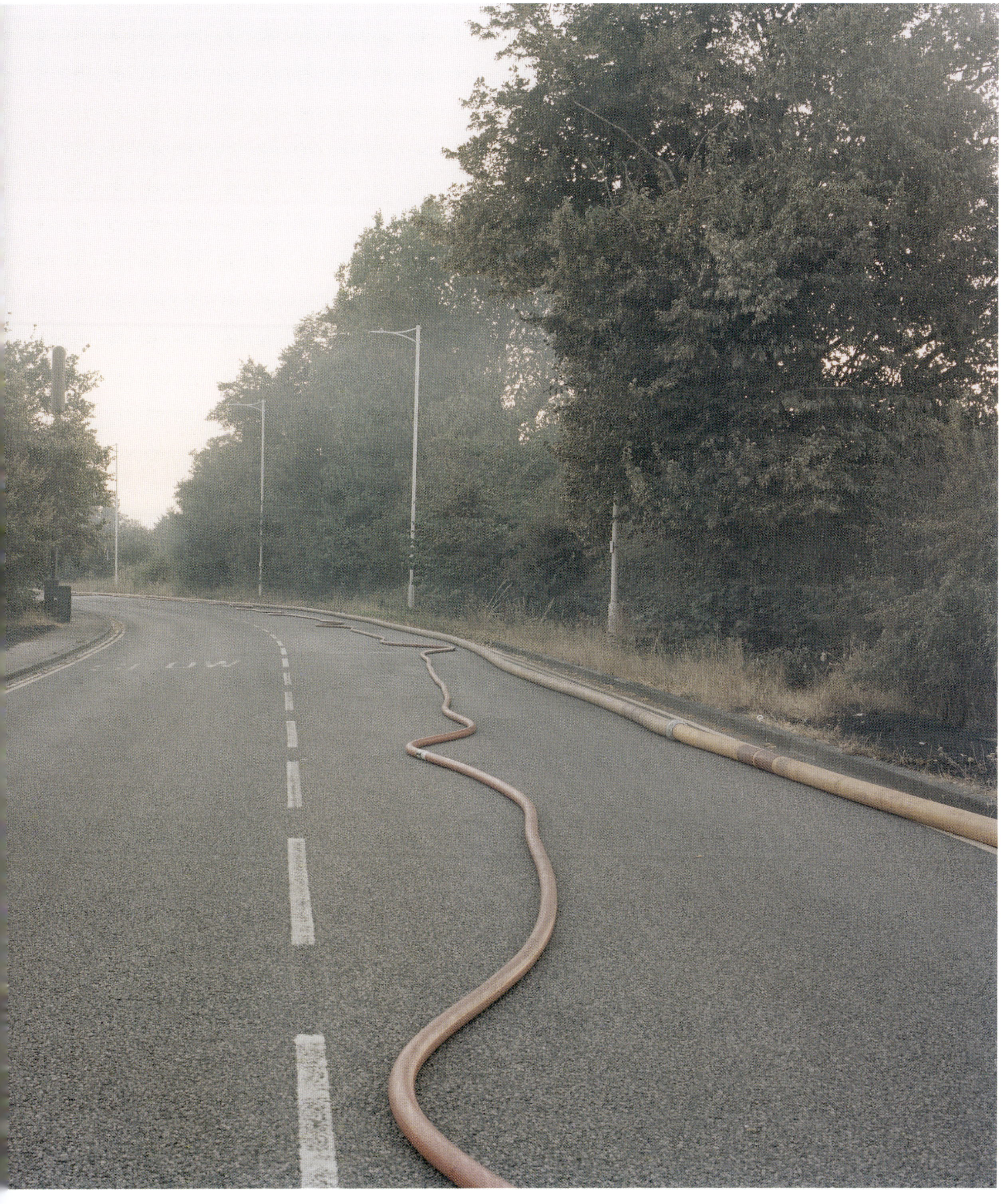
SLOW

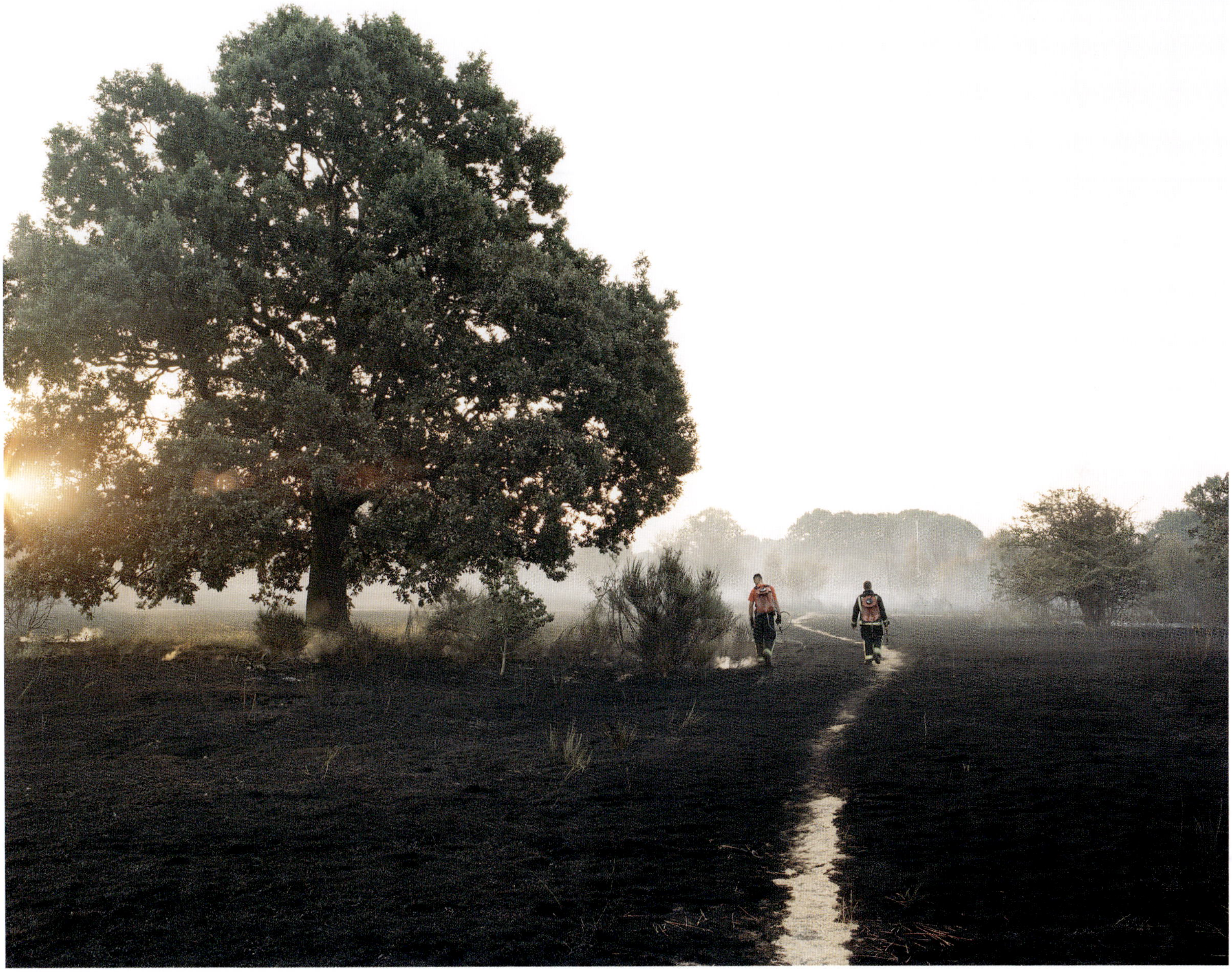

Wanstead Flats, England, July 2018

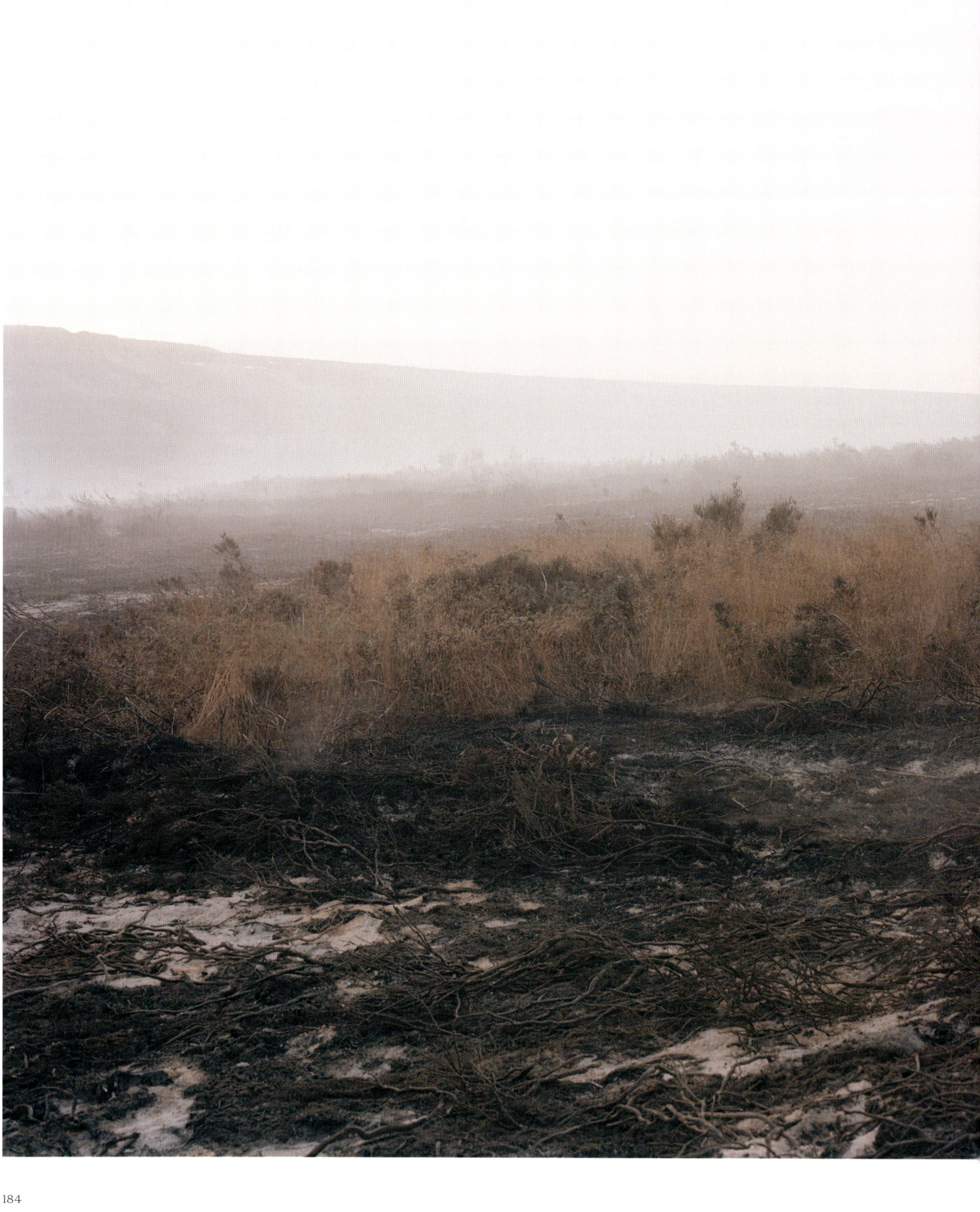

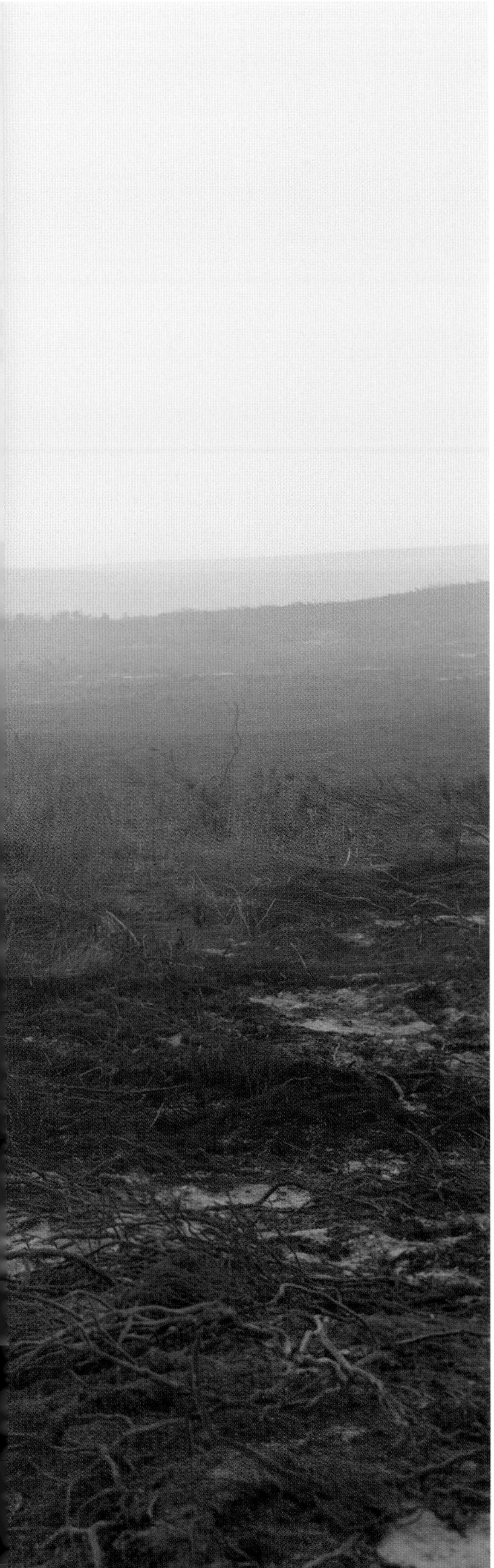

Saddleworth Moor, England, June 2018

Vale

Robert Darch

'That uncanny element was, for me, [a way of] talking about loss. There's something under the surface. There's something there that's not quite right with what you see.'

Illness is often understood as its own kind of landscape. Susan Sontag describes the kingdom of the well and the kingdom of the sick as separate territories. Hilary Mantel wrote about the sickroom as its own terrain: the world reduced to the edges of the bed, and the ceiling stretching above. Robert Darch's *Vale* was created in response to a prolonged period of chronic illness following a minor stroke in his twenties. When the body is incapacitated, the imagination becomes a refuge. Darch found solace in fictive worlds, daydreaming about everything that lay outside the claustrophobic limits of his home. Later, after moving to Devon, he embarked on a project in the surrounding area that brought some of those narratives to life.

Vale tilts between the halcyon and the sinister, imagining Darch's lost time and lost youth through a mixture of portraiture and landscapes. Young people stare uneasily at the camera, at odds with their surroundings. There are shadows in the trees and rotting carcasses on the ground. Despite the constructed nature of various shots, many of these images came about organically. One day, Darch discovered a swarm of bees on a chopped down log, on another, he came across an abandoned house overwhelmed by ivy. These deliberately eerie elements were fine-tuned by taking behind-the-scenes pictures on a horror film, but they also speak to something deeper about rural spaces. For every moment of blue-skied idyll, there is another where the atmosphere shifts and a sense of the unknown descends. There are mysteries that lurk down the lanes and in the depths of our mind, glimpsed out of the corner of one's eye. Blink, and you might just catch them.

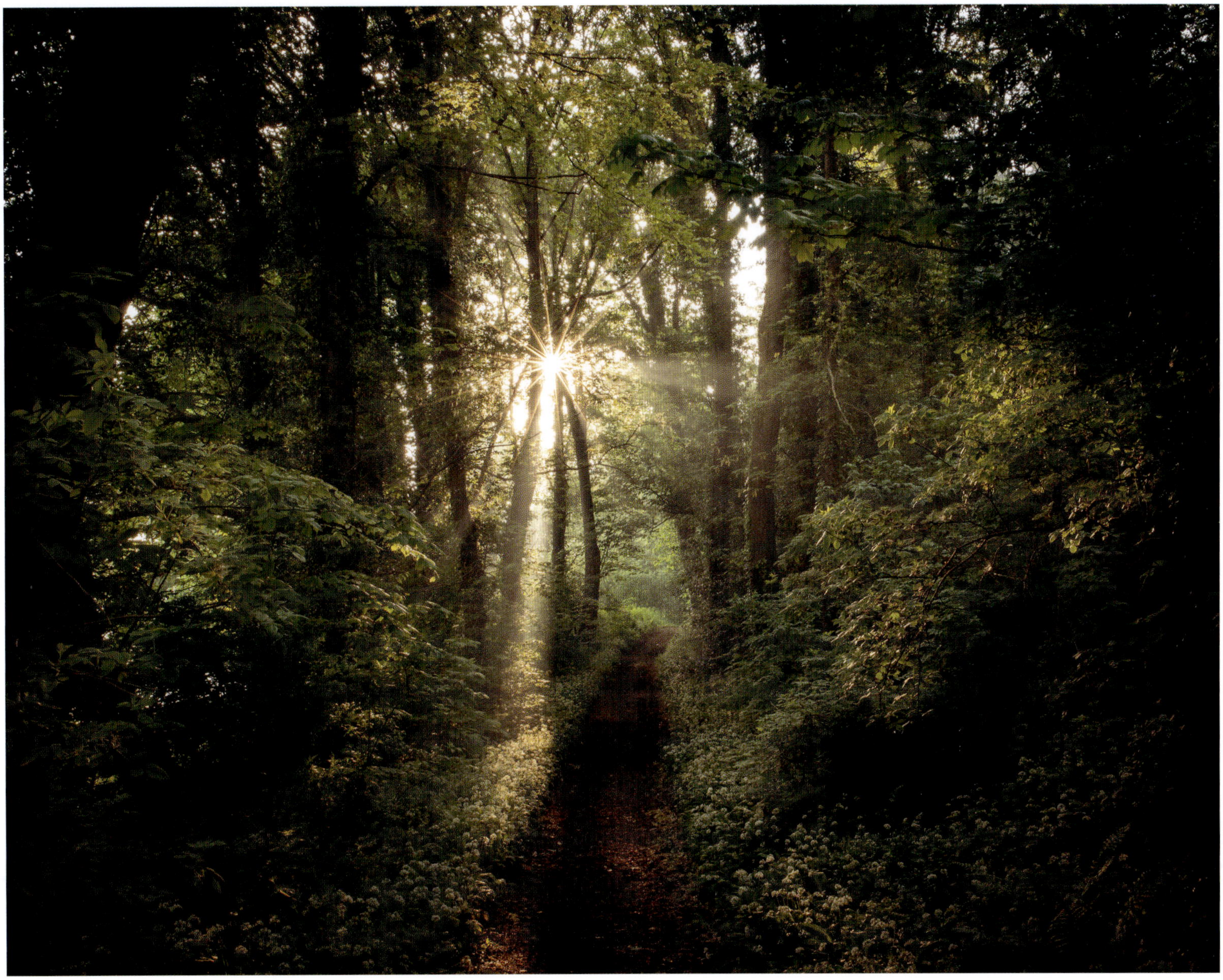

Dawn, Devon, England, 2014

Gus, Oliver and Ben, River Exe, Devon, England, 2014

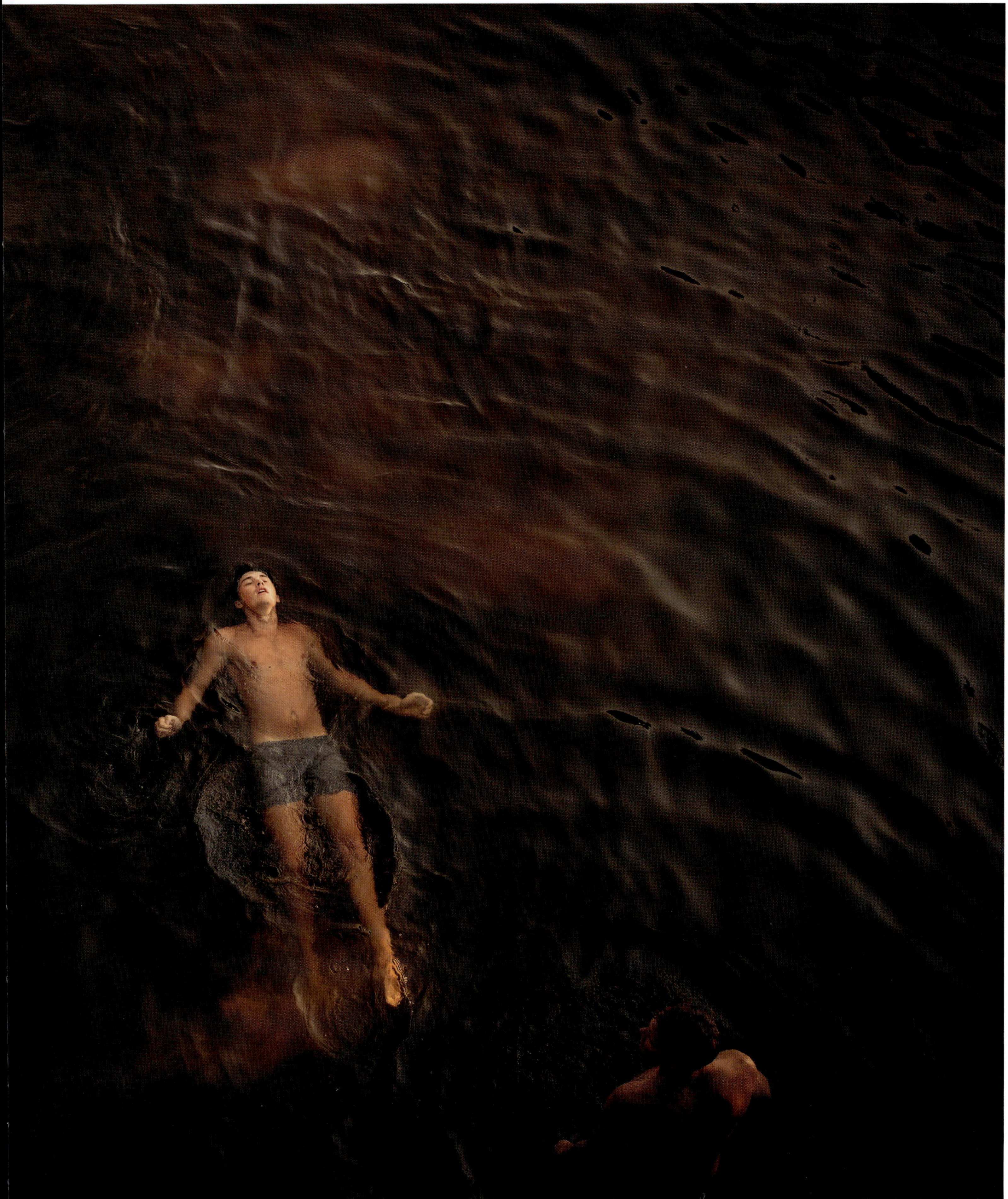

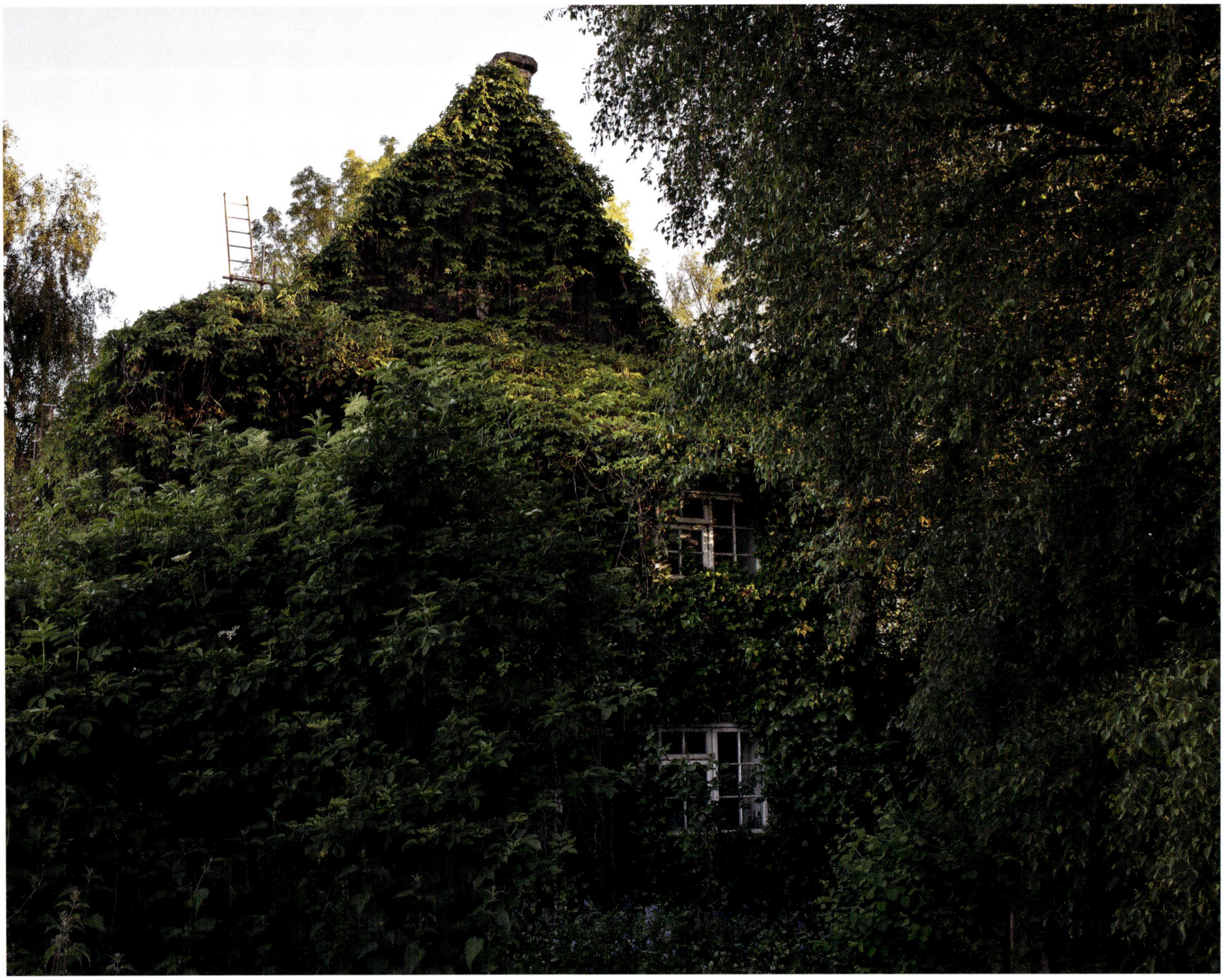

The House, Devon, England, 2014

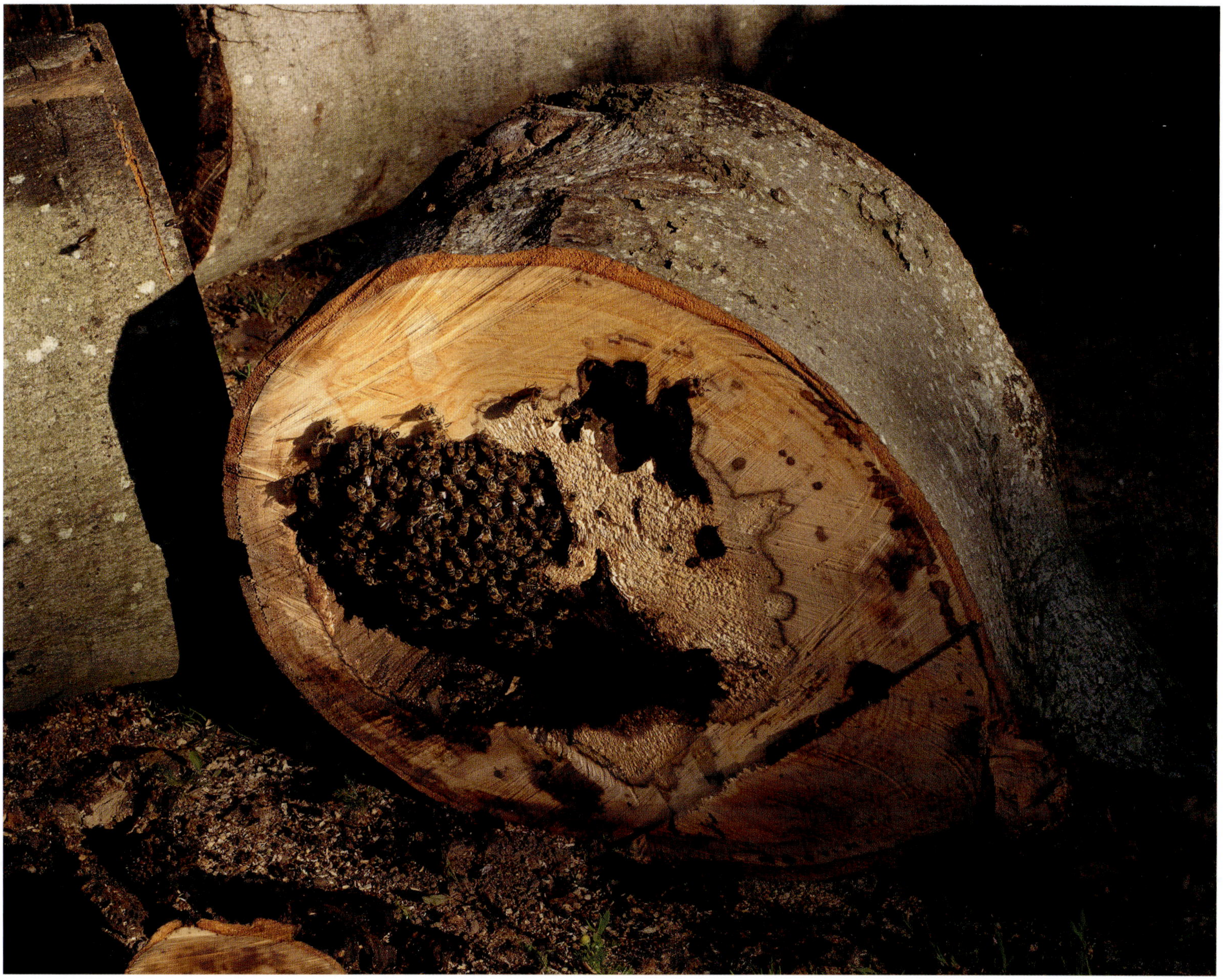

Swarm, Devon, England, 2014

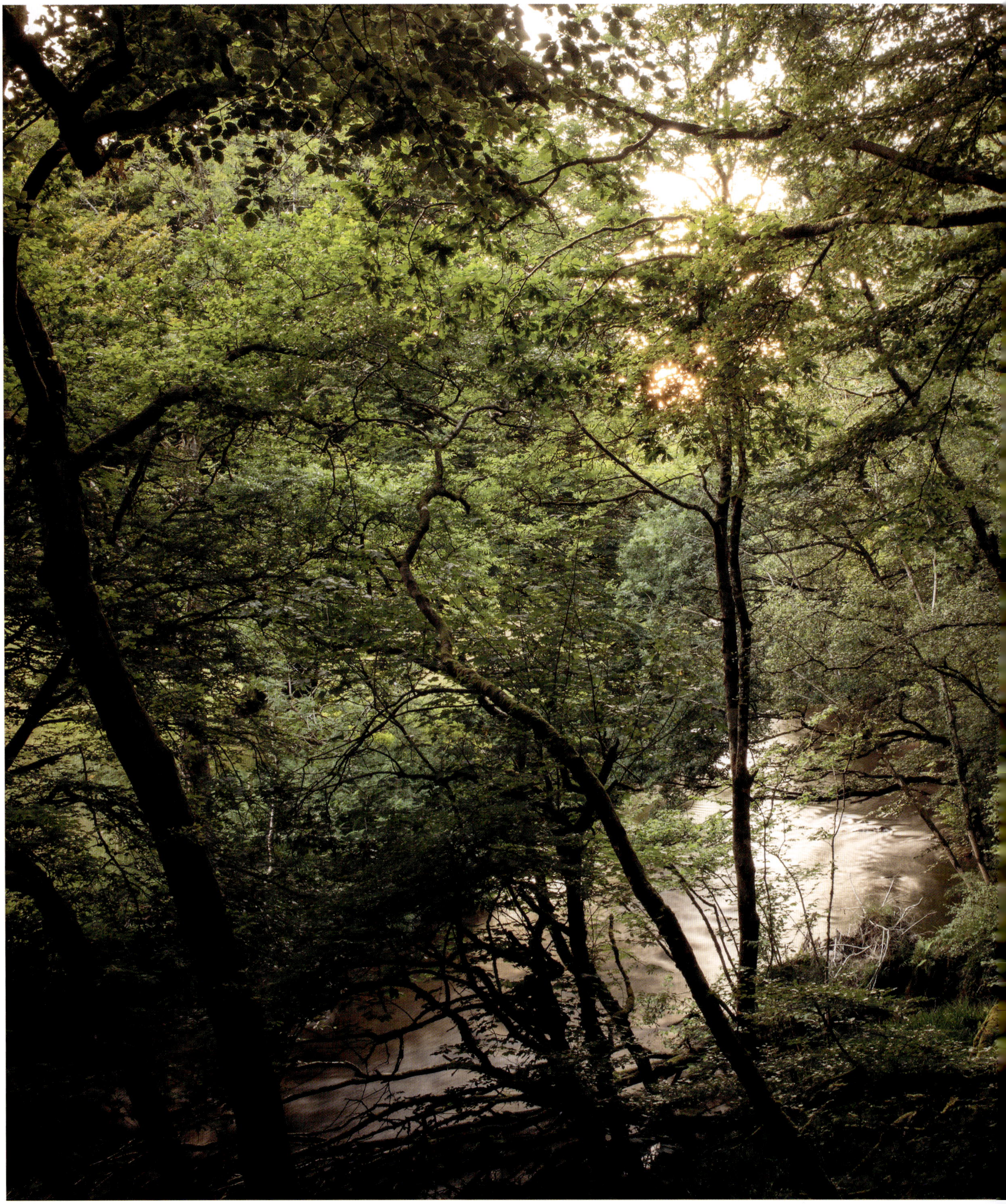

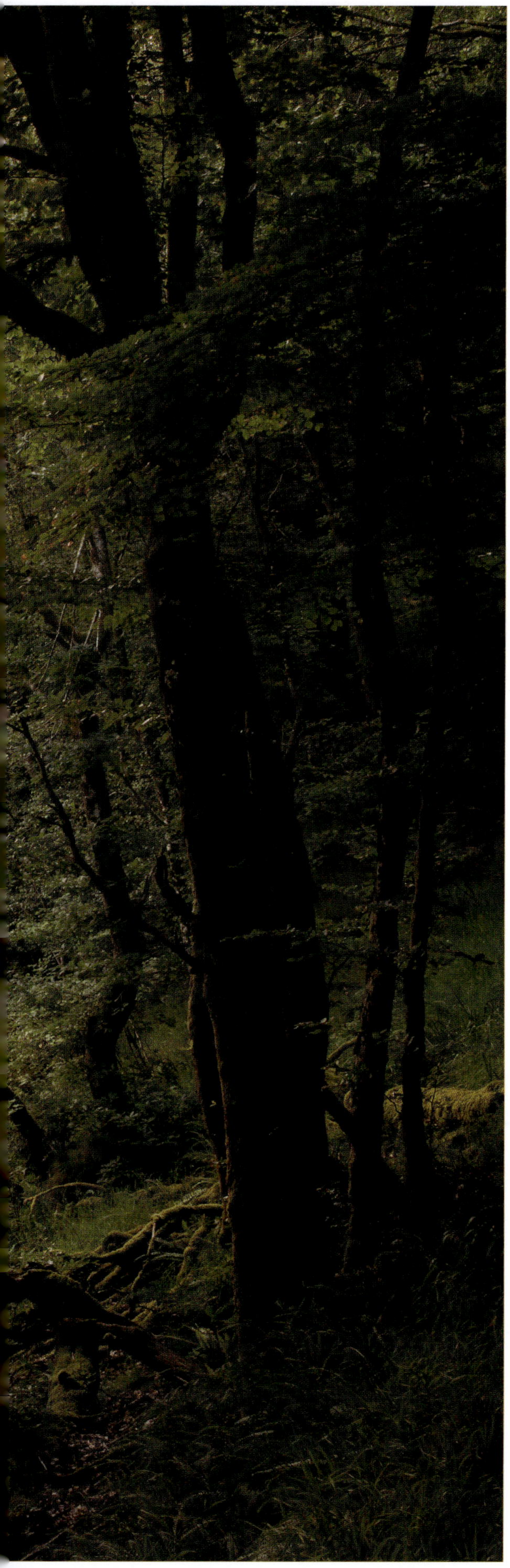

The Barle, Somerset, England, 2014

The Floods

Joseph Wright

'I found it quite calming. To me, it seemed to almost simplify the environment, because a lot of the mess of the woodlands was masked by the water. It was all underneath the surface.'

'What would the world be, once bereft; Of wet and of wildness? Let them be left'. The penultimate lines of Gerard Manley Hopkins' *Inversnaid* come to mind when looking at Joseph Wright's *The Floods*. Wright's photos of his local woodland, hit by heavy rain between 2012 and 2015 are moody, murky, damp images, with trees and bushes erupting from the submerged undergrowth like limbs. Sometimes they are reflected in the stagnant water below, dark doubles reaching out across mist and waterlogged ground.

A flood is a shapeshifter. Like snow, it covers what is usually seen and temporarily alters our known terrain, making it alien, impassable. Most faiths have a flood myth: a story of destruction and cleansing, the world subjected to a deluge so that it can start over again. But the areas photographed by Wright don't seem to be deserving of any special ire or disaster. They are marginal places, found on the edges of towns and villages or hemming roadsides: little strips of nature usually seen in passing through car windows. 'Edgelands' are a general preoccupation for Wright, but these are a local concern too – all the sites pictured are found within walking distance of his home in a village just outside Swindon. When the floods hit, he visited them many times, drawn to this new, swamp-like kingdom. 'As I walk about, things are resolving themselves in my vision and in my mind,' he explains of his process, noting that he found this temporary inundation surprisingly peaceful. Here though, the still waters and strange new world offer only a short-lived resolution, the flood merely a visitor, leaving mud and mess in its wake when it finally retreats.

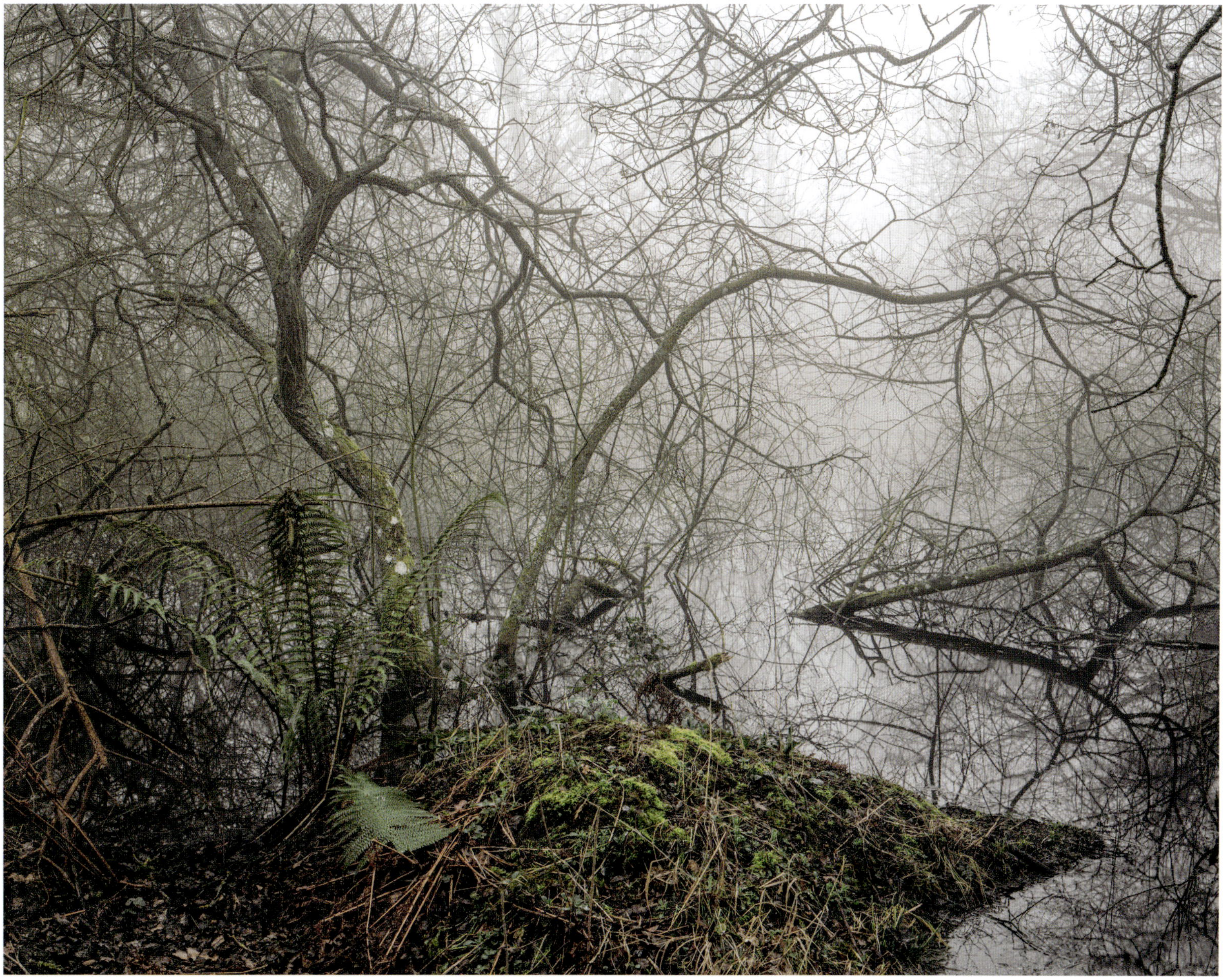

The Floods #06, North Wiltshire, England, 2014

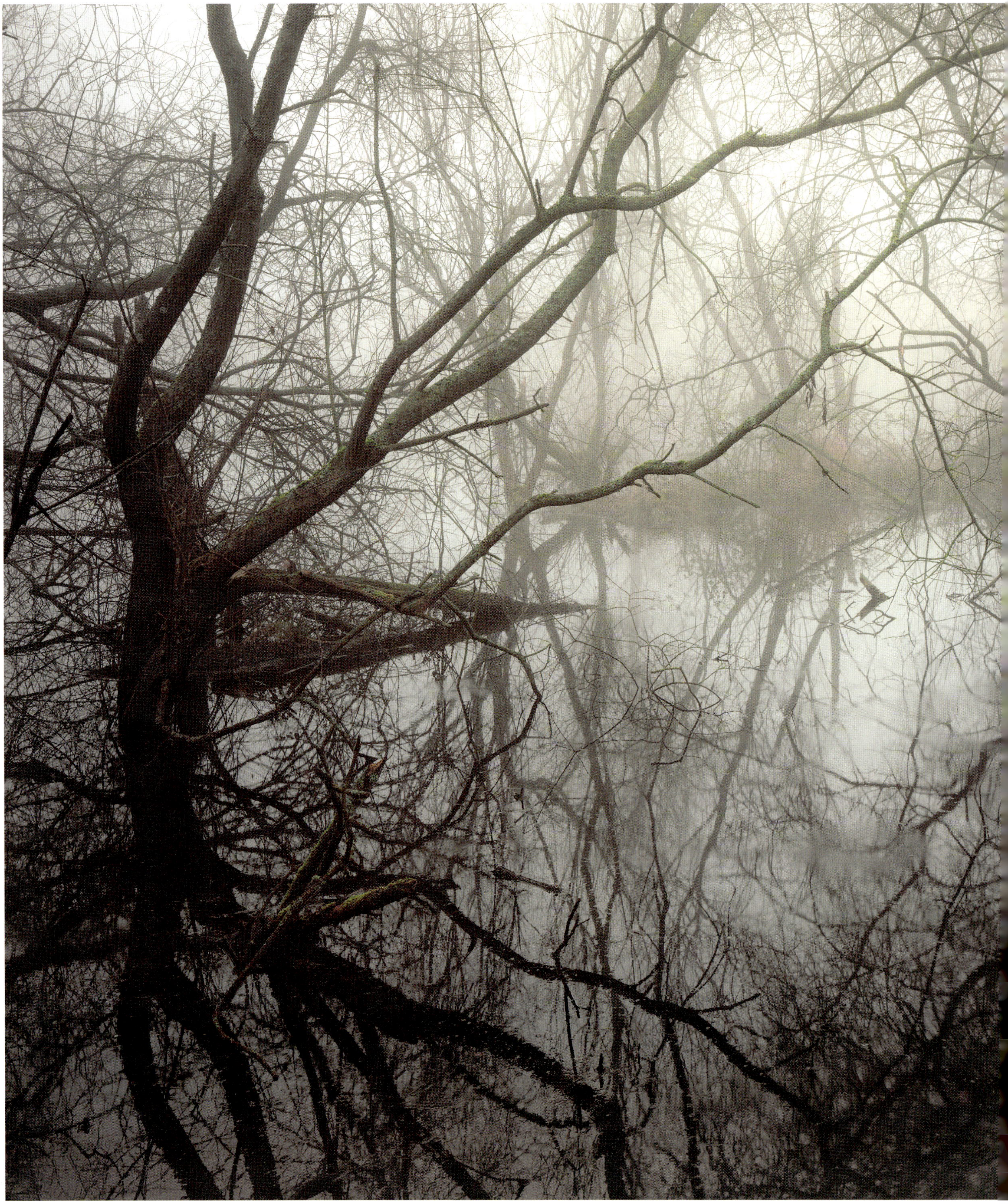

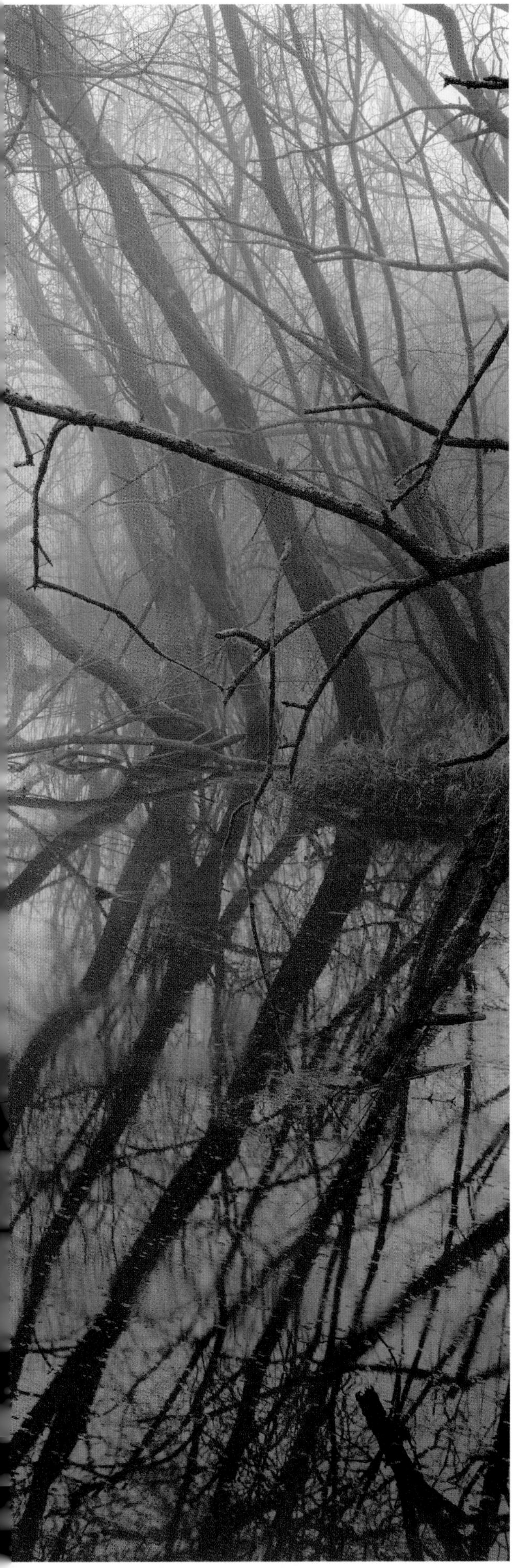

The Floods #01, North Wiltshire, England, 2014

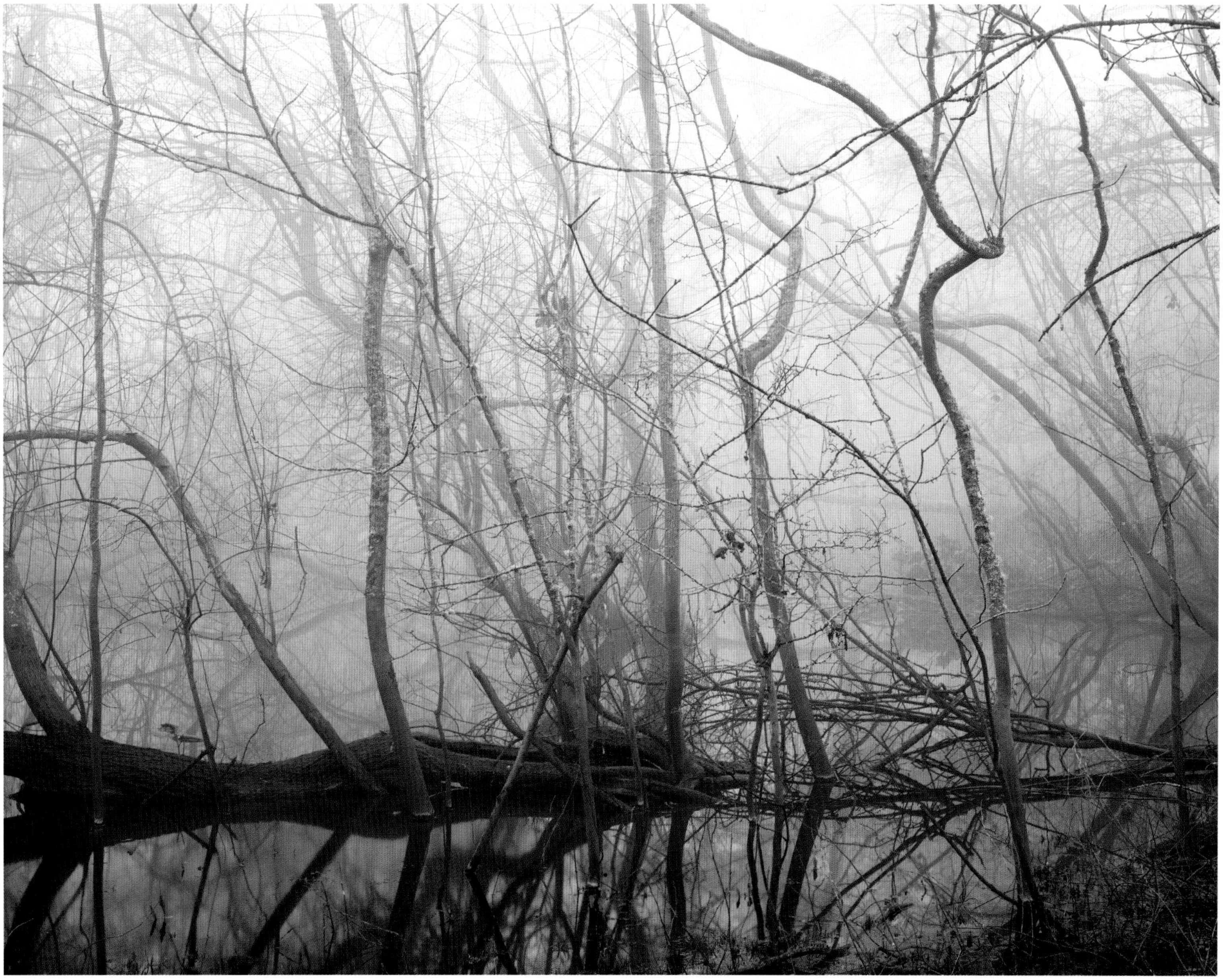

The Floods #05, North Wiltshire, England, 2014

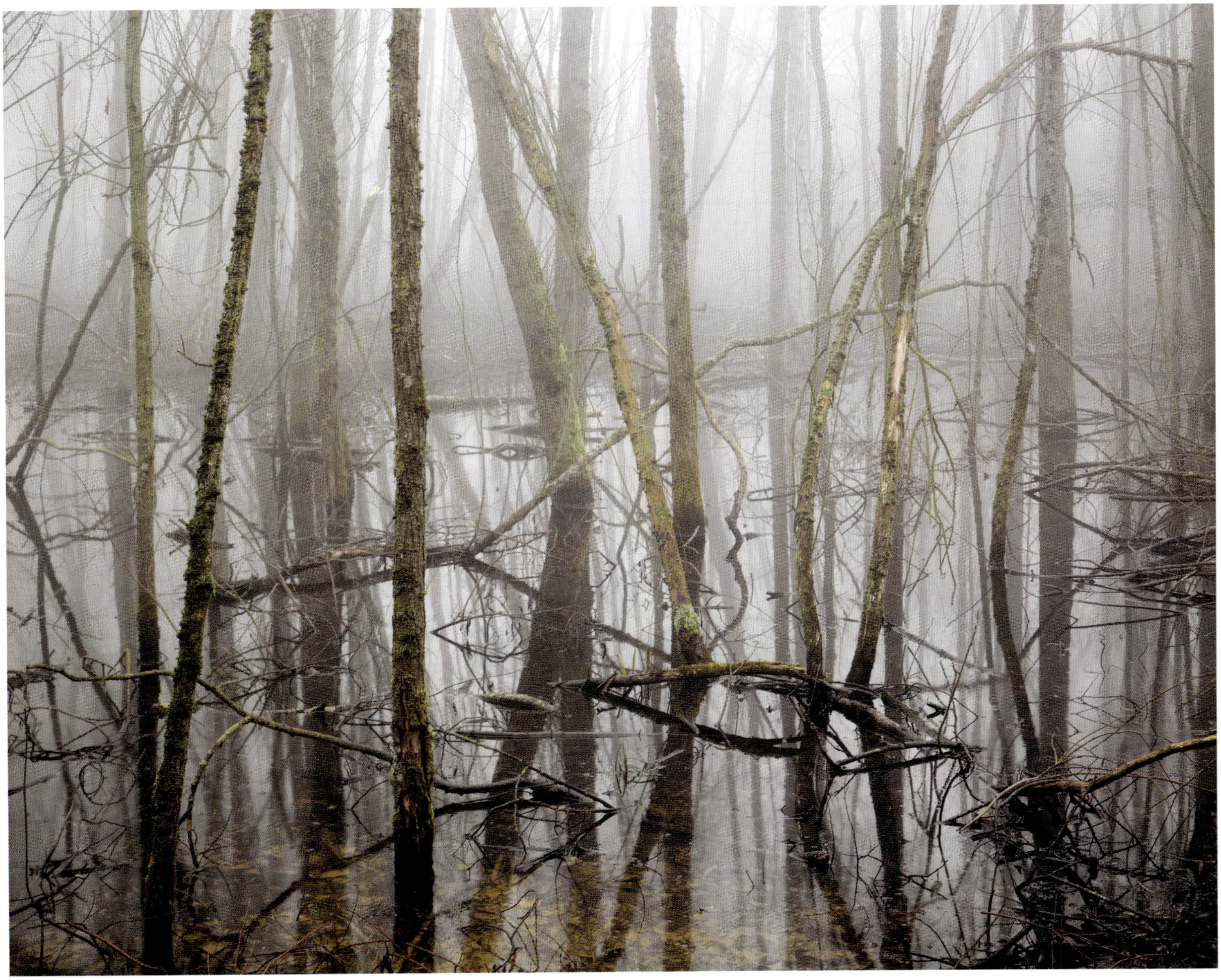

The Floods #02, North Wiltshire, England, 2014

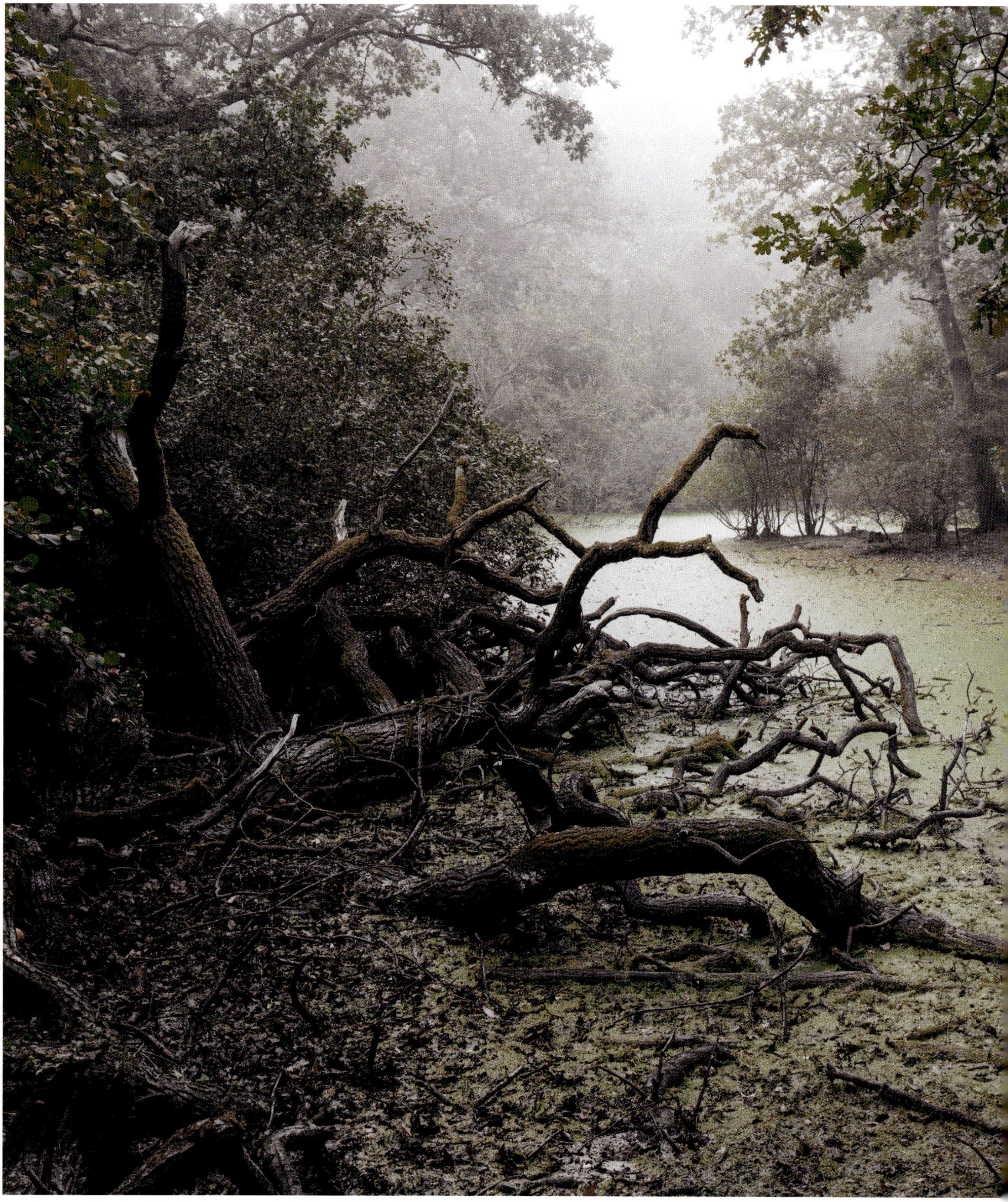

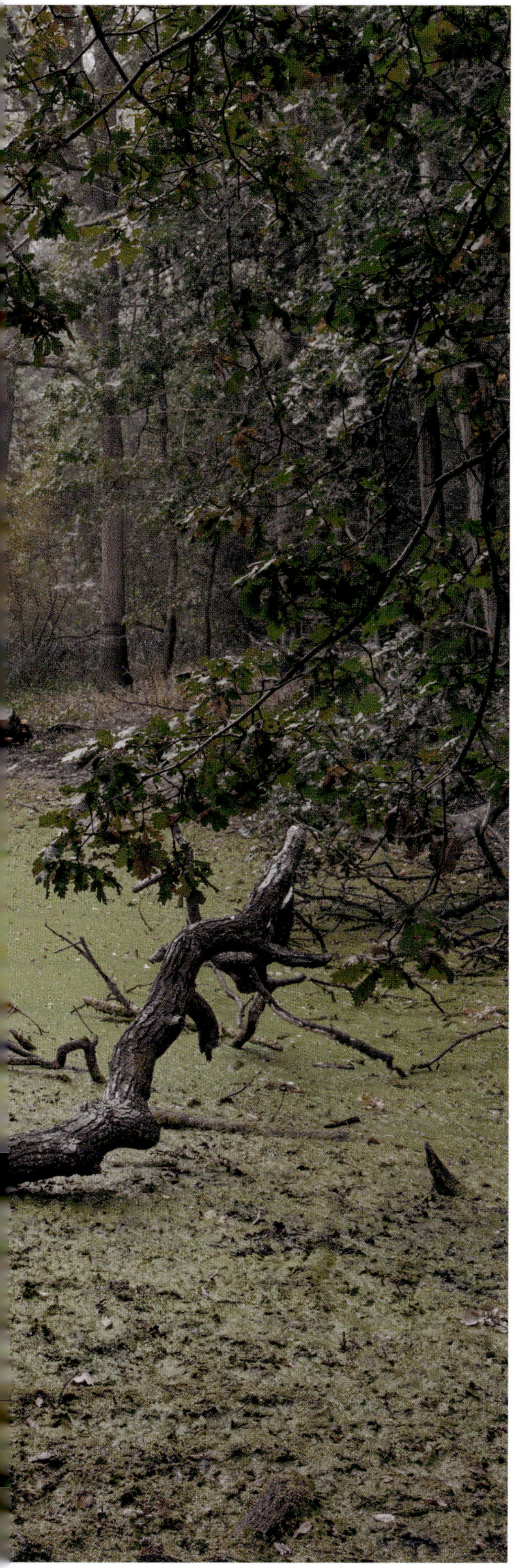

The Floods #30, North Wiltshire, England, 2014

The Moth

Jem Southam

'The stories that we carry in our heads about the world that we live in map on to the world that we travel through.'

Jem Southam is a storyteller. His work rewards those who return to it, digging down into the layers and excavating previously unnoticed details. *The Moth* (1983-2018) begins with a photo taken over thirty years ago of a solitary man on a beach, his face turned away towards the waves. Southam wanted to construct a narrative exploring what this man could be imagining. The idea came, in part, from time Southam spent with his brother, who was living in a care home with dementia. Southam imagined his brother's mind to be a little like the tin mines that riddle Cornwall's landscape, full of caverns and holes. His images, featuring that same landscape, take on the elegiac aura of a distant, vividly remembered time.

Much of his work involves returning to the same site to develop a deep and evolving relationship with the land. In doing so, Southam assesses his own response to the images he's taking and environments he's absorbing. What myths and references do we carry with us, superimposed on what we see? How do we filter this external realm through the web of tales, clues, religious texts, traditions, known histories, shared symbols and folkloric ideas that are woven into individual perception?

The resulting large format photographs never veer into nostalgia, but rather hint at something both lost and eternal. It is a Blakeian vision of England, unafraid of darkness, even when suffused with light. Southam, who is also Professor of Photography at the University of Plymouth, combines academic precision of thought with something wordless, something that can be felt before it is necessarily understood. These images are akin to a dream sequence, the known world refracted and retold in richly coloured fragments.

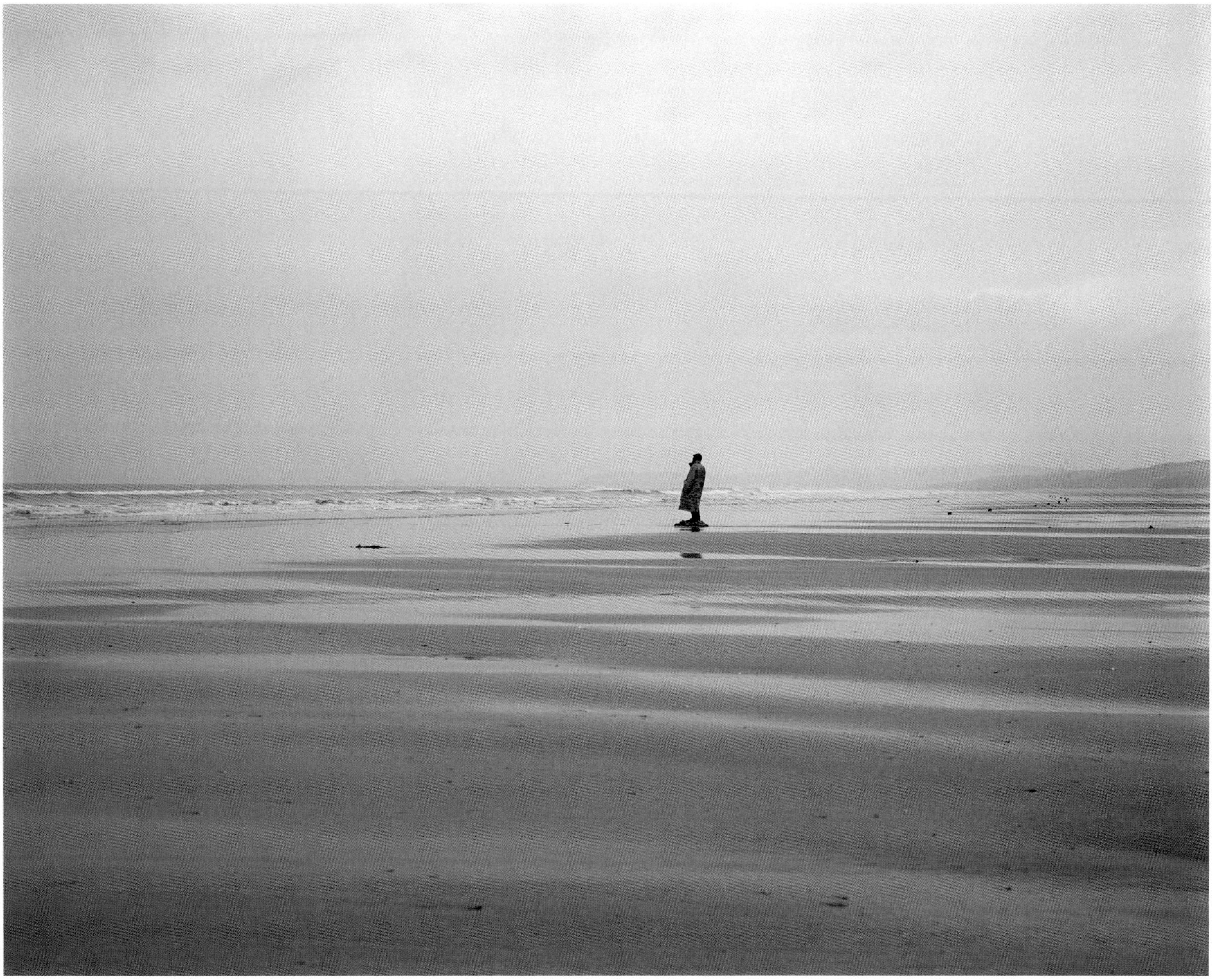

Man on the Shore, Gwithian, Cornwall, England

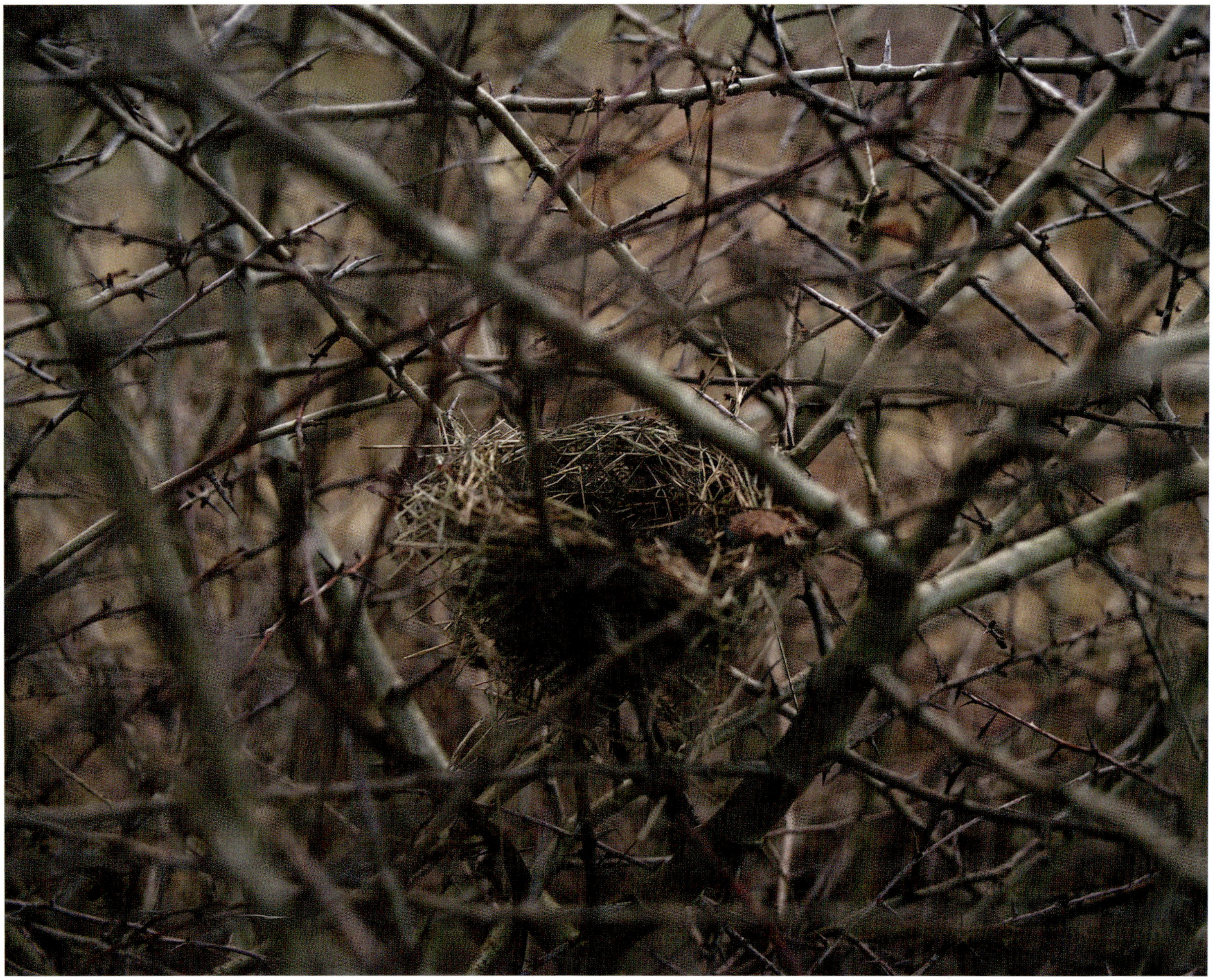

The Nest, Red River Valley, Cornwall, England

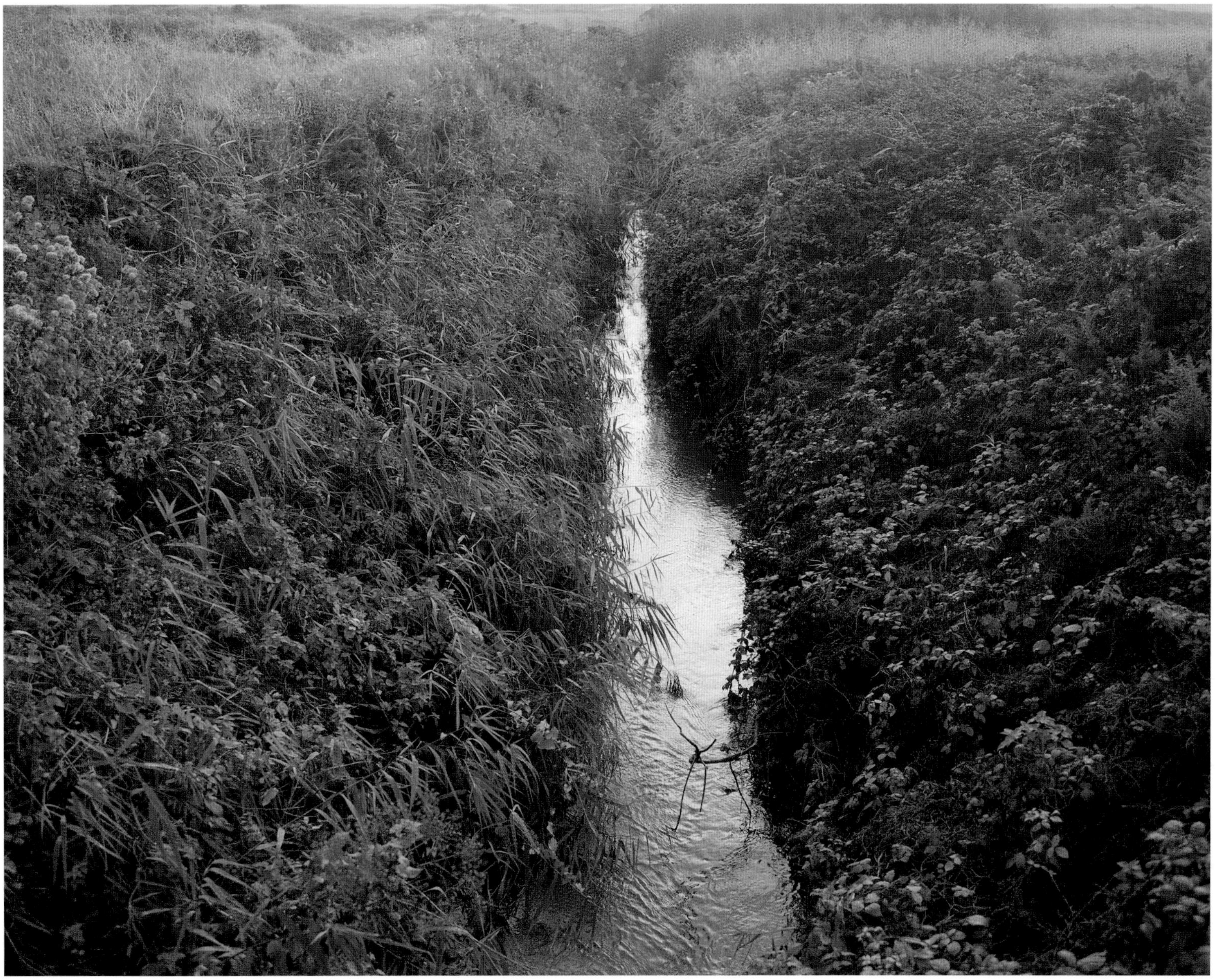

Red River, approaching Godrevy, Cornwall, England

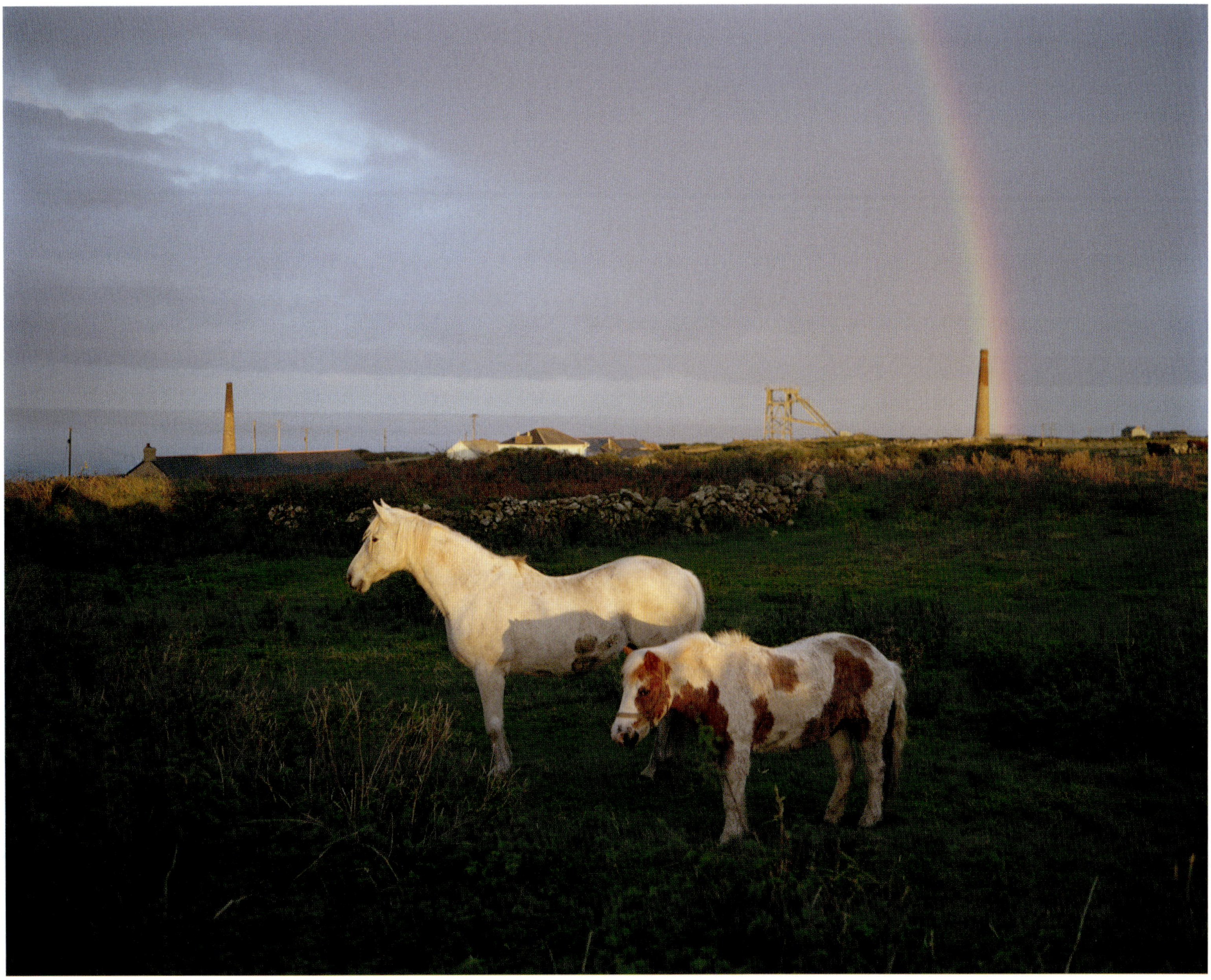

Two Horses, Pendeen, Cornwall, England

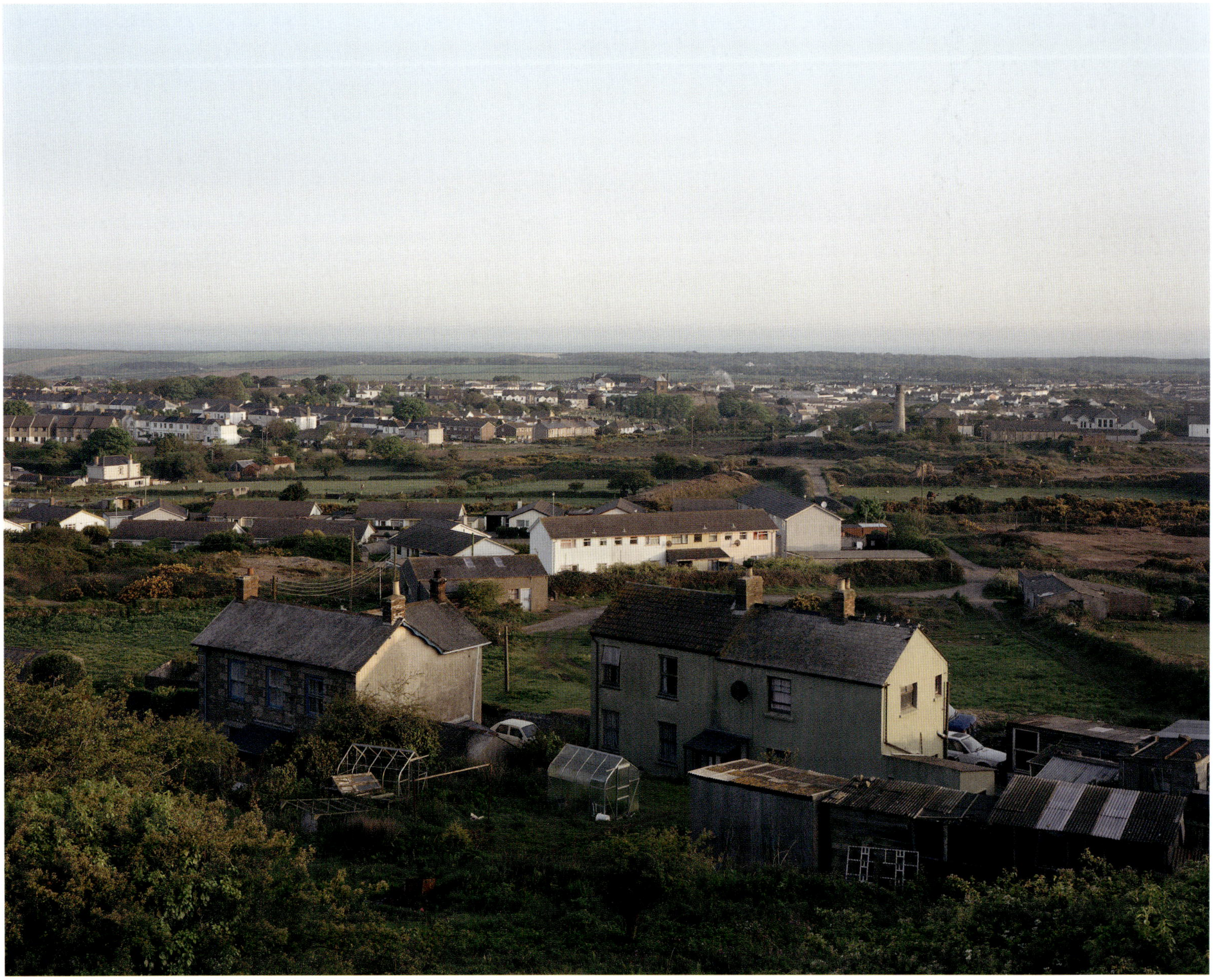

Dolcoath, Cornwall, England

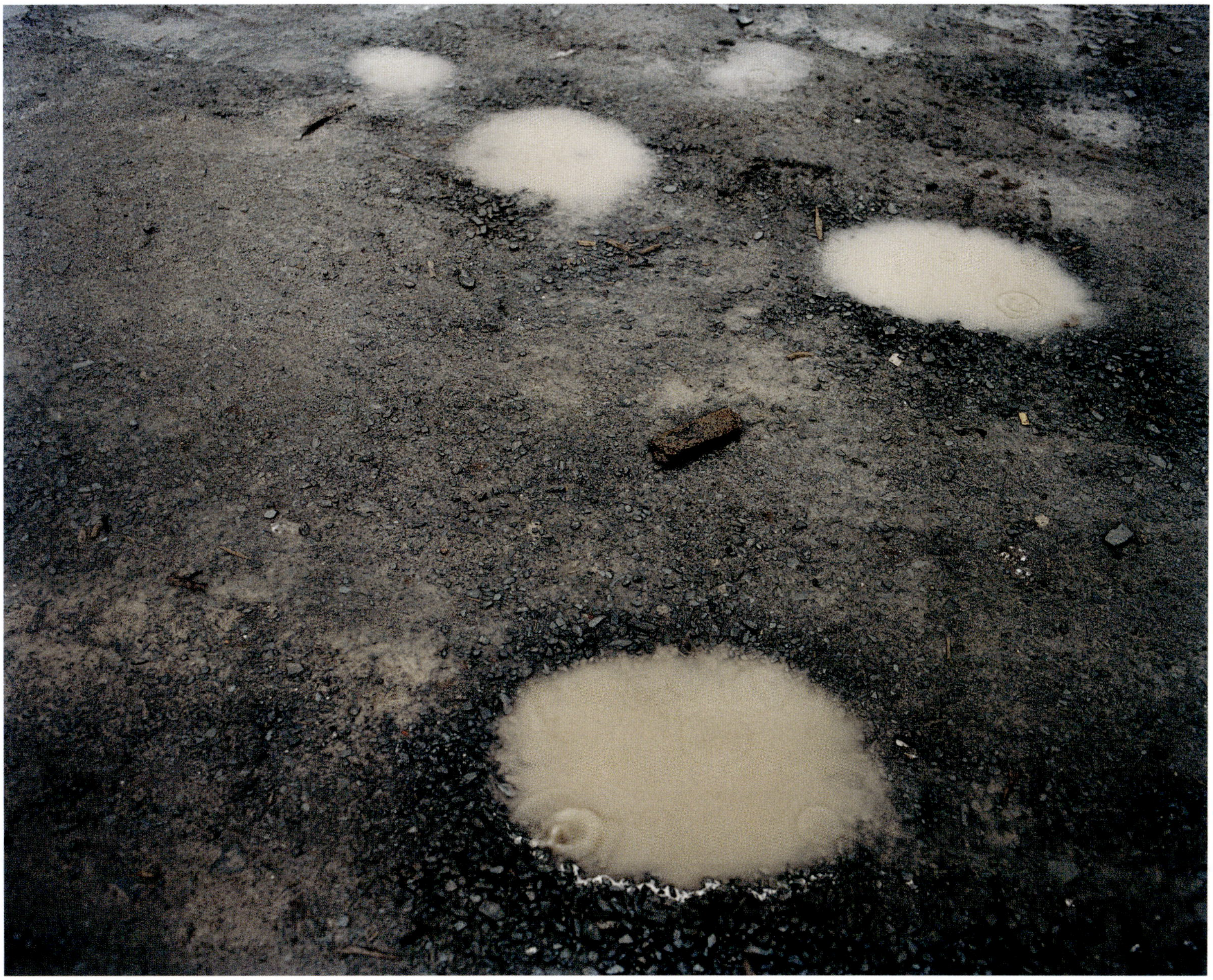

Puddles, Tuckingmill, Cornwall, England

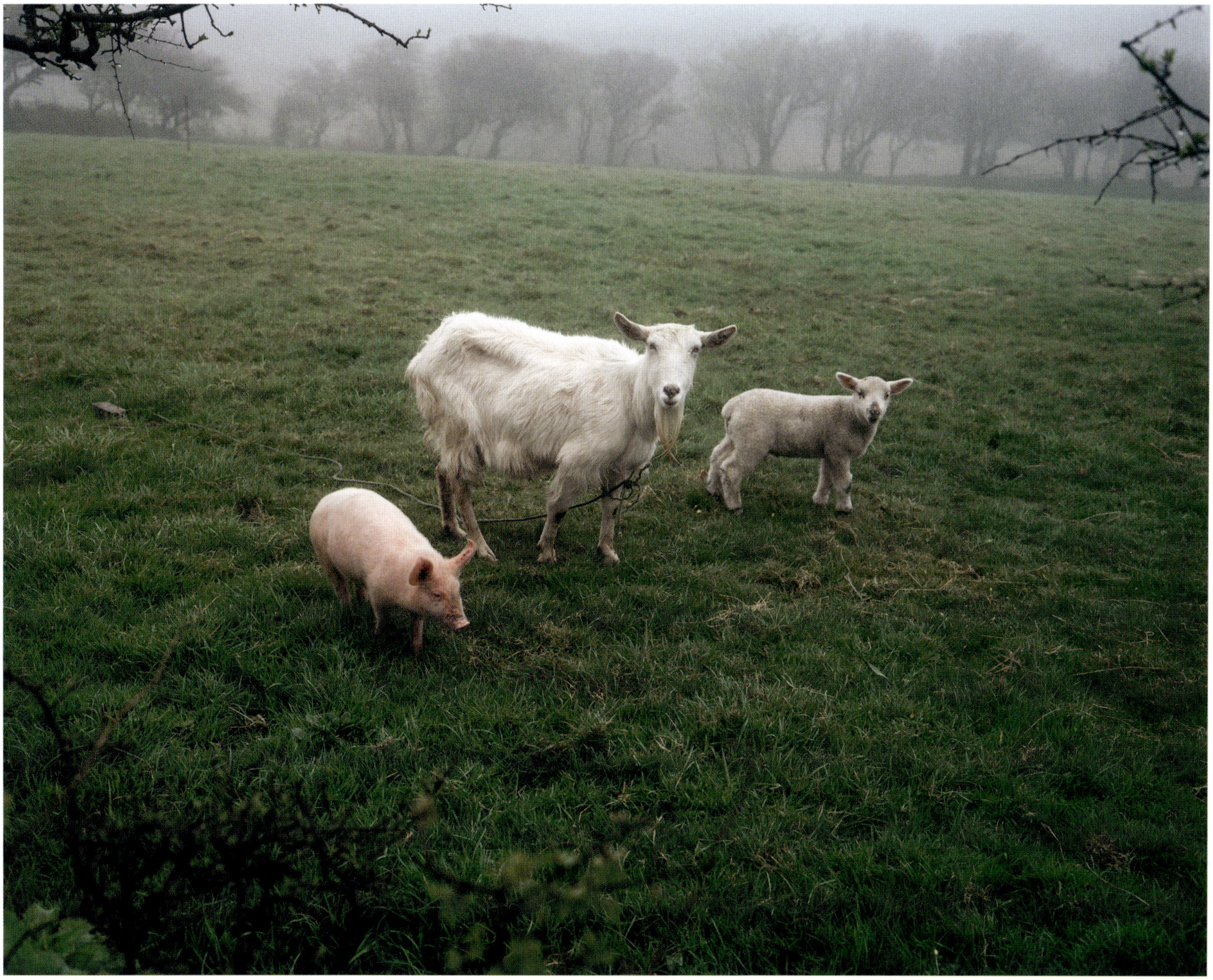

The Pig, the Lamb and the Goat, Bolenowe, Cornwall, England

Sensation of Landscape

Harry Cory Wright

'When you press the button, it's special: a little bit reverent, a little preconceived, a little loaded. It's expensive. This feeds into a feeling that you're elevating what you're seeing.'

Harry Cory Wright's photographs induce a sense of wonder. There is something in the vigour of the colours, the span of the skies, the clarity of each individual head of blossom or blade of grass, that provokes a response at once bodily and imaginative. Perhaps it is a yearning, as though we too want to be plunged into the salt sting of the dunes or follow the paths that disappear into mist. These photos recall the formalism of classical paintings, the half-remembered lines from poems that lodge themselves deep in our memory. No wonder that Wright's latest book is titled *Sensation of Landscape*. For the photographer, this sensation is something first felt by him, then passed on to the viewer – a reverent sharing of what was, initially, a private moment.

Wright uses three different 10x8 inch cameras: heavy, tactile tools. For the last twenty-five years, he has favoured the same 240mm wide angle lens, compressing time and space with each, decisive click. The darkroom was, for most of his career, the crucial next stage, with its alchemy of chemicals and ritual use of shadows and light. But as processing becomes more challenging and digital technologies expand, Wright has embraced the possibilities of working with high-end digital scans made from his negatives. All the craft and verve remain – in fact, it has been heightened and made more robust, new technical horizons offering a fresh vitality, another way of looking at images both old and new.

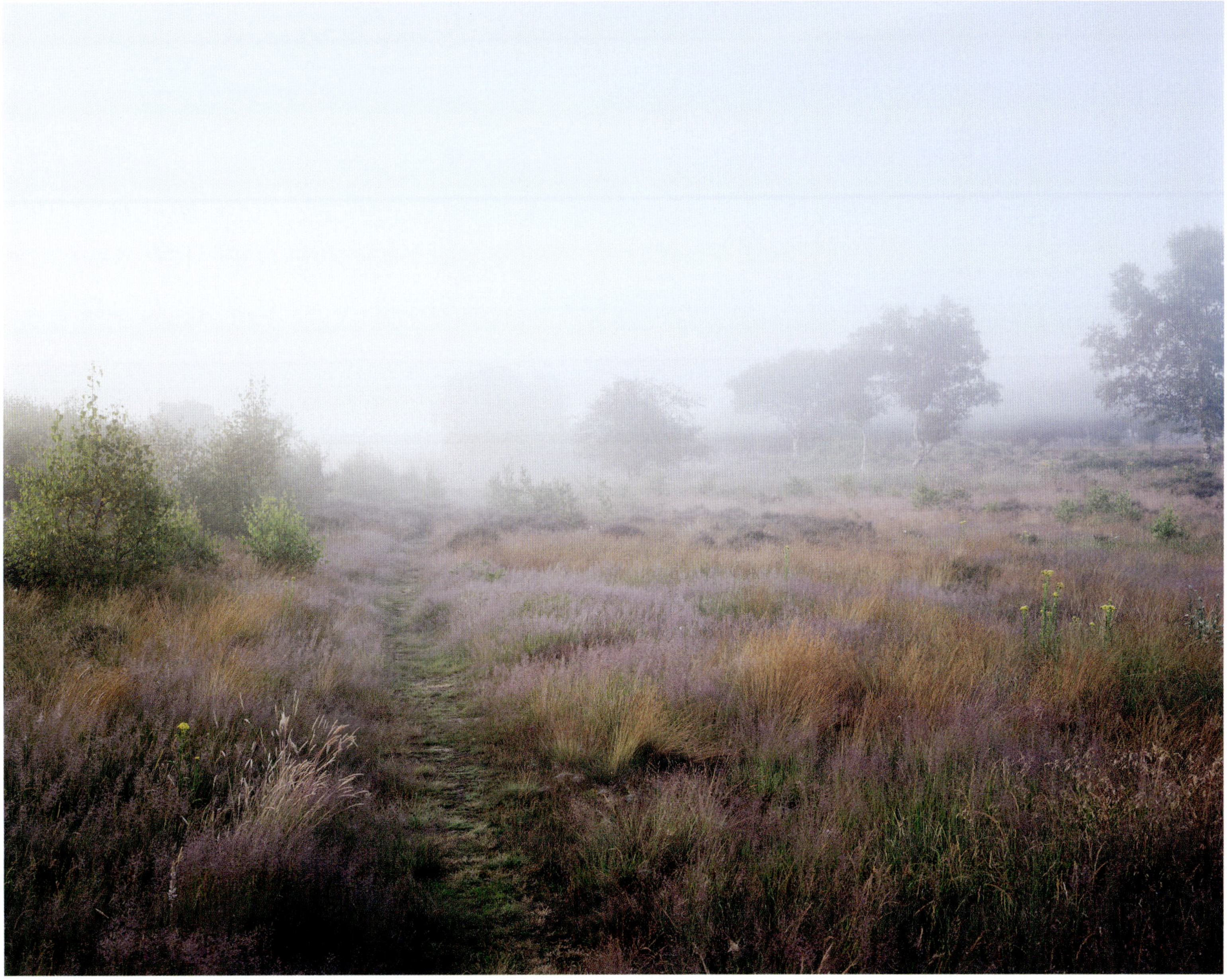

Heath Sunrise, Dunwich, Suffolk, England, 2019

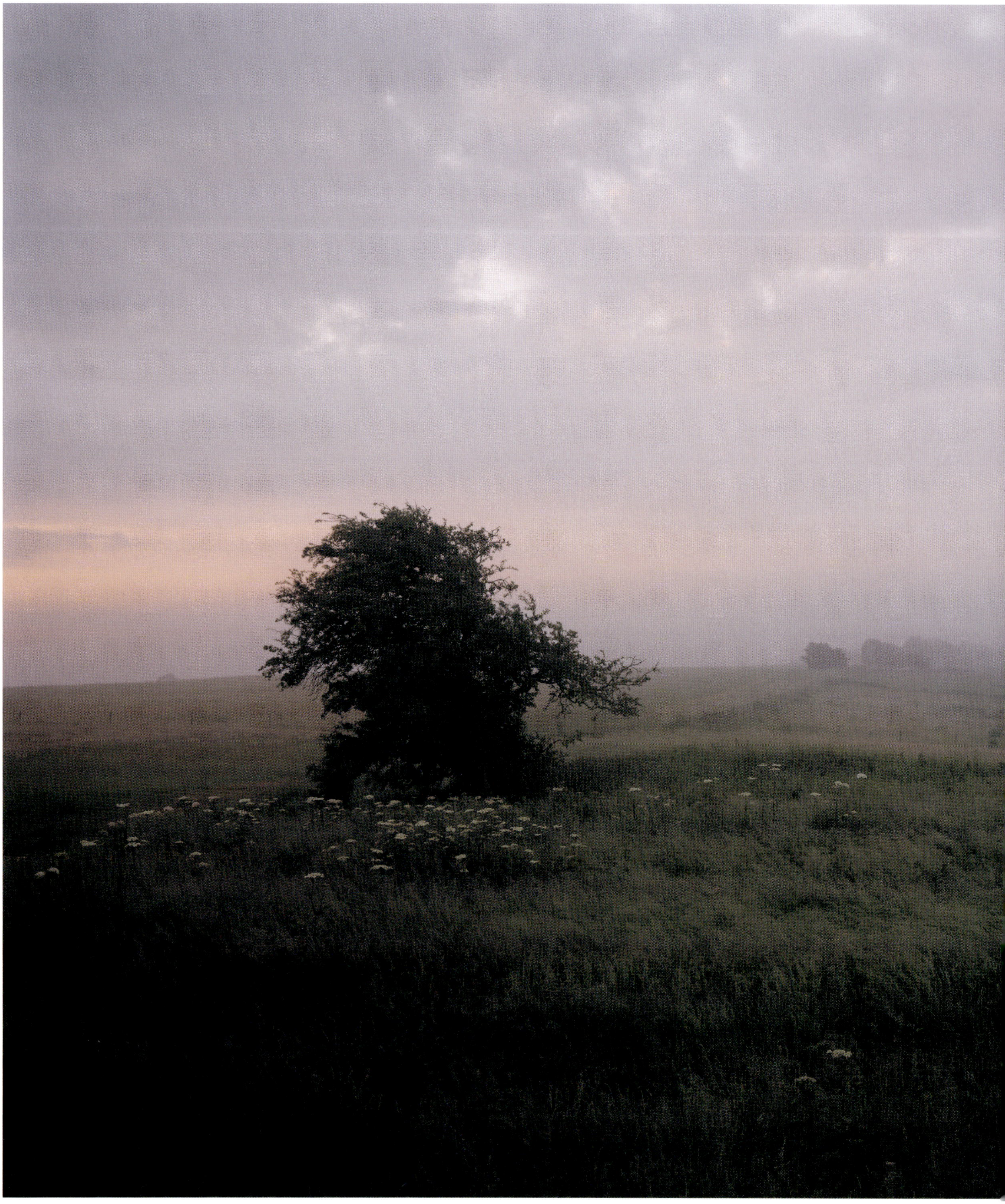

Barbury Castle, Journey through the British Isles, Marlborough Downs, England, 2006

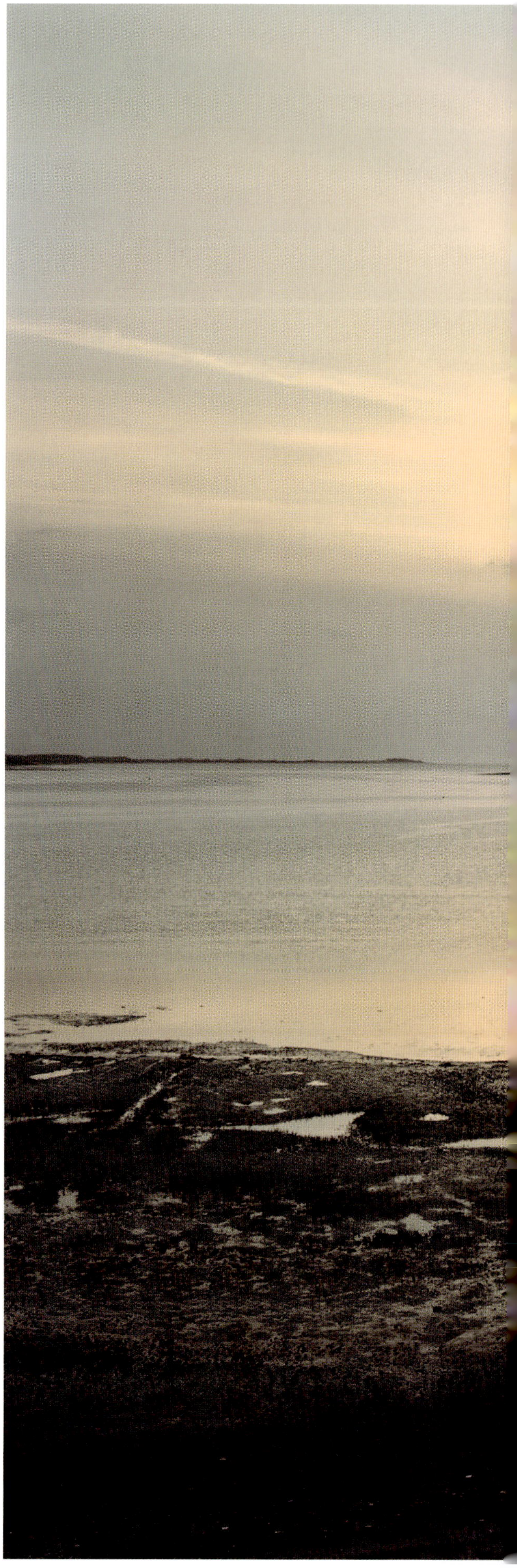

Exposed Flats, North Norfolk, England, 1998

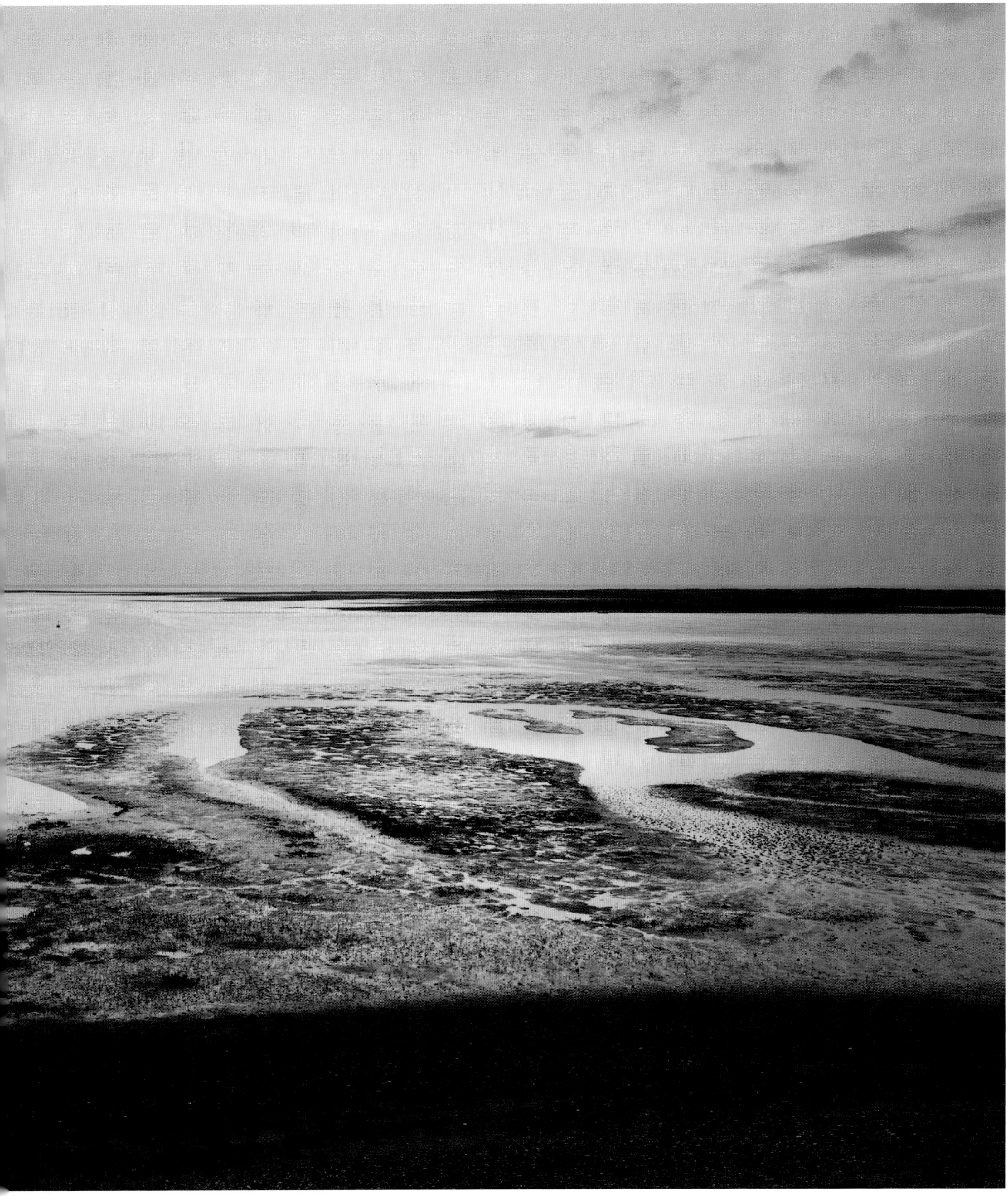

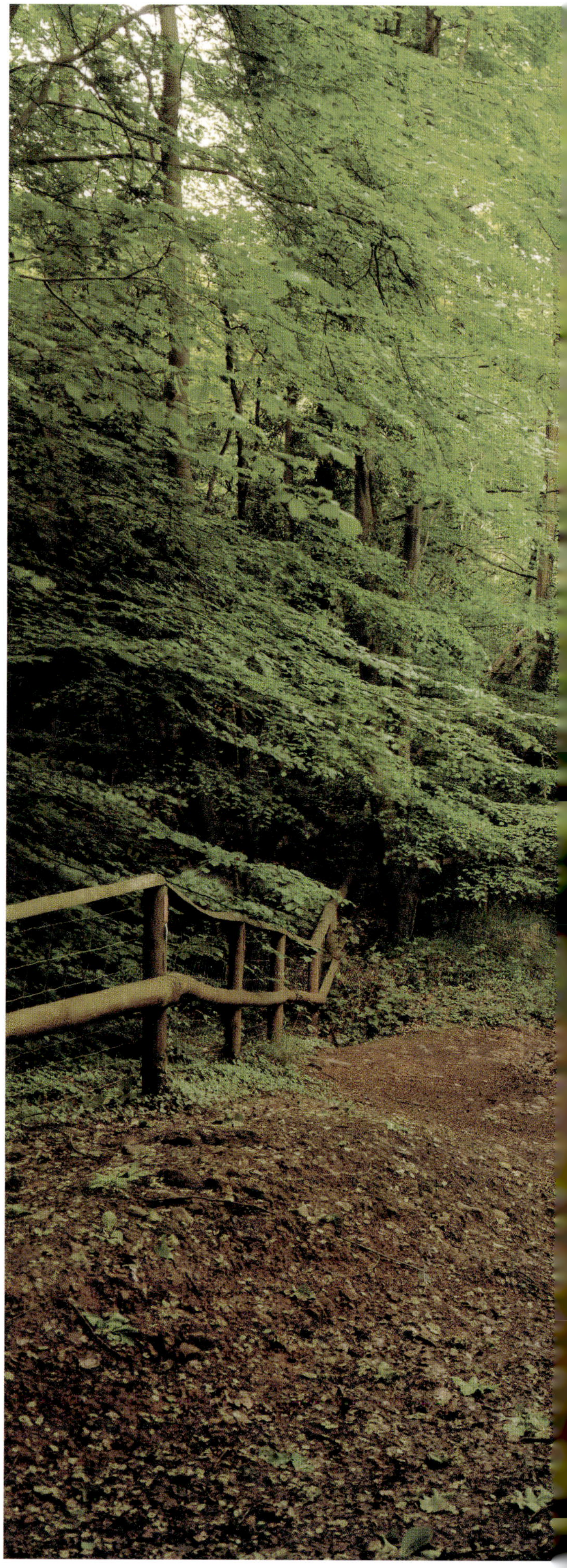

Holly and Beech, Day 67, Wye Valley, England, 25 May 2006

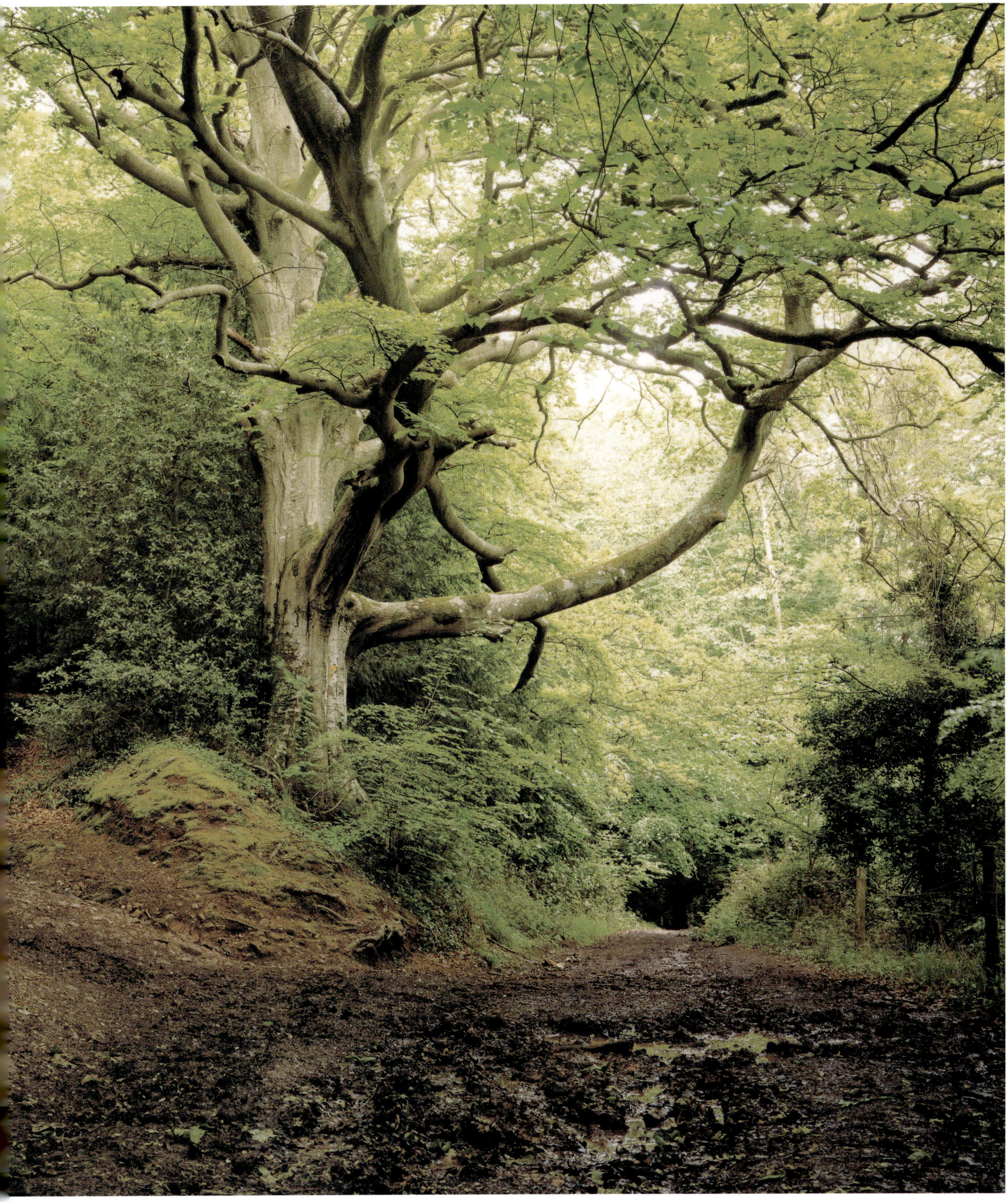

Morning Gold, North Sea from Suffolk coast, England, 2019

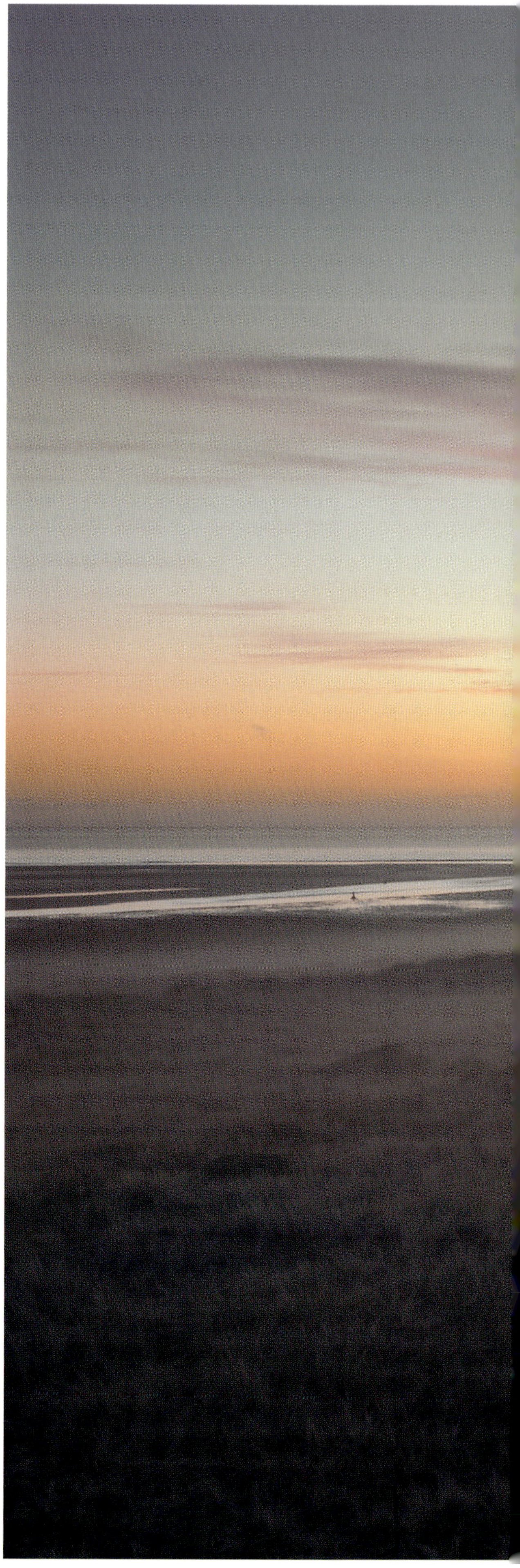

Norfolk Dunes, North Norfolk, England, 2020

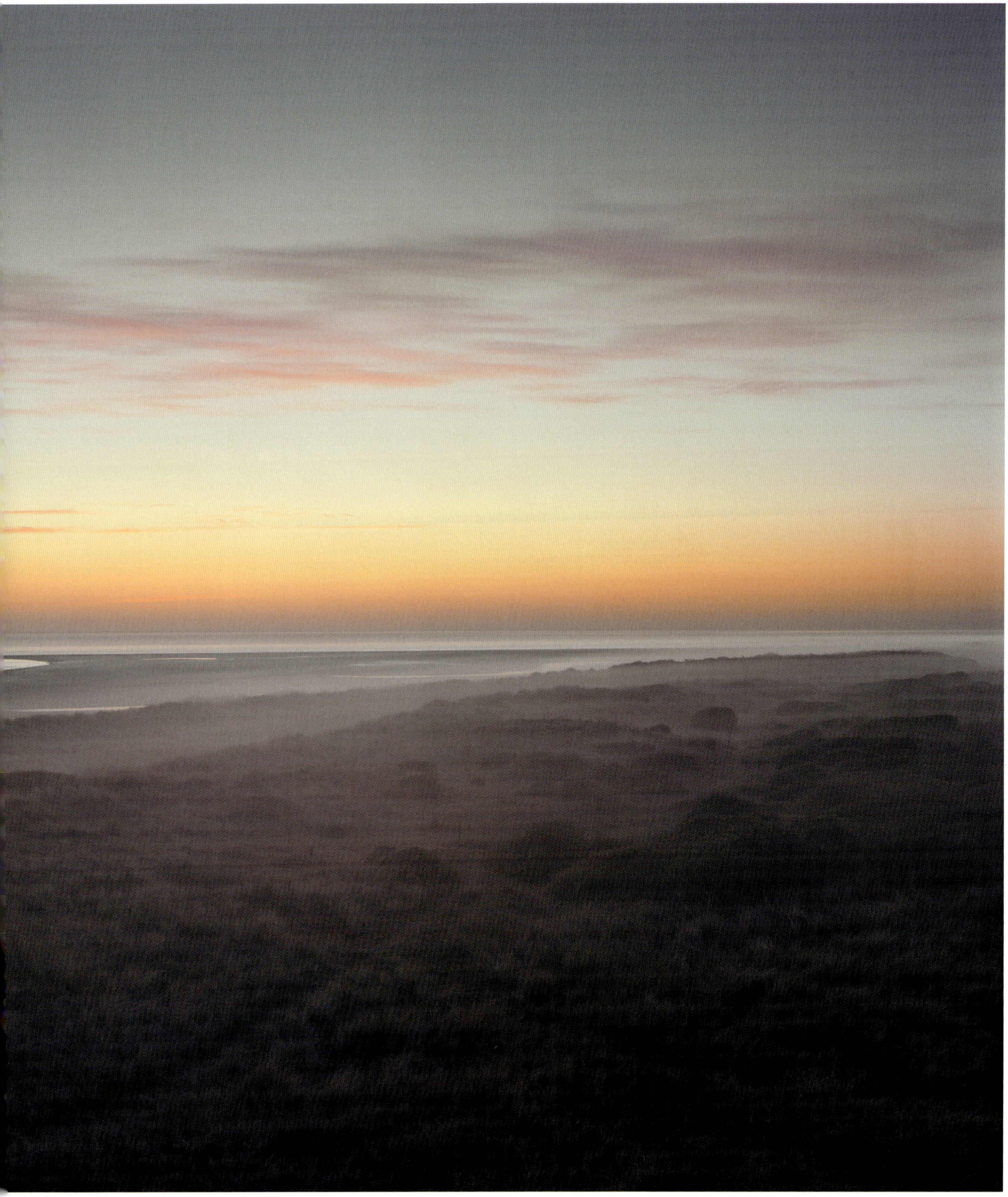

This Pleasant Land: New Photography of the British Landscape
First edition, second printing
Published in 2022 by Hoxton Mini Press, London

Text and interviews by Rosalind Jana
Front cover photograph by Toby Coulson
Back cover photograph by Robin Friend
Design and colour repro by Richard Mason
Sequence by Friederike Huber and Hoxton Mini Press
Copy-editing by Octavia Stocker
Production by Sarah-Louise Deazley
Production and editorial support by Alison Evans

A CIP catalogue record for this book is available from the British Library.

ISBN 978-1-914314-29-2

Hoxton Mini Press is an environmentally conscious publisher, committed to offsetting our carbon footprint. This book is 100 percent carbon compensated, with offset purchased from Stand For Trees.

Printed and bound in China by C&C Offset Printing Co., Ltd.

For every book you buy from our website, we plant a tree:
www.hoxtonminipress.com

FSC www.fsc.org
MIX
Paper | Supporting responsible forestry
FSC® C008047